Chasing Sunsets

A PRACTICING DEVOUT COWARD'S CIRCUMNAVIGATION
with his wife
and son

Lawrence Pane
Carole Wells Pane
Ryan Pane

Copyright © 2005 by Lawrence Pane. All rights reserved.

No part of the publication may be reproduced, stored in a retrieval system, or transmitted, in any form or by means electronic, mechanical or by photocopying, recording or otherwise, except for the inclusion of brief quotation from a review, without prior permission in writing from the author.

10 9 8 7 6 5 4 3 2 1

ISBN 0-9765695-0-7

Library of Congress Control Number: 2005922876

Published by Raymond Hill Publishing, P. O. Box 3561, Burbank, CA 91508-3561

Book layout and cover design by Ernie Weckbaugh of Casa Graphics, Inc., Burbank, California.

Manufactured in the United States of America by DeHart Media Services, Santa Clara, CA, USA

Cover Photographs by "Pilgrim" and Philip Pane

Dedication

To Patricia Mulryan
whose dream it was,
who bought and named "Dolphin Spirit,"
designed our wonderful logo
and sailed with us in spirit, protecting us constantly.

TABLE OF

Introduction		page 7
Chapter 1	Across the Pacific to the Marquesas Islands	page 13
Chapter 2	Marquesas and Tuamoto Islands	page 27
Chapter 3	Tahiti and the Society Islands	page 45
Chapter 4	Cook Islands, Nuie and Tonga	page 59
Chapter 5	Fiji and Passage to Australia	page 77
Chapter 6	Australia	page 93
Chapter 7	Indonesia	page 115
Chapter 8	Singapore, Maylaysia and Thailand	page 139
Chapter 9	Sri Lanka to Yemen	page 153
Chapter 10	Red Sea to the Suez Canal	page 167
Chapter 11	Israel, Jordan, Egypt and Cyprus	page 159
Chapter 12	Turkey	page 203

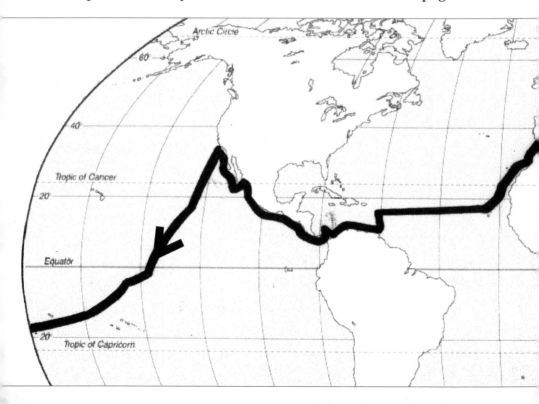

CONTENTS

Chapter 13	Greece	page 227
Chapter 14	Sicily and Malta	page 245
Chapter 15	Italy	page 261
Chapter 16	Spain and France	page 279
Chapter 17	Land Travel in Europe	page 293
Chaoter 18	Spain, Gibraltar and Portugal	page 305
Chapter 19	Crossing the Atlantic	page 321
Chapter 20	Martinique to Trinidad	page 337
Chapter 21	Venezuela	page 359
Chapter 22	Curacao to the Panama Canal	page 377
Chapter 23	Panama to Mexico to San Diego	page 397
Chaoter 24	Re-entering the Real World	page 411
Appendices/A World of Photographs		pages 415 / 433

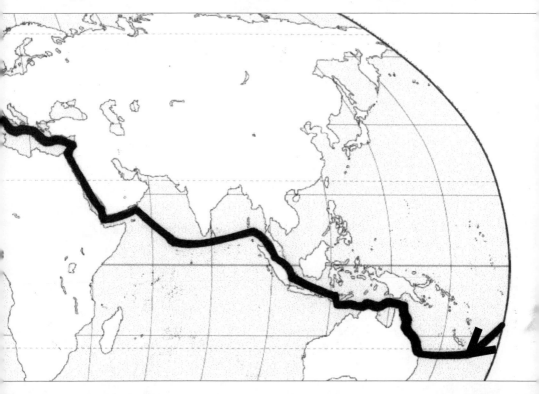

CHASING SUNSETS

Acknowledgements

We owe thanks to so many that the following list has to be regarded as representative only:

Our relatives:
Carole's mother, Vivian Wells
Carole's brother and his wife, John and Janet Wells
My father and mother, Cesare and Dulcie Pane
Ryan's grandparents, Joe and Lenore Mulryan
My big kids, Jenny Bell and Philip Pane

Our friends
Ross and Lyn Dee Rankin, who were always there as support
Lynette Ballas, Carole's good friend, who regularly looked in
  on Carole's mother
Florence and Richard Dommes for the wonderful quote that ends this book

Our Suppliers
Jim Leishman at Pacific Asian Enterprises, Dana Point, for the
  Mason 53, a truly wonderful sailing yacht
Forespar, Costa Mesa, who provided the mast and mainsail furling
  system to ease our passages
UK Sailmakers, San Francisco, who made us the sails that took us
  around the world without a problem
Ken Englert and Joe Carpio at Maritime Communications,
  Marina del Rey, who provided the best electronics, service
  and friendship
Kathy Rupert at Mariner's General Insurance, Newport Beach,
  who worked tirelessly for us
Pantaenius Insurance, who were absolutely magnificent when they
  were needed

Our Editors
Ernie and Patty Weckbaugh, who were kind and gentle and guided
  us along the right paths

Our special sailing companions
Pat and Tash Stolle on "Marita Shan"
Steve and Tammy Guay on "Sky Bird"
Kurt and PL Mondlock on "Osprey"
Steve Whitmore and Sue Angus on "Pilgrim"
Gary and Dorothy Woods on "Gigolo"

Introduction
Who, Why, and How

"Arrested in Sudan."
"Exploding depth-charges in Sri Lanka."
"Mum walking naked in Rome."
"Discovering mosaics in Turkey."
"The creatures that lit up the Indian Ocean"
"Stalked by whales in Tonga."
"The lightning strike in Panama."
"The Portuguese church constructed out of human bones."

In "Dolphin Spirit's" salon, we are reminiscing, sitting on cushions upholstered in Antalya, typing on a computer bought in Singapore, sipping a lemon liqueur made especially for us in Ladispoli, and listening to a CD found in Madrid. Baskets from Tonga, daggers from Yemen, and carved figures from Lombok and Luxor surround us. The engine is operational because of an oil cooler found in the Cape Verde Islands, filters bought in Thailand, and fan-belts from Australia. The Navtex was installed in Gibraltar, the stove bought in England, and most of the electronics were replaced in Panama after we were hit by lightning.

For Carole it all started with an ad in the *Los Angeles Times*. Ryan's introduction was a charter in the Australian Whitsunday Islands, when he was less than a year old. I had a dream I didn't realize was achievable until I met and married Patricia. She had the drive and determination to give our joint dream reality and momentum, and only death could stop her.

For ten years we had worked hard, played often, created Ryan, made so many plans including sailing around the world, and had even bought the perfect boat, "Dolphin Spirit." Patricia's death, after a two-year battle with cancer, shattered everything. Only one thing was clear: Patricia had been adamant that, should the worst happen, I was still to sail around the world with Ryan, as we had planned for so long. Focusing on that seemed to be a way of moving on.

Gradually life settled down. Having been with a partner for as long as I could remember, I was not prepared for the loneliness of being single. Even though surrounded by family and friends, there was no one to turn to and talk, share, or just be with.

In addition, I was absolutely petrified at the thought of entering the world of dating ("Male, fifties, widower, six-year-old son." You can just see the line forming to be with this person!). Helpful friends arranged dinner parties where, by pure chance, a single lady just happened to be present. Such evenings were by no means torture, but were uncomfortable, even though many of the ladies were delightful company. "You must meet J.... She has just been divorced/separated/widowed" was a statement I came to dread.

Most mornings I would read the *Los Angeles Times*, sharing the comics with Ryan as he ate his cereal. On Friday this page is next to the Personal Ads. In common with most L.A. males, married or otherwise, I had occasionally skimmed through the "Women Seeking Men" section, trying to decode the initials, and wondering why so many attractive, personable women were unattached. Now, unsettled and unsure, I perused them with a different perspective.

Loneliness won out over terror. I made one selection from the ads, and called the number. Totally unprepared for leaving a message, I blurted out a string of widower, child, sail around the world, tall, can we meet, reverting under stress to an almost unintelligible Australian accent. Surprisingly, I did have enough presence of mind to leave my phone number.

Carole: *At forty-six I thought my life was ending. I had loved him, been his wife for ten years. Now he had left and I was devastated. That I did not handle it well is an understatement.*

Luckily for me, my brother, John, had just purchased a powerboat, a Hatteras 58, and invited me on many trips to Catalina. I had always loved looking at the ocean and found solace, when I wasn't seasick, sitting in the cockpit, watching our wake. Janet, my brother's wife, and I would joke about the sailboats next to us, comparing their cramped quarters with our spacious ones, complete with dishwasher. However, watching their graceful movements and billowing sails, I fell in love with them. How wonderful to be on a sailboat, but how improbable that it would ever happen to me.

Not being ready to date, and yet not wanting to be all alone, I began searching the personals. Reading somewhere that it was better to take control, I started running my own ads. "Tall, curly headed blonde, 46 looking for..." I met many interesting, respectable people, but I did not want any relationships, just companionship.

Coming to the realization that I was still desirable, I was able to let go of the past more and more. My work as an elementary school teacher, which

Introduction

I always loved, became important again. I started redecorating my house. I took classes. Happy with being by myself, I decided not to run any more personal ads, and just let life, for the time being, stay as is. Except...

....my ad had one more week to run, and I had always called back those who responded, even if I did not choose to meet them. This day would be no different. I called the first two messages, thanked them for answering, and told them I was no longer available. But then there was something in the third man's voice. A strange accent—was he English? He was the widowed father of a six-year old. A child! I never had one, but really wanted one. He had plans, plans to sail around the world! How wonderful to be on a sailboat. But, I called him back and told him, as I had the others, I was not going to date for a while. The man was so interesting I found myself giving him my phone number, something I had never done with anyone else before a first meeting.

I was substitute-teaching during my holiday time to earn extra money. That day, the third grade class' reading assignment was a book called, Alexander's Terrible, Horrible Day. I Think I Will Move to Australia. *The phone rang. "Larry" wanted to know if I would please meet him for cocktails on his boat, the "Dolphin Spirit." Next thing I knew I was in my red Acura Legend driving down the Santa Monica freeway, at rush hour no less!*

What was I doing? This was not what I planned. I wasn't going to date for awhile, and I never, NEVER, meet anyone for a first date at any place other than Starbucks. What was I doing driving all the way to Marina del Rey to meet a stranger on his boat?

From the marina entrance I called, and waited for him to appear. Seeing the tall, good looking, well built fellow walk towards me, I breathed, "Thank you, L.A. Times." *Over cocktails, I found out his name was not Larry but Laurie, he was not English but AUSTRALIAN and his son, Ryan ALEXANDER and I were born on the same day of the year.*

By Monday, we had already seen each other three times. By the following Friday he was bringing Chinese food to my house, and showing me videos of families sailing around the world (hardly subtle). Even though I had never been out of the United States, I knew I wanted to go wherever he went. The following Sunday he took me on my first sail and I met his son Ryan, who handed me a bunch of wild flowers he had picked that morning while on a lizard search. On the back of the boat that afternoon, I read Ryan the book about Alexander thinking he would solve his problems by moving to Australia.

No, we did not sail into the sunset the next day. Neither of us was really ready for a relationship, but we became good companions. Well meaning friends told me to watch out, as Laurie was just beginning to face his wife's death, and I was heading for a disappointment. But I liked this man. We were honest with each other. He could use an easy relationship. I was now two years away from my divorce and becoming more comfortable with that at last. Neither of us knew where this would go, but we were happy with it. A year later he asked me if I would marry him and sail around the world.

And still we did not sail into matrimonial bliss. I get seasick! I wanted to go but was afraid to give up my job, my tenure, my family, my house, my independence. What about storms? Sea snakes? Tsunamis? Laurie listened and listened, again and again, and slowly quieted my fears. We took classes in "Medicine at Sea," attended talks on provisioning, and he began teaching me how to sail. Knowing he wanted to do this circumnavigation more than anything in his life, I said I would go with him, but not marry him until I was sure I had some chance of sticking with the entire trip. What if I hated it? What if all my fears...?

Carole was wonderful and brave to even consider a relationship with an emotionally disturbed Australian, who was adamant about sailing around the world with his six-year-old son. With her acceptance, preparations began in earnest. During the year before our departure, we worked at our usual jobs, looked after Ryan, and:

Read every local, national, and international magazine that had even the faintest connection to sailing and cruising. We even subscribed to powerboat publications, for some reason thankfully long banished from memory.

Read every book by the Pardeys, the Dashews, the Roths, Earl Hinze, and every author who had cruised, sailed, or thought about it.

Attended every seminar, talk and lecture held within a 100-mile radius having to do with matters even remotely related to cruising.

Took courses on emergency medicine, weather forecasting, sail repair, engine maintenance, refrigeration, navigation, celestial navigation, tuning the rigging, ham radio, etc., etc., etc. It didn't matter that, at some of the courses, we knew more than the instructor, as there was always the chance that we would learn that one new thing that would make all the difference.

Assured family and friends we weren't crazy, undergoing mid-life crises, or not in full possession of our faculties. We repeated these discussions every time a water-related incident appeared in print or on TV.

Wrote lists of spare parts, provisions, galley equipment, repairs, new equipment, boat modifications, charts, tools, books, CDs, videos, school supplies, as well as short and long term "To Do" lists, and "Lists of Lists."

Determined our departure date. Revised our departure date. Fixed a latest-possible departure date.

Undertook the quantum leap from writing lists to actually doing it.

Introduction

Made out timetables and schedules for doing this. Redid all the timetables and schedules when they inevitably became outdated.

Worked on a cruising budget. Despaired at the published information, much of which seemed to relate to experiences prior to 1985, or to life styles that would result in immediate mutiny, or worse.

Developed close relationships with all the local service providers for masts, rigging, engine, refrigeration, sails, electronics, batteries, haul out, anti-fouling, paint, varnish, upholstery, computers, and more. Noted how none managed to keep to the agreed timetable, so that our carefully worked out, interlocking schedules, had to be scrapped again and again.

Bought charts, cruising guides, pilot books, light lists, nautical almanacs, and other essential publications. Made the choice between them, clothes, and food, for occupancy of the boat's storage areas.

Tried to get boat insurance. Because we were crossing the Pacific most carriers wanted either three in the crew, or a premium roughly equivalent to the cost of the boat. Finally, the tireless work of Kathy Rupert at Mariners General Insurance led us to Pantaenius, who not only was happy with the two of us, but had a reasonable premium. Of all of the things that we did before leaving, signing with Pantaenius would turn out to be one of the best.

Decided on what clothing and personal possessions could be taken along. Set absolute maximums. Halved these in the light of apparent reality, and halved them again during the actual storage process. Dealt with Carole's resulting emotional breakdown.

Found homes for Ryan's lizards, parakeets, rabbit, fish, cat and kitten. Dealt with Ryan's resulting emotional breakdown.

Decided on how our land-based property and possessions were to be maintained, rented, sold, disposed of, cared for or stored.

Determined how to handle land-based affairs—banking, credit card payments, insurance, IRS returns, mail, and other essentials.

Sailed as often as possible. Convinced ourselves that an afternoon's sail, once a month, was really good experience for an ocean crossing, as it was better than not going out at all, which was all that doing everything else we needed to do really allowed.

Finally I (*Carole: Note it was "I" not "we"*) came to the conclusions that there would never be enough preparation, that the boat would never be perfectly ready, that the provisioning would never be complete, and so I decided we would go anyway.

Carole: *The preparation was fun, and then came the realization that we actually were to go...but not everything had a storage place...I wanted to practice man-overboard one more time...there were dishes in the sink...*

Key dates:

March, 1996—"Dolphin Spirit," Carole, Ryan and Laurie, left Marina del Rey.
November, 1996—Arrived in Australia.
January, 1997—Carole and Laurie were married on a powerboat.
May, 1997—Carole and Laurie were remarried by other cruisers, on a sailboat.
August, 1997—Arrived in Kupang, Timor, Indonesia.
December, 1997—Celebrated Christmas in Thailand.
April, 1998—Transit of the Suez Canal signaled the Red Sea was behind us.
November, 1998—Began winter lay-over in Antalya, Turkey.
November, 1999—Began winter lay-over in Barcelona, Spain.
December, 2000—Arrived in Martinique after crossing the Atlantic Ocean.
November 2001—Hit by lightning, San Blas Islands, Panama.
December, 2001—Transit of the Panama Canal signaled we were on the final leg.
April, 2002—Arrived in San Diego and completed our circumnavigation.

Across the Pacific to the Marquesas Islands

Year One
March 16 to April 15

The 2,000 miles from Fiji to Australia took us 10 days to sail, exactly the same amount of time we took to cover the 120 miles from Los Angeles to San Diego. What was to be a simple departure evolved into one of the more protracted farewells in history. We should have left the previous October to go to Mexico for a shake-down cruise, but boat upgrades and additions got in the way. The mast rework, confidently predicted to take three weeks, took three months. Perhaps I should have paid full price instead of insisting part of the work was warranty. Mostly it was my fault, as I kept adding "essential" items, many of which actually turned out to be pretty useful. Then we really had to go on a last skiing trip to Snowmass, Colorado, where Carole broke her arm.

Carole: *Thank Goodness, we won't possibly be able to leave this year! I won't be able to help with the lines. It will be too hard for me to climb up and down the companionway at sea. I couldn't possibly cook! No, I did not do it on purpose, I really wanted to go, though part of me was almost glad it happened.*

It had been our first day of skiing, the eve of my 50th birthday, and I had been so looking forward to both events. A rank novice, I spent the day with the bunny class on the appropriately named Fanny Hill. The day's lessons were over. All that was left was to slowly pole the couple of hundred yards to where Laurie was picking up Ryan from his class. A classmate came alongside and spoke to me. I turned my head to answer, moved slightly, just enough to cross my skis, and the next thing I heard was a loud crack. When Laurie saw me I was sitting on a ski-mobile on the way to the hospital.

Carole's accident gave me the excuse to do even more work on the boat while we waited out the healing process. It also gave more time for the proponents of the case against our taking Ryan along to state their objections. Friends and relatives vociferously propounded the belief that children must have a formal education, in the company of their peers, to allow them to take their place in a competitive world. Accusations ranged from, "You are destroying his life" to "Poor little fellow, being taken away from his friends." The same relatives and friends then continued on to say, "Won't it be wonderful for him, seeing the world like that." We were damned as selfish and uncaring in the same breath that praised our endeavor.

As part of our planning, we had consulted child psychologists about the effects of taking Ryan out of a "normal" environment. They assured us that a child gains most of his mental growth and social skills from adults, that Ryan's development would therefore not be held back in any way, and would probably be accelerated. All of this had little effect on the opposition, and we spent many sleepless nights debating and wondering, "Could so many people be wrong?" Sheer stubbornness on my part, and a "They haven't done it, so what would they know?" attitude kept us going.

Ryan (16): *After six years at sea, I can truthfully say that there is no better life for a kid than cruising. I loved it, and didn't want to stop sailing after we had completed the circumnavigation.*

Ryan's grandparents were very upset, and from their perspective, rightly so. They had just lost a daughter, and now her son, their only grandchild, was being taken away. All this was on top of their normal concerns about storms, shipwrecks and pirates. My family simply thought I had gone crazier than usual, as they were accustomed to my traveling to strange parts of the world. Friends took the "Are you sure about this?" attitude, and waited to see what happened.

Carole: *One of Laurie's friends, ex-Navy, took me aside to confide how quickly storms can brew up. Comforting!*

At last it became obvious we had to go, ready or not, or miss the whole season. After all, we had waited four weeks for Carole's arm to heal. Our very good friends, Ross and Lyn Dee Rankin, volunteered to collect and forward our mail, pay our bills, and generally act as the clearing house for our land-based activities. Carole's brother, John, looked after her money and the leasing and maintenance of her house. It was sheer co-incidence that, within four months of our departure, Ross bought a new airplane, and John a new powerboat!

Departure

The departure process began with an "open boat." Friends and relatives gathered to commiserate with Carole, and cheer her up with statements such as "Well, it is cozy, isn't it!" "When will we ever see you again?" "You are so brave!" Actually it wasn't too bad, except for having to make "Dolphin Spirit" artificially clean and tidy in the middle of last-minute modifications, packing and provisioning.

Carole: *"Now the fun part is over and you have to go and do it," said one of my friends. With a shock, I realized that she was right. Getting ready had been fun—planning, attending classes, shopping—but now here I was faced with the cold reality of having to actually let go of the dock lines.*

"Bye, Granma." Ryan's sad little voice and wave demanded sympathy and a hug, but we were too busy backing out of the Marina del Rey slip to go and comfort him. His third-grade classmates, Mrs. Demerey their teacher, and some of their parents waved with his grandparents from the dock.

Ryan (16): *No matter how many times I ask him to, Dad will not change that paragraph. I remember that day very well, and I was not sad, just saying goodbye as I had been taught to do. I was excited and very proud to be the center of all that attention.*

My eldest son, Philip, and Bill, Carole's friend Lynette's husband, were on board, with everyone trying not to trip over the clutter of unpacked provisions and spares, and last-minute presents brought by good-intentioned well wishers. Someone gave us a wood-covered log book that was lovely to look at, but designed by a person with a hatred for varnished surfaces.

March 16 took us just "26 Miles Across the Sea" to Avalon Harbor, on Catalina Island, where Carole's brother John, their mother, his wife Janet, and her parents, were waiting to participate in the second departure. Lynette and the rest of her family came by ferry. An arrival party, a few "parting is such sweet sorrow" celebrations, and we set off on the next leg to distant Newport Beach (again 26 miles), and a slip at the Bahia Corinthian Yacht Club. Three days, and we had moved less than 20 miles of the 3,000 we had to cover to get to the Marquesas Islands.

Ryan (8): *Carole woke me up to have a breakfast of green eggs and ham as her way of celebrating St. Patrick's Day. Was I surprised when I poured milk on my "Lucky Charms." It was green, too.*

A pod of gray whales followed us on the way to Newport. Though we didn't know it then, they were the only whales we were to see until Tonga.

Another arrival party, final, final farewells, and we were off again—to San Diego, in dense fog. This marked the first and last use (until Italy) of our new electronic fog horn. More friends, and my son Philip, met us in San Diego for another round of farewells (no arrival party this time), before we settled down to final provisioning and preparations.

Our crew, Nate Axel, joined us a couple of days before we were to set off. Because of her arm and her uncertainties about sailing, Carole desperately wanted an extra person on board. Nate had done a lot of the electrical work on the boat in Marina del Rey, and was foolish enough to express an interest in sailing with us. With a wide grin and curly, bushy, red hair, Nate had no sailing experience, but was a willing worker and a great cook. We agreed he would crew for us until Papeete, Tahiti.

Carole: *Nate was so thrilled to be on board, he hugged me. I tensed and felt a little irritated. We were leaving in just two days and I was so nervous—how could he be so happy?*

In common with most first-time cruisers, we believed everything we read, and over-provisioned to the hilt. Certainly we needed all the fresh fruit and vegetables we could cram in for the long Pacific passage, but it was Italy where we finally ate the last of the spaghetti bought at Costco. A fact we ignored was that very few of the locals in the South Pacific actually starve, and that equally few rely solely on fishing or farming for their sustenance.

To this day, we have never vaselined our eggs, and they have kept well. No cans have had labels fall off, or rusted, no flour spoiled. Our wine bottles stayed unbroken and very drinkable. Perhaps this simply emphasizes the value of a good, dry boat like "Dolphin Spirit;" perhaps the authors we revered were in leaky boats and didn't tell us; perhaps they simply wanted to make their already wonderful life seem more exotic; or perhaps they simply wanted to discourage others, and keep the anchorages to themselves.

Carole: *My house had four closets of essential clothing. I left 20 sweatshirts behind, but I desperately needed the six I brought (I did actually wear two in the Mediterranean). I carried aboard only a vital dozen cookbooks, and bemoaned at length the 103 left behind. Calvert School had a great program for Ryan, but I couldn't possibly teach him without boxes and boxes of my own materials. Laurie gritted his teeth and tried to store everything.*

One great find, that did turn out to be absolutely essential, was the Snap-Ware rectangular plastic jar. We purchased 40 of them, as, to prevent cockroach infestation, we always throw out the cardboard boxes some food comes in. Not only did each of the jars hold five pounds of flour, cake mixes, breakfast cereals, rice, Jell-o®, crackers, cookies and candy bars, but the contents stayed fresh for months, some for years. The shape allowed me to use our storage spaces efficiently

With "Dolphin Spirit's" waterline visible only to divers, we finally decided March 26 was THE DAY, so I went to check out. The Immigration and Customs people were quite polite to an Australian, checking out an Australian registered boat which had never been checked in. Thankfully, I had a complete document trail.

Patricia and I had purchased a U.S. federally registered boat in her name. As a Resident Alien, I could not be even a part owner of such a boat. We politely inquired why, and were told it was so that, in the event of a war, the boat could be requisitioned! When Patricia died, the federal registration was canceled, so as an interim measure I took out California State registration for "Dolphin Spirit." As almost all countries require a country, not a state, registration as a condition of entry, I then took the only option available, Australian registration. For Customs, I had to produce marriage and death certificates, old registration, new registration, and letters from lawyers. We were leaving, not entering, but I was determined to start as we hoped to proceed, by complying with all official requests, no matter what.

Finally it was all done and we cast off. I like to think it was simply because I was preoccupied with contemplation of our impending passage, but it was probably sheer incompetence, coupled with a nasty cross wind, that caused us to crash into the fuel dock. Apart from an exploded fender, "Dolphin Spirit" was undamaged. My already nervous crew stayed mercifully silent. Full of fuel, water, provisions and foreboding, we headed out into the choppy Pacific on a bleak, cloudy day.

When I compare the extensive pre-departure ritual that we now employ with the almost casual first departure, I shudder. Actually, I did do just enough then to avoid charges of complete incompetence.

Carole: *Mom's phone was ringing and I suddenly realized I had to pull myself together. It wouldn't do either of us any good if I stood there crying, saying my final good-bye. A few hours ago, sipping an orange juice by the marina pool, watching my hopefully soon-to-be-son, and beginning my trip journal, I had been in seventh heaven. Now, just minutes before we were to sail out of San Diego's Sun Marina, my knees were shaking, and I was on the verge of fear.*

Looking at the newspaper lying next to the phone, the speed at which my life had changed was brought home. The headline story was Steve Reeves attending the Oscar ceremonies. In the midst of our preparations I, the former wife of an actor, hadn't even remembered it was Oscar time. My life had been transformed!

Back on the boat, I finished the final preparations for our first meal at sea, checked THE PATCH (Dramamine) was still behind my ear, and promptly threw up. It was time to let the final dock lines go, and bid farewell to my old life, the land, my country.

Laurie looked so forlorn after the fuel dock incident that I didn't have the heart to tell him to go back to the Marina. How I was to wish, over the next few days, that I had. Sailing down the channel, I served our first meal, a late lunch, which the guys instantly devoured. Laurie had recovered and was looking relaxed and confident, or at least so my fevered brain interpreted. Ryan, cute as a bug's ear, kept his eyes peeled for the first shark as a signal to throw his mother-replacement overboard. Soon, the men were looking for dessert, and I for the barf-bag.

Taking pity on me, Laurie stood both of our watches that first night, while I lay in my bunk begging my insides to adapt to this new life. Thwack, shudder, creak. The wind died. We rolled, the sails banging back and forth. Never had I heard "Dolphin Spirit" making such noises. I had already vomited twice. Tomorrow I WILL tell Laurie I have to go back. We will be only a hundred miles out. Surely, helping him get ready was enough!

That first day, everything seemed to be conspiring against us. The skies were grey, the seas lumpy and confused, and the wind fitful, finally dying and leaving us rolling. I didn't want to use the engine, conscious of the miles ahead and the doldrums to be crossed, so we rolled and banged all night. In the midst of this ruckus, the G.P.S. stopped talking to the autopilot, something akin to your brain not telling your feet what to do. We switched to the back-up autopilot, while Nate investigated and found a loose connection. The morning sun brought the wind. Thankfully, we had weathered the worst day of the passage. Wish we had known it at the time.

Ryan (16): *I remember that day and night very well. While I can't recall what I was thinking, I do remember the sun setting as we passed a group of rocks and being somewhat struck by its strange beauty. I was only eight at the time.*

Just before we left, Dad and Mum bought me my own sailing dinghy I named "Cool Dolphin." It was lashed down on the fore-deck waiting for me to take it on my first sail when we got to the South Pacific. I was very excited about this whole trip, and don't remember thinking about leaving my old life.

Coast Guard planes buzzed us twice those first days, the last time about 300 miles off shore. They suddenly swooped out of the clouds to just over mast height and called us on the radio, grabbing our attention immediately. Carole felt safe, believing the U.S. was keeping track of her whereabouts. Maybe they were. We were leaving U.S. waters, our bow persistently pointed away from land, so we obviously weren't smuggling stuff in.

Departure

Carole: *If I ever thought of it at all before I met Laurie, I just assumed boats anchored every night. I know many of my friends thought so too, because it was mentioned several times in Laurie's presence. He manfully resisted the impulse to burst into laughter (it was very early in our relationship) and pointed out the need to carry several miles of anchor chain on board to accomplish this. The "sailing through the night" concept generated weeks of questioning from me and patient answers from Laurie.*

Each day we slowly sorted things out and got more organized. Carole overcame her seasickness. Ryan began lessons. We started to fish seriously. There is no way to really prepare for a long passage out of sight of land other than by actually doing it. Boredom was not a problem, as there was always something to be done, but day after day of seeing nothing but China-blue water all around took some getting used to. Carole drew us into her fantasy that we were stuck in the same circle of water, unmoving, with only the clouds on the horizon changed by some power, just to keep up the illusion of motion. Sanity was not high on our list of priorities.

Ryan (16): *Should it have been? Based on reactions of friends today to my stories about the trip, we had abandoned our sanity when we left San Diego.*

Most of the passage was spent on a port tack and therefore heeled to the right. Whilst I kept the boat as upright as possible, to maximize comfort and speed, walking about was an art to be learned afresh. Even standing still required a feet-apart stance that soon became second nature, as pain was a great teacher. The refrigerator was on the "up" side, so opening the door required caution, and at least three hands. Fortunately the galley had been designed with long passages in mind, and we could easily wedge ourselves in place without needing straps or other restraints for safety. The gimbaled stove and adjustable fiddles (metal bars to keep pots and pans from moving) meant cooking was not a problem.

Carole: *It was a long time before I would even attempt to boil water while we were at sea.*

A chance remark at a seminar we attended led me to design and install what became my favorite safety device. Instead of jack-lines running along the deck onto which we could snap our safety harnesses, I installed spectra lines running chest-high, fore and aft, on both sides of the boat, and clipped onto these. Jack-lines won't stop you falling overboard; these lines would, and saved me on innumerable occasions. They also made great places on which to hang the wash out to dry.

We were not sportsmen, but fished for food and trailed a 300-pound breaking-strain line—anything big enough to break that wouldn't be welcome on board anyhow. If a large fish was hooked, the line often went around the electric winch—who needed the exercise of hauling in a dorado bigger and stronger than we were? I did not reduce sail or slow the boat for a fish. Getting it on board was one thing, but subduing a five-foot long, 30 to 40-pound piece of frantic muscle was something else. Then there was cleaning up afterwards! Who knew that a dorado could fling blood more than 20 feet? One of the advantages of our center-cockpit boat was that fish were landed at the stern, and well away from our living space.

Ryan (16): *Later in the trip, when I became the fisherman for the boat, Dad did compromise a little and let me have fun pulling in the fish.*

Carole: *A fish would always be hooked just as I was about to serve lunch. I'd hear the squeal of the line and have to run up to the cockpit to drive the boat while Ryan (with just a little help from his father) brought the catch in. Then I would wrap and refrigerate the already prepared lunch while Laurie cleaned and barbequed the fish. Not a real complaint, as the fish was delicious, and the next meal was ready to be microwaved.*

The sight of the dorado we just hooked, swimming above our heads in the clear Pacific swell that was always approaching our stern, never ceased to awe us. These swells, even minus fish, were mesmerizing. Smoothly they would loom over our stern, then equally smoothly lift us to the top and drop us into the next trough. Widely separated, the motion was easy, the ride exhilarating.

Carole: *Sitting for hours in the pulpit with only cobalt blue in front of me, it gradually dawned on me why they call this blue-water sailing. When I first noticed the huge swells, "Dolphin Spirit" was already sliding smoothly down one, and her easy handling of them gave me a lot of confidence in our floating home. On later passages, when the seas got ugly, I would think back on this time and be reassured.*

Flying fish and dolphins escorted us on many days and nights. We saw flying fish every day, singly, and in shimmering clouds of tens to hundreds. Most mornings there were three or four unfortunates on the deck. The very first flying fish to come aboard flew straight through a port hole, across the salon, and landed in the bookshelves on top of *The Complete Sherlock Holmes*.

Although we had not seen another yacht since we left San Diego, through the Pacific Maritime Radio Net's daily radio schedule we realized we were not alone, as some eighteen other boats were making the passage at the same time. When we did check in on day six, the experienced net controllers noted our position, and told me to make more easting, or risk missing the Marquesas. Every day we would provide our position, weather, sea conditions, barometer reading, and record the information from the others. Then I would plot all the positions to see where everyone was on the big ocean. This had two benefits. We felt less lonely, and got an ego boost when we made more miles in a day than the others.

Carole: Some of them, including "Marita Shan," "Osprey," "Blue Ribbon," "Pacific High," "Promises," "Gigolo," "Topaz," and "Sea Bird" were to share our lives over the next few years.

When we reached the Marquesas, it was interesting to watch arrivals, and match boats and faces with the voices we heard over the net. The last sentence is a sneaky attempt at self-congratulation. "Dolphin Spirit" is a fast boat, and we did make a very quick 19-day passage (24+ days was the norm). At one stage we were even thinking of 16 days, but then we reached the doldrums, and the wind died.

Our average for the whole passage was 163 miles per day. As we were traveling in our "home," comfort was a high priority, as was safety. Sail was adjusted to minimize heel during meal-times, and we always reduced sail at night, for safety. This did bring down our average speed, but maintained a happy, contented crew.

"Dolphin Spirit" boat rules require someone to be in the cockpit 24 hours a day when at sea. During the day it was a loose arrangement, but at night we kept formal watch hours. Everyone, except Ryan, stood three-hour watches, me 8pm to 11pm, Carole 11pm to 2am, Nate 2am to 5am, me 5am to 8am. As it turned out, the watch-keeper had little to do except listen to tapes, gaze at the stars, watch the moon/sun rise, marvel at the phosphorescence in the wake, make log notations, tweak the auto-pilot, and then wonder how the three hours passed so quickly. (*Carole: In your wildest dreams. I spent a lot of time watching the wind speed—30 knots, 35, 40, 25, 38, 42, "LAURIE!" I had no real sailing experience and so it was really frightening to be in the middle of the Pacific, isolated, alone, rushing through the water.*) All sail adjustments were made without leaving the cockpit, mostly with the push of an electric winch button. The autopilot did the steering. A fully covered center cockpit meant that we stayed dry even through the numerous squalls. All the comforts of home really, only better—a 360-degree ocean view.

Carole: By the third day my seasickness had eased and our days began to settle into a routine. Breakfast by eight; school for Ryan, sometimes in the salon, often on the stern seats, perhaps the most spectacular classroom in the world; lunch about noon and dinner at seven; bed by eight so I could get up for my watch at 11pm.

I have a hard time falling asleep, and knowing my watch was coming up in three hours— now two—now one— didn't help. Not wanting, at that early stage, to change the Captain's watch schedule, I did not say anything. Later, I "asked" Laurie if I could have the first watch.

One sleepless night, in mid-Pacific, just south of the Equator, I joined Laurie at the helm. He must have been in a romantic mood, and asked me to come onto the deck with him, properly harnessed, of course. We lay on the deck enthralled with the glorious Southern Hemisphere stars, blazing from horizon to horizon. The only sound was the gentle swish of "Dolphin Spirit's" wake. On other such nights, Laurie would say, "Listen!" and we could hear the breathing of dolphins and see the lightning flash of their phosphorescent passage through the dark water.

Although I worried a lot, most nights on watch I had an easy time, helped by my bag full of books-on-tape, CDs, and my comforting See's chocolate suckers. It did take some getting used to the eerie feeling of rushing, almost soundlessly, through the dark sea, under the canopy of stars. Being all alone, with everyone else asleep, was somewhat unnerving in those first days of adjusting to ship-board life, yet it was a relief to have some time to myself.

Laurie had the radar on "Watchman" mode, so it beeped every few minutes to remind me to look around. It was the tenth night out when I spotted my first ship on the horizon, and just had to wake Laurie to watch it pass. I thought it was an event. He was not terribly amused! (Laurie: It was at least 12 miles away.)

Ryan (8): *I really wanted to stand a watch and often Carole woke me to share her watch, but I just couldn't stay awake. Most times I would just sleep the rest of the night in the cockpit. One night Carole forgot to close the companionway hatch and I woke up just in time to stop myself falling through.*

Carole: *After Nate left us and I began taking the 8pm watch, I would often stretch the duration to four or five hours if things were calm and peaceful and I was awake and alert. If Laurie was merciful he would then let me sleep to dawn. Mostly there was no mercy. Of course I always fixed Laurie coffee, tea or soup when I woke him, but he usually got me up empty handed. I guess he somewhat compensated by staying on watch for the two minutes it took me to make my own drink in the microwave.*

The weather was a little too boisterous at times, but we had no major storms, just days of 15 to 25-knot winds and six to eight-foot swells. The Captain (I took the title, and Carole and Ryan allowed me to maintain the illusion) kept promising gentle Trade Winds south of the Equator, and had to put down a near mutiny when we got only two days of them. However we caught fish, didn't break too much equipment, had plenty of food and water, 183 video tapes to watch, 318 CDs to listen to, and more than 200 books to read. Prepare with the essentials is our motto. The cruiser without reading material is a frightening sight, dinghying to every new arrival at an anchorage with a desperate "Any books to swap?" cry.

Ryan (8): *My first Easter at sea— a great day. The Bunny found me from his underwater base in the middle of the Pacific. Must have ridden his yellow jet-ski to do it.*

Carole: *Poor Ryan worked the hardest on "Dolphin Spirit," as he had school for two to three hours every day, his own chores, his journals to write, his books to read, and his games to play. He also supervised the fishing, watched for birds and dolphins (we saw birds every day skimming the waves, never at rest), made sure we ate on time, and generally kept us shipshape.*

One of our early lessons was that, when at sea, things go bump in the night. The boat was never still, there was the constant sound of the water brushing by the hull, and the occasional whine of the auto-pilot motor, but the really annoying sounds were those that surfaced during the enhanced-hearing period which occured just as we were falling asleep. It was then the sounds of the cans in the cupboards caroming off each other in spite of being held by paper towel rolls, of wine glasses clicking together even though firmly wedged in place by tissues, of the toaster-oven rattling under its cocoon of towels, began to dominate. Diligent re-padding stopped most.

Brain atrophy was a real possibility during the long passages, so we all memorized lines of sea-related poetry, and would recite them to each other. By the time we had finished cruising Ryan had more than 50 poems he could recite at will, from Byron to Blake, Shakespeare to Wordsworth.

Ryan (8): *Carole stopped vomiting. She began to make us proper food, not the frozen stuff Dad and Nate heated. My school work got going. Carole started teaching me Spanish. We read "Old Yeller" together, often sitting in the stern.*

Dad and I built Lego in the cockpit almost every day. He found the little pieces, I put them together, and we watched the fishing lines at the same time. I watched some of the movies we had on board. Whenever Dad finished a bottle of wine, I put a note in it and threw it overboard. I hoped someone would find them and write to me. A year later, I got a letter from some kids in Vanuatu who found one of my bottles.

Notes from the log:
    March 28— all the screws in the jib roller-furler fell out.
    April 1   — wing on wing. G.P.S. notes speed of 12 knots over ground.
    April 4   — half way mark. Caught 25 pound dorado. 15 foot swells.
    April 6   —NE winds of over 20 knots for the sixth day.
    April 10   —crossed equator at 0915.
    April 12   —SE trades at last. Oranges, apples, potatoes and onions still okay. Removed outer cabbage leaves. Tomatoes in refrigerator good.

Carole: *One night during the first week, Nate came below to tell me Laurie said the barometer was falling and we were in for a storm. Nate and I rushed around putting everything away and tying everything down. Laurie then came below, asked why all the portholes were closed, and was puzzled when we said that it was because of the storm. It turned out that the storm was only a possibility and days away, but it illustrated how nervous we were.*

That night was black and it seemed as if we were rushing off the edge of the world. For the first time I felt empathy with Columbus' crew and their fears. The clouds had hidden the stars and there was no moon (our first moonless night). Only later did I come realize how much the moon meant to us. We would often time our departures depending on the phase of the moon so as to have light at night and because of its apparent influence on the weather. Somehow that silver track, leading to us, always to us, was reassuring.

All hell broke loose on the 15th evening, as we were quietly sitting in the cockpit contemplating the sunset. The mainsail outhaul block at the end of the boom disintegrated; the outhaul line snapped; and a block pulled out of the mast, all in one split second. We went from the serenity and stability of sailing, to a maelstrom of flapping sail and slapping lines.

The nasty job of controlling the flapping mainsail and getting it all back together would have been much more difficult in worse weather. Of course we had spares for everything, and the hardest job was feeding the new outhaul line down the 22-foot long boom. It was eventually accomplished (Nate's idea) by tying fishing line to a small plastic bottle, and blowing the bottle down the boom using the deck salt-water wash down pump. We were sailing again before it got really dark.

Carole: *I sat calmly in the cockpit offering assistance. Inside my inner child was screaming, "Can you fix it? Is it almost fixed yet?" but not a*

DEPARTURE

word of that passed my lips. With Nate there to help Laurie I was not needed, but what about after Papeete when he would be gone and I would be the only other adult on board?

Things we didn't have: Champagne—we had only one bottle on board, a major oversight. Early in the passage Carole used this as an argument that we left too soon, a year too soon—a lime squeezer; peanut oil (but we did have olive, walnut, corn, vegetable, engine, transmission and other assorted oils); enough fish hooks or lures or line. The things we had too many or too much of were far too numerous to mention.

The lack of champagne meant we had to toast Poseidon with wine (Australian) as we crossed the Equator. Ryan swam across, some 2,000 miles from the nearest land, becoming probably the first eight-year old to do so. The water was 83 degrees; the sea was almost flat; there was no wind, so there was no real danger.

Ryan (8): *I was in a life jacket, attached by several lines to the boat, much to my dismay. I wanted to swim, not be barely able to touch the water. Dad's too protective. He let Nate swim without being tied to the boat.*

Ryan had a blast and joined a very select group of mid-ocean, cross-Equator, swimmers. We didn't see the fabled magenta line across the ocean, and missed the floating ice cream stand Ryan was promised, but three new shell-backs were christened by the Captain, who had crossed twice before (ho hum!). A shell-back is a person who has crossed the Equator on water (flying doesn't count).

Before we left we had signed up for a service that allowed us to call a telephone number through the SSB radio, mainly so Carole could speak with her mother. Those listening in (the frequency was of course available to all) must have been really entertained. Carole was new to radio protocol, and her mother had never heard of it, so they continually talked over each other. No matter how hard I tried to stop it, their ritual of saying goodbye, then thinking of something else to say, and doing this at least 20 times, persisted until I timed it one day, and showed Carole how much it actually cost.

We sighted just four ships on the whole trip, two only on radar, one as a glow on the horizon, and the last, to make up for it, at 2pm on a clear day, on a collision course. All of us were reading in the cockpit, and didn't look up and take notice until it was only a mile or so away. It was a very large tuna boat that was just changing direction to miss us. After 17 days at sea, we had become complacent.

Although it sounds pretentious, clear skies full of brilliant stars, the silver path of the moonlight directly to the boat, glorious sunrises and sunsets, and the perfect dark blue of the ocean, all become commonplace after a couple of weeks, engaging our attention for only a short time, compared with the awe-struck hours at the beginning of the voyage.

On the 19th evening, just before sunset, Carole pointed and screamed "Land!" None of us believed her at first, but I checked the radar, and there it was. Nineteen days out of San Diego on the "Dolphin Spirit," nineteen days of water, water and still more water, and the Marquesas Islands were finally in sight. After wanting land for so long, Carole's last words to me before she went to sleep that night were a request to stay at sea, well away from the islands. She was very aware that the biggest danger to cruisers is not the sea, but the land.

To ensure that I would remember the passage, as Nate was taking off the running backstays, he let go of one, and the block at the end caught me squarely on the mouth, splitting a lip. I bled my way into harbor.

Carole: *Laurie lost 15 pounds on the passage. I threw up and didn't eat much, and HE lost the weight!*

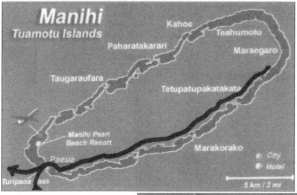

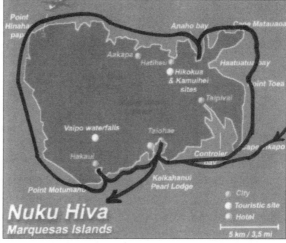

Marquesas and Tuamoto Islands

Year One
April 16 to June 1

Carole: *Our first South Sea island, and not a single canoe paddled out to meet us. No strumming ukuleles, no leis. Didn't anyone care we had just crossed 3,000 miles of the Pacific? Even the other yachts ignored us, except to check we didn't anchor too close to them.*

Taiohae Bay, the main harbor on Nuka Hiva, is the water-filled crater of an extinct volcano and a magnificent sight, even taking into account our land-starved senses. Black cliffs, partly covered with dark green rain forest, surrounded the bay and gleamed with waterfalls after the daily inch or two of rain. We could count over 20 cascading into the deep valleys that sliced toward the island's interior. Rain squalls chasing the sunlight across green mountains provided more than adequate entertainment and beauty. Wet clothes were cool in this land of perpetual 90-degree-plus temperatures and 90% humidity, so rain was just ignored.

Our first anchoring at an exotic island was a disaster. The anchor chain pile had collapsed somewhere in the Pacific, and the anchor wouldn't drop. Carole nervously took the wheel while I ran below to untangle the mess. She started following a boat (*Carole:* You told me to.), which then turned and came towards us. Her anguished scream got me out of the anchor locker in record time. We avoided a collision, found a spot, and anchored successfully, in spite of the murky water and horrendous roll.

Carole: *What a disappointment! The scenery was gorgeous, but the rolling, the humidity, the rain and the brown, shark-filled water was not what*

I expected. Where was the turquoise water I was promised? I had risked my life for this?

Trying to get out of the swell, we raised the anchor, and blew the anchor winch fuse with only half the chain on board. A still nervous Carole had to drive again, circling the anchored boats and dodging the small ones, a task she managed well—a fast learner! Finally re-anchored and still rolling, we put out a stern anchor to keep our bow to the swell, and became reasonably comfortable. Water shaded from reddish-brown near the rocky beaches, where muddy run-off from the daily rain kept the water almost fresh, to grey where we were anchored. Swimming was not inviting, and was made even less so by the number of hammerhead sharks Ryan and Nate caught from the deck.

Ryan (8): *A seven-foot-long hammerhead swam past the boat, but the locals we invited on board caught only small ones. They then killed them by holding their tails and bashing their heads on the deck. My Dad wasn't happy about this. Carole and Nate wouldn't cook them so we gave them to some other locals who paddled past.*

A brand new 90-plus-foot sailboat being taken by a professional crew from New Zealand to Los Angeles anchored nearby. They put out a stern anchor, but someone forgot to secure the bitter end of the rode, and the lot went overboard. Several crew immediately donned snorkel gear and were attempting to dive for the anchor, when I dinghied over to advise about the sharks. The water exit was even faster than the entry. Dragging with makeshift grapnels, they recovered the anchor the next day.

Taking my French phrase book with me, I went ashore. My first task was to check in with the Gendarmes, post the necessary bonds ($US1,095 per adult, $US550 per child), buy the visa stamps ($US30 per head), change money, and find fruit. The Gendarme spoke excellent English, which was fortunate, as my high school French, spoken with an Australian accent, left much to be desired. He had visited Brisbane, so we chatted about Australia before getting to business. The bank's computer expired in the middle of the money changing/bond posting transaction, so the procedure went beyond the 11am bank closing time. To avoid any international repercussions, I was sworn to secrecy and carefully smuggled out the back door.

Then I was off to get what I really went ashore for—fruit—but no fruit was in any of the four stores. No fruit in a tropical paradise, where I walked past trees loaded with succulent pamplemouse, (a large tropical citrus called pomelo in Australia, and pumelo in the U.S., about the size of a small soccer ball, and absolutely delicious), where I had to dodge falling mangoes under a tree when I sheltered from the rain, and where coconut palms, paw paw (papaya) and banana trees grew everywhere. All trees were owned by someone, so I just couldn't pick what I wanted. The fruit-aholic is ingenious by nature, and within a day we had local sources, traded for with our dwindling supply of fish hooks, line, tapes and baseball caps.

Check-in accomplished, but fruitless that first day, I returned to take Ryan, Carole and Nate ashore for lunch at one of the small hotels.

Carole: *Walking on land after 19 days in a boat was disorienting. Not only did the ground move, the smells and sights were so different from those of California.*

The only savages in the Marquesas were the No-Nos, almost invisibly small black flies with the bite of a rabid pit bull. We employed a "go ashore dripping with bug spray" policy and avoided serious injury. Friends on "Osprey" were really hit (several hundred bites per person) and couldn't swim for a couple of months, as infection was a real possibility. Other bite victims scratched, were infected, and had problems recovering.

A dinghy ride to shore and walk through down-town Taiohae went something like this. After checking out the resident manta ray and waving to the cockpit loungers on the other yachts, we pulled in to the concrete dock. Unfortunately the tide was out and we were faced with a six-foot barnacle-covered concrete wall to scramble up. The top of the wall was where the locals clean fish, but we managed, this time, to avoid the oldest and smelliest of the guts and fins. A toilet and shower block was right on the dock, but unusable for all sorts of reasons, best not described.

The only real street followed the seashore. To our right was the administration center, with post office, gendarmerie, hospital and local government offices. Directly ahead was the jail, looking very picturesque from the outside. Parading down the street to the left (there are no paved sidewalks, so everyone walks on the road), we waved a casual "bon jour" to the passing cars, all of whom drove at less than 30-miles-per-hour, and were tolerant of foot traffic.

The local open-air dinner/dance area was being decorated with fronds and flowers for Saturday night's event. Dinner was 2,000 francs ($US31) per head, but did include all the lobster you could eat. The dance could be attended separately for 500 francs. Dinner was by reservation only, and we sadly noted that all the tickets were sold. Next was a small store selling souvenirs, clothing, cameras and film. The postcards were mainly of Tahiti, or of bare-breasted Polynesian beauties. Under the same roof was the Nuka Hiva helicopter service, which boasted one helicopter and a landing pad on a hill overlooking harbor and town. It seemed to be well utilized, perhaps as a shuttle to the airport on the far side of the island. The planes came in from Papeete daily and mail service was therefore quite good. Socrode Bank, the only one in town and the site of my midday smuggle was next, with the elementary school behind it.

Carole: *Such an exotic setting, and then to see a regular elementary school. The buildings, Disney character murals, and equipment, could be in any town in the U.S. I was dripping sweat and the rain was pouring down, so California it wasn't, but there were the classrooms, the blackboards, the rows of desks.*

Over the bridge to the first store, the "Chinese store" to the locals, "Loto" to the yachties, as it sold the local version of lotto (spelled "Loto") and had a sign up advertising that fact. Canned goods, bread, drinks, ice cream, very limited vegetables, eggs, cosmetics and some hardware items were on the shelves. Prices were very high for sodas, reasonable for canned butter, and cheap for bread. The store opened at 5.30am and we needed to get there soon after if we wanted fresh bread. Non-French speaking transients were common, so communication was no problem.

At the back of the store was Fred, the local refrigeration mechanic. We needed help as our engine driven refrigeration had failed during the passage (fortunately the 110V parallel refrigeration system kept working). Fred was a young Frenchman, ex-navy, who had married a local girl and settled in. As he didn't advertise, and didn't charge us for his time to diagnose a faulty compressor, I was glad his wife had a good job at the airport. His English was excellent, a real bonus in the technical environment of refrigeration. May he prosper!

To digress from our tour, we ordered a replacement compressor from the States, to be delivered by air. There were daily flights from Papeete, so we, the shipper, and the U.S. freight company, expected no problems. I became very friendly with the local post office person, given that we had only marginal grasp of each other's language. After I had been to his office every day for two weeks expecting the parcel to be there, the following exchange (translated and condensed) took place:
"Are you waiting for a package?"
"Yes."
"Only mail comes by plane, packages come by copra boat from Papeete."
"When does the copra boat arrive?"
"There is one every three weeks."
"When is the next one due?"
"Next week."
"Will my package be on it?"

"No."

(Story to be continued)

Over a second bridge was an intersection, where a rather steep dirt road headed off up into the mountains, bordered on both sides by houses, all of which were set back with lawns, mango, banana, and paw paw trees everywhere. About a mile up this road were probably some of the best views, and certainly the best store in Taiohae in terms of wares and presentation.

Carole: *The view of "Dolphin Spirit" in the bay was worth the up-hill walk and sweat. I was able to replenish some canned milk and we bought a delicious beef roast—it was beef wasn't it Laurie?*

Back on the main road, just past the intersection on the left, was the produce market. Again, if we didn't get there before 7am, the shelves were empty. Pineapple was always coming tomorrow, but the smiles made the lack of goods acceptable. Under the same roof we could buy lunch and dinner—dish-of-the-day only—for around 500 francs ($US5.50) per plate. Overlooking the intersection was another store, no bread, but more hardware, stationery supplies and fishing tackle. A little further on the right was the fourth and last store, the biggest, but no bread. It had no sign, but in a town of 800, advertising didn't seem necessary. They sold lumber, and were adjacent to a mysterious pile of coconut husks, guarded by a horse.

Next was the hotel where we had our first exotic meal—steak and salad—on a patio overlooking the bay. Flies guarded every table during the day, so the American style of eating with one hand, leaving the other free to wave, was a definite asset. Carole decided on a salad and later became very concerned about her future health when she remembered advice not to eat lettuce because of the possibility of nasty resident worms. She survived. The worms, if any, didn't. Pizza was the specialty at night, which was also fly free.

Over another bridge, and we found some of the authentic old Polynesia. The seashore was lined with a number of "mare," stone platforms that once supported houses and places of worship, and stone statues of varying antiquity and origin were scattered around. In the semi-twilight, with the rain beating down and no one else around, it was very easy to imagine the original Polynesians living there.

Ryan (8): *Some kids were swimming in a stream so I joined them. It had just rained so the water was running really fast and was very muddy. When I fell over, the current bumped me along the rocks at the bottom until the biggest kid grabbed me and helped me get up.*

The secondary school, next on the right, had volleyball courts, buildings, obviously a school, just in a dramatic setting. Past the soccer field and some houses was another hotel, this one comprised of individual thatched units and a central dining room/bar. A can of Pepsi was 250 francs ($US3.80) and a bottle of reasonable French white wine was 2,600 francs ($US40).

The paved road stopped here. Paving, when it existed, was reinforced concrete, and there were no curbs. As the sheer drop was often several feet to the storm drain, careful driving was a must. The dirt road turned away from the shore and wound up the hill to Rose Corser's hotel, which had become the informal gathering point for yachties. The patio and dining room overlooked the anchorage and the town, a magnificent view at any time of the day, but especially at happy hour.

All that was left of the town was back past the gendarmerie, up the hill, to the garage, where a number of men seem to gather each day, and where occasionally a car was to be found. The road along the shore led past the helo pad to the main wharf, where the copra boat from Papeete loaded and unloaded every three weeks, and where there was a petrol station.

The whole street was bordered on the one side by palm trees and the sea, and on the other by houses, mango trees, coconut palms, frangipani, hibiscus, shrubs and trees. The mountains seemed to rise right out of the roofs. A later Sunday stroll found everything shut up, and everyone out and about. The adults played bocce, a type of bowls which I had thought was Italian, as I had seen only Italians playing it before this; the teenagers played volleyball, and the children swam in swarms in the sea.

We took our dinghy to one such swarm and were almost swamped as everyone wanted to clamber on board. Ryan had a terrific time with all the kids. Children really don't need a common language to communicate and relate to each other. Good will seems to be enough. It kept away the sharks as well.

Ryan (8): *The kids were diving off a rock, but Dad wouldn't let me do it. I wanted to swim with them, but they wanted to sit in the dinghy. We were nearly washed onto the rocks since Dad couldn't start the engine with all the kids around.*

The only problem with this stroll in Paradise was the heat and humidity, especially after the afternoon rain. Carole had never experienced the combination before, and was quite uncomfortable. Ryan was in the same situation, but played the nonchalant macho-male to perfection. After noting, more than several times, how great it was to be in a place with real rain and proper temperatures (my youth, in tropical North Queensland had been spent in such a climate), I naturally couldn't complain, regardless of how I felt.

Taiohae, with a population of 800 or so, was the largest town in the Marquesas and the nominal capital, although the real government rested in Papeete, Tahiti. There were some moves towards separation and self-government, but things advance slowly in the South Pacific. Everyone seemed to have a car, TV, mangoes and pamplemouse in the garden, and fish for the catching. Apart from the regular dances, slide shows and lectures, there seemed to be few "diversions," and little "entertainment" to our sophisticated eyes. Who knows what drives the local economy, but we tried our best to help by purchasing as much of the bread, baked every second day, with which we could stuff ourselves. It was wonderful and cheap, the only food bargain on the island.

The people were nice, but we had to make the first move. Perhaps they were jaded by the constant flow of yachts, up to 1,000 per year. Being friendly and relatively inconspicuous, we were rewarded. Having Ryan along was a major plus.

Nate went ashore often and made a lot of friends. He brought two back to the boat one night. One picked up Ryan's guitar and entertained us for an hour or so with local songs. It was worth every one of the numerous margaritas he inhaled regularly during the concert.

Carole: *My only problem with Nate's bringing the locals on board was that he didn't ask ahead of time, and they invariably arrived when we were eating. I felt we were on display—"Here look at how the yachties live."*

Local Marquesans drove Toyota and Nissan 4WD vehicles, with a handful of Land Rovers and Citroens thrown in. Most seemed to be less than five years old and diesel-engined. Diesel was approximately $US4.50 per gallon, but the island has only 30 miles or so of roads, so there is little opportunity to use a lot of fuel. Unfortunately, we had to buy about 100 gallons of it.

The fuel pier was exposed to the ocean swells and provided our first Med-moor (tying up at right-angles to the dock instead of alongside) experience. We dropped a bow anchor, reversed to within a few yards of the pier and threw lines to the attendant. Because of the swell, getting close in just wasn't feasible. Another line pulled across the fuel hose and also was used to transfer the bill and subsequent payment, in cash. All this sounds fairly humdrum, but the bottom was a mixture of rock and junk, with doubtful holding ability, the swells were bouncing us all over the place, reversing is not the best feature of "Dolphin Spirit," and we were very new at the game. I can say now that I was really, really concerned, but hid it, of course.

Tiring of the muddy water and the rolling of Taiohae Bay, we moved five miles west to Tai Oa Bay, universally known as Daniel's Bay.

Carole: "Only five miles," he said; "Only round the corner," he said. So we made the mistake (never repeated) of not putting everything away properly. Smashing into tall waves and bouncing in all directions caused some of my favorite dishes to be broken. With me throwing up almost continually, Laurie not finding the entrance to the bay and keeping us at sea for three hours instead of the promised one, that little jaunt remains as one of the worst days in memory.

To set the record straight, it was my last navigation mistake on the circumnavigation, but it was a good one, at precisely the wrong time. I didn't trust the G.P.S., which took me right to the entrance, so went past, and then turned around to follow "Pilgrim" in. Thank you Sue and Steve, you saved me from a watery death at the hands of a mutinous crew.

Carole: In Daniel's Bay I broke down and cried and cried. There was no way I could face going to sea again. Climbing those huge waves really scared me, I was miserably sea-sick, the worst I had ever been, and the thought of doing it again was simply terrifying. Laurie did what he could to help, but I could see no way forward.

Daniel and his wife Antoinette have been welcoming yachts to "his" bay with fruit and fresh water for almost 30 years. The only requirement was that we sign the visitor's log, now in its third volume, where we were yacht 333. The crews of the four yachts in the bay (we met "Pilgrim" and "Camelot" there for the first time) were treated by Daniel to a "goat roast," with the goat (shot by Daniel that morning) and breadfruit cooked in a pit by heated stones, and the rest of the meal provided by the yachties.

Carole: Very carefully I moved the goat meat around my plate, and equally carefully made sure that none of it passed my lips. Whenever Ryan looked my way I pretended to be eating and enjoying. I do eat meat, but prefer not to know where it comes from, other than out of a shrink wrapped package.

This was our first real yachtie get together and it was great to meet the other sailing wives. They all seemed so competent, which made me even more depressed. In paradise, the enormity of what we had done hit me. Late at night, sleepless, I'd go on deck and have a good cry.

Besides goats, Daniel had horses and a few cattle, as well as the usual fruit trees and vegetable garden. We never found the reason for the cattle, as they were not used for milk or meat. He piped fresh water to the beach from a mountain stream and made it available to all visitors. Occasionally

Daniel traveled to other parts of Nuka Hiva, but seemed content to sit and let the world come to him. A cursory glance through the visitor logs showed boats from every country of the world, including Switzerland and Poland.

The TV show "Survivor" was shot there in 2002. Reports from subsequently visiting yachts indicate that some of the magic has gone. As the water was muddy and we were still rolling, we passed up a five-mile walk to see a 2000-foot-high waterfall, and moved on to the north coast of Nuka Hiva and Anaho Bay.

Carole: After our experience going to Daniel's Bay, I wasn't anxious to head out again. I knew that we would be sailing past the airport, and I kept thinking when I see it I will ask Laurie to put me on the next plane home. When I did see it, the seas were calm and I kept my mouth shut. My reward was the picture-perfect South Pacific I had been promised. All I could think was that this paradise had to be a movie set.

White sand beaches, gently waving palm trees, towering cliffs, waterfalls, clear water, coral reef, gorgeous fish, friendly people, unlimited fresh water, and a calm, calm anchorage—at last, we could put down a glass and have it still there when we reached for it again. At last we could snorkel and see fish that were thirty feet away. At last we could clean the growths off the side of the boat. The colony of goose-neck barnacles on the stern had become almost like family.

Naturally, we had protected the bottom of the boat with anti-fouling paint before we left the U.S. This worked very well, keeping it free of marine growths. However, the pre-departure loading of provisions, etc. made our original water-line discoverable only by a scuba diver. In addition, we spent almost the whole trip heeled over to one side.

Barnacles have to be one of the more intelligent of living things. I am amazed that a barnacle spore, drifting in the middle of the Pacific, and suddenly seeing a fiberglass hull whipping past, can realize, "Looks like a pretty good place to me; think I'll grab hold." If the ones at the stern of the boat are bright, consider the Einsteins at the bow! That amazement didn't stop me turning the lot into fish food—nature can be wonderful on another boat.

On one side of the dinghy passage through the reef we noticed a local, Peter, with a net set on the coral in knee-deep water. He was catching fish on the incoming tide, killing each with a quick bite just behind the eyes. As we watched, fascinated, he caught a small octopus, dispatched it in the same fashion, then held it out to us. He seemed surprised when we turned it down, but we had just spent the low tide walking on the reef and watching the octopi scuttle in and out of their holes. Who eats the floor show?

Ryan (8): *Dad gave me our fish spear and I was poking around in the tide pools when I saw a flash of green behind a rock. It was a five-pound parrot fish. I jabbed it with the spear, which bounced off the big scales, but the fish jumped out of the pool onto the coral and I speared it. Everyone was amazed. It was only later that I told them how I really caught it.*

Carole: *It was my first reef walk. Laurie turned over rocks and coral and pointed out the myriad of different creatures. There were lots of pretty wriggly things that I was admiring until Laurie's words sank in. Sea snakes! Our lives were in danger! Laurie calmed me down to the extent that I found the next octopus. After that, I swam with a constantly turning head.*

A newly arrived sailboat was charging all over the anchorage in full-throttle reverse, trying to set its anchor on hard coral pan. They came to a stop, all the crew gathered around the bow, then they reversed to just off our bow. "Is this yours?" they asked, pointing to an anchor hanging off theirs. I nodded, so they dropped it, right there, 20 feet off my bow, and left. Fortunately, their antics had wrapped the chain around a number of coral heads, so we didn't drift back closer to the reef, only a hundred feet behind us. Unfortunately, the chain wrapped around the coral heads made it very difficult to get re-anchored properly.

Leon, whose family lived in a house on the hill overlooking the bay, became our friend. His brick bungalow would not look out of place in any U.S. suburb, was serviced with electricity from his generator, and had most modern conveniences, including running water. The four groups of families around the bay had a single source of piped, pressurized water, from the streams in the surrounding mountains. We traded canned goods and sugar for pamplemouse, bananas, limes and coconuts.

The local restaurant opened when you wanted it to, and was closed at all other times. They would cook our fish, or provide us with theirs, and we could even specify the variety, being assured that it would be caught just before we arrived. Cold beer was available, as was a pig roast for parties of ten or more. The restaurant would also dispose of our garbage for 300 francs ($US3.50) per bag. Could anything have been more convenient?

Carole: *I saw my first sarongs and immediately all the clothes in my wardrobe (the ones Laurie let me bring anyhow) were no longer desirable. The problem now was to find one to fit. What's hard about fitting a sarong did I hear you ask? I am tall, and wanted the sarong to gracefully touch the ground as it did on the shorter Polynesians. Finding material the correct length was difficult.*

All of the children went to school at the village on the next bay, over the hills, living there for the week and coming home only on weekends. Anaho did have a "Catholic Camp," a group of buildings where children came for the equivalent of the U.S. "summer camp." The week after we left, a party of 25 Swiss (adults) were arriving and staying at the camp for three days. Apparently this was a somewhat unusual event, but Anaho was taking it with aplomb.

Leaving this paradise, we went back to the rolls of Taiohae to get our refrigeration compressor, which, of course, was not there. After the conversation related some pages earlier, the Post Master promised to receive our parcel and send it immediately back to Papeete on the return boat. It would be waiting for us when we arrived. Confident we had taken care of everything, we set off for the Tuamotos.

Carole: *I decided to stay on board to Papeete. Anaho had restored my equilibrium.*

As if to say that we were doing the right thing, the Trade Winds finally arrived, bringing clear skies and calm seas, and blew "Dolphin Spirit" gently and quickly from the Marquesas Islands to the Tuamotos. Our first landfall was Manihi Atoll, in the northern part of the Group. With a couple of exceptions, the Tuamotos are all atolls, and are probably known to most of the world merely as the site of the French nuclear tests in the Pacific. Those tests were held in the southern part of the Group, and that area was out of bounds to yachts.

Carole: *Our first view of Manihi was a line of palm trees rising out of the water, as the highest land is only three feet above sea level.*

Ryan (8): *Dad and I didn't tell Carole about the eight-foot shark that swam under our bow just before we entered the pass.*

Most atolls have passes in the surrounding reef which enable boats to enter and leave the central lagoon. These passes are of varying widths, depths and straightness, and most have strong currents, as they form the only passage for water in and out of the lagoon. Naturally, Manihi, our first pass, was one of the narrowest, and had two dog-legs to be traversed.

The procedure for running a pass was quite straight forward. First, everyone gathered round a copy of "Charlie's Charts," (a cruising guide which diagrams and describes the passes), and memorized all the salient features. Then the tide tables were interpreted to determine the approximate time for a slack tide. The direction of the pass was then correlated with the tide time and sun position to determine if the sun would be above and behind the boat during passage. Negotiating coral-filled water with the sun in your face is something like flying without radar through clouds filled with mountains. If all auguries were satisfactory, one crew member took the wheel, another climbed the mast to act as lookout and course fine-tuner, and the pass was run.

Nothing could be simpler! Unfortunately, "Charlie's Charts" were essential, the only game in town, and out of date. Coral grows, markers come and go through human and natural causes, and cyclones and storms move things around. The lookout aloft becomes essential and cannot relax. The Captain did, and we hit coral, not badly, but enough to put a major dent in an ego, and some minor scratches in the keel. The remaining bends were negotiated without incident, and we anchored off a very pretty beach, reef and motu (a small island that, strung together with others like it, makes up the atoll).

This was our first real coral experience. We had to learn to trust the water colors as the only true indicators of water depth:

Dark blue	—deep and safe
Pale blue	—okay, but getting shallow
Pale green	—probably too shallow
Yellow	—definitely too shallow, brace for impact
Brown	—too late

Manihi has a thriving pearl farming industry, with the farmers scattered on motus all around the atoll, and the oyster beds filling the lagoon. The village at the pass, contained the only bank, post office and primary school. There were 156 children attending the school, most of whom came in from the pearl farms to stay with relatives and friends in the village for the school week. The village population was less than 150 adults, so kids seemed to be everywhere. We watched a bra clad young lady cleaning fish and beating off the attentions of a six foot moray eel and some small sharks, a few yards from a group of kids playing soccer.

The largest shop sold all sorts of canned and frozen goods, but the only fresh vegetables were onions and garlic, and there was no fresh fruit. Here, as throughout the South Pacific, we found frozen chicken legs, but never thighs or breasts. The local live chickens seemed to have the normal number of appendages, so perhaps the frozen ones were a special breed.

One of our propane cylinders needed refilling. French cylinders have different connections to those of U.S. cylinders, but I had an adaptor with me. As cylinder exchange was used, there were no refill facilities. I had to upend the French cylinder and gravity fill mine through the adaptor and hose, a process that took over an hour. There was no propane, only butane, and butane attracts flies. I set the French cylinder in the branches of a tree so that I could have shade, and spent the hour waving away flies, and watching the comings and goings at the bakery across the street. The man who came out holding a huge rat by the tail was of particular interest, as the bakery had been our principal bread source.

Carole: *They did tell me about the shark months later, but I read about the rat for the first time here. What else is there Laurie has hidden from me?*

The anchorage was deep (60 feet) and full of coral heads to guarantee an anchor chain wrap. Anchored next to us was a French couple with a high school age daughter. She came over to help Carole and Ryan translate a Patricia Kass song they were using as a tool to learn French. Carole and the mother went to the local school the next day to donate some of the school supplies we had on board. At dinner that night the family told stories of untouched anchorages in the northern part of the lagoon, so we decided to set off and explore.

The general depth of the lagoon was 40 to 150 feet, but travel was made a little complicated by the shallow coral heads (6 to 200 feet in diameter), and more so by the buoys and lines that supported the pearl farm oysters. These were scattered all over the lagoon, mostly above water. We dodged and twisted, survived several heart attacks and a few cases of minor hysterics, and found a lovely anchorage tucked in behind a reef. The water was crystal clear, the sand blindingly white, the blue ocean visible across the motu, palm trees everywhere, and fish that leapt from water to line to barbeque with eagerness.

Carole: *Nervously I drove "Dolphin Spirit" through the lagoon, with Laurie on the bow calling directions using finger pointing and hand signals. It was my first extended boat driving experience, and it was in such a dangerous place. We had to twist and turn, so I had to learn fast, and didn't hit anything, which was a great relief after the scrape getting in.*

Kaliong and Ken, the pearl farmers on this motu, made us very welcome, inviting us ashore for lunch—grilled chops with macaroni and cheese. They then joined us on the boat for dinner and a video. Fractured French on our side, and equally mangled English on theirs, made for interesting conversation. The next day, they took us fishing off a coral head in the middle of the lagoon. Suicidal fish seemed to be everywhere. Ken, age 16, drove the boat by sitting on the outboard (120-HP). As a parting present, they gave us a double handful of misshapen black pearls.

Ryan (16): *Dad wouldn't let me drive the dinghy sitting on the outboard. It really looked so cool. I caught the biggest fish that day. They were biting a lot. Thinking back on this time now, I was really a dumb kid, with my backwards baseball cap, long shirts, and long baggy shorts. It took me several months to completely dismiss these impractical things, and move worrying about being cool to very low on my priorities list.*

Ryan and I decided to swim ashore one day and were a little perturbed to be shadowed by a big barracuda. He looked at us; we looked at him, and managed the previously impossible feat of swimming forward at speed while maintaining a continuous look backward under the arm, between the legs and over the back. Somehow a barracuda is more intimidating than a shark, even to Ryan.

Nate learned how to turn the local giant clams into clam chowder, so we went snorkeling and collected enough for dinner. Let's simply say that perhaps the locals didn't really want anyone to know how to do it right, as Nate's concoction was best left un-tasted. Poor Nate had equally bad luck with an octopus. At great risk to life and limb, he had captured one and then spent hours stopping it from crawling out of a bucket. Perhaps he should have spent those hours beating it against a rock as we had seen the locals do. There may be truth in the story that, after such beatings, one cooks the rock, as it is more tender.

Ryan (8): *Nate and Dad seemed to be enjoying the clam chowder when Carole told me to bring my chowder and help her with something in the galley. I gave her a kiss when she poured our chowder out of a porthole into the sea.*

Across the motu, the waves crashed onto the reef. We spent hours standing there watching colorful fish swimming in the transparent water, right at eye level as the waves built up in the shallower water—a real life aquarium, with an ever-changing population.

Further north we wound our way, and found another delightful anchorage. We were later told we were the first yacht to come that far. This may account for the welcome we received from Mahiri, his wife Remuna, their three children, and four hired hands. This pearl farm was extremely well set up with solar cells and a generator to supply power, telephone, satellite TV, and some of the most gorgeous sunsets we have ever seen. Remuna had visited Las Vegas, Disneyland and most of the California attractions the previous month. Is isolation a thing of the past?

Ryan (8): *This was a really great place. I could jump over the side at any* time for a swim. Every time I went fishing I caught fish. I even caught a five-foot black tip reef shark. Carole wouldn't go swimming after that.

We had dinners ashore with the local family (mostly fish and spaghetti with a unique sauce of mayonnaise and catsup) and enjoyed many visits. Their houses were built on stilts above the water of the lagoon, so dinner swims by, and washing up entails dropping the pots and pans into the water and allowing the fish to do the work. These people were by no means disadvantaged.

Carole watched octopi strolling from inlet to lagoon, Ryan snorkeled and found moray eels and myriad fish, and I did as little as possible.

Carole: I had been snorkeling with the guys when the "Jaws" music started in my head, so I swam to shore where a little stream ran across the motu from the sea to the lagoon. Movement caught my eye. Two octopi were swimming along the stream. Just as they reached me, the water shallowed, so they turned over and walked the rest of the way to the lagoon. I was enthralled, and the sight remains as one of the most special moments of the entire trip.

On our last visit to Mahiri's family, the tide was low. This meant that the ladder, from the work boat we used as a dinghy landing to the pier on which the houses were built, was close to vertical. I was at the top of the eight-foot climb, with both hands full of gifts, when the work boat moved away from the pier. This made the ladder about six inches too short, and I fell the eight feet into about a foot of water covering the reef. Apart from the obligatory cuts and scrapes, I had no serious damage. There must be some truth in the "fortune favors the foolish" saying.

Carole: Watching him fall that distance, I couldn't believe he hadn't broken both of his legs at least. Just as I was starting to relax, I was reminded that there was danger all around, and no nearby hospital.

We had learned the secret of traveling with big boats inside the lagoon—stay close to the shore where there was deep water and no buoys. All too soon it was time to employ the technique and we dragged ourselves away. Waiting for the tide at the lagoon entrance, we saw our local friends speeding past on the way to their pearl farm oyster beds. Acting the seasoned veterans, we passed on our fund of pass-knowledge to an Australian boat waiting to come in. Safely out (my ego somewhat restored) we settled down to an overnight sail.

Rangiroa Atoll, the largest in the Tuamotos, is so large that all of the island of Tahiti can fit into the lagoon with room to spare. After our experience with the tiny pass at Manihi Atoll, we were thrilled to see that the two passes into the lagoon were each about 400 yards wide, with depths to match. Everything is relative however, as the tidal flow causes six foot high waves at the entrances.

Dauntless as always, we plunged in, and the pass was easy. There were 15 yachts already at anchor just off the Hotel Kia Ora. This, the largest hotel, was six miles from the main town, and the gendarmerie wasn't even on the same motu, but across another pass. The tidal currents were so strong that our five-horsepower outboard was barely sufficient to make headway. Checking in with the gendarmes was an absolute requirement, the post office was there, as was the shop that sold fresh bread, so we had to get across.

Picture this: blue skies, dark blue water shading to pale green near the shore and dotted here and there by the black of coral heads, white sand beach, palm trees and assorted flowering shrubs fringing the beach, and you get some idea of what we were forced to look at every day. Life can be hell!

Just inside the pass was a small, flat motu, surrounded by a reef in 10 to 30 feet of water. The fish there were very accustomed to snorkelers and divers, and gathered around the dinghy waiting to be fed. It was quite an experience to be surrounded by several hundred sergeant major and butterfly fish, all trying to get at the cracker crumbs, and to have all those little mouths (some quite large) nibbling at our hands and arms.

Carole: *Cracker crumbs were plentiful, as I had just discovered that all the boxes of crackers kept (in their boxes) in a storage area behind the salon settee, had developed a peculiar taste. Tearfully we converted all our Wheat Thins, Triscuits and Water Crackers into fish food, and from then on used that area to store only canned food.*

The Kia Ora offered shark dives, but we didn't participate. Catching hammerheads in the Marquesas, and black tips in Manihi, was enough shark for us. Besides which, we saw at least one every time we went snorkeling, so why pay for the privilege? One cruiser came back from a solo drift snorkel in the pass, still wide-eyed. He had glanced around and noticed he was being shadowed by a 10-foot tiger shark, thereby providing another reason why solo snorkeling is never a good idea.

Carole: *Laurie told me about all the sharks months later. I never saw one while I was swimming, but I heard the music from "Jaws" in my mind every time I went snorkeling.*

The hotel had $US600-per-night bungalows built out over the lagoon, each with their own steps to the water. We went to the Friday-night buffet.

The attendees were people from ten of the yachts, and hotel guests who seemed to be American, English and Japanese. The dinner comprised cold salads, rice, baked potatoes, barbeque steak, lamb chops, fish and sausages and one of the more extensive dessert bars we have seen. We could have been anywhere, as there were no local dishes. For approximately $US100 per couple we received one pre-dinner drink each and the dinner. Not cheap, but the post-dinner show of Tuamotan singing and dancing was new to us. I was forced to make the obligatory fool of myself during that part of the show when the audience was required to demonstrate that it was impossible to move hips forward, backwards and sideways at the same time. Surgery was not required the next day, but it was a close call.

Carole took notes at the sarong fashion show and learned all the ways to tie them. Now all she had to do was find a store and buy one.

Ryan's sailing dinghy, the "Cool Dolphin" was at last christened and was perfect for these waters. We quietly zoomed in and out of the yachts as Carole zoomed us in and out with the video camera. I was relegated to First Mate, and tended the main sheet, while Captain Ryan lounged at the tiller, steering with a finger tip, waving casually to the other captains.

Ryan (8): *The best part of sailing my dinghy around was that, as captain, I got to give orders to Dad.*

We rented bicycles and pedaled the six miles to town. The motu was less than 100 yards wide at the widest, so the view from the road was always beach, palms, ocean, and reef. The scenery made it so easy to pedal along that the miles just flew by. We found out the real reason on the way back, forcing our way against the 15-knot wind.

Unfortunately, the bank and post office were closed for some sort of local holiday, but the shops were open and the drinks were cold, if expensive. The long push back into the wind simply made the pina coladas at the hotel taste better. Hey, we may be on a yacht, but that doesn't mean we can't use the shore facilities. Besides which, the hotel lounge had a glass floor so we could watch the fish swimming by as we sipped.

The Club Med "sailboat," a 20,000-ton cruise ship with masts, called in for the day, anchoring off the hotel with us. The boats it used to ferry guests ashore were bigger than most of the cruising yachts. The hotel was on the ship's Papeete/Raitea/Morea/Bora Bora/Rangiroa one-week tour.

Carole: *This was the first time on our voyage that we met real tourists. They were amazed at our adventures, and green with envy that we would still be lounging in Rangiroa, when they were back at home, at work.*

Our dinghy was always tied up so that it floated just on the other side of the hull from our bed. The soft slap of the ripples against the dinghy was a lullaby every night, until one night it stopped, and I awoke with a start about 3:30 a.m. It took a while to realize what had woken me and when I got to the deck the dinghy was long gone into the darkness, as the fitting the painter was tied to on the dinghy had broken.

When it got to be light enough, we hailed a passing local fishing boat and headed off down-wind to search. About four miles away, there was the dinghy pulled up on shore at a pearl farm factory. It was intact, as was the outboard and all of our snorkeling gear. The pearl farm workers had seen it drifting past, gone out and pulled it in. They refused any reward. The fishermen just asked for a gallon of fuel. Thanks again to such great people.

We watched the sun set from the cockpit—again—and it was gorgeous—again. As Carole said, "Every view is a post card." As I said, ad nauseam, "Someone has to do it."

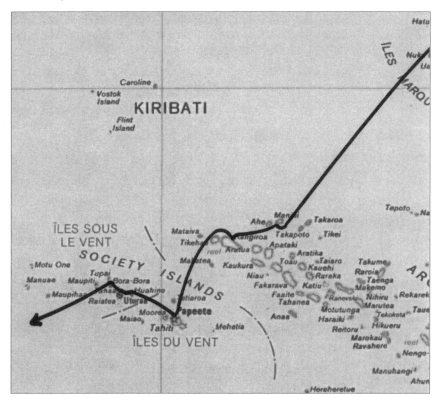

Tahiti and the Society Islands

Year One
June 1 to July 13

Carole: *"See you in Tahiti," we would call to other cruisers as we left one anchorage to go to another. How nice it was to not have to say goodbye to new friends, and to know that our trip was really just beginning. Sadness at leaving any place was fleeting, as we had so much to look forward to.*

Planning to arrive at Papeete at daybreak two days later, we left Rangiroa at 1600 hours. Of course we sailed to perfection and therefore hove-to at midnight outside the Papeete harbor entrance. This allowed us to savor at length the sight of the full moon setting over the dark, jagged mountains of Moorea, across a calm, silver sea.

Sailing legend has it that one of the great experiences of life is to sail into Papeete harbor at sunrise. While it was a thrill to bring "Dolphin Spirit" in at dawn, it must be said that having to dodge an inbound freighter and two of the high speed Moorea ferries, did take a little of the romance away. Murky water and rusty container ships also didn't help. Once inside we decided to experience decadence in full, and tied up at "Le Quai," which is right on the main street of Papeete.

Boats moor "Mediterranean Style," at right angles to the quay, either bow or stern in. "Dolphin Spirit" has a mind of her own in reverse, so we quickly decided to drop a stern anchor and go in bow first. The critical audience of already moored yachts, the cross wind, and the small space available, helped the decision immensely.

Naturally, we dropped our anchor on top of one from a previously moored yacht, and a later arrival dropped theirs on top of ours. Leaving was therefore a comedy of smelly mud, tangled anchor chains and interlocked anchors, that cost us a boat hook, a reasonable amount of skin, and the lasting enmity of several yachts.

Bow in did give more privacy, but required us to crawl over the anchor to get to solid ground. Judging the last step was a real art form, particularly when the swell from the ferries made the boat bounce up and down a couple of feet. Nate fell in, and weeks later, in Moorea, we met a young boy who instantly recognized Carole as "The lady who screamed getting on and off the boat."

Carole: *Laurie expected me to step backwards into space with only a little rail to hold onto, and the water slurping below. No way! Eventually I did, of course, but the trips ashore never got easier. I really don't remember screaming, but then I have tried to forget everything about that terrible yawning space. I wasn't glad to leave Papeete, but I never missed that terror-filled step ashore.*

Ryan (8): *It was only two feet!*

In 1962, when I first sailed into Papeete, the jagged green mountains rising straight up from the shore line were a dramatic sight. Today, the mountains cannot be seen for the multiple-story buildings that line the water front. Then, we sat and watched local dancers performing against a background of Moorea and the sunset. Today, we could still see Moorea across the container wharf, but the dance floor was buried under a divided highway. Papeete was now a city, with traffic jams, noise, pollution, rush and bustle and hustle. Swimming was banned in the harbor because of pollution. While toilets were handled by septic systems, all other effluent went directly into the harbor.

We were meeting lots more cruisers and many "old" friends had arrived. "Marita Shan," "Sky Bird," "Osprey," "Soliloquy," "Magnum Bonum," and "Pilgrim" were tied up nearby. The yachties congregated at Les Trucks to eat, as it seemed to be the only affordable food in town. A collection of mobile restaurants, each had its own specialty—waffles, Chinese, pizza, lamb-on-a-spit, ice cream, hamburger—you name it. They were cheap (average 800 francs, $US9 per meal) and generally delicious.

French restaurants were right in the stratosphere of prices, so we can't say we often ate at them. Ice cream was cheap, delicious and plentiful. Baguettes were a bargain at 38 francs ($US0.50 approx.) per loaf, all warm and crusty. There were shops, shops, and more shops, with almost anything you could want, albeit at incredibly high prices.

Carole bought only some material for a pareo (***Carole:*** *A sarong by another name. I gave up looking for one the right length, and settled for an equally fetching [Laurie's description] shorter version.*). Ryan roller skated up and down the quay and I used the unlimited fresh water to clean everything.

Ryan (8): *I got to roller-blade up and down where the yachts were tied up. Getting on and off the boat—no problem! Sometimes I just jumped, though I did almost fall in a couple of times. One night, Dad and Carole took me for a special treat, ice cream with burning sparklers stuck in it.*

We were in the "high rent" district. A little farther around the harbor, boats could anchor and stern-tie to a palm tree with less traffic noise, but no power and water, and questionable security. Past the airport, Maeva Bay offered a gorgeous anchorage inside the reef, but many boats moved to Papeete because of the rolly conditions in the bay. "Promises" had to rush back from the city when they received word they were dragging. Carry that portable VHF at all times!

Carole: *Watching Jan back "Camelot" into the tight space near us without her husband Bill directing her, made me feel dreadfully inadequate. That feeling went away, with time, but to this day Laurie has not let me dock "Dolphin Spirit," not that I would want to.*

Two local teenagers tried to steal a dinghy. One worked at distracting attention while the other drove off in the dinghy. Not the smartest of moves around a group of yachties. Several of us detained the one, while a couple of dinghies quickly caught the other, as the young thief had picked the smallest outboard in the place. It was our first experience of theft, and practically our last until we got to the Mediterranean.

The refrigeration drama, started in Nuka Hiva, came to its climax here. Expecting to find my package there, I went to the special post office for packages. Nothing. Using my best Franglish, I worked my way up the food-chain to the head man, who mercifully spoke reasonable English. A short explanation from me, a Gallic shrug from him, and we were stalled.

"Can you speak to the post office in Nuka Hiva?" I asked.

"Of course, all I have to do is pick up that phone," he boasted.

"Would you please do that now?" I begged.

This seemed to pose a bit of a problem, but eventually another Gallic shrug and some button punches, and we were connected. Yes, the parcel had arrived. No, the parcel had not been sent back. How can he be so sure? It was obvious, he was looking at it. Would he please send it on the next boat. Of course. When was the next boat leaving? In three weeks.

I then intervened and asked if the afternoon plane for Papeete had left yet. No it hadn't, but parcels could not be sent by plane I was told from both ends. Fine I said, please buy a passenger ticket on the plane, and put the parcel in the seat. If I had suggested blowing up the Louvre, the astonishment wouldn't have been greater. I persisted and got eventual agreement, picking up the parcel from the head-man's office the next day.

Carole: *It was about this time I began to regret telling Laurie before we left, "You look after everything above deck and I will look after everything below." That was fine when we were sailing, and duties seemed equally divided. In port however, I seemed to be always cooking, teaching Ryan, or cleaning, and Laurie lounging about reading at the rate of a book a day.*

Most cruisers divided tasks into "blue" and "pink" jobs, and many a get-together was enlivened by discussion on the category for many middle-of-the-road ones such as cleaning the stainless, and cleaning the shower area. We decided that, while at sea, up and down worked well, but in port "blue" jobs would include hanging out the washing occasionally, in exceptional circumstances, doing the dishes, sweeping and washing the floors and other miscellaneous chores. The newly developed "mauve" category (all three of us working together) would include cleaning the stainless.

I agreed with Carole's decisions, because she left in the "blue" category my favorite task of clearing a blocked toilet, and then rebuilding it.

Hiring a car for the day we took a pretty drive around Tahiti, finding a black-sand beach where Ryan got blissfully knocked around by the waves. The drive up into the mountains was a cool break. Petrol was around $US5 per gallon, so small cars were the order of the day, and we hired the smallest and cheapest. Seeing my 6'4" unfold from the car provided much amusement to the onlookers, who generally stuck around to see how I got back in.

Ryan (8): *We walked up into the mountains to see a big waterfall. Dad wanted some photos so I had to get into the water and stand near the bottom of the waterfall. It was cold, cold, cold. You have no idea how many times I had to do this or that so that Dad could take the perfect picture.*

Diesel for the boat could be obtained tax free as we left (35 francs per liter versus 75 francs with tax, $US1.55 per gallon versus $US3.33), a real bonus to the budget.

It was nice to be in "civilization" again, but it wasn't Polynesian, it wasn't French, it wasn't cute or smart or dramatic or cultural, just a cosmopolitan center, so different from the idyllic tropical island that the mind goes into culture shock.

Carole: Not for me. I enjoyed our days of city life, well stocked grocery stores featuring delicious cheeses, freezers full of known meat, fresh milk, and restaurants. However, many things were so expensive. A group of us got together to share the cost a bunch of celery ($US5).

Our shotgun had been handed over to the Customs officers in Nuka Hiva, and we got it back when we checked out of Papeete. This was a little strange, as we were to visit several more islands in French Polynesia. In common with most other cruisers, we found that having a gun on board was more trouble than it was worth. Almost every country requires guns to be surrendered on entry, which negates any defensive worth they might have. A non-declared gun found during a Custom's search often results in immediate confiscation of the boat. Pepper spray and Mace provided us with equal feelings of security, even though we never had to use them.

Moorea was a pleasant few hours sail from Papeete, and we anchored in 12 feet of calm, clear water on a sand bottom, inside the reef at the mouth of Oponohu Bay, where a Moorean we had met in Nuka Hiva suggested we stay. It was a lovely spot, ocean on one side, saw-tooth mountains on the other.

Carole: We saw the moon over Moorea from Tahiti, and a rainbow over Tahiti from Moorea. Both were the stuff of dreams, and here we were living them.

Entering the anchorage took a bit of maneuvering as it was almost surrounded by coral. Anchoring in 12 feet sounds great, but we draw 7 feet 6 inches, so watching the depth drop 20 feet, 18, 15, 12, "Laurie, drop it now!"

The boat next door to us had the movie South Pacific, so naturally I had to have us all watch it. I think it was filmed on Moorea. Even if it wasn't, the sharp peaks, green slopes, palm trees and blue water that surrounded us were the reality that the movie pretended to be.

It was starting to dawn on me that I could relax. There was no rush to work, only one student instead of 30, no TV programs to watch, no newspaper to read, nothing really pressing to do. Laurie had shown he could look after us and the boat. We were spending months in places I had once dreamed about spending days in.

If only I had known we would survive, life would have been perfect.

I actually stood on the bottom when I was cleaning the hull. Ryan spent many hours ashore playing soccer, swimming and catching fish with Jerome, the son of a Frenchman and a Scottish lady who had sailed to Tahiti from France, and were there for a few years hoping to save enough to start sailing again.

Ryan (8): *Jerome was the first boy I met on the trip. He and the local kids never seemed to go to school, so they were always ready to play when I finished my schoolwork. The water was very shallow for a long way out and there were lots of little fish. Jerome's house was right on the water and we spent a lot of time making different fish traps from plastic bottles and coconuts. Carole always let me bring him on board to sleep over, and especially for dinner, because whatever she made, Jerome said, "Yummy!"*

Carole: *"Yummy!" Yes! For the years since Ryan's mother had become sick and Laurie had to get most of the meals for Ryan, they had been simple and overly take-out dependent. Casseroles, for example, were not dishes Ryan had met. His body language did not bode well for happy meal times and rampant bribery was often the order of the day—from Laurie, not me.*

"Gigolo" came into the anchorage and we met Gary and Dorothy who were to share many adventures with us over the next few years. I taught Carole to stand up in the dinghy, to stay dry if we were heading into the wind and waves. Dorothy saw Carole doing this, and much later (***Carole:*** *When she knew better.*) confided that she thought Carole must be a real sailor. "Blue Ribbon" arrived and we began our regular bridge games with Dave and BK. Somehow, real bridge was not the same as the game we had been playing on the computer. For one thing, we were not allowed to keep re-dealing until we got a good hand.

Dinghy driving became an art. Kurt on "Osprey" drove standing up, using a plastic-pipe tiller extension to stay in control. Steve on "Sky Bird," not to be outdone, fitted his dinghy with a lashed down kitchen chair, and drove around sitting in style. Kurt continued for years, but Steve's experiment lasted only a day.

There was a local barbeque on the beach every Saturday and Sunday. Chicken and French fries (frites in French) for 500 francs ($US5.50), with bottles of Hinano beer for 200 francs. One Saturday was a special celebration of some kind, and we got roast lamb for free, just because we came ashore and were friendly.

Carole: *It was here that Doctor Laurie provided us with his most memorable treatment. I was starting to get a sore throat, so Laurie gave me some pills, which I then took faithfully three times a day. A couple of days later, he sheepishly sidled up and asked how I was feeling. "Much better," I responded. "That's good," he said, "because I've given you Lomotil." Lomotil is a sure and certain cure for diarrhea.*

Nate left us here to head back to California. He had been a great help on the passage to the Marquesas, but it was now time for us to be alone and do things as a family.

We took lots of walks on Moorea to find fruit, so we actually got exercise. A road went round the island, and it was delightful to walk under the palms, mango and breadfruit trees, surrounded by hibiscus and frangipani flowers, with green mountains on one side and the blue water on the other—walks to be savored and remembered. One of our favorite pictures, "Dolphin Spirit" at sunset, was taken on such a stroll.

Playing tourists, we visited the Tiki Village for dinner and traditional island dances. The Village is a collection of native houses, maintained in the old traditions, supporting traditional arts and crafts and manned by volunteers. Most Polynesians we have met spoke Tahitian, French and English, generally in that order of fluency, but the Tiki Village guides seemed also to speak German and Japanese. One noted that he spoke Australian, but I found that difficult to believe.

I wandered off, only to have Carole call me back urgently. She simply pointed, and there was Ryan, surrounded by grinning Tahitians, and showing me the fish tattoo on the back of his hand. Momentarily I went up the wall, before I realized that Carole had been there all the time, and would never have let such a thing happen. It was, of course, temporary, but hand drawn and very realistic.

Ryan (8): *Dad really looked mad. He was so funny. The "tattoo" lasted more than a week.*

The Village was on the lagoon, with some guests coming from the hotels by out-rigger canoe. The food was cooked in traditional pits, the sunset made the weak Mai Tais irrelevant, and the show was superb. Ryan was particularly fascinated by the fire dances. Of course I was not impressed by the swaying grass skirts, and got up to prove, once again, that Tahitian dancing really can be performed only by Tahitians. Carole recorded my antics on video for later blackmail use.

Carole: *We met some tourists who lived not far from my mother, so I asked them to telephone her on their return. This began the custom of asking Californians we met to call my mother and tell her I was doing fine. We didn't get onto email until we arrived in Turkey, and telephoning was very expensive.*

The manager of the Moorea Club Med convinced us that we should move to that anchorage, through a pass only a few miles away. We found the pass and twisted our way into it until I became concerned about the lack of water and room, turned around, hit a rock, scraped off, and got out of there as fast as possible back to our comfortable Oponohu anchorage. More damage to my ego than to the boat—four passes and two groundings was not an impressive record.

The West called, so we moved on to Huahine Island, a horrible overnight passage with 30-knot winds, confused seas and a seasick Carole. A couple of books slid off the nav station seat and neatly switched off the autopilot. The resultant abrupt change in direction went unnoticed until Carole commented on the easier ride and on the Club Med ship going in the wrong direction. Confusion reigned. As it turned out, this was one of the worst nights of the circumnavigation.

For some reason, now banished from memory, I had to go into the forepeak. I was too tired, or too careless, and forgot to hold the door open, so it closed behind me. This allowed the handle on the toilet in the forward head to come down and effectively prevent the door from opening more than a crack. Carole and Ryan were un-stirring and there was no other way out. Half an hour of work, timing pushing with rolls, and I managed to inch the toilet handle up enough to allow the door to be lifted off its hinges, and I was free.

Carole: *I was so sick. It was supposed to be a short overnight trip. The boat was rolling and pitching. There was no way I was going to leave my spot in the cockpit, where Laurie had wedged me in with pillows and blankets. Poor Laurie had to be up the whole night. He had gone below and a long time passed without his re-appearing. I didn't care where he was or what he was doing. All I wanted was the rolling to stop.*

Ryan (16): *I slept the whole night and took very little notice. Little did I know that as I got older, I would want to be on watch at these times.*

The anchorage in front of the village of Fare was crowded, with all yachts anchored far too close to each other for comfort, but the village itself was delightful, with shops and businesses strung out along the shore under huge trees. It looked very much like a North Queensland town, or an 1800s Western cow town with palms, sand and beautiful water, in the place of cactus, dust and more cactus. We had drinks ashore with the other yachties in a small bar with the waves lapping under the floor.

Ryan made friends with a young boy on a neighboring yacht. His father, Brian, was Californian, mother Polynesian (now divorced and no longer around), step-mother French. The wife and the fifteen year old daughter went topless, much to my delight and Ryan's complete indifference. I guess eight-year-olds take almost anything in stride. Brian built hotels and was between jobs.

Ryan (8): The snorkeling was good. I saw my first lion fish, which is very pretty, but has poisonous spines.

The rest of our group went to Raiatea, while we sailed with the California/French couple (mainly so Ryan could continue to be with his new friend) to the southern part of the island, where the father's Polynesian relatives (through his first wife) had considerable tracts of land, and where one of his old hotels was located. There we met the patriarch who owned half the island (bare feet, ragged clothes, battered pick-up with missing headlights), and another major land owner (bare feet, bicycle with no brakes, ragged clothes), which taught us not to judge by appearances, especially in the South Pacific.

Ryan (8): The water was shallow and the bottom almost completely covered with black sea slugs. I had great fun picking them up and throwing them. Carole was disgusted and screamed every time I took one near her. One day she accidentally swam into shallow water and started screaming because she kept touching the slugs with her body.

The family had land along the beach, and had a barbeque set up, so we joined them a few times for breadfruit, sausages, steaks, and fish. Brian led us through a very complicated reef passage for a few miles, to one of his old hotels for lunch. The view was great, the hotel very nice, but empty. We found empty hotels through most of French Polynesia outside of Papeete. The tourist industry seemed to be really hurting. Everything was so expensive, food, transportation, clothes, even souvenirs, that it must frighten people off. Scared us, and we were such cosmopolitan sophisticates.

The short, four hour sail to Raiatea was calm, and we anchored behind Taoru Island, just inside the reef entrance. Snorkeling, with beautiful live coral, in depths ranging from four feet to a drop off to 100 feet or more, Ryan found lots of sea anemones with attendant clown fish, our first white-tipped reef shark, and a number of the very poisonous but beautiful lion fish. We could have moved to any of the four marinas on the island, but chose to stay where we were, as we planned to head off soon for Bora Bora, where we had heard there were kids.

Carole: Saw my first clown fish, and was enamored. Also saw a sailboat on its side, high and dry on the fringing reef and was reminded that we were in dangerous, coral filled waters. Relax Carole, relax!

It was a wet dinghy ride to the town of Utoroa, a seemingly solid concentration of tourist shops. Both sailing cruise ships "Wind Song" and "Club

Med II" were there, so the place was full. We had seen the ships often in Moorea, Raiatea, Papeete and Rangiroa, and delighted in commenting that the poor passengers had only one week of the good life, while we had it every day. Their "Today is Tuesday so this must be Raiatea," compared with our "What month is this?"

Raiatea and Tahaa islands are within the one encircling reef, so we sailed half-way round Raiatea and up to Tahaa, before exiting a pass to head for Bora Bora. We wanted to see the famous island with only one palm tree, but unfortunately, the tree had died, and the island was under water, but we do have a photograph of the water where it once was. The dolphins escorting us out of the passage were some consolation for our loss.

Just ahead of us in the pass, "Marita Shan" did an abrupt right-angle turn and nearly hit the reef before Pat regained control. Tash had switched on the vacuum cleaner, and the resultant power drain had switched off the auto-pilot. Later, in New Zealand, Pat increased his battery capacity from 400 amp-hours to 800. I reassured Carole that it wouldn't happen to us, as we had 2,000 amp-hours of house battery capacity. Besides which, I never use the auto-pilot in a pass.

Carole: *In addition, vacuuming was not high on my priorities list. I am a cleaning fanatic, but only when company is coming.*

From Raiatea, Bora Bora was an impressive jagged pair of mountains in the west, exuding all the mystery and romance that the name conjures up. As we sailed closer, the peaks became less and less majestic, still nice, but definitely not the "Bali Hai" of legend. The island is completely surrounded by a very lovely lagoon, with only one entrance through the surrounding reef.

"Blue Ribbon" was anchored just inside the pass and invited us over for lunch, but we decided to be decadent and picked up a mooring at the Bora Bora Yacht Club. This was really a restaurant, one of the best and most expensive in French Polynesia, with a good marketing gimmick. They had moorings at 2,500 francs ($US30 approx) per day, fresh water at 300 francs a fill, and garbage disposal at 250 francs a bag, but all of these charges were waived if we ate at the restaurant.

At the next table, on the one night we ate there, were Californians off a cruise ship. They lived a couple of blocks away from where we once kept "Dolphin Spirit" in Marina del Rey. Carole naturally asked them to telephone her mother, and they did.

We stayed two nights, then moved to a delightful anchorage near the entrance pass, between a small island and the reef. The water was shallow and clear and there were kids, lots of kids. On board the seven Australian boats, "Dolphin Spirit," "Mahini," "Skerryvore," "Wise Cat," "Aphrodite," "Kiley" and "Bon Accord," were 15 children. The other boats in the anchorage, from the U.S., Canada, and Sweden, had none. I am not sure what that means, but it must have some relationship to the national psyche or libido. Needless to say, Ryan had a ball.

John and Lois on "Topaz" had a grandson visiting, and invited Ryan to go snorkeling with them. As it happened, he had put off doing his school work that day, so we wouldn't let him go. This was an act of sheer stupidity on our part, demonstrating that we still carried with us the land-bound regimentation of our past. Kids are more important than school when they are so rare. We tried not to make that mistake again.

July 4 was celebrated with a party on board "Dolphin Spirit," all decked out with Christmas lights for the occasion. It was an intimate gathering of everyone in the anchorage, some 30 yachties, a mixture of Americans, Canadians, Australians, and two brave Swedes. It was notable that the Americans went back to their boats at a reasonable hour, while the Australians partied on. Afterwards, there was no wind and the sky was full of stars, so we lay in the dinghy and just drifted, with the lights on "Dolphin Spirit" and the stars reflected in the calm water.

Bringing into full service all my extraordinary powers of perception, I discovered by accident the place where the tour boats fed stingrays on the reef. We went there at the same time as a tour boat, and were warned to stay away, as the place was reserved for tourists. Not sure whether to take this as a compliment or an insult, we ignored the warning, as it was unmarked, open reef, and had a great time swimming in about four feet of water with 15 or so rays, all three to four feet in diameter.

Ryan and I did the swimming. Carole jumped in too, but then thought the better of it and chose to observe from the dinghy, through our viewer. She missed the sensation of having a ray suddenly appear from behind her, some six inches below her stomach, and take approximately two hours to pass. Those tails (with barbs) were long! Ryan's eyes seemed bigger than his goggles.

We made sure that every cruiser in the anchorage knew about the rays and went there at feeding time. Those hotel people learned that it doesn't pay to be nasty with the "Dolphin Spirit" crew.

Ryan (8): *I caught fish every day; 10 in half an hour was my best effort. Fishing was quickly becoming my favorite pastime. It was always on my mind, even during school lessons. I was constantly looking out to learn new techniques, though it was better to learn them from the locals than my father. If he knew so much about fishing, how come he let me fish all the time instead of him?*

While Ryan was playing with Nat, one of the five kids on "Wise Cat," Carole and I, with Dave and BK off "Blue Ribbon," rented bikes and rode the 20 miles around the island. Fortunately, the road was mostly dead flat, with only one hill, which we walked up and down. Up because it was up, down because none of the bikes had brakes that we would trust to stop us. Shipboard life strengthens the upper body, but allows the legs to deteriorate sadly.

The central mountains revived some of their majesty with dramatic apparent shape and size changes as we circled them. Several stops to enjoy the views and partake of liquid refreshments, allowed the geriatrics to make respectable progress. We chose to ignore the young Japanese couple that passed us three times while we were on the first half of the island. They were obviously professional bike riders!

Ryan rode with us on another day to Bloody Mary's restaurant. All they serve for lunch is pizza, so Ryan was in heaven. The island ride was delightful (there needs to be new adjectives. I have used gorgeous, wonderful, lovely, delightful, etc. to death. It is very hard not to lapse into superlatives when describing the water colors, the flowers, the trees, the mountains and the combinations that make up the continually changing views, so I won't try.), with the towering mountains on one side and the lagoon on the other.

Each time we rented bikes, I returned to the boat with the bike-basket and my back-pack loaded with pineapples, other fruit, and loaves of bread. We began to think we were finally starting to settle in and really enjoy this cruising life and some of the unique pleasures it offers.

Ryan (16): *As the trip progressed, my parents became much more casual and laid-back, and much easier to deal with. I suppose I was getting older as well.*

Bora Bora was the best place to be during the Bastille Day celebrations. Every night for a week from July 5 there were song and dance competitions between the different islands and villages. I happen to love Tahitian drums, and put up with all those swaying grass skirts just to feel the beat. The singing was wonderful, the spectacle stunning, and it was all free. We went several times and consumed huge amounts of video and still film.

Around the dance arena was a small village of temporary thatched buildings, housing restaurants, electronic game arcades (even in paradise), and my favorite, the spinning wheels. Here you buy a number, and if the wheel stops spinning on that number, you win. The prizes were what fascinated me. None of the usual stuffed toys and plastic garbage, the prizes here were cans of butter, sacks of sugar and flour, boxes of biscuits and other useful articles. Imagine—prizes that are useful—what a concept!

Beautifully decorated, many restaurants even had walls made completely of flowers, leaves and fronds. There was a competition to pick the best, and choosing one became not just a search for the best food, but for the prettiest and most fragrant.

Each night we formed a dinghy convoy to navigate the couple of miles back to the anchorage in the dark. Flashlights in hand we would wend our way through the reefs and coral heads. Each driver had to decide whether the lead dinghy was correct and follow it, or incorrect, and therefore go another way. Some nights we were a neat snake of lights, others a disorderly rabble.

It was here that we really linked up with the boats that were to be part of our lives for the next few years.

"Marita Shan" Pat and Natasha (Tashi)—Canada.
"Sky Bird" Steve and Tammy—Seattle
"Gigolo" Gary and Dorothy—Sunnyvale, California
"Osprey" Kurt and PL—Seattle
"Pilgrim" Steve and Sue—San Francisco
"Soliloquy" Joe and Madeline—California
"Blue Ribbon" Dave and BK—Texas
"Camelot" Bill and Jan—San Francisco
"Promises" Dave and Heather—Seattle
"Magnum Bonum" Egon and Silvija—Sweden
"Topaz" John and Lois—Connecticut

A very diverse group, from widely varying backgrounds, it was hard to imagine another circumstance where all would meet, let alone become friends.

The boat names were equally diverse. Cruisers generally become known by their boat name, so pick one that you are happy to be called by. "Gigolo" skated close to the edge in this regard. We became "the Dolphins" which wasn't too bad, and much preferable to "the Spirits."

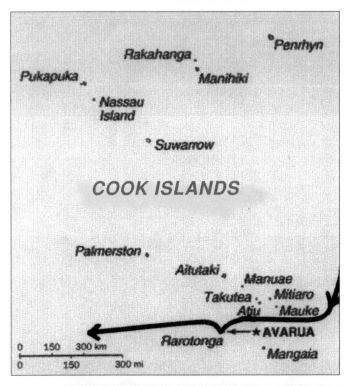

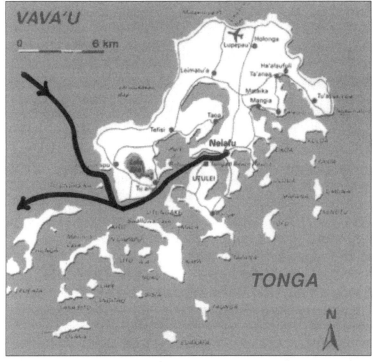

Cook Islands, Nuie and Tonga

Year One
July 15 to August 29

One of the fallacies of cruising is you have all the time in the world to do things. Certainly there is more time to spend in each place than is available to land-based mortals, but key schedules, mainly weather and season-related, have to be kept. For example, you cannot enter the South Pacific before the end of the cyclone season in March, and you must be out, in Australia, New Zealand, or north of the equator, by early November. That leaves only seven months to cover French Polynesia, Cook Islands, Tonga, and Fiji, all at less than six knots. Stay too long in one place, and you have to hurry through another. The main problem is that it gets better as you go west, something that is hard to appreciate when lolling in Bora Bora lagoon.

Realizing this, I hauled up the anchor (with Carole saying, "Do we have to leave?" and Ryan in tears over leaving his friend Nat on "Wise Cat."), and set course for Raratonga in the Cook Islands, a four-day sail. Just about every type of weather occurred in those four days, starting out with no winds, then light ones from the north-east (we were heading almost due west), then from the south-west, then from the west at 20 to 25 knots. We were beating into head winds and, as everyone knows, gentlemen don't sail to windward. Where were those confounded south-east trade winds when we needed them? So far we had a total of only four days of trades. All that was predictable about the weather was that it was unpredictable, and that the forecasts were wrong, even those from Arnold, the New Zealand weather guru everyone consulted.

Carole: *This was the first time we had sailed in a group. With us were "Marita Shan," "Sky Bird," and "Promises." It was nice to be able to chat on VHF with the other ladies, sharing recipes and complaining about the weather. Poor Heather on "Promises" was serving orange juice, with both hands full, when a wave knocked the boat sideways. The resulting bruise on her bottom was so impressive that all the ladies had to see it and relate lurid descriptions to their husbands. One whole cheek was black.*

The winds stayed over 20 knots, right on the nose, and the seas got rough. The generator set and the inverter both stopped working, as did the engine-driven refrigeration system. One of the sensors in the gen set had a broken lead, right at the unit, so it was not repairable. I bypassed all sensors, so the gen set was working again, but without cutouts for temperature or oil pressure. The inverter simply decided to start again. Don't you just hate equipment with a mind of its own? I pretended I had fixed it, but I will get mine when the machine gods decide it is time.

Carole: *It was the first time I realized how fast "Dolphin Spirit" is. We all left together, but we arrived hours before everyone.*

Arriving at Raratonga at around 3am, we hove-to until daylight. Avatui Harbor was a small hole, dredged and blasted into the reef. It was completely destroyed in the 1983 cyclones and had only just been rebuilt. We tied up against the wharf—concrete, with huge black tires as fenders. Our white fenders turned black instantly, and transferred the black to our once white hull. The swell coming into the harbor kept the boats in constant motion, making getting on and off a circus act, and fraying the lines almost as fast as we could replace them.

Agriculture sprayed us and brought back old memories of arriving by plane in Australia. Immigration, Health and Customs visited. Ryan's first words were "Southern Fried Chicken" and sure enough, there was a fast food shop just off the wharf. Chicken and chips for lunch (It was nice to speak Australian and New Zealand again, where chips are chips and not French Fries.), pizza for dinner, delivered to the boat. After French Polynesia, prices were almost reasonable.

The Customs Officer wanted to take away our shotgun. To make life easier, I suggested that he seal it in a locker on board, and he readily agreed. Not able to find a seal in his briefcase, he left, promising to find one and return. The next day I saw him on the dock and asked about the seal. "Can't find one," he said. "Promise me you won't shoot anyone and we will forget about it."

Ryan (16): *I don't remember why, but I was exceptionally frightened here, during the dark, dark nights. Perhaps it was the strange sounds made as we rubbed against the concrete. The days were pleasant, the nights unbearable.*

Ryan naturally made a beeline for the nearest local to get the scoop on fishing. He just goes up to people, says hello, gives his name, asks for theirs, and settles in for a conversation. We could always find Ryan by the circle of adults and children he attracted every time he started fishing. The adults were always helping him with tips and giving him lures and gear.

Ryan (8): *Fishing in the Cook Islands was quite an experience. I was fishing off the dock using my little gold hook method, but catching only small fish. Some of the local men came up to see what I was doing and taught me the proper way to catch fish—jagging. Just get a huge treble hook, with a big weight, throw it out into the middle of the harbor, pull it back very quickly and "Bam!" you've got fish.*

Don Silk was the Harbor Master, a very pleasant man, always ready to chat and share a glass in the cockpit. Ask him politely and he will tell you about his very adventurous background, and may even allow you to buy a copy of his book *From Kauri Trees to Sunlit Seas*. Don't hesitate, it is a great read.

Carole: *After a rough passage "Magnum Bonum" limped in with a broken G.P.S. As there was no chance of repair or buying another, they were preparing to use celestial navigation when Laurie loaned them one of our two hand-held G.P.S.s. Cruisers help other cruisers, and we were just fortunate to be in a position to assist.*

All the cruisers in the harbor got together at Trader Jacks, a restaurant/bar on the beach, run by New Zealanders, as are the Cook Islands in general. The town was spread out along the water front, so we had to walk miles to shop. There was a road running right around the island. For variety, we caught a local bus and did the full circle.

"Dolphin Spirit" was in the right place at the right time yet again; this time for a local dance and song festival, held in one of the sheds on the dock. There must be something about grass and leaf skirts that make the wearers (male and female) sing so melodiously and dance so fluidly. Great dancing and singing means great food to follow, and this was no exception. There were speeches, in English, but the combination of the amplification equipment, wind, and accent, made them, perhaps mercifully, unintelligible. I can still see the smiles on everyone's faces.

Paw paws were only 20 cents each, so I subsisted on a paw paw diet. The lady seller pulled me to one side and, in a sotto voice, warned me that paw paws, in the quantity that I was obviously eating them, were likely to have a laxative effect—well that's not quite what she said, but that was the idea. Oranges were 20 cents each and there was ice cream! We managed to buy duty free NZ chardonnay and champagne, so life became livable again.

Carole: *Raratonga was such a pleasant change, with a supermarket full of reasonably priced goods. Everyone spoke excellent English and I could understand the New Zealand accent because of long exposure to Laurie. He gets upset when I say Australians and New Zealanders sound the same, but they do!! The dust blowing off the land beyond the wharf kept everything coated with grime and we were constantly bouncing in the swell, but it was a lovely place to be. I always cook ahead of time for a passage, since I never know how I will be feeling. This time I made the usual red- cabbage salad, coca cola beef, spaghetti, chicken and rice, chili, and a vegetable beef soup. Fortunately I prepared the meals as soon as we came home from the market because...*

The wind began blowing directly into the harbor and the swell was increasing, so preparations for leaving began in earnest. Don Silk came down to warn us to move, as an island trading boat was arriving, and the 70-year old female skipper had a reputation for driving straight in. She did, and we were pleased we had gone outside the harbor, as "Dolphin Spirit" would have been some 10 feet shorter had we stayed. After tying up again to the wharf, the wind kicked up some more, and we decided that it was all too much, so got our clearances and headed off for Tonga, via Nuie.

The winds were 20 to 25 knots from the south-east, with confused seas. For once, the wind direction was perfect and we were soon doing over 10 knots, but the seas were pounding us, so we reduced sail. "Marita Shan," "Sky Bird" and "Promises" all left with us, which was a good thing as events unfolded.

The weather changed, the wind died completely for a few hours, and then swung round to the north, again giving us a very nice sail. It was too good to last, and we ran into a line of major squalls, each with 25-plus knots of wind and driving rain. At the end of the third squall, one of the cockpit cover zips came apart, and we struggled for half an hour to repair it. Just then the fourth squall hit. This one had 40 knots of wind, which whipped up some large seas, so we started the motor, to drive directly into them and ease our motion a little.

It was dark by then, and what we hadn't seen was that one of the large seas had washed a line off our bow, which wrapped around the propeller, and pulled the propeller shaft/gear box coupling apart when we put the motor into gear. We were on a sailboat, but no motor meant we couldn't stop at Nuie, and getting into the Tonga anchorage would be difficult, if not dangerous. The motor is there for convenience and safety, probably in equal proportion.

Steve and Tammy ("Sky Bird") offered their help, so we hove-to for several hours to await dawn, and allow them to catch up. At dawn the seas were too large to attempt a dive to cut the line off, so we sailed on, with Steve and Tammy in sight.

Carole: *My peaceful sleep in the salon was disturbed when Laurie told me the dreadful news. I know we were on a sailboat, but that night, without an operating engine, I was frightened. How comforting when we at last saw "Sky Bird's" lights. Tammy radioed that they would keep watch, and we could sleep.*

The next day the seas had calmed down, so Steve came over in his dinghy and stood by while I donned scuba gear and went in. It was an eerie experience diving in mid-ocean with just shades of blue in all directions. Much as I fought it, I kept imagining the shark suddenly appearing out of the haze. Even in calm seas the swell moved the boat up and down several feet, so it was quite a task to cut the line free without being knocked about.

Carole: *Laurie was tied to the boat, and we had another line streaming behind just in case, but I was nervous. What if he was knocked out by the boat? Would he keep breathing? Could I pull him up fast enough when the shark came? If he cuts himself, I'll pull him up immediately because the blood will bring sharks. I was exhausted with worrying.*

Ryan (8): *I sat with my finger on the electric winch button ready to haul Dad on board the instant Carole saw a shark.*

The line cut off, Steve and I disappeared under the floor boards for several hours, and put the coupling and everything else back together. It was terrific having someone else on hand to help, and particularly Steve, who works like a demon, and can bend and fit into confined spaces far easier than I can.

Nuie was one day away, so we headed there. The last night was dead calm, and we motored around the island, arriving at the "harbor" just as the moon was setting, so it was too dark to pick up a mooring. A low, flat island with no lagoon or fringing reef, Nuie has no harbor. There is an indentation in the land, a small concrete jetty, and eight moorings, all completely open to the ocean, the waves and the wind. Even in calm weather there is such a swell that dinghies cannot be left tied to the jetty. A crane was provided to lift them out of the water so they aren't pounded to pieces.

By the time it was light enough to come in, the wind had started up and was blowing 20 knots. We approached the mooring, I put the engine into reverse to slow down, and found that I couldn't get it out of forward gear, as the changing mechanism had come loose in the console in the cockpit, a malfunction totally unrelated to the coupling problem. Carole was up front wondering why the mooring was passing by at such speed. We were bouncing up and down at least five feet each way because of the swell, so she had no easy task anyway. Back to sea we went while I feverishly made repairs.

On the second approach to the mooring, Rod ("Basho") was on hand in his dinghy to help. We slowed, Carole missed picking up the mooring buoy, so Rod threw her a line, which she also missed. By some miracle, Carole managed to hook it out of the water and we tied up. Rod then discovered he had tossed us a frayed line and had tied his end to a weak plastic fitting on the buoy, not to the mooring line.

I then found that putting the engine into reverse to slow the boat had pulled apart the coupling again, so that, at the time we were getting tied up, we had no drive. The rocky shore was only some 200 feet behind us, with the wind and waves driving us straight on to it. If Rod hadn't been there with his line, however frayed, we would have been on the reef before we realized what had gone wrong. If we had been early enough to have gone in to pick up the mooring by moonlight and missed it, we would have been without drive and without wind, and the waves would have driven us onto the reef. That was as close as we ever want to come to losing "Dolphin Spirit." Just writing about it gives us the shakes.

Ryan (8): *Dad took me with him to the bows to check the lines, and I got soaked by the waves. It was fun until Carole insisted I put a life jacket on.*

The wind and waves were so strong that we pulled the mooring buoy about 15 feet under water. I tried to free-dive on it to attach another line, but couldn't manage, so we called the local dive operation. They came immediately, and attached a second line to the buoy, with a back up line to another buoy.

After working unsuccessfully for a couple of hours to get the coupling back together, I realized that a large press or vice was needed. We were bouncing around so much that it was difficult to launch our dinghy, so

Gary from "Mahini" took me to the jetty. A well timed leap and a desperate scramble, and I was ashore with all the bits of the coupling.

A man in a pickup was about to drive off the jetty when I stopped him and explained what I needed. "My brother," he replied, so I piled into the back of the truck, and off we drove to the local Fish Cooperative. The brother opened up the workshop, and a large vice had the coupling back together in five minutes. "Dolphin Spirit" was still there when I got back, much to my relief.

Two hours later, when the coupling was finally back in place and we theoretically could motor again, I was even more relieved. Those two hours contorted into a tiny space, not knowing what was happening above, and not able to spare the time to check, were not the happiest.

We spent a very uncomfortable night at the mooring, with waves breaking over the bow of the boat. Both mooring lines were fraying and under terrible strain. (We were told, months later, that we had dragged the mooring some forty feet until it jammed in a crack in the coral.)

Carole: *Laurie, Ryan and I put on life jackets (Ryan cried and fought against it) and we spent the night in the cockpit with one of us awake at all times. I knew we were in danger, and I would have been even more frightened had I known that Laurie was so concerned he had the anchor ready to drop.*

All I could see was the reef behind us, and the waves coming over the bow. While watching the divers attach the mooring lines earlier, I had seen the water was full of sea snakes, and all sea snakes are poisonous. The divers told me that the mouths on these were too small to bite, but I didn't believe that. However, I was determined to battle sea snakes and waves to get myself and Ryan ashore when the mooring lines broke. Morning finally dawned.

There was no way to really test if the coupling would hold under load, but we tried some dummy runs the next morning, still tied to the mooring. It was lucky that we did, because my repair efforts had loosened an oil line, and the gear box was empty—no drive again. A quick tightening of the fitting and a refill and we were once again as ready as possible.

We set the mainsail as insurance, left the anchor ready to drop as further insurance, and I cut the mooring lines, as they were impossible to untie. The coupling held and we were away to Tonga, more relieved than you can believe.

Neither the divers nor the good Samaritans ashore would accept payment or gifts for their efforts and help. We really regretted that we couldn't stay to enjoy their island. Those yachts who have been there in better circumstances have painted a glowing picture of terrific diving, great scenery and wonderful people. We can vouch for the people; the rest will have to await a future visit, probably by plane! As a closing note, the local divers recovered our lines and gave them to other cruisers, who gave them to us in Tonga.

Carole: *Even as I re-read this now, years later, my heart pounds and I can hardly breathe. This was definitely the scariest day of my life.*

"Basho" stayed another day. As they were leaving shore the swell was so large that they had to throw the children into the dinghy. Rod then managed to leap in just as the dinghy was swamped and smashed up against the wharf, holing one of the tubes. Kerry had to jump into the water and swim for the boat. They made it.

Something positive. Carole was not seasick through all this, even though the motion of the boat was worse than it has ever been. She also was not seasick all the way to Tonga! In Nuie she saw a sea snake and survived. So did the snake.

Carole: *I saw hundreds, thousands maybe! Laurie can't avoid small distortions of the truth when they make for a neat turn of phrase.*

The sail to Tonga was uneventful, apart from winds from the wrong direction, which forced us to sail towards Samoa, to minimize the pounding and the affects of the large swells.

Carole: *During this passage we seemed to be riding on top of the waves looking down at the pale purple shimmering sea below. A pretty sight, but we were exhausted by the dramas of the previous days.*

We arrived in tolerably good shape, in a dead calm, at Neiafu, the capital of the Vava'u Group. I had spent some weeks there on a chartered yacht in 1991, and had been very vocal with other cruisers, extolling the virtues of the place, convincing several to go to Tonga instead of Samoa. There were strong rumors of keel-hauling and walking the plank if Vava'u was not the drop-dead gorgeous place I said it was. Fortunately, it was all that, and more.

To check-in, we pulled up to the Customs wharf and were boarded by Immigration, Customs, Health, and Agriculture. These four very large gentlemen (a Tongan weighing less than 200 pounds goes on a crash eating course) crowded around our salon table to do the paperwork. We were prepared, with pots of tea and a five-pound box of biscuits, so everyone was happy and the papers got filled out, one set at a time.

The cruisers who arrived before us had warned that we had to hand over all our oranges, so Carole turned them into orange juice, which was exempt for some reason. All potatoes were confiscated except for those we were allowed to keep for dinner that night.

Agriculture: "How many do you want for dinner?"
Carole: "Three."
Agriculture: "Keep six. He looks hungry." (pointing to Ryan)

Carole: *I didn't mind giving up the potatoes, until I went ashore and found none for sale.*

It pays to be polite with officials, and tea and two five-pound boxes of biscuits (the first didn't last long) can't hurt.

Ryan (10): *One of the officials asked Dad if he had ever shot the shotgun, and Dad said no. I was sitting on the settee, and reminded Dad that he had shot it once to show me how it worked, a year before we left. For the next few countries, Carole would take me into my cabin and sit with me while Dad was dealing with the officials. I was only helping Dad remember.*

The Kingdom of Tonga, the Friendly Islands of history, myth and legend, is north of New Zealand, west of Tahiti, south of Samoa and east of Fiji. This remoteness makes it one of the few places in the world that has not come under European political domination. However, under the influence of the Wesleyan Missionaries, the ancient Tongan laws and taboos have been replaced by a new set, based on the Ten Commandments and Wesleyan Methodism.

Written by Missionary Shirley Baker, and originally known as the Code of Vava'u, the set of codes were in force all over Tonga by 1850. As a result, Tongan men and women swim fully clothed in the warm, clear waters, and men must wear shirts at all times. Sunday is a true day of rest. Nothing may be done on that day except go to church, sing, stroll, visit friends and relax. Shops and restaurants close, any contracts signed are legally invalid. In Tonga even Seventh Day Adventists observe Sunday as their Sabbath.

Tourists and cruisers were expected to comply with the Sunday customs, and that meant no fishing, swimming, or boat repairs. Charter and cruising yachts were permitted to sail. We found hearing hymns interpreted by the melodic native voices, supported by the wind in the palms and the murmur of the sea, was a very acceptable reason to stay at anchor. Going to church in a Tongan village was an experience not to be missed, even for the non-religious.

We soon become aware of, and under the spell of, Faka Tonga—the

Tongan Way. Faka Tonga is keeping it simple, and doing things the easy way, with a minimum of fuss and bother. By way of example, there are no traffic lights in Vava'u and no stop signs. Combine this with the fact that all Tongans are first generation drivers, and you have the potential for disaster. The Tongan solution is to set the speed limit at 35 miles per hour, and keep the roads so full of potholes there is little chance of exceeding this speed, and having your car survive.

Some years ago, I flew into Nuku'alofa, the capital of Tonga, from Nadi, Fiji, on an Air Pacific flight that departed Nadi at 2:40am. When I asked the airport manager (Tongan) why the plane left at that ungodly hour, his astonished response was, "So we can get to Nuku'alofa on time, of course." Faka Tonga!

Perhaps one of the best illustrations of the uniqueness of Tongan culture was provided by Mark and Patti Fields, who were the owners of Dolphin Pacific Diving. Patti arrived first (from California) to supervise the construction of their base, and to install the equipment. Because she was a woman, and therefore could not possibly know what she really needed, the local suppliers refused to sell her the lumber and other hardware she wanted. "Get your husband to come," was the constant refrain. In desperation she asked one of the Moorings' employees (male) to do the buying for her. He had no problems.

Mark arrived, and as a modern, liberated male, often did the food shopping. The women shopkeepers refused to believe that he knew a banana from a pineapple, made all the selections for him, carried his purchases to his car, and constantly admonished him to "get a new wife."

Beer bottles stuck neck down into the ground marked some graves, while others were crowned with elaborate creations of wood, stone and yards of flapping cloth. Tongan cemeteries were small and scattered throughout the towns and villages, with no apparent separation from the houses and farms surrounding them. This was not lack of reverence, but an attempt to make death, as well as life, more convenient to all.

Neiafu had a great old-time feel to it, trees hanging over the streets, faded paint on the wooden-floored stores, dogs and pigs wandering everywhere, and just the occasional car. Some of the stores had the same glass-topped counters I associate with my youth, and maybe even had the same goods in them. The Post Office was a huge rambling structure, where standing in line for the one stamp-seller was just perfect, allowing us to exchange pleasantries with the locals, and enjoy the cool breeze blowing through the open windows and doors.

The stores were well stocked, and the open air market had plentiful fruit and vegetables, most at reasonable prices. The bakery was a couple of streets off the shore, with several pigs feeding just outside the door, a dirt floor, wood-fired ovens, and great buns and bread, cheap at 60 cents a loaf. Carole took exception to the dead pig on top of one of the ovens, but where else would they keep it—on the floor?

Pigs were everywhere. Every household had at least one, and they all roamed freely. No one had a really good answer to how the pigs found their way home each night. The one I liked best noted that all the household pigs are called the same name. In the evening, the housewife simply goes to the door and yells "Fred" and her pigs—all Freds—come running home, to spend the night in the wallows dug in the front yard (Faka Tonga).

Uniquely Tongan was the margarita we had at one of the local hotels. Carole took one sip and almost spat it out. I did the same, and took it to the bartender to enquire about its composition. "Tonic water and tequila" was the response, and no he wouldn't take it back, as that was the way he had always made them, and I was the first to complain.

The Moorings Charter Yachts publishes the cruising guide for the area. Long ago, they determined that the village and island names were too long and hard for Western tongues and ears, and gave all 36 anchorages numbers. This has so taken hold that, when I asked one Tongan which village he lived in, he replied, "Number 6."

We were in Anchorage 6 when a young lady and a young girl paddled out in their patched outrigger canoe to sell baskets and shells. As we were talking to them, their canoe started to fill, eventually stabilizing some six inches under water. Naturally we rescued both distressed females and, after hauling up and emptying the canoe and engaging in a lot of sympathy buying, we towed them back to shore. A few days later we were talking to a local chief, and recounted the story. "Best salesladies in Vava'u," he said.

Almost every day we were visited by boats selling baskets, shells, tapa and fruit. One local minister of religion arrived in a 20-foot half-cabin motor boat, accompanied by a support group of village elders. If the mixture of God and Mammon and old and new religions was meant to be intimidating, it worked.

The prices were negotiable and trade items (new, not used) were often welcome, perhaps mixed with cash. Carole had brought along all the free Lancôme gifts she had collected over the years. Each lipstick was carefully uncapped by the ladies, to ensure it was unused, before being accepted as a trade. Bargaining was the order of the day. Ryan was no help in this regard, as he tended to say things such as "I really like that, Dad" and "That's cheap" and "We wanted one of those."

Carole: *Tongan baskets are the best in the world. We didn't buy nearly enough of them. We have used the ones we bought on a daily basis and they are still beautiful, many years later.*

On a previous visit, I remember standing in the rain, up to my ankles in the stickiest mud in the world, negotiating with an eight-year-old girl for some shells. She was soaking wet, had a huge smile, and was a tough enough bargainer to give Donald Trump a run for his money. Ryan, then three, was equally unconcerned about the conditions, and spent the time determining the solubility of pig droppings. The sea was a step away to wash in, and it was warm (the sea, not the droppings), so who cared. (**Carole:** *Obviously I wasn't there!*)

"Promises" had a major electrical fire on board, destroying a lot of their wiring and equipment. I helped Dave, a banker in his previous life, to do the rewiring. What Dave lacked in technical knowledge and practical experience, he made up by carrying the most extensive range of spares I have ever seen. Next to the ultimate of towing a second boat, this was as good as it gets.

By this time there was quite a group of cruisers in Vava'u, but with 36 different anchorages, none were ever crowded, unless it was an intentional gathering for a beach BBQ, or some other entertainment. A group of us had an anchorage almost full, when one of our friends arrived (for reasons which will become obvious, they will remain nameless). In what can only be described as a mental aberration, they decided to try the "drop it on the fly" anchoring technique, for the first time.

Occasionally used in Europe, this involves dropping the anchor while the boat is still moving forward, letting out the required scope, then simultaneously snubbing the anchor and stopping the engine. The anchor sets and the boat spins around, perfectly positioned and at rest. In this instance the practice did not quite live up to the theory, and the resulting chaos saw three anchor chains tangled, two dinghies almost sunk, and several near misses to yachts and dinghies. We were charitable, and did allow them to live this down, but not for a couple of years.

Carole: *Since we were all together again, one of the ladies held a "girls only" coffee break on board her boat—Starbucks, of course. We were by now feeling comfortable with each other and so were able to tell some of our stories. My divorce was nothing compared with the lady who lost a child to a rapist, and another who lost her son and his girlfriend in India. We all had suffered from depression, and all were so pleased that the sailing was such a catharsis.*

On a happier day, we had a group over to watch **Babe**, *a movie we had just received. Tammy's four kinds of popcorn and Heather's lemon cookies kept the hunger pangs at bay. It turned out that my ex-husband was the voice of the horse, and I didn't even recognize him. On with my new life!*

Ross and Lyn Dee Rankin, with teenage children Blake and Autumn, arrived for a two week visit. Ross had been Patricia's (Ryan's mother) oldest and best friend. Patricia and I had chartered in Tonga when Ryan was small and had a wonderful time. I was really unsure how this double whammy would affect me. Naturally, the memories flooded back, some quite painful. We anchored in the same places, did the same things, but everything was different because Carole was there. Thanks to her mostly, and with able assistance from Ross and Lyn Dee, I did not dive into depression, but thoroughly enjoyed the new experiences.

Carole: The Rankins brought us a new inverter and a suitcase full of essentials such as sugar-free Jell-o. Making Jell-o in a still anchorage is a breeze. At sea, with a breeze, it is impossible.

Ross and Blake were keen scuba divers, so the 100+ feet of visibility in Tongan waters had our air-compressor working full time. Lyn Dee on the other hand was a reluctant snorkler until the wonders of a huge bommie (location I want to keep secret, as it is the loveliest snorkel I have ever seen, and don't want it spoiled) made her a convert.

Carole loved this bommie, so we snorkeled it every day we could. I took the opportunity to pick up and kill (by taking them to shore) every Crown of Thorns starfish we saw. These eat living coral, and have devastated a lot of the Great Barrier Reef. Yes, I know that killing them meant disturbing the natural course of events, but nature can have its way on another bommie, not mine. The Crown of Thorns got back at me with a very painful jab from the spines one day, when I got careless.

Carole: For our first guests from home I wanted to be the perfect hostess, but the food I had saved for their use had gone stale, and supplies from town didn't match my still largely California-based standards for entertaining. I felt so incompetent, but the Rankins soon put me at ease. Lyn Dee and Autumn went really yachtie, even washing their hair in salt water.

Another Tongan secret, probably now known to all, was an island where low tide exposed a coral rock shelf. This shelf had a number of large holes worn in it, making a series of spa baths, all sand bottomed and populated by fish, coral and crabs. Each small wave pushed a surge of warm, crystal water into the waist-deep pools. The tide did not stay out long enough.

When we tow a lure, it is often dived on by the sea birds. This day one misjudged and got hooked. He was a big gull and took off, pulling the line into the air and into the rotating blades of the wind generator. It took a long time to stop the wind generator, haul in the very unhappy bird by hand, control his huge wings, sharp beak and sharper claws, and unhook him. A longer time was needed to unwind the several hundred turns the line had made around the wind generator axle. The bird flew away unhurt and hopefully wiser.

A special highlight was Swallows Cave, a large cave accessed by dinghy. We snorkeled, to discover that the cave was filled with fish, and that just outside was the most wonderful reef wall. There was nothing else to do but return that afternoon with scuba gear. The fish parted to allow us to sink through them, then formed a shimmering silver ceiling, that turned into rivers of silver as we moved towards the cave entrance. Over the lip we went, surrounded by these silver streams, to a wall of coral visible for over 150 feet in all directions, including down. We returned three times just to experience the thrill again.

Mariner's Cave can be reached only through an underwater tunnel. I had done a lot of practicing, with Ryan breathing through my spare scuba mouthpiece, so he could go through the tunnel. As it turned out, I couldn't leave the dinghy, so Ryan went through the tunnel with Ross, and was so thrilled with the experience he couldn't talk for almost three seconds on surfacing.

Ryan (8): *This was the second time I had been to Tonga, but I can't remember much about the first, as I was only three-years-old then. I really enjoyed it this time. It was where I learned to row my dinghy properly and got my rowing license, made especially for me by Dad. I chased after some tuna that were boiling in the middle of the bay. Steve off "Sky Bird" took me fishing about a mile off shore, and we caught some huge fish. The swim into Mariner's Cave was very exciting and it was spooky inside. There were lots of pigs on every beach rooting for shellfish. One day, we somehow got a sea snake in the dinghy, which caused lots of excitement until Dad flicked it over the side.*

One Saturday we went to Aisea's feast. I had been to it many years ago, and noted that it was not as good this time around. Heated stones in a covered pit cooked the banana leaf wrapped food, which included suckling pig, octopus, taro, noodles, several types of fish and bananas. The promised lobster was absent, and the roast pork was terrible, but the rest of the food was good, if not plentiful. We all thought we had eaten just the first course, when dinner ended.

The young dancers who entertained us had the traditional oil coating on their arms and shoulders. Spectators showed approval by sticking paper money onto the oil during the dance. Good dancers became surrounded by fluttering notes and flattering admirers. Traditional dancing, in the unique knees-together Tongan style, was still taught in the primary schools. Aisea told us that an ideal dancer was pump, soft and supple, with long hair and a ready smile. All the ones we saw seemed to fit this mold admirably.

Ryan caught fish in the anchorage, and some of his friends were there, so we all had a good time. There were three dinghies sailing around, two Australian and one U.S., so we staged a miniature Americas Cup. Naturally, the good guys won—work it out for yourselves.

Catching fish in Tonga is quite a feat, as they are very intelligent. We were in one anchorage, after a prolonged fish-less period, when I noticed a school of quite large black fish boiling around some cheese balls Ryan was throwing over the side. Quickly I rigged a hook onto a light line, put a cheese ball on it, and threw it and a few other cheese balls, to the school. The water boiled and all cheese balls vanished, except for the one with the hook. Eventually it got soggy and fell off the hook, at which time one of the fish detached itself from the school, swallowed the ball, and returned with a disdainful flick of the tail.

Ryan now had his dinghy rowing license (he had to be trained, practice, and pass a solo test) and rowed his own dinghy everywhere. He could visit his friends on other boats whenever he wanted, and spent hours just rowing around the anchorages greeting everyone, checking out the fish and generally having a great time. While we were anchored off Neiafu, Ryan left his rod unattended for a moment (something he had been told never to do) and a fish took it right over the side in a flash. Even though Ryan was at fault, we couldn't abandon our fish diet, so found a replacement rod and reel ashore for prices very competitive with those in the U.S.

One of the anchorages was off an "uninhabited" island, who's only inhabitants were an Austrian, his Tongan wife and child, and a German baker, who ran a small "hotel" and a unique restaurant, cafe, bar and bakery. The bar had swings for seats; the bakery had the most delicious bread in the world; the restaurant cooking was all done on open fires; and the whole thing was lit by kerosene lamps. We tied our dinghy at the end of a pier, 300-feet long and one-foot wide, walked ashore (screaming if necessary for equilibrium), climbed the hill, turned left at the pig pen, climbed more hill, and we were there. Great place Hans and Meile.

Carole: *We would call them on VHF to make a reservation, as the restaurant had only six tables. Hans would ask if we had eaten there before, and if so, what we had. There were no menus, and they cooked only one main course each day, so wanted to be sure we ate something different each time. We had several great nights there. Laurie offered to find water on the island, as this was a major problem for them. Laurie is a water diviner, a fact he doesn't share with many. It is true; I have seen him do it.*

Their son Lope was about Ryan's age, paddled a dugout canoe (his anchor was an old Singer sewing machine), and loved to fish, so he and Ryan got on very well. They swapped boats one day. It was really funny to see how these kids, so competent in their own craft, simply could not control the other. After going in circles for a while, they swapped back. Both caught lots of fish. We had Lope on board for videos and video games, a new experience for him.

Our sighting record was seven humpback whales in one day. One mother and calf we followed for hours in the dinghy. As the calf breached time and time again, the mother would slap her flipper as if in applause, then breach herself as if to show how to do it better. Another day saw us, again in the dinghy, following a whale miles out at sea. It breached many times, once right next to us, a wonderful and scary sight, as we were twelve feet long to its forty-plus.

Carole: *That day, on the way to anchorage 16, we had caught a huge wahoo. A lot of our friends were at the anchorage, so I invited them over for sashimi. Naturally I wanted to clean the boat up first—the Rankins were still with us, and to my eyes the place was a mess. When "Whales" was called on VHF, and everyone took off in the dinghies, I felt I had to stay behind, continue the cleaning and get the dinner ready.* <u>*What was I thinking?*</u> *I was so upset with myself when they returned with stories of great breaches. It was my fault I hadn't gone with them. Old habits die so hard.*

A specialty of Anchorage 16 was the weekly pig roast, and the operator boasted that he needed only one shot to kill the pig, and this single shot was the signal to all that the roast was on. One day we heard a shot, then another, then another—obviously a three-pig night was planned. Full of anticipation we dinghied ashore, to be told that the roast was off. Apparently slightly inebriated, the operator had missed with all shots, and then sprained his ankle trying to catch the pig.

In "Dolphin Spirit" this time, we followed two large whales until they stopped. We stopped. The whales turned, swam under the boat, and stayed there. We looked down at them a few feet below our keel, each bigger than we were, and I will swear they looked back. After what seemed hours, but was probably only a couple of minutes, they swam off. We took the hint and went in the other direction.

Ryan (8): *I climbed to the first spreaders and looked down. Because the water was so clear the two whales seemed to be touching the keel. They looked at me, too.*

Aisea claims that his fellow villagers were the best whale hunters in Vava'u. Chasing the whale in dinghies, they used spears and dynamite to kill it, then immediately sewed up its mouth to prevent sinking. Occasionally the whale would sink, only to bob up again when thoroughly decomposed. "Fortunately," Aisea grinned, "The prevailing winds always blew the carcass to another village's beach."

The floating, newly-caught whale was then towed to his village and everyone went to work cutting it up. There was no refrigeration, so all the butchery, and much of the eating, had to be done on the day of the catch. The resulting carcass was then pushed out to sea, where it floated off, presumably to that other village. Regretfully, Aisea reported, whale hunting was stopped when the down-wind village successfully complained to the government. Actually, whale hunting was stopped by Royal Decree, but I prefer Aisea's version. He gave the impression that whale safety remains very wind-direction dependent, even now.

Our six-months old computer had died in Bora Bora. It was there we found the true meaning of "World Wide Warranty," which is, "Ship it back to us from anywhere in the wide world, at your cost, and we will repair it and ship it back to you." In any practical way therefore, warranty does not apply to cruising equipment. We sent the CPU back with the Rankins, and my son Philip brought it back to us in Fiji.

As another warranty example, the new U.S. purchased radar on "Marita Shan" died, so Pat took it to the registered dealer in Papeete who repaired it, for immediate cash payment. "If you want warranty, get it from the dealer you bought it from," was the policy. With very few exceptions, you are on your own once U.S. waters are left behind.

Chasing Sunsets

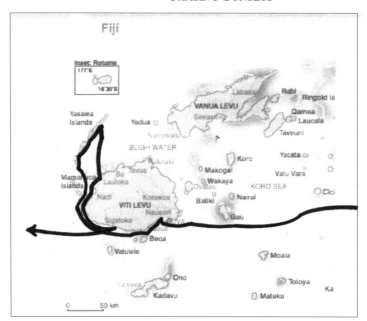

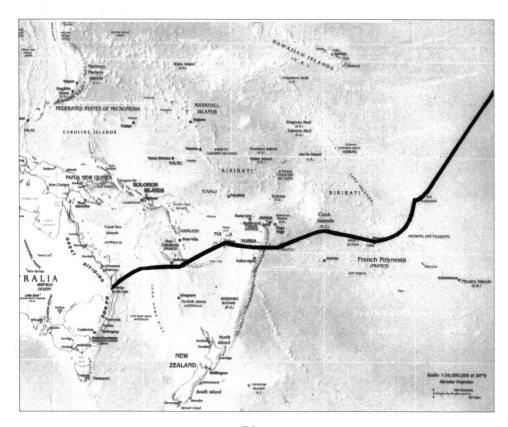

Fiji and Passage to Australia
Year One
August 30 to October 30

Time caught up with us again, so we left Tonga for an easy three-day sail to Suva, Fiji. I knew that the pass into the harbor was on the port side of a wreck on the reef—how's that for directions that inspire confidence! We found the wreck, started in (it was pouring rain and blowing 20 knots), and then I looked further left through the binoculars to see a second wreck that the pilot directions had neglected to mention. We cruised up and down a bit, conferred with charts and G.P.S., decided on the first wreck, headed in and found we were right—Ho Hum! Just another pass entry.

For the record, that week three boats ran into the reef while entering, one needing to be towed off at a cost approximating to its value. One of the others was "Sudade," a 90-footer with a professional crew, which hit in broad daylight. They made a turn a little too soon. We non-professionals felt justifiably smug, forgetting our own mistakes in the glow of someone else's.

Three other cruisers had arrived before us, so we all dinghied across to the commercial wharf, and the four-story building that housed most of the check-in offices. Health was first. A very pleasant gentleman handed out two forms, each to be filled out in triplicate. This got us health clearance and a bill for $Fiji30 ($US22) to be paid at the down-town Health Office. Next came Customs—three forms here, two in triplicate, one in duplicate. Then Agriculture, two floors up—only one form, also in triplicate. Then the Port Captain—two forms, one copy only of each, plus a payment of port fees of $Fiji15. Then back to Customs to prove we had done all the above.

Because so many boats were checking in, Immigration sent a man down to the dock, otherwise we would have had to pile into taxis for the five or so miles to the Immigration office. Only one form here, single copy, but one for each person on board. After all this, we were legally in Fiji. It took only three hours. More paperwork than most places, but smoother flowing, and they provided carbon paper (3M take note).

My policy has always been to go along, uncomplaining, with any local requirements. It is their country and their rules. If you don't like it, just leave and go somewhere else. In this instance we were having a very pleasant time with the Fijians, joking and laughing and generally helping the time to pass. They knew that the paperwork was just "make-work" and so did we, but it had to be done. A late-comer captain arrived, not one of our group, and immediately started complaining. All the officials spoke fluent English, and really didn't like hearing their country maligned. Their attitudes changed dramatically towards us as well, making the rest of the form-filling time unpleasant.

To leave Suva and cruise to any other Fiji destination required us to obtain permission to visit the new islands from the appropriate Government Department, a form we then had to carry with us at all times, and which we were supposed to show to the chief of each village we visited. Armed with this form, we went to Customs, where we filled out the same form we completed on entry, again in triplicate. This allowed us to sail to the next major port, Lautoka, visiting the islands we named, en route. Arriving at Lautoka, we had to check in—same form, same carbon paper. Check out in Lautoka was simply a stamp on the copy of the check-in form—there is a God! I really have no problems with the paperwork. It is the Fijian way. A few forms are a small price to pay for permission to spend time in such a delightful place.

It was civilization again, as Suva was a large city on a busy (therefore polluted) harbor. We anchored off the Royal Suva Yacht Club, and used their facilities and dinghy dock as a base for land-cruising. All the cruisers gathered there in the evenings for a delicious, cheap dinner. It was there we celebrated PL's ("Osprey") birthday with Carole's superb lemon cake.

Ryan (16): *We had lemon cake so many times (I kept asking for it) that I can't remember this time, but I can remember being out in my rowboat one day, and somehow it was half full of water. The wind was blowing very strongly and Dad had to come out in the dinghy to get me.*

There did not seem to be a taxi driver or storekeeper, either in Suva, or later in Lautoka (the second largest city), who wasn't of Indian descent. In downtown Suva, almost every face was Indian, with most of the women in traditional saris complete with the dot on the forehead. Shops advertised the latest in fashions, and sold only saris. I didn't know there were different styles and fashions before this. The produce market sold bulk spices and curries, and the supermarkets were heavily stocked with goods appealing to the Indian palate. Parts of Suva could have been directly transplanted from any city on the Indian sub-continent.

Away from the main island of Viti Levu, we saw only Fijians in the villages, lots of sulus (men's traditional skirts) with not a sari or whiff of curry. Many of the villagers could have been of mixed blood, but the way of life was Fijian, not Indian in any respect. Fortunately, the friction between the races, so evident in past years, was not visible.

Our first move was to hire a taxi to take us on a voyage of discovery for about three hours, for the princely fee of Fiji$30. The driver was Indian, and took us to his home for tea and to meet his ten children, ages six months to 20 years.

Suva had certainly changed since I was first here in 1961. There were traffic lights instead of policemen in white sulus and white gloves, a definite regression. Suva market was probably the best we have seen, with all kinds of fruit and vegetables at reasonable prices, and no bargaining.

Ryan (8): *Carole and I went ashore in the dinghy to the Yacht Club. I was in the bow ready to grab the landing when I fell in and cut my ankle very deeply on all the barnacles. Dad washed out the cuts with bleach and then peroxide to kill all the bugs. It hurt a lot, but I didn't cry, even when the bleach hit. It must have worked because I didn't get infected.*

Carole: *These things always happen when I am alone with Ryan. At first we laughed when he fell in, but that stopped as soon as we saw blood everywhere. Ryan was so brave. Even today, he asks why I laughed when he fell in. I didn't want him to think I would be mad when he surfaced, because he had gotten his clothes wet and he'd have to go back to the boat to change, and he did look comical falling in.*

"Magnum Bonum" caught up with us and returned our G.P.S., together with a thank-you bottle of wine and a wonderful pencil sketch by Egon, who taught art in his previous life. They could buy a new G.P.S. here, because Suva was by far the best place in the Pacific to buy equipment, electronics and outboards, which were less than half U.S. prices. Labor was well trained, efficient and cheap. We arranged to have varnishing done, but only two coats were applied before rain, and the desire to swim in clean water, drove us to the outer islands.

Of course leaving Suva wasn't without its little bit of trauma. Our engine stopped when we were in the middle of the pass. I swung into action, tearing up the cabin floor to get at the engine, while Carole stayed at the wheel, trying by sheer will power (there was no wind) to keep the boat off the reefs on both sides of us. Both efforts were successful; the engine started again, and the boat stayed unscratched.

At every village we visited, we were required to make a gift of kava root to the chief, asking his permission to anchor, walk through the village, swim, photograph and fish. The half-kilo of kava root cost between $Fiji10 and 12 at the Suva market. Ashore at the village, a child or adult would always appear and act as self-appointed guide to the chief's hut. A village elder conducted the kava ceremony in Fijian, with everyone seated cross-legged on floor mats in front of the chief. The ceremony seemed to have a common central core, but did vary considerably from village to village, from a 60-second mumble, to a ten-minute, almost religious happening. It does seem that it would be better to make a present of things that the people need, rather than a narcotic for old men, but it was the custom and the tradition.

As it is suicidal to sail at night in these coral-filled waters, we broke our passage to Malolo Lailai by anchoring for the night in a "mainland" bay, solely occupied by a huge hotel. Saved on kava. The smaller islands call Viti Levu the mainland and mean it. Malolo Lailai, a name that runs trippingly off the tongue, has no village, just the famous Musket Cove, an airstrip and two hotels. Saved on kava again.

Normally we were the biggest boat in most anchorages. Not a big deal, but sort of nice in a round about kind of way—what the hell, it's good for the ego! When we entered Musket Cove, there was a 150-foot sailboat, two 130-footers, an 85, a 75 ("Condor" of Sydney to Hobart race fame) and two 65s. Put us right into our place it did, with our measly 54 feet.

Ryan (8): *I met several kids here, including the ones on "Condor," went to parties ashore with them, and generally had a great time. "Condor" rigged up a line hung off their spinnaker pole that allowed us to swing way out over the water before dropping. Dad copied it in other anchorages, but I was the only one that used it.*

Carole: *Laurie had been teaching Ryan to dive off the deck, and he had become an expert by Fiji. We would stand on deck, me with pretend megaphone announcing each dive; Laurie grading, deducting points for splash, legs not straight, toes not pointed, and feet not together. A grade of eight or less was considered an abject failure and greeted by boos and howls of derision from the assembled multitude (2).*

Near the Musket Cove Resort there was a store, with fresh bread every day, fresh fruit (expensive), ice cream, a reasonable variety of canned and packaged goods, and soft drinks. The morning stroll there was very pleasant, exchanging smiles and "Bulas" with everyone we passed.

On the other side of the airstrip was another resort, Plantation Island, which had an excellent bar and restaurant, and there was a third restaurant. Variety was possible! Musket Cove operated a "$2 bar," where all drinks, beer, soft drinks, gin and tonic, rum and orange, etc., were $Fiji2. They also put on a barbeque every evening, where they provided the BBQ and fuel, and we provided the meat. Salads were available, would you believe for $F2. It stayed open until the last person left.

Carole: *It was here I persuaded Laurie to write an article on what we wished we had known before we left home. Naturally it was immediately published by a national sailing magazine, and got Laurie back into the writing mode again. He had several articles published before we sailed and now would have many more. Even I had an article published, fulfilling a childhood dream of becoming an author.*

The Musket Cove Yacht Club invited us to become life members, at a cost of Fiji$1. The condition of membership is sailing to Fiji in your own boat, so it is a little exclusive. No certificates or anything fancy like that, but our boat's name got carved into one of the beams over the patio. The Club had nice facilities, restaurant, pool and the associated resort.

Carole: *There was also a laundry ashore, but we didn't use it. Luckily for me, we have a water maker, a washing machine that turns into a dryer, and A LAURIE. The machine takes too long to dry the clothes. The sun is much faster and that's when A LAURIE comes in handy for hanging out the clothes on the lifelines and the safety line.*

Laurie did tell me about the other ways of washing, but thankfully I never had to rely on them. The "Bucket Wash" involves filling a bucket with water, adding soap and clothes, then sailing to the next port. The suitably agitated clothes are then rinsed and hung to dry. Actually I did use this a few times for "nappisanning" out stains, and it worked well.

However, I never used the "Dinghy Wash" (and never saw anyone else using it either), but for the record here it is. Thoroughly wash out the dinghy to remove all traces of oil and gasoline. Partly fill with sea water and add Joy detergent (excellent with salt water) and clothes. Stand in the dinghy and rock back and forth—now you know one reason I never used this method—until the clothes are well agitated. Rinse in fresh water. Get husband to empty the dinghy.

Sunflower Airlines flew in and out every hour or so, a 10-minute trip by small plane from Nadi Airport. My son, Philip and his girl friend, Patricia, flew in, taking videos all the time, as the approach was over the yachts at anchor. Jenny (my daughter) flew in sitting in the co-pilot seat, trying not to scream at the pilot that he was too low, too fast, too ...... and then she was down.

We walked around the island a few times for the exercise, and because it was very pretty. Steady walking by a fit person will complete the circuit, mainly on the beach, in about 90 minutes. We know this because others have done it. Our times were a little different, and you, gentle reader, can decide whether they were more or less, and by how much. There is no prize for a correct answer.

Eagle-eyed Ryan discovered an island that appeared only at low tide—our own island—well it was until the tourist boats from Plantation Resort discovered it, too. The water around the island was an astounding pale green, with the sand covered with small starfish. A little way off was a reef of lovely coral and the usual clouds and crowds of multi-colored fish.

The one downside to this paradise was the occasional stone fish, an ugly little brute, almost indistinguishable from the surrounding rocks and dead coral, but with razor sharp, extremely poisonous spines. Sneakers were some protection, but while we were there a tourist stepped on one, and almost died.

Carole: *On July 8 we began a new tradition for Ryan, his half-birthday celebration. As both our birthdays are on January 8, two weeks after Christmas, there is a very long drought between presents. I baked Ryan half a cake, gave him half a birthday card, and sang half the "Birthday" song. He did get a whole present.*

Ryan (16): *Thanks Mum. I'm glad we have the same birthday so that you know how long it is without presents between our real birthdays and the next Christmas.*

Fiji seemed to have more coral than any place we have been to. The reefs were everywhere, many uncharted, and so sailing between islands required constant observation. Nothing spoils a good day's sailing quite as much as a close encounter of the coral kind. I made a wrong turn once and we sailed into a horseshoe shaped reef. Luckily, we backed out with no damage except to my ego (again).

To illustrate the dangers, about a year after we left Fiji, our friends Bill and Jan lost "Camelot" on a Fijian reef. They are both great and careful sailors, but this day the small things added up to disaster. A way-point had been set some 800 yards off a reef, and Jan was just going down the companionway and Bill was going up, when they hit.

The weather was calm, but overcast that morning, and the tide was just past full. Propping the boat up to prevent it falling on its side as the tide fell further, they called for towing assistance. No tug would leave port without pre-payment in cash, something that just was not possible, of course. Another cruiser arrived and stood by waiting for the tide to rise. Unfortunately, as it did, so did the wind and waves, and "Camelot" started to pound up and down. The end came so suddenly that Bill and Jan had to struggle to get off safely, and escaped with nothing but the clothes on their backs.

Both Bill and Jan are better sailors than I will ever be, and hindsight is wonderful to have, so the lessons to be learned from this are in no way to be construed as criticism of them.

1. Never sail on a day when the water colors cannot be clearly seen. This includes flat calm, sunny days, as the mirror sheen on the surface blocks the colors.
2. Never set a way-point closer than one mile from land or reef in day light, and two miles at night. The G.P.S. is accurate, the charts are not.
3. If you do go up on a reef, first look after the boat, then get off your valuables to another boat or some safe spot.

This Musket Cove easy life eventually palled, and we headed north to the Yasawa Group of islands, stopping at the southern end of Waya Island, and anchoring off a pretty little village. We dinghied ashore to meet the chief and present our kava, and were met by a group of children who claimed us for their own (Ryan wins again).

After the presentation ceremony two gorgeous nine-year-old twin girls took us to their hut, where their mother had tea and fruit for us. We became very friendly with the family (never met the father then, or on two subsequent visits) and had them to the boat for lunch and a video after church one Sunday. They insisted on bringing the food, fish cooked in coconut cream, breadfruit and yams. Carole made brownies and popcorn for the movie.

Church was conducted in a shed, with a bare concrete floor and corrugated iron roof. A large mango tree overhung the roof. Most of the village attended, bringing woven mats to sit on, as there were no chairs. The smart ones sat where they could lean back against the posts which supported the roof. We weren't so clever, and even though we were provided with cushions (the only ones in the church), sitting through the service was a strain on the back and bottom.

All the children sat in a group in the middle of the floor, with one of the mothers behind them holding a long bamboo pole. Any child who was not attentive, or somehow was not behaving properly, was promptly tapped on the head with the pole. Even the "good" ones got the occasional rap, probably by way of reminder to stay good. The choir sat off to one side and sang beautifully, with no instrument accompaniment. The minister started the service in a low key, but became very animated and vehement, with much finger waving, when delivering the sermon. We weren't sure of the subject, as it was delivered in Fijian, but clearly it was directed at me and I was suitably chastened.

Ryan (8): *I didn't have to sit with the kids, and got to wear a lei.*

On a subsequent visit a few weeks later, we found the church gone and the mango tree chopped down, as a new church was being built. The new structure will certainly be more comfortable, but will it look nicer, or have more character than the old? We liked the sound of the branches rubbing on the roof and the baaaing of the goats coming through the open walls.

There was a sand bar across the pass between Waya Island and the smaller island that the village was on. The local boats, often laden with up to thirty people, traveled back and forward through the pass every day. At low tide, there was often little or no water over the sand, so everyone piled out and they pushed, pulled, and dragged the boat over by sheer force, generally laughing and singing. At other times, they just got a good run up and ploughed through. Made interesting viewing, but I was certainly glad that I didn't own one of the boats.

"Teacher Appreciation Day" was being celebrated at the local school, and all the yachties were invited. The school had four teachers and about 60 kids in eight grades. Their standard of work appeared to be about the same as an Australian or U.S. school, with most of it in English. There were the usual speeches from the parents (in Fijian), the dignitaries (in Fijian), the headmaster (in Fijian and English) and the kids (in English). I made an impromptu thank you speech (in Australian) on behalf of the cruisers. The kids entertained with songs and dance. The kava was circulating amongst the parents and teachers, and soon some of the ladies got up to sing and dance. PTA meetings must be more interesting than the ones I have been to.

A few of us yachties were invited to lunch in the headmaster's house; four dishes, sort of Chinese style, one fish, one meat and a couple of unknowns, but all very good. Even Carole had some. The twins' mother made me a special lei, apparently bestowing on me the status of a village chief, at least in her eyes. Carole was given a flower lei, and later on many of the children she had been photographing gave her their leis. Ryan, also leied, marched with the kids, carrying half of a banner, and out of step.

Fiji and Passage to Australia

Carole: *We had given the school a lot of supplies. As Laurie said, the school seemed very familiar, with one room even having a copy of my favorite kindergarten reading book,* Mrs. Wishy-Washy. *Somewhat out of place in this brown-skinned land was a poster of Linda Evans telling children about skin care. Not to be found in a California school was a poster over the toilet reading, "Keep seat down and flies out."*

Further north we went, to Blue Lagoon, near Turtle Island Resort, one of the most exclusive and expensive in the world. Yachties were banned from the neighborhood of the resort for fear that we would lower the tone of the place. The movie "Blue Lagoon" was filmed here, hence the name. As a New Zealand production crew was filming *Swiss Family Robinson* while we were there, I would expect it will be called Robinson Bay by the time we return.

The film crew had made a full scale model of a partially sunken ship, and were towing it around. It made for some very interesting pictures. Away from the shoot, this was a very pretty place, with nice snorkeling and pleasant beaches, Carole got to sit out and relax on the sand (the third time she had done this on the whole trip so far!) while Ryan and I looked for shells and crabs.

A word about Ryan and fish. He was fishing crazy, and dangled a line in the water at every opportunity. While in Fiji his record was, counting only those over ten pounds, three tuna, one mackerel, one sweet lip, one cod. We have lost all record of the smaller fish. He still had to beat his Bora Bora effort of 10 fish in half an hour, all eating size. Amongst the cruisers he was a legend, seeming to be the only one who can catch anything. In the group of yachts we were traveling with, Ryan was the only child, and there was real competition to see who got to be with him or have him on their boat. He was well liked, and seemed to have the ability to mix with all ages, from 6 to 66.

Pat (60+) on "Marita Shan" became Ryan's best friend, and Ryan often spent the night with Pat and Tash. After one such episode, he asked Pat to ask Tash if he (Pat) could bring his tooth brush and sleep-over on "Dolphin Spirit."

It was at this anchorage that Ryan and Kurt indulged in some of their regular roughhousing play and Ryan made his usual comment that Kurt had "beat him up." A thoughtful Ryan then got out our medical encyclopedia. After a short while he asked for help, as the encyclopedia didn't have prices for injuries. What he was planning was to present Kurt a bill for his "injuries." We decided that he should look up appropriate medical terms and create a bill with costs he considered matched the seriousness of the hurt. He did that and wrote out a long list of injuries, together with their prices. The next day I took Ryan across to "Osprey" and witnessed the formal presentation of the bill. A fishing expedition settled the debt to the satisfaction of both parties.

While at another anchorage, one of the villagers took Kurt, Steve, Pat, Ryan and me across the island to a place where a World War II fighter plane was lying under about ten feet of water in the lagoon. Ryan and I swam out, and dove down to examine it. It was still recognizable as a plane, even though the pilot's seat was occupied by a large sea anemone with attendant fish. The plane was supposed to be a Spitfire, but we experts could agree only that it was a single-engined, single-seater.

The chief at this village was a woman, and perhaps this was why the kava ceremony was short. It was only in recent times that women were allowed to drink kava. Perhaps it was coincidence, but whenever the men went alone to make the presentation, we were invited to drink. Whenever the wives (co-captains, first mates) were present, the ceremony was very short, with no drink offered.

For the record, kava tastes as it looks, like dirty dishwater. It is impolite to just sip, so I usually drank about a cup full per ceremony, and finished up with numb lips, but no other apparent side-effects.

Carole: *It was somewhere in Fiji that I started serving our main meal at lunch. We spent many evenings with cocktails on our boat, or on others, and it was difficult to break these off to cook the main meal that Ryan demanded once a day, every day. Under the new system the meal was cooked, eaten and cleaned up by early afternoon, the leftovers made into soup or sandwiches were an easy evening snack, and Laurie and I didn't overeat.*

Needing fuel, we made a trip to the marina at Vuda Point, near Lautoka, on the mainland. This was a circular hole in the land, man-made, lined with concrete, and entered through a channel that had been blasted in the reef. It was designed as a cyclone-hole, presumably safe to leave your boat there during cyclones. Only open for a few months, and yet to go through a cyclone season, the claim was unproven.

Ryan spent his spare time trying to catch the small crabs on the concrete wall, using a hand spear and a fishing line baited with a wad of chewing gum. As always he attracted a fascinated following of locals, and became quite famous in the area. Next door to the marina was the "First Landing" restaurant, where we dined in the open; right on the beach, under the palms—a Carole restaurant—so we spent many evenings there.

Fiji and Passage to Australia

Carole: *Our table was right at the water's edge. The romantic tropical setting of surf, sand, sunset and palms, was completed by the ripples massaging our feet as we ate our curried chicken pizza.*

It had been almost six months since we set off from Marina del Rey, and we still hadn't listened to most of the CDs, or read all the books we brought along. Carole had come to realize that clothing can be reduced to a swimsuit and a pareo and had, as her Australian project, a major review of the clothes she brought along. Of course, she did have 12 swimsuits. Ryan and I made do with three each.

Fiji is the end of the line for South Pacific cruisers. From there the choice is either Australia or New Zealand to spend the cyclone season (November to March). Most of our group went to NZ. This made our farewell get together at the "First Landing" particularly significant, as we had been sailing together for five months, and some would not be going on past NZ.

Dick and Jeanne Lamar, friends of the Mulryans, and in their seventies, had asked to come on an ocean passage, so they joined us in Vuda Point. They had the honor of participating with us in one of the true Fijian scams. We were walking along the street when this very friendly Fijian came up to us, smiled, said "Bula" and asked Ryan's name. Naturally we obliged, and chatted a little about where we were from and the usual trivia.

Within a minute, another Fijian came up to us with music sticks and a toy canoe, all carved with Ryan's name. No, it was not a present, they were for sale, and the kicker was that we "had to buy" because they now couldn't be sold to anyone else. Carole walked away in disgust, but I relented (once a sucker, always a sucker) and negotiated a price—$10 for the three pieces. Two paces behind us, Dick and Jeanne became the proud possessors of a wooden man with their names on his legs.

Carole: *As did the Rankins before them, the Lamars brought a suitcase full of relief rations, otherwise known as stuff we couldn't get in the South Pacific. This included the essentials such as See's chocolate suckers, Lipton onion soup, and brownie mix.*

We prepared, with some trepidation for the 10 day sail to Brisbane, as the crossing had a bad reputation—not as bad as the one to New Zealand, but bad none the less. There were eight boats leaving on the same day from Vuda Point, seven going to New Zealand, one (us) going to Australia. I did try to talk everyone into going to Australia, but not for the obvious reason. The Fiji to New Zealand passage will result in hitting at least one storm front. The New Zealand to Australia passage across the Tasman Sea is always rough and stormy. By way of contrast, Fiji to Australia is above the storm belt and relatively peaceful. In addition, repair costs and facilities in Australia are at least equivalent to those in NZ, and you get to leave a month earlier after the cyclone season to cruise the Great Barrier Reef. NZ can be visited by 747 for the four weeks it will take to see it all twice.

We asked Immigration and Customs if we could check out from Vuda Point, instead of having to bring our boats to Lautoka, using the excuse that we were an organized rally. Immigration said OK, but Customs said NO, until Dave ("Promises") and I went to their offices to beg and plead. They eventually came to us after we agreed to pay an hourly rate per officer, plus transport costs. It saved us all time, inconvenience and money, so it was a good deal.

Carole: Jeanne started what we later adopted as a family passage tradition. Every day of the crossing, she had a small gift for each person. We looked forward to noon each day when the presents came out. Ryan got such things as fishing lures, and a pirate flag, Laurie batteries and a small screw driver set, while I received a shell necklace and dish towels.

The nine days to Australia had everything—35 to 40 knot winds on the first day, then a couple of days of good winds, then no winds, then good winds. Dick practiced real navigation with a sextant. Using our combined skills (I write numbers down really neatly), we often managed to place "Dolphin Spirit" within five miles of where the G.P.S. said we were. I could do celestial navigation, but carried four G.P.S.s so I wouldn't have to.

Carole: So far you have been spared the gory details of my sea-sickness, but this one is too good to miss. It was the third hour of the passage. As was my normal practice, I was in my bunk and feeling fine, in spite of the rough seas. Dick had been asleep in the salon, when I heard him get up and deposit his lunch in the galley sink. "I'm not getting up until that gets cleaned up," I thought. Then I heard Jeanne and Ryan use the barf bags we kept in the cockpit for my use.

Still I was feeling fine and quite proud of myself, as Ryan had been seasick only once before, and here was I, the seasick maven, in total control. Deciding to join the others in the cockpit, I crawled out from the barrier of pillows and moved to the edge of the bed, just as a wave hit us hard. It threw me back across the full width of the queen bed, and I hit my head on the hull. As I flew across the bed, so did the contents of my stomach. We never used that bedspread again.

Laurie cleaned up after all of us. Not once in our sailing was he seasick, not even when he was head down in the engine room for hours, surrounded by diesel and oil fumes.

Fifty miles out of Brisbane the weather got really nasty, with lightning, driving rain, 35 knots of wind on the nose, and 12-foot steep-fronted seas. When Carole spotted land, but with a huge thunder storm over it, she insisted that we turn around, and not go anywhere near it.

Carole: The land I so longed to see was engulfed in the blackest cloud. I heard the loudest thunder and saw the bright, white streaks, so begged Laurie to turn the boat around. He did and I went to bed much relieved, not caring if it took another day to get there, as I didn't want to be anywhere near that lightning. As soon as I fell asleep, Laurie headed in again. He didn't wake me for my watch (Laurie: I may be crazy, but I am not stupid.). *The next morning we were right in the middle of the storm with lightning striking the water all around us.*

There was lightning hitting the water, but the nearest strike was over 20 miles distant. In Carole's defense, it was spectacular. Making another bad decision, I choose to take the northern passage through Moreton Bay, which forced us to sail against both wind and tide, and take over 12 hours to cover the last 40 miles inside Moreton Bay. The water was shallow, and we had to tack back and forth across the channel—TACK—real cruisers don't tack without several hours of deliberation, and here we were tacking every five minutes. You would think that Australia would offer a better welcome to its returning prodigal son.

Carole: A huge slab-sided, bright orange Swedish-flagged car-carrier was coming up quickly behind us. I offered to call them on VHF to make sure they saw us, as I was the only one on board who spoke Swedish. Ryan immediately piped up, "Carole, I don't think that 'I love you' and 'Thank you very much' will cut it."

However, we made it, but not without a final flourish. Right at the mouth of the Brisbane River, I had to go below to call Customs on the radio, so handed over the wheel to Dick. When I came back on deck, my first comment was, "We're not moving." Sure enough, we had gone out of the channel and were aground, with the tide falling. It was quite serious, as the area we were in dried out completely at low tide, and if we had fallen on our side the returning tide would have filled "Dolphin Spirit."

Carole went below and calmly called for help on the radio, while I worked at getting us off. I put up the sails, and the 30 knots of wind heeled us over enough to reduce our draft and allowed us to slide off, with help from the engine. Carole, still calm, called off the rescue vessels. Ho-Hum, another day at the office.

Carole: *Calm! It must have been an Oscar winning performance. Laurie hadn't told me he was putting up the sails, so when we suddenly heeled over and I went sliding across the cabin, I thought "Dolphin Spirit" was a goner.*

All this meant that we were at the Customs/Quarantine Wharf in time for Customs and Immigration, but had to wait at the wharf overnight for Agriculture. None of us could go ashore (It was Jeanne's birthday and they were looking forward to an evening on the town), or receive visitors (not even my daughter). We were tied up outside of an Australian yacht, and the lady on board didn't like it at all. She spent the night yelling at us to adjust our lines and put out more fenders.

Agriculture showed up early the next morning, took our remaining fresh fruit and vegetables, Spam (anything but the Spam!), honey, eggs, and all dairy products (including canned and powdered milk), and charged us $A114 for the privilege. However, he did take all our garbage. At the time we thought that he was being nice, but in retrospect he had to, given the nature of the quarantine regulations.

Perhaps the wait was worth it, because the morning's motor up the river (about six miles) to our central city marina berth was very pretty. "Skerryvore" had just completed her circumnavigation, and we passed her all decked out with flags. She is less than 30-feet long, and one memory from Fiji is of them struggling back on board with a kava bowl that seemed to be larger than their dinghy. Baby Kim had been born in the Caribbean, and this would be the first time she had slept on land. Our fleet celebrated when she began crawling. Then she stood up, and commemorated the event by turning on a tap and flooding the boat with kerosene. What does land have to offer to compete with that?

We tied up at Dockside Marina, and immediately became the most photographed sailboat in Brisbane. While we deserved this honor, it really came about because sightseers had to look past us to see "Mercedes," a 140-foot power yacht, which had just been launched. Its dinghy, complete with 150-HP outboard, was named "Benz." The owner was from Florida and owned—you guessed it—a Mercedes dealership. If that doesn't tell you that the cars are overpriced, it should, but the captain very nicely invited us on board for a tour.

My parents came to the dock to see the boat their crazy son had sailed in. My father was so proud of our accomplishments, and so disappointed that his knee problems stopped him from coming aboard. Mum just looked, and I could hear her thoughts of "There is no way you would ever get me out on that." When Ryan was six months old we took him on a sailing charter in the Whitsunday Islands. Mum pulled me to one side and said,

"Promise me that if there is any wind you won't leave the dock." She was not a sailor.

After a week there, meeting my family, recuperating, and being tossed about by the wakes of the new "wakeless" river ferries, we sailed to Mooloolaba. It was hard to believe that it was the same Moreton Bay that fought us so grimly on the way in. The seas were calm, the sky blue and the breeze perfect. Millions of jelly-fish occasionally slowed us down as we ploughed through. I can remember sailing racing catamarans in the same area, being brought to a shuddering halt by jelly-fish, which caused me to wrap myself around the forestay, as I was out on trapeze.

We were given my parents' car. Ryan started school and trotted off every day, complete with school uniform. He was in a Grade 3 class, as the school year finished on December 13. With the personal schooling he got from Carole, Ryan seemed to be well ahead of his peers in most areas. I helped in Science by dissecting a crab, obviously key to Ryan's intellectual growth.

When we checked in, I was asked by Customs for payment to cover the Australian Government import duty and sales tax on the boat, some 35% of its assessed value. I argued that, while I was an Australian (non-Australians didn't have to do this), I was leaving within the year to continue our circumnavigation.

"Don't worry," I was told, "We will give you back your money then."

"With interest?" I asked.

They fell about laughing. Finally we reached an agreement that we were to leave within 12 months, and the payment would be waived.

Chasing Sunsets

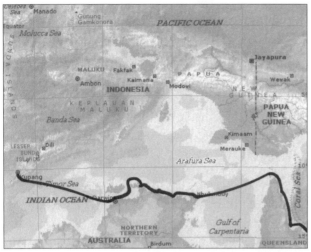

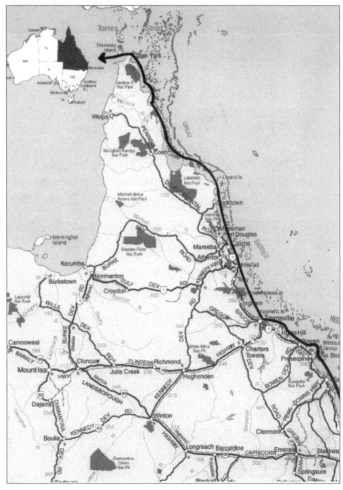

Queensland, Great Barrier Reef, North Australia, and Darwin

Year One and Two
November 1 to August 24

Mooloolaba Yacht Club was a perfect place to spend the cyclone season. The beach was just 100 yards away, beautiful soft, white sand, clear blue water, waves, the works. We could walk along it, or along a path in the bordering sand dunes, for about a mile to the town and school. It was summer, so there were a lot of swimmers and sun-bathers, but because of the space it was never crowded.

Our days became; take Ryan to school; work on the boat; walk on the beach; lunch under the pines; work on the boat; pick Ryan up from school; swim/surf on the beach; barbeque dinner; collapse into bed exhausted. Ryan made a best friend, Andrew, off "African King," docked just 10 yards from us and they became inseparable. His parents were originally from South Africa, and their name is King,

Ryan (8): *Andrew and I spent many hours in front of the television and playing cards on the large tables in the Club, when we weren't body surfing at the beach with his older brother.*

Carole: *Each day I'd walk Ryan to school along the beach with him (and occasionally me) skipping along the water's edge. Stopping for coffee on the way back, I'd drink it while reading a novel watching the waves, the surfers and the strollers.*

Australian breakfasts of baked beans or spaghetti on toast with eggs, or steak and eggs, or lamb chops and eggs, certainly set you up for the day.

Lunch can be an Australian meat pie, all hot and runny, with or without a scoop of peas, a sausage roll, greasy and flakey, or fish and chips laced with vinegar and eaten out of the newspaper wrapping. In spite of my apparent disparagement, these all became quite addictive and Laurie and I would often take the walk to town to indulge.

Of course Thanksgiving is not celebrated in Australia, but there were enough Americans on boats to kick start the function, Australians never turn down an excuse for a party, and so the Yacht Club was made available for the day. The turkeys were small (we were lucky to find any), but everyone brought along a dish so there was more than enough food for the over 100 attendees. Carole made a cranberry/mandarin/orange jelly (American translation—Jell-o salad) and felt bad when very few people took any. I moved it from the salad section to the dessert area and it vanished in seconds. An example of cultural diversity.

Another excitement was the Sydney to Mooloolaba Yacht Race, as the 40 or so competitors all came in and tied up at the Yacht Club. The first boats arrived at about 4.30am, and most were in by the afternoon. Why is it that racing crews seem to think that they have to get drunk as fast as possible after a race? By early afternoon young bodies were everywhere, and for two days the Club was a place to steer clear of. According to the locals, the crews were well behaved this year, compared with last year when they were "animals."

The Yacht Club was a social centre for the town. There always seemed to be meetings in the conference rooms, the restaurant was full, as was the bar and the lounge. They had slot machines ("pokies" in Oz-speak), a TV set for the kids and Barbeques free for anyone to use. Every Tuesday night the cruisers (a lot of Australians, a few Americans) got together for a pot luck BBQ and chat session. Carole was a regular hit with her artichoke-rice salad. Good chardonnay at $A8.50 per bottle ($US6.75) and beer at $A2.00 per glass helped to lubricate the good will.

To educate the taste buds of the Americans, we had bugs brought in—Moreton Bay Bugs—that look just like a deformed insect with a lobster tail. I defy anyone to tell whether they are eating lobster or bug. The other Queensland delicacy of mud crabs (the best tasting crab in the world) was the highlight of many a seafood dinner. Most also became barramundi addicts, as I have been all my life. The barramundi is a great fighting fish for the angler and the loveliest, lightest, white-fleshed fish ever. Queensland was the place for seafood.

Christmas Eve was spent with Ryan sewing his own stocking under Carole's direction. Santa found him, probably because of the masthead strobe, and left a body-board and case. Carole received one of our black pearls done up in a necklace, and I was not forgotten with a large fishing reel for the stern. The Thomsons, friends of the Mulryans, adopted us and had us to their house in the mountains for a Christmas Eve feast.

A first for Carole, the California native, was Christmas Day on the beach wearing a swim suit, watching Ryan surfing with his new gear. We had organized lunch with some of the other cruisers at a table under the pandamus palms and she-oaks on the beach. To be certain that we got that particular table, Carole had cruisers in relays sitting at it from 7am. Even a short sharp rain shower (equivalent to Los Angeles' annual rainfall) didn't dampen the festivities.

My daughter Jenny was just recovering from the removal of a melanoma from her leg. Queensland is the skin cancer capital of the world, and I came from North Queensland, the capital of the capital. One of the Brisbane stores is aptly named "The Cancer Store" as it sells only clothing and other things designed to reduce the risk of skin cancer. "Slip, Slap, Slop" was the anti-cancer theme—slip on a shirt, slap on a hat, slop on the sunscreen.

Carole: I met Bernice, Laurie's first wife, Jenny and Philip's mother. She and I got along very well swapping advice on how to make Laurie better, and noting he hadn't changed stories with wives.

Carole entered recipes into the computer and passed the 600 recipe mark. Everyone continued to be amazed at the dishes she produced from our galley. Her other occupations, apart from cooking, cleaning, washing dishes and clothes, and teaching Ryan, were polishing the stainless steel on deck (with a tooth brush!), lemon-oiling the wood below, playing bridge on the computer, and reading all the classics—Steinbeck, Victor Hugo, Tolstoy—she had put off reading in high school.

Carole: It was here that I became renowned as "The Toothbrush Queen." In my days of blissful ignorance, I thought stainless steel was actually stainless. I had discovered by watching Heather, BK and Jan, that the rusty stainless steel on deck could be cleaned—Laurie certainly never imparted this knowledge. Now I had my opportunity. Listening to Spanish tapes, I spent the next two months of my spare time attacking the crevices and corners with my trusty toothbrush. I got every bit of rust off the boat and we looked so smart. One week after we started sailing again the uselessness of my effort was obvious.

We played bridge with Dave and B.K. off "Blue Ribbon" and George and Jenny off "African King." Unfortunately, "African King" was sold and the family became land people, therefore untouchables. Ryan was particularly sad as all too soon he and Andrew had to say goodbye.

Carole and I went on a pre-wedding honeymoon trip to New Zealand and drove all over the North Island. Our cruiser friends gathered in Auckland to see us, a great reunion and planning session for next year's trip.

Carole did as promised and packed six suitcases of stuff we could do without. We took these back to the U.S. to store, but unfortunately brought back six suitcases and three large crates of stuff we absolutely had to have (more See's suckers, onion soup, videos). However, we really did cut down on clothes and other things, so we could actually find what we wanted, when we wanted it, and move through the boat without needing climbing equipment. Carole has been quite wonderful in this regard, ruthlessly searching out and discarding the unnecessary and the unneeded. I was lucky to make the cut.

Carole: *Probably the only reason he survived was that we had just been married during our trip home. Laurie had wanted to get married in Fiji, on that disappearing island, but we decided to wait until we got to Australia, when I would have my mother fly over. Then we got to California and everything just seemed to fall into place for a wedding there. It was so rushed that Laurie forgot/didn't have the time to tell his daughter. His father was particularly disappointed.*

Laurie wanted the wedding on January 8, Ryan's and my birthday, so he would have only one date to remember. We made it on January 19, doing, in one week, all the organization, finding the minister, buying the perfect cake decorated with real seashells and starfish, and sending out invitations. The ceremony was on board my brother John's powerboat, "Lucky Ducks," in Newport Beach, California. The entire wedding party wore Brisbane tee-shirts with dolphins on them, and blue jeans. The bride could be distinguished by the lace on her white tennis shoes and the crown of flowers—oh, and perhaps by her wide smile.

I'd weathered the first year and was starting to think I might complete the whole trip.

Back in Queensland, the weather gods were still creating cyclones further north (four in five weeks), but apart from the last cyclone, which brought 30 to 40 knots of wind and very heavy rain for about four days, the weather was close to perfect in Mooloolaba.

The day after we returned, our new 240/110 volt transformer stopped working. Australia is 240-volt so we needed the transformer for shore power. We installed another new one, having to run the gen set every day for refrigeration and to charge batteries in the interim. That made it our third transformer, an expensive business. The supplier gave us our money back on the original, U.S. sourced transformer, as did the second supplier (Australian), but we were out the installation costs for each of them.

My father had been so thrilled to be wheeled down to the boat when we arrived. He had been in bad health and confined to a wheelchair for a while, but maintained he was going to stay alive and see us arrive. Sadly, his health then declined even further, and he passed away quietly. Dad had arrived in Australia from Italy at age twelve, and through sheer hard work and determination, assisted by a great choice of wife, had created a cane farm out of North Queensland wilderness, and raised three children, all with at least one university degree. He was so proud of us, and we of him.

Ryan went back to Mooloolaba State School every day and had fun being with the kids. All the children who were in the "continued good behavior" category went on an outing to an island for fishing, swimming and a BBQ. Ryan was, of course, included, and, of course, caught fish.

Ryan (9): *I spent one night in the local aquarium with my class, sleeping in a tube in the shark tank. It was fun waking up to see a seven foot shark staring at me through the glass. My sister Jenny came with us, and she was more scared of the sharks than I was.*

To get her bottom cleaned and painted, we had the boat hauled at the yard next to the Yacht Club. They used a platform-on-rails system which required precise alignment of the boat and expert arrangement of the supports. I watched, heart-in-mouth, but all went well. New cockpit cushions, a new cockpit canopy and windows, and upgraded refrigeration completed the repairs. Dave ("Blue Ribbon") had installed three plates in the freezer and one in the refrigerator, an arrangement much more suited to tropical waters. It proved its value again and again over the years. The leak in the Avon dinghy became unfixable so we bought a new, red, 12-foot inflatable-bottom Zodiac and new 15 and 25-HP Yamahas to drive it.

All then left to do was install the new BBQ, re-mark the anchor chain, service the diesel engine and gen set, run out and check the sails, varnish everything that looked like wood, polish everything that looked like metal (Carole's area of management), re-program the auto-pilot, swing the compass, repair the washing machine, store all the stuff we said we would get rid of but didn't, provision, store provisions, finish off the minor repairs (a list that never seemed to get shorter), check off all the lists, check off the master list, do the things that weren't on the list, and we were ready. Where did the last few months go?

Before departure we tried painting markings on the anchor chain, but that lasted about three anchorages, and in any case couldn't be seen accurately at night, or in bad weather. We tried those commercially available tags, but they lasted an even shorter time, with the same visibility problems. The lasting answer was plastic wire ties. I put one at 30 feet, two at 60 feet, three at 90 feet, one at 120 feet, two at 150 feet, and so on. These did not interfere with the winch, lasted for months, were easily seen in daylight and by flashlight, and any missing or worn ones could be easily replaced at any time. I usually did replacements when pulling in the anchor on a calm day.

Carole: On Mother's Day, Ryan gave me the greatest gift of all—he told me he was going to call me "Mum" for the day. Four months earlier, the night before Laurie and I were married, he started to ask, "Do I have to…..?" when I cut him off with, "Of course not. Don't worry; life will go on the same as before." He had been relieved.

Going to bed that Mother's Day night he asked if he could call me Mum from then on—and he has. Even at those times when he is very, very mad at me, he has never called me Carole or said, "You're not my real mother." I have a son! At 51 I became a mother!

"Marita Shan," "Osprey," "Sky Bird," "Pilgrim," and "Soliloquy" arrived from New Zealand. "Topaz" and "Gigolo" had spent the season in Mooloolaba with us. We hired a mini-van and most of us went for a farewell tour of the Southern Queensland and Northern New South Wales highlights, with me as driver, guide, and token Australian.

I started by impressing everyone with an overnight stay at O'Reilly's Guest House, in the mountains behind Brisbane. Set high on a ridge, it is totally isolated, surrounded by forested mountains. Wonderfully colored parrots climbed all over us during the day and that night we went on an organized walk to spot rare nocturnal animals. We actually saw a couple, but no one really cared, as a walk through the Australian bush at night is, by itself, unforgettable. A lunch of billy tea and damper overlooking mountains and forests, with Brisbane and the sea in the background, was a fitting finale.

Typhoid shots injected, and malaria tablets collected in preparation for visiting the Far East, we set off again, full of trepidation. After almost seven months tied to a dock, we wondered if getting back into the cruising routine would be difficult—fishing, swimming, looking for shells, drinking wine while the sun sets, lying on the sand, walking under the palms—the problems were obvious.

Taking this into consideration, we decided to start off with a simple overnight sail from Mooloolaba to Bundaberg, around the outside of Fraser Island, the largest sand island in the world. Just to remind us who was the real boss, we were presented with a mixture of motoring in no wind, pretty sailing under an almost full moon, and pounding into head seas and head winds.

My new, super, dinghy-support system collapsed, and we almost lost both dinghies overboard. Naturally, this happened at night, when we were smashing into head seas, so I was well baptized by the time I had righted matters. Carole made sure I was secured to the jack lines, and blinded me with a flashlight every few seconds, checking that I was still on board. In Bundaberg the $A500 dinghy supports quickly became scrap lumber, and the dinghies moved into a new mounting configuration that was both stable and actually allowed us to see forward. Naturally, as this new system worked, it cost nothing. Such is the law of cruising.

To press the "take nothing for granted" lesson home even more, we had problems in a river. Bundaberg is some ten miles up the Burnett River, which is quite shallow in parts. In spite of Carole's vehement protests I decided to try to make the trip up river with the tide almost out. The channel winds like a snake, but was well marked with buoys that must be precisely aligned. "Marita Shan" took up her normal position behind, following what Pat calls his "half-a-million dollar depth sounder."

Of course we went aground, got off with difficulty, and decided (Carole demanded) to anchor and wait for the tide to come in. In finding an anchoring place, we went aground again, got off again, and finally anchored. To give Carole her due, she never said, "I told you so!" but the pressure to do so was almost unbearable. I had no excuse, but I was tired, frustrated by the dinghy support situation, needing to prove my manhood for the day, stubborn, and generally not in the mood to be told I couldn't take my baby where I wanted to.

With the tide rising, we blew up the river, hitting bottom only twice more, but never actually stopping. The Mid Town Marina in Bundaberg had allocated 60 feet of space for our 56 foot boat (I count anchors in this circumstance), between a very wide catamaran and a trawler. Thankfully, we had people on the dock to catch lines, and I made a masterful approach, missing the catamaran by almost two inches.

Carole: *He had the gall to act nonchalant about it, obviously quickly overcoming the complexes listed at the end of the previous paragraph.*

I had lived in Bundaberg for about six years in the 70s, so acted as tour guide for our group of cruisers. We went on the Rum Distillery tour (**Ryan (9):** *The adults had free rum to drink. All I got was water.*), saw my old house, walked the streets, shopped, and then left after two nights. Motoring down the river at high tide, we anchored overnight at the mouth so as to get an early start the next day. The five boats all agreed to leave at around 5am, so, naturally, all were up and gone by 4:30am, with us just starting to stir.

We were always happy to be the last to leave, as we didn't want to get to anchorages too much before the others, and it was always a great ego trip to blast past them in mid-passage.

"Osprey" has a simple regime for departure. PL stays asleep in bed and Kurt pulls up the anchor and gets going. On this morning I happened to be up, standing on the bow, watching everyone leave without us. Kurt had pulled up the anchor and was motoring while he coiled lines and did last minute clean-up of the deck. With Kurt at the stern, "Osprey" headed straight for us and passed our bow only feet away. Kurt looked up and we exchanged whispered pleasantries, so as not to awake the sleeping spouses. We were that close. Kurt's story continues to be that he was in perfect control in spite of his back being turned, and as evidence offers the fact that we did not hit.

Our destination was Pancake Creek, some 60 miles away. We had a delightful sail, with dolphins jumping and spinning all around us, and were securely anchored by 2:30pm. Then it rained, and kept raining all night. Welcome to sunny Queensland! The next morning was fine, so Ryan and I went trolling in the dinghy, got bites, but caught nothing. We decided to stay a second night as we were enjoying ourselves, and on no schedule. The time was spent walking on sand islands exposed by the falling tide and covered with all sorts of interesting animals and things to turn over and examine.

Carole: *Daily school for Ryan continued. I had schooled Ryan the first year using the Calvert system, which was really good. However, we wanted Ryan to learn about each country we visited, when we were actually there, as well as give him a deeper grounding in Spanish, music and art, and Calvert was too rigid to allow this. As soon as we set sail again, I moved Ryan to my curriculum and daily lesson plans.*

One of the problems with home schooling is to separate the teacher and the parent. We developed an elaborate charade where, every morning, Ryan would say goodbye to his parents and hello to "Teach" (me) and "Prince" the principal (Laurie). On occasions, Teach would phone home to get permission for Ryan to go on a field trip, or to advise that he was not feeling well and would a parent please come to pick him up. In the afternoons, it was goodbye to "Teach" and "Prince" and hello to Mum and Dad.

It seems silly, but I think that it did help and Ryan really threw himself into it, insisting that we call the school to get him a day off whenever that was necessary. We kept it going for five years.

On to Cape Capricorn—a lighthouse, huge sand hills, and sand flats exposed by the tide and covered by millions of bright blue soldier crabs.

Ryan exhausted himself herding them into squadrons, and then chasing them until they decided to call it quits and bury themselves in the sand. The smart ones led him into soft sand where he quickly sank to his knees and couldn't get out. He really didn't appreciate our walking away and leaving him there. Later, he scraped his shin on the only piece of wood on 20 miles of open beach.

Great Keppel Island had a lovely anchorage and a short dinghy ride to a charming resort with $A12.50 hamburgers. It is known for its shark attacks and sells clothes with a bite taken out in strategic places. We had to fight off the red and blue rainbow lorikeets to get food into our mouths, much to Ryan's delight. Lorikeets are a parrot, about the size of a pigeon, with brilliant coloring. They congregate in flocks of hundreds, and are very friendly to anyone who offers food. The only problem comes when, with two lorikeets on your head, several on your shoulders and arms, and more on your lap, you try to get food into your own mouth.

After lazing on the beach and swimming, we arrived back at our boat to be called to come over to "Marita Shan." As we were dinghying across, the flags on the other boats all went up, and their occupants, in best clothes, got into dinghies to join us.

Deciding that being married on a powerboat made our first ceremony null and void, our friends set up a second one on "Marita Shan." The ladies dressed Carole in a white mosquito net veil covering her from head to foot, with a garter and posy of flowers. Ryan and I were given bow ties and toilet paper boutonnieres. Rings (painted hose clamps), and a better looking license than the real one, were special details. The ceremony was written by Steve, off "Pilgrim," a lawyer in previous life, but it was funny in spite of that. He had paid his $5 in the 60s and became an ordained minister of the Universal Church. Afterwards we had a tremendous feast (prawns, mussels, pork, beef, chicken, and salads to mention but a few of the culinary delights), a special cake that took Tash three days to make, champagne, the works. We were thoroughly caught by surprise, and that was very difficult when communication between boats was by radio, open for all to hear. Thank you everyone, it was a very special day.

The next few stops were Pearl Bay (pretty, nice beach, the usual stuff), South Percy Island (prettier, nicer beach, more usual stuff), Scawfell Island (you guessed it), Brampton Island (resort, $A12.50 hamburgers again, see above for superlatives) and Thomas Island. We were now well and truly into the Whitsunday Island Group. I had mixed feelings, as Thomas was the favorite stop when Patricia and I chartered in the Whitsundays, and to complicate matters, Ryan had been conceived there. Apart from an initial jolt when we sailed into the anchorage, the memories were all pleasant, helped by Carole's quiet support.

As we were getting low on fresh stuff and—horrors—had run out of fruit, we headed for the Abel Point Marina in Airlie Beach, to enjoy the delights of civilization. Just behind us was a Colombia 32 called "Dolphin Spirit," and the owner's first name was Larry. Too many coincidences! Careful questioning discovered that WE WERE FIRST with the name—law suits will follow.

Ryan shook me awake one morning, all excited because he had found a young man, shirtless and shoeless, asleep in the cockpit. He was crew from a trawler in the marina, and had no idea how he got in our cockpit. The last he could remember was "a great party." We found his missing wallet a couple of months later, on the deck, stuffed under some chain. Shirt and shoes were never found.

The Whitsunday Group forms one of the great cruising areas of the world, terrific scenery, usually perfect weather, calm seas, steady winds, protected anchorages, wonderful snorkeling and diving. Unfortunately the terrible weather hid most of these from us for the three weeks we were there. Even more unfortunately, our visitors didn't get to experience the fabulous Whitsundays.

Joanne, a teacher friend of Carole's, arrived armed with the usual suitcase of supplies, the latest videos, and Tevas, the sandal of choice for cruisers. John and Shirley Thomson, with sons Kyle and Iain were next. They were Queenslanders, living just behind Mooloolaba, so were allowed to join me in saying nasty things about the weather. John sadly missed his daily stock market report, and a week on board was not long enough to train him in proper cruising relaxation.

I got into an argument with the owner/operator of the local crocodile farm when I said that, in my youth, we had caught a 20-foot crocodile in our barramundi nets. He was adamant that they grew no bigger that 18 feet, and won the argument through sheer volume. He had the microphone, but I was right!

Ryan (9): I think I started the argument by saying something like, "My Dad caught one bigger than that." This was the place where I was kicked by a kangaroo. His big toe scratched me. Dad then told stories about how kangaroos hold dogs with their front legs and rip out their stomachs with those big hind leg claws, so I guess I got off easy. Lots of the females had joeys in their pouches. Some of the older ones were so big their feet stuck out the top of the pouch.

The solitude and excellent snorkeling on Black Island was only a couple of miles out to sea from Cid Harbor, so we decided to dinghy there, with the Thomsons, for a picnic. Seven of us, with food and equipment, were an easy load for the dinghy, and we zoomed across the calm sea in style. We must have been enjoying ourselves too much, because the afternoon wind increased, and getting back was a wild wet ride against it. In a smaller dinghy we never would have made it without being swamped. All the visitors were sick. Carole never had a twinge, and was so proud of it that Ryan and I didn't mention we were equally unaffected.

My daughter Jenny, with her friend (now husband) Brad came on board at Hamilton Island. This has to be the only tropical island paradise polluted by high-rise apartment buildings. Whatever happened to the "no building taller than a palm tree" planning rule? To Ryan's delight we were again boarded by dozens of brightly colored rainbow lorikeets and a few white cockatoos. These climbed all over us and "Dolphin Spirit" with absolutely no fear.

That day was memorable in other ways. On the passage to Hamilton, the circuit breaker switching the main G.P.S. failed, I broke a Teva strap and lost a lens of my glasses. To top it all, I screwed up a very simple approach into the marina slip, under the critical eyes of the mainly charter boat novices. The sneers were almost audible.

Carole: *Laurie persists in talking about the very few times his boat handling wasn't brilliant, and neglects the many hundreds of times when it was.*

It was here that Ryan and Jenny flew, but attached to a hang-glider which slid down a cable from the top of a mountain to the bottom. They were winched back up, all thrilled and ready to go again. We sailed, in good weather, to Whitehaven, a glorious, blindingly white, crescent beach. Jenny swam ashore with Ryan paddling a surfboard alongside her. With a whoosh of exhaled air, a large turtle surfaced a couple of feet in front of them. All three were petrified, then took off in different directions.

Ryan: *Dad had promised to look out for sharks while we were swimming, and he didn't see a huge turtle! Jenny was very mad at him.*

A goanna (Australian monitor lizard) joined the cruiser group BBQ ashore at Cid Harbor. He was over six feet long and managed somehow to swallow a whole T-bone steak. It was his territory, so we got out of his way. His coming marked the end of the good weather, and we had wind and rain for the remainder of our stay.

Jenny had to fly out of Hamilton Island, so we took "Dolphin Spirit" back there. Most of our cruiser friends decided to tag along as passengers. It was a windy, rainy day, and not all suitable for sailing in coral-filled water. However, I had successfully navigated this channel more than 30 times over the years and Jenny had a plane to catch, so we went, crawling at less than two knots over the bottom into the squalls.

Under the eye of five captains and their first mates, in an area I knew like the back of my hand, I went aground on a bommie (coral head). The good thing about having experienced people on board was that everyone knew what to do. The bad thing about having experienced people on board was that everyone knew what to do, and told me. We were only lightly aground, so shifting the passengers to one side heeled us enough that we were quickly off, but OH, the chagrin and embarrassment.

We were ready to leave the Whitsundays, thoroughly disappointed with our time there. The wind had blown 20+ knots almost every day, it had been cloudy when it hadn't been raining, and cold (for cold read in the low to middle 70s—I am just a tropical flower!). Enough—we were heading north to Townsville, Cairns and Darwin, my old stomping grounds.

A very pretty sail took us to an anchorage behind Cape Edgecumbe, near Bowen, before the winds blew up to 30 knots again. Just at dark, a dinghy drifted past with two people on board calling for help. We had our dinghy on deck, and couldn't raise any of the trawlers anchored in front of us. Finally we got through to Bowen Air-Sea Rescue, just as we got our dinghy in the water, and the drifters managed to start their motor.

A howling wind woke us around 3am. When we went to sleep there had been a line of trawlers anchored in front of us and now one, with all lights blazing, was right on our bow. We called them on VHF with no response, called Air-Sea Rescue on SSB, but they were unable to help. Then we resorted to the loud hailer, waking "Marita Shan" but not the trawler. By now very concerned (read close to frantic) we spent the rest of the night doing distance calculations. Daylight showed that none of the original trawlers had moved, and that the object of our concern had come in while we were asleep, and was anchored like a rock. One of those nights to forget, not helped by "Marita Shan" telling the story again and again.

Cape Upstart offered a calm anchorage, Cape Bowling Green an ugly, rolly one, and then we were in Townsville at the Breakwater Marina. Right in front of us was "Sudade," a black, 90-foot sloop we saw in Papeete, just after the captain had broken the boom by wrong use of the hydraulics, and in Suva, just after the new captain had run it aground on a reef at the entrance. The third captain was very nice, and we never saw them again, so either he sailed in the other direction, or the next incident sank the boat.

My brother, Des, and my sister, Shirley, came on board in Townsville and sailed with us to Cairns. They left behind spouses and families, and the three of us were together for two weeks for the first time since 1957. We proved that we hadn't aged at all in the past 40 years, and that we all had very retentive, and extremely selective, memories.

It was a family period. We got together with my uncle and family in Ayr, uncle and family in Ingham, aunt and family in Townsville, and a cousin from Tasmania who was visiting Townsville. Our cruiser friends gained the impression that I was related to everyone in the place. We rented a van and drove a group of cruisers to the farm where I grew up, and all around the area. One highlight was the cemetery in Ingham, where the Italian population has raised magnificent tombs and mausoleums. Some of them are house size!

Carole: *A lot of time must have been spent designing one's home for eternity and selecting the photographs to be exhibited. Me, I'll select my college graduation picture. Who cares if no one recognizes me.*

Then it was off to Cairns. We spent one night at beautiful Orpheus Island, where Ryan, Des and Shirley pulled in more that 30 eating-sized fish in half an hour. Ryan had, at last, found people as fanatical about fishing as he was. Later, to our horror, we discovered that the anchorage was a no-fishing zone. No wonder the fish were so plentiful.

Carole: *Shirley not only caught the fish, but she cleaned and cooked them as well. I worked hard at scenarios that would keep her aboard longer.*

Shirley showed another of her true values that night. A large powerboat dragged down on us and no shouting of mine could rouse anyone on board. One bellow (there is really no other description that comes close) from Shirley and heads popped up everywhere. Proving that certain intellects are found all over the world, they were then very indignant, because it was obvious that we had dragged up-wind into them.

A moment of excitement at the entrance to the Hinchinbrook Channel saw us mistaking a channel marker and going aground—again. I got us off—again. In all fairness, it was raining, with poor visibility, and the marker that caused the problem was bigger than the channel marker, and in the place where the channel marker was shown on the chart. I still got the "How can we ever trust you again?" bit from Carole and Ryan, and both of them went bananas every time the depth went under 50 feet for the rest of the day. Des and Shirley accepted the explanation that we wanted them to experience every aspect of cruising, including going aground.

Carole: *Laurie always says being at sea is much safer than being near land. He's right. As usual, "Marita Shan" was following right behind us. I frantically called them on the radio, "We're aground. Turn. Turn now!"*

Memorable days were spent anchored up a creek on Hinchinbrook Island, looking for crocodiles, and fishing for barramundi and mud crabs. Missed the first two and caught only a small mud crab (a three-for-oner, female, pregnant, missing one claw), which we returned to the water. In the mornings, the water was mirror smooth and we had wonderful dinghy rides up into the mountains.

At Dunk Island, one of the nicer resorts on the Reef, we met another boat who convinced us to visit Fitzroy Island, a place we had previously decided to pass. We stopped, the weather was great, the water clear, the coral and fish outstanding, and the island walks enjoyable. The best snorkeling was off a beach, appropriately named Nudey Beach, which always had at least six topless females spread around it. It was purely coincidental that Des and I had to go ashore at regular intervals to check the dinghy, defog the mask, repair the snorkel, adjust the fins, and complete several other vital procedures that never occurred at other spots.

Next stop, Cairns. Cyclone Justin, in March, had damaged the city marina, so we went to Yorkey's Knob Half Moon Bay Marina, some seven miles north. Getting in was a little tricky, given our deep draft, but we avoided going aground, and the marina and facilities were quite delightful. Again, we hired a mini-bus for a drive to Port Douglas and on to Daintree, where we went on a river cruise to see crocodiles and other assorted tropical flora and fauna.

Carole: *A yellow snake was curled up on a branch. Almost everything that moves in Australia is poisonous, particularly the snakes. We were in the region noted for the most poisonous snake in the world, the taipan, and Laurie would persist in telling stories of his encounters with them during his childhood on the farm. As a result, I was always on the lookout and thankfully most of the ones I saw were either crossing roads, or, better yet, dead on the road.*

Ryan (16): *What about that snake we saw on the beach in Cyprus just near your feet, the huge python in the tree in Costa Rica just above your head, and the cobra in Bali...*

Carole: *Ryan and I continue to have the "snake argument," with me on the "only good snake is a dead one" side and Ryan extolling the virtues of and necessity for, snakes. Neither ever changed the other's mind.*

It was in Daintree that the habit I don't have—exaggeration—caught up with me. We were in Far North Queensland, just a few degrees off the equator, having drinks on the main street of a town with a maximum population of 1,000, in one of the most casual and laid-back areas of the world.

Instead of just saying that, I announced to the assembled gathering, that I would pay everyone $5 for every suit they saw that day. At that mo-

QUEENSLAND, GREAT BARRIER REEF, NORTH AUSTRALIA, AND DARWIN

ment, the street filled with men in suits, and just as quickly they were gone, and the street was back to its sleepy self. No, we weren't hallucinating; although that was the theory I pushed to avoid paying the bets. We were right next to the Court House where there was a lawyer's convention, and they had just finished a formal session, requiring suits, and were hurrying back to their hotels to change out of them.

Our cruiser group had dinner at a restaurant called Going Bananas, in Port Douglas. The food was Middle Eastern/Turkish/Greek/Chinese/????, and delicious. The owner, Alex, wore a skirt and a large moustache. He gave couples jelly snakes to eat (one partner at each end chewing towards the middle), gave the women and me strawberries soaked in liqueur, gave me a kiss (is there a trend here?), played with my hair, and generally acted as your typical "mine host."

As it was Shirley's birthday, she got a glass of liquor (she didn't drink before this), a leaf crown with a sparkler burning at the front, and a tattoo on her upper chest. She took it all in good spirit. I, on the other hand, got very concerned every time Alex walked behind me. Ryan was in seventh heaven as Katie, Kurt and PL's daughter had joined them. He had a real crush on her. Pity she was 15 years his senior, as they made a good pair.

Carole: Katie often flew in to the best spots as we sailed into them. PL and I often asked ourselves why we hadn't taken this option and had to be on the boat for the whole journey. My fear of sailing never really went away. In the Marquesas I told myself I'd go to Tahiti, in Tahiti to the Cooks, in the Cooks to Tonga. Now I was in Australia I could at least sail up the coast—it must be safe inside the Great Barrier Reef—to Darwin. Indonesia? Well I doubt it. I'm not going to chance getting malaria.

Sailing "Dolphin Spirit" to the outer reef was not possible because of the weather, but it was a "must see," so we took a day trip on the tourist boat "Reef Magic." The sea was bumpy, even for that large boat, but when we got there the fish and coral were terrific. It was next to impossible to get Ryan out of the water, even to eat. We saw a giant wrasse (about 60 pounds) and all the other myriads of "normal" reef fish.

Carole: It all started out so well for me. The trip over was rough, and although most of the passengers were sea-sick, I had my sea legs and felt fine, a real pro! I was snorkeling a little way from my family, when I heard someone calling and saw motioning from the deck of the catamaran. In a panic, knowing a huge shark had been sighted, I wildly swam for the boat. False alarm. The attendant had been signaling for a snorkeling instructor to return and take out some children. Nevertheless, my panic attack foolishly kept me out of the water for the remainder of the day.

On the way back, I was on the bridge, chatting with "Reef Magic's" captain as we approached the marina and happened to make some remark about difficulties in following the channel. "Not a worry," he said and promptly headed straight in across the mud-flats, totally ignoring the channel. Now he said there was plenty of water, but I swear that our wake was mainly mud and sand—several hundred horsepower can do great things.

Provisioning complete, Des and Shirley safely returned to their families, it was time to head up the coast to Cape York, the tip of Australia, and then west, through the Torres Strait, across the Gulf of Carpentaria to Arnhem Land and Darwin.

Carole: *Provisioning for a leg of the journey was always a treat, buying everything we would need for the next months. Candy bars, popcorn and cookies were items I would pass up in my previous life, knowing I could get them the next day if the need struck. Now I bought by the cart load. Who knew when we would see them again, if ever. What if we were marooned and a mint chocolate cookie could save me?*

North from Cairns, settlements were small and scattered, and most of the anchorages were completely deserted. We anchored alone under the reef behind tiny Hope Island and couldn't get out for three days because of high winds, strong enough to stop our launching the dinghy. On the last night, a charter powerboat with seven men came in. They invited us to a BBQ ashore, after dark. Carole decided not to go, and spent all the time Ryan and I were ashore with a can of Mace in one hand and the radio microphone in the other, ready for any sign of murder or piracy. The lawyers, doctors and businessmen were actually quite good company. We left the next day, in spite of the wind.

Lizard is one of the better islands on the Reef, so of course the wind was so strong we could hardly move off the boat. We missed diving with the 800-pound gropers at Groper Hole, we couldn't get to the great snorkeling spots, but Ryan and I did actually get ashore for a walk. The weather certainly had been against us all the way up from Mooloolaba.

"Morning Glory," Rupert Murdock's huge yacht was anchored nearby. We had not seen it since Papeete. Rupert, whom I had met several times when I was President of the Australian American Chamber of Commerce in California, was not on board (I called and asked, hoping for a tour of the boat).

The mainland coast scenery, pure white silica sand hills alternated with darker sand hills, trees, huge brown ant hills and rocks, framed the multi-blue colors of the sea. Bush fires sent plumes of smoke up every few miles, and there were no people in evidence. On Morris Island, another tiny speck of land surrounded by a huge reef, Ryan and I were dive bombed by gulls, and found the grave of a pearl diver who had died in the late 1800s. Portland Roads was a surprise—several big, modern looking houses hundreds of miles from the nearest town of any size.

By that time, we were sailing in a group with "Marita Shan," "Sky Bird," "Osprey," "Pilgrim," and "Soliloquy." By far the slowest boat, "Soliloquy" always trailed us, with Joe, her captain, noting that he did this to keep the pirates off our tails, and that he was always successful. For some reason, "Soliloquy" arrived first at Portland Roads, and we heard Joe, over the VHF, plaintively asking where everyone was, and where should he anchor.

Ryan (9): *I sailed on "Sky Bird" from Portland Roads to Shelburne Bay and caught two Spanish mackerel, 5 and 15 pounds. Dad also caught two little 5 pounders. We had a fish BBQ on "Dolphin Spirit" for 15 people that night. Tammy and I dinghied around trying to catch more.*

The Escape River bar is five miles out to sea, and clearly marked on the charts. I knew from experience how dangerous river bars can be, but dismissed this one as probably just a shallow spot. Shallow it was, with all the other attributes of a bar—steep, breaking waves being the most noticeable—and it took me totally by surprise. There was no choice but to try to pick a spot where the waves were lowest and head in, no channel markers here. We leaped and plunged, the depth gauge went to zero several times, and we were through into calm water, shell-shocked but undamaged.

"Pilgrim" hit an uncharted rock at the mouth of the river, and got off with minor damage. All boats anchored off the desolate looking pearl farm. The winds and poor holding had a few dragging, and kept the rest of us sleepless. We were solid—a big anchor and lots of chain equals security.

Because "Pilgrim" hit on the way in, we all waited for them to lead our parade out the next morning, on the theory that they couldn't possibly find the rock again. "Pilgrim" did not at all subscribe to this theory, but finally headed out, as the alternative seemed to be to spend the day circling. The theory worked, we all made it safely, "Pilgrim" resumed communications, and the fleet headed for Cape York.

There are two ways around the Cape, through Torres Strait via Thursday Island, or hugging the Cape. The Torres Strait route is longer and more coral filled, so we took the sensible, practical alternative, one missed by Captain Cook, but then he didn't have G.P.S.

Almost every day, a Coast Watch plane flew low over us and called on the radio to check up. That we were being looked after was a nice feeling, even though we knew that they were mainly interested in drug runners and illegal migrants. They would select one boat to report on the fleet, seemingly taking perverse pleasure, if a co-captain was speaking, in asking detailed questions about each boat's rig. I guess it was boring up there.

We had a double celebration as we rounded Cape York, passing the most northern part of Australia, and putting 10,000 miles under our keel since we left Los Angeles. Out of the Pacific for the first time, we entered the Arafura Sea.

Ryan: *Mum and I baked blueberry muffins to celebrate.*

Carole: *Because we were sailing almost daily, my seasickness was a thing of the past. Knowing I was going to get seasick was always on my mind when we set out. There was some comfort in reading of others with the same problem, but not much.*

The two-night sail from Cape York to Gove, across the Gulf of Carpentaria has a fearsome reputation. The whole Gulf is quite shallow, and any wind builds up short, steep waves that really batter a boat. I had spent a lot of time there in a previous life managing a seafood company, as it is a major prawn fishing area.

Carole: *"Topaz" had crossed a few weeks earlier, in very bad weather, and Lois said it was the worst 36 hours of their lives. We had a perfect passage, with light winds and flat seas. Ryan and I began learning how to bake bread, as we had run out.*

"Sky Bird" had bypassed Escape River, and gone on to a less protected anchorage so as to get an early start across the Gulf. The rest of us began the crossing together and soon we were ahead of the pack. By the end of the day, we were so far ahead as to be out of VHF radio contact, but there was no way I was going to ask Laurie to slow down. By morning we were close enough to "Sky Bird" to be in VHF contact, and I was happy again. The crossing ended before we actually passed them, but we tried.

Gove exists solely as a port to ship bauxite and alumina to the east coast for processing. The yacht anchorage was crowded with over 50 boats, most of which had processing plant workers and miners living on board. Gove Yacht Club had showers, washing machines and a bar, all the essentials.

Ryan (9): *I met a really crazy boy who lived on one of the permanently* *anchored boats. He went to the local school, but was on holiday, so we rode bikes all around. The reason I say he was crazy was because he did very dangerous stunts with his bike and just laughed when he crashed.*

The fuel dock was on the far side of the harbor, designed to serve only the freighters and ore carriers. Our dinghy was commandeered as fuel barge. Steve ("Pilgrim") and I spent the day ferrying jerry-jugs back and forth to our fleet, while Steve ("Sky Bird") shuttled water from shore. Filling the jugs with diesel was a three-man operation, Pat ("Marita Shan") on the dock to operate the pump, and two in the dinghy 20 feet below. It took several hours to get the diesel smell out of the dinghy at the end of the day.

The nearby township of Nhulunbuy provided Carole and Ryan their first real experience with aborigines. Unfortunately, most of the ones we saw were standing around, dirty, with tatty clothes, some of the men drunk, and generally giving the appearance of idleness and dissipation. There were exceptions, of course, and these were not so obvious, as they were working, or otherwise occupied. We had to wait for an hour to get a taxi back to the Yacht Club, as it was pay-day for the locals, and all taxis were fully occupied shuttling between grocery stores and pubs.

Because the whole area is aboriginal reserve, we needed permits to land at any place between Gove and Darwin. A long time ago, the Government of the day gave the most worthless looking land to the aborigines as a reserve. Then it was found to contain incredibly pure and huge deposits of gold, wolfram, tin, uranium, bauxite, and iron ore. A "small" conflict of interest surfaced, and sent ripples throughout the entire Australian community. Unfortunately, the aborigines seem to be their own worst enemies, closely followed by the whites who profess to be helping them, closely followed by the politicians.

The second day out of Gove, we had to negotiate a pass between two islands, charmingly called Hole in the Wall. Forty feet wide and two miles long, it boasts current flows up to 15 knots, reversing with the tide. The idea is to go through at slack tide, or close to it. 15 knots behind you means no control over the boat, and 15 knots against you means going backwards, with no control over the boat. Either way, fiberglass doesn't bounce well.

We went through with about eight knots behind us, hitting the dizzying speed of 14 knots over the bottom. Carole was oblivious, snapping pictures of the rocks blurring past, and calling out to me to look at particularly pretty formations. I, mesmerized by the rock fangs zooming past, inches from the hull, and with about as much control of direction as a skier going over a cliff, was noticeably reticent.

Carole: *For once I have to thank Laurie for not telling me something. "Sky Bird" had decided to go, so Laurie followed. I am always happy being* *second into an unknown place and stood at the bow admiring the scenery. If I thought it was going by rather quickly, that concern was immediately superseded by the sight of another magnificent rock formation rising out of the brilliant blue water.*

Safely through, we turned left and anchored in a very pretty bay. Ryan and I went ashore to explore this remote, almost pristine place. We found tracks of wallabies, goannas, snakes, and dingoes, and a cave where many seemed to spend a lot of time. Over the sand dune, out of sight of the boats, and we were in the Australia as it has been for thousands of years. We stood and listened to the hush of a virgin landscape, and then started to hear the real sounds of the bush, the hum of an insect, the rustle of a lizard moving through the dry grass, the distant thump of a wallaby's progress. It was a new experience for Ryan, and a forgotten one for me. This is the oldest part of the oldest continent and one of the few places where humans, if they have ever visited, left no impressions.

Carole: *Ryan conspired with "Marita Shan" to get us to stay another day to explore, while the rest of the fleet moved on. I didn't want to leave the company of the others, so we too departed a couple of hours after they did. Tash and I maintained an elaborate charade over the radio, acting as if we were still at anchor, arranging to meet for lunch, asking how the men were getting along ashore, and other inanities. I guess nobody looked back, because we certainly surprised them all as we sailed past.*

An overnight passage and several day sails took us to Port Essington, our last stop before Darwin. We went ashore and walked to the point to see the signal cairn, built in 1845 to guide ships into the settlement of Victoria, which survived only 10 years before everyone died of one disease or another. Not a terribly hospitable area, made even less so by the resident crocodile that cruised past in the evenings. Raised in crocodile country, I have a real respect for them.

Again "Sky Bird" decided to get a head start, so had left Port Essington the evening before in real style, weaving through the anchored boats with "Don't Worry, Be Happy" blasting over the loud speakers and Steve dancing and singing on the deck.

Tides in the Darwin area rise and fall at least 20 feet, and sometimes 40 feet. These tides create strong currents in the island passes that lead to Darwin, so planning the last passage became a real task. We knew we would have the current against us for part of the way, so chose to buck it in the deepest water, where we thought there would be the least effect. We were wrong. In 300 feet of water the currents were bringing up sand from the bottom in huge boils. Doing over eight knots through the water, we were crawling along at less than two knots over the bottom.

Anchoring out in Darwin is complicated by the huge tides. Tie your dinghy to a dock at high tide and return at low tide to see it dangling feet above the dry sand. Come in at low tide, and have to walk at least a mile to reach the shore. We chose to go to the Cullen Bay Marina, which is a lake behind a lock, so the water level is constant, regardless of tide. It also kept away the large crocs that infest the harbor.

Carole: *The previous year a lady on one yacht tried to swim to another. I don't need to tell the end to that story.*

This was our first lock experience, and our last until the Panama Canal. The lock operators decided to put "Marita Shan" and "Dolphin Spirit" through together in a staggered formation, as the lock was not wide enough to take us side by side. The problem then became length, as it wasn't 100-feet long, and we combined to 110 feet. Creative diagonalization, combined with aggressive fendering and fending, got us both through with no damage.

Settling in, we hired a car to take a four-day tour through Kakadu National Park with Pat and Tash. We saw crocodiles, birds, huge termite mounds, strange rocks, aboriginal rock paintings, stayed in a motel shaped like a crocodile (we slept in the left hind leg), toured cultural exhibits, and drove through gorgeous countryside. Floating up Katherine Gorge, between immense cliffs, was a highlight. We swam under waterfalls and in rock pools between rapids, drove up and down mountains, and saw the sun set twice one evening.

All Kakadu roads are unsealed dirt, often badly rutted and corrugated and always lacking adequate signs. We had booked for a river cruise and rolled up to the appropriate spot (we thought) to find the river, but nothing else. Remembering a possible sign some miles back, we retraced our tracks, found the sign, an ancient "Road Under Repair," and drove on, eventually finding habitation.

They told us that the place we were at first was the correct place to be, but now it was about 15 miles away and we had only 15 minutes left to get there before departure. I was driving, and headed off in a plume of dust. There were no other vehicles on the roads, so I was soon speeding along at around 60 mph, safe on sealed highways but dicey on these wide, but rough, bush roads. The inevitable happened. We crossed a series of corrugations in the road, the rear of the car floated past the front, and we came to rest gently against a pile of dirt, but facing in the wrong direction. Everyone was mercifully quiet as we waited for our dust cloud to pass so we could see to proceed. The car wasn't scratched, we weren't even shaken—physically, but mental scars persist to this day.

A more sedate pace got us to the river bank. Pat jumped out of the car and ran shouting to the boat as it was pulling into mid-river. It returned, and we saw lots of crocodiles.

Carole: Laurie and I argue about it to this day. I say we spun into sand on the side of the road, which brought us to a gentle stop, while he says it was his superb driving skills.

When we returned to the marina we discovered that the boat next to us had left, crashing into us, not once, but twice. He had not noticed our awning poles and these had caught in his rigging.

To assist cruisers in buying the best Australian wines, we hosted a wine tasting aboard "Dolphin Spirit." We offered six white and six red to choose from, carefully selected after exhaustive private tasting of our own over a period of some months (others might say years, but I consider that pre-wine-tasting-idea drinking doesn't count.). By all accounts it was a resounding success, with my only complaint being that the lousy sods drank all the wine.

The countdown to departure for Indonesia on August 25 started. Ryan's computer ceased functioning, and had to be rebuilt. The technician ignored the 110V signs and plugged it into 240V, so we had to search for and find the only 110V power supply in Australia to replace the melted one. The generator set got a new heat exchanger—specially built, as no such part was available in Australia. The refrigeration ceased working while we were in Kakadu. Tiring of having to peer over two dinghies, and not seeing any opportunity to sail in Indonesia, we sold Ryan's dinghy.

Carole stocked the freezer with meat, as Indonesian meat was reported to be somewhat unreliable. Then came the provision shopping and the storage, and then the fresh fruit and vegetables. Around all of that, we had to fill up with diesel, petrol and propane, top up the water tanks, fill out the check-out paper work (we got Indonesian cruising permits in Queensland [three month lead time] and visas in Darwin), check we had enough charts (charts are like money—you never have enough), information on anchorages (no cruising guides for Indonesia), money, malaria pills, clothes, wine, mosquito repellant, sunscreen, hats, batteries, paper, spare parts....

Carole: I guess I made the decision to continue on, threat of malaria and all. I must confess that this decision was really shaken on the day the mastless cruising boat limped in. She had been hit by a freighter in Indonesia, and the freighter had never stopped.

Indonesia

Year Two
August 26 to October 22

Steve ("Sky Bird") and I raced along the tree line, trying to keep the dragon from leaving the beach until we had shot some good video. He/she was about nine feet long, and was obviously starting to get a little exasperated with us. Suddenly, we both realized that this was not a lizard we were harassing, but a bad-tempered carnivore, one who can bring down a fully grown buffalo. Our pace slackened a little (let's face it, we took refuge behind a tree), and the dragon lumbered off into the forest.

Rindja Island, together with next-door Komodo Island, is the home of the Komodo Dragons, lizards that grow up to 12-feet long. I have always thought that they would be just basically an expanded gecko—wrong! We saw one 10-feet long, weighing over 200 pounds. As he garumphed past us, about five feet away, flicking out his tongue at every step, and fixing his eye right on me, he went way up in my estimation. My foot fitted neatly into one of his prints, and he had razor sharp claws and infectious, bacteria-covered teeth—sort of a streamlined crocodile, with an attitude.

Our anchorage was in Lehok Uwada Desami, at the southern end of Rindja. The place was gorgeous, no people, beautiful clear water, surrounded by high mountains, pretty beaches, and great coral for snorkeling. Komodo Dragons, five to ten feet in length, paraded up and down the beach from 0800 to 1100. Monkeys had the sand in the early mornings and late afternoons. Deer appeared at 1700, and pigs made visits at irregular times. All this within a couple of hundred feet from where we sat in the cockpit, entranced.

Carole: Ryan dinghied me to shore to show me the monkeys. The fleet of boats was left behind in a calm pearly mist. The water, reflecting the sky, was a pale pink, as the sun had just set behind the mountains ringing our anchorage. If only I could paint—a photo does the scene no justice. On the beach we saw ten small monkeys and a black pig followed by a piglet. Until we got close, Ryan swore they were a dragon and a deer. Further down the beach he got his deer wish with a whole family, buck, doe and fawn. Several audacious monkeys were circling them.

My journal that day: Made delicious ANZAC cookies, roast leg of lamb, mashed potatoes and coleslaw for lunch. Dinner was left-over chicken and the coleslaw, in pita bread. Laurie cleaned the outside of the boat. Amazing how dirty the waterline gets, with scum, algae and barnacles. Then he spent the rest of the afternoon fixing the engine, which had been overheating.

Ryan and I were trying to sneak up on a pig feeding on the beach, when it took fright, and raced up into the grass at the top of the beach, straight into a dragon that was coming out. Both shot up into the air in a cloud of sand, with a wild shriek from the pig, and took off in different directions. Naturally, I didn't have a camera to record it. The area was saturated with pigs, probably accounting for the number and size of the dragons, which apparently love a pork diet. We climbed the hills behind the anchorage, following well-worn pig trails, immersed in very potent pig perfume.

Back to the chronology. Preparations to leave Darwin for Indonesia finally were done, the latest repair finished, the last cabbage bought and stored away, food for the passage cooked and frozen, the malaria pills started, so off we went. As six boats were leaving together, the usual group of "Dolphin Spirit," "Marita Shan," "Sky Bird," "Soliloquy," "Pilgrim" and "Osprey," Immigration and Customs came to us, at 6am, a pleasant variation to the normal bureaucracy.

A cold was being passed around amongst the cruisers. Remember that we had been on land for a few weeks, in contact with land-based people, and therefore subject to land-based contagion. We had never been healthier than we were during the past 18 months, with the only sickness being "sea," and that confined to Carole. Perhaps all our defenses were lowered as a result, because nearly everyone sailing that day had the cold, was just catching it, or just recovering. We all shrugged it off in a couple of days, so the healthy cruising life must have benefits.

For those of you interested enough to dig out an atlas and try to follow our Indonesian wanderings, please note that the place names that are used have been spelled as they appear on our charts. British, Australian, American and Indonesian charts seem to have different spellings, and even totally different names, for certain places. We have no idea what is correct, or even if there is a correct.

Through the South Pacific and around Australia we had excellent cruising guides, even though all contained some errors and omissions. There were no real guides for Indonesia, so we ("Gigolo" doing the lion's share) made compilations of cruiser reports including those from Seven Seas Cruising Association members. When doing the SSCA summaries, we made a serious error in not noting the dates. Things were changing rapidly in Indonesia with respect to facilities and treatment of visiting yachts, generally for the better. Of course, the attitude of the cruiser has a large bearing on the attitude of the people and officials.

Any yacht entering Indonesia when we did, had to hold a previously obtained Cruising Permit. Obtaining this was a relatively simple process, but it did take a couple of months. We applied directly to a company in Jakarta; others went through a New Zealand organization. Costs ranged from $US250 to $US400. The only exception was entry at Bali, where the officials allowed you to stay if you had no Cruising Permit, provided you left Indonesia from Bali, and visited no other place in Indonesia. Arrivals without a visa were issued a two-month, non-extendable visa, at no charge. As we wanted to stay longer, we obtained a Sponsorship Letter from the Indonesian company, and got visas from the Indonesian Consulate in Darwin. These took 24 hours to get, cost $A100 ($US75) each, and were valid for two months. The benefit was that we could get a month's extension at any time.

Carole: *Why did we pay all that money to go to Indonesia? The guide books were less than reassuring. Wear shoes at all times as there are worms in the dirt that get into your feet. The water is not drinkable. All of the snakes are poisonous, except for the pythons, which swallow humans. The dogs and cats have rabies. Malaria is prevalent, so we have to take malaria tablets, which may or may not work, so we also have to carry a malaria test kit. If we get ill, can we find a good doctor in Indonesia? We carry our own needles, so if we need an injection, it will be with a sterile needle.*

It was a delightful four-day sail to Kupang, Timor. From our reading, we really expected a bad trip, and instead had great winds, just behind the beam, almost flat seas, and clear skies. Sailing in convoy, we saw no other vessels until we had to wend our way through a well lit trawling fleet on the last night. Because we had made such good time, we then attempted to slow down, so we would make landfall after dawn. Thanks to a following current, the slowest we could achieve, without putting out a drogue, was seven knots. This was our introduction to the Indonesian currents, which were invariably against us, no matter what we wanted to do.

No sooner were our anchors down, when a boat came out from shore with Jimmy on board. For a fee of $US50 he cleared us in through immigration, customs, health and the port authorities. He must have been very persuasive because, after a few minutes of filling in forms, he left with our passports (I am paranoid about letting them out of my hands, let alone out of my sight, and here I handed them over to someone I had known for nine minutes!). That night, about 7:30, there was a knock on the hull announcing Jimmy, with the passports and completed check-in paperwork. As part of his fee, he organized vans and drivers to take us around, got fuel, acted as interpreter, and cleared us out when it was time to leave—a bargain.

In the past, Indonesia in general, and Kupang in particular, enjoyed a bad reputation for "officious" and corrupt officials, thievery, rudeness, and a general poor attitude towards cruisers. We found none of this in any of the places we visited, and did not have a bad experience in Indonesia, perhaps because of our policy of smile and comply. Frankly, if we had taken note of all the negatives we read, we would have never entered the country.

As an example of the new officialdom, on check-out from Kupang, we were invited to visit the Port Captain, who gave us a long speech. The gist was that we should not pay any charges or fees to any official while we were in Indonesia, as we had already paid for our cruising permits. So many of the reports we had read went on at length about problems with officials, and the need to bribe.

While we were waiting to see the Port Captain, one of the officials came over to us and walked by, staring intently at each person. We squirmed a little, wondering what was coming. He then conferred with a couple of his colleagues, and came back to us. "Professor," he said pointing at the white-bearded Steve ("Pilgrim"), "Film star," to Pat ("Marita Shan"), "James Bond," to me, "Businessman," to Kurt ("Osprey"), and "Convict," to Steve ("Sky Bird"), then retired giggling to the safety of his desk. With the possible exception of the last named, we were all quite pleased.

Carole: *On my first visit ashore in Kupang, one look at the restaurant walls and the dirty linen on the table was enough. I had a much wiped can of coke for lunch. Ryan and Laurie just ordered and ate. Amazingly, they lived.*

The water-maker stopped working due to a crack in the control box on our second night in Indonesia. No water-maker in Indonesia, where any local water use was close to suicidal! There was no way this could be fixed ashore. The other cruisers offered to run their water-makers longer each day to help. Kurt went one better, and gave me a clamp that, together with a powerful resin/glue mix, gave us a temporary fix that lasted until we received replacement parts shipped into Bali.

The part could be imported duty free, but the international carrier that did the shipment automatically paid the duty, and therefore required me to repay them before I could collect the package. Naturally I protested, and was told that it was not a problem, as all I had to do was apply to the appropriate Ministry, and I would get my $US900 back. I should live so long!

Kupang was a great introduction to Indonesia. It was a small city, essentially untouched by tourism, with streets full of small shops and vendors, all for the locals. Bemos (small Japanese vans with seats, designed to carry ten Indonesians, but always loaded with at least 20) were almost wall-to-wall, every one blowing their horn, every one stopping to ask if they could take us somewhere (fixed price 400 rupiah—$US1=2,800 rupiah). My 6'4" unfolding out of one usually attracted an interested group of voluble, 5'3" Indonesians. Although we were always a focus of attention, we never felt threatened or remotely in danger.

Traffic generally kept to the left, as in Australia, and opposite to the U.S. I say generally, as both sides of the road got good use, regardless of direction. We saw no accidents, as it was live and let live, blow your horn if you want to do anything, and then do it. Want to stop for any reason, then stop, middle of the street, wrong side, no problem. No one complains, and all the traffic just patiently maneuvers around. Coming out of a side street was simple, just keep moving, and everyone will dodge you somehow. The average Indonesian driver would last 30 seconds in Los Angeles or Sydney. The only disadvantage was the noise of every driver constantly blowing his horn, to indicate that he was passing, dodging, turning a corner, going left or right, stopping, or starting.

Carole: PL, Sue and I went for a walk through the back streets. This must have been a pretty, white-walled city once, but now it was run-down and dirty. We passed a cemetery where many women were cooking food next to the graves. Not being able to speak Indonesian we couldn't find out the reason for this.

The ladies in our group were a little put off by the piles of live dogs, all neatly trussed, ready for the market, and then the pot. For some reason, the similarly stacked chickens excited no comment. Ryan expressed a desire to try dog, rat and snake, but Carole turned pale green, so the subject was quickly changed. As some of our shore-side meals were unidentifiable, Ryan may have gotten his wish. Carole never ate meat to ensure that she didn't try anything exotic.

Chasing Sunsets

Ryan (9): *I was disappointed because I didn't get to eat dog or rat, or at least, not that I know of.*

Jimmy took us on a tour of the island to see villages, rice paddies, and general life on the farm, Indonesian style. A highlight was a fishing village, with acres of small silver fish spread out in the sun to dry. Some were being salted and packed into boxes. The chickens and children ran freely over the fish, adding their own unique flavors, but there were no seagulls—in fact we saw only a couple in all of Indonesia. The fishing boats were unique; a hull, with two masts that supported a large rectangular bamboo platform, from which nets were suspended. They were permanently anchored about a mile off shore for most of the year. The fishermen paddled out to them every evening, and brought the catch ashore in the morning. We saw one being built, no nails, all wooden pegs, and this was a boat about 30 feet long and 10 feet wide.

The village market was spread out on the sand, and we quickly became the focus of a group of adults and children who followed us everywhere. This was a real market, not one for the tourists, so the vendors didn't really know how to deal with the strangers. One lady simply hid her head, and wouldn't look up until we left. Naturally, the occasional young male had to show off, but even this was restrained.

Our next stop was a stand of special palm trees, where the workers climb more than 50 feet to the top, with no ropes, toeholds, or support, to extract juice from the leaves. This is then boiled down to make a very sweet sugar, and an alcoholic drink. As a side line, the same people make silver jewelry, both traditional, and for the occasional tourist.

Up and down mountains we went, to Carole's consternation, as she hates looking out of a window and seeing only tree tops a thousand feet below. Arriving at a "traditional" housing compound, we self-consciously wandered around, as the people who lived there just sat and stared at us. Jimmy asked us for donations—"only to buy flour for the poor people"—who were then forced to line up, and unhappily sing a song of thanks. The sordid experience left a bad taste, and we told Jimmy so, in no uncertain terms.

The next stop featured entertainment by a family group. This show was clearly "pay for services," so we were much happier. Father played a three foot tall, 20-stringed instrument, with semicircular sound box that "concertinaed" up for travel. The oldest son played big drums, young sons played small tuned drums, mother orchestrated the performance, daughters danced, all in traditional costumes. For me, the best was the youngest daughter, aged three or so, in everyday clothes, not part of the performance, who simply joined in the dancing, imitating her elders with a huge smile, and obvious enjoyment.

Indonesia

Ikat, the traditional weaving is unique because the threads are tie died before being woven. The final patterns are quite intricate, so the calculations that go into the dyeing are mind-boggling to me. The whole process from growing the plant, hand-rolling the thread, dyeing, to weaving, takes almost a year, with two to three months for the hand weaving. All weaving is done by women, sitting on the floor, staring at a blank wall, who tension the threads by leaning against a belt around their back. They were either alone, or two or three to a room One girl we spoke to was 23 and had been weaving for seven years—she could still smile! An old lady, in another village, was set up on the dirt at the back of her hut. She looked about seventy, was about the size of my leg, and had lost her smile.

Carole: *My bottom goes numb just thinking about it. A lifetime of sitting on hard ground, all day every day, strapped to the frame. So many women are still doing that today, working as they did for centuries, with no relief.*

An overnight sail took the fleet to Ende, on Flores Island. One advantage of group passages is that there are several eyes seeking potential dangers and giving a warning to the fleet. Around midnight, we received a "Heads Up" call from "Pilgrim" to beware of fishing boats strung across our track. Fortunately, they were well lit. About this time, Pat woke to take over watch duties on "Marita Shan." Over the VHF came the urgent, "Turn, turn, turn. Land dead ahead!" from him. We managed to convince him to properly adjust his radar, and convert the green arc into discrete fishing boats.

In the morning, the final approach was past a volcano, with steam and sulfur emitting vents all over the slopes down to the sea. As we could sail within a hundred yards, it was exciting, and not as dangerous as it sounds. The anchorage was deep (50+ feet), and the beach had a pounding surf. Landing and getting off in the dinghies was very chancy, reminding everyone of several similar Mexican anchorages.

Waking up in the morning in this anchorage was a reminder that we were in Asia, and in a very different culture and life-style. We were accustomed by now to the early calls to prayer from the mosques, and Carole and I generally got up then to enjoy the sights, odors and sounds of the town coming to life. The smoke and smells of the cooking fires lay as a fine mist over the harbor and fringing town, and shrouded the mountains behind. Fishing boats, sails furled, paddled quietly past, the occupants waving to us. Occasional faint voices could be heard. Somehow coffee tasted better these mornings.

Herry (Jimmy's brother) had organized a tour that necessitated a 5am start, while it was still dark. Getting to shore, several dinghies were swamped, and one overturned, trapping Madeline ("Soliloquy") underneath, where she couldn't be immediately found. After several panic and concern-filled minutes, she escaped with no physical damage, but was in a state of shock for some time. Kurt and PL made it close to shore, when PL stepped out into a hole, and she too disappeared for a moment. We managed to get in, terrified, but without incident. Big dinghies do have some advantages. Dry clothes required a second, this time uneventful, dinghy run, but Madeline decided to recover on board.

The road wound through the hills, past clusters of squatting blanket-draped figures breakfasting around fires. The smoke, the shadowy forms, the smells, the flickering flames, and the overhanging trees, made the whole experience surreal.

Carole: *Thinking of that drive brings back the smell of Indonesia, a mixture of smoke, cooking oil, fish and dirt, sometimes nice, sometimes overpowering. I see ladies, huddled on their haunches beside the road with smoke from the cooking fires drifting around them, adding to the unreality of the early morning mist. Other women carrying bundles and pails on their heads—chickens and bananas—walked along the road. Children everywhere in school uniforms, white shirts, dull red shorts or skirts, and all this at 5:30 in the morning.*

Then the sun rose and broke the spell, but it was a memorable half-an-hour. Almost immediately we were under another spell, as we entered a region of rice paddies. These brilliant green terraces rose above us to the hill tops, and disappeared into the valleys below. We were so in awe of the time and effort necessary to construct the stone walls that seemed to be everywhere, we left the van and walked for a mile to get closer looks and prolong the experience.

The road was cut into the side of the mountains. Maintenance was not a priority. In places we inched around, or over landslides, through huge potholes, or past washouts that allowed an unrestricted view of the valley floor, far below. The bridges were suspect, to say the least. One, of infamous memory, had deteriorated to a single lane, with seemingly tire-wide gaps in the few planks that were left. We gingerly walked across it, leaving the driver to take his chances with the van.

Carole: *My hand was over my mouth most of the way, to muffle my screams. If there was atmosphere to be absorbed I couldn't give it attention and save my life too.*

Our primary target was an extinct (?) volcano that had three lakes in it, all different colors. When we saw them, they were red, brown, and pale blue. The colors are reported to change with the seasons to black, blue, and white. There was a path from the end of the road to the crater, some two thousand feet higher. As we were walking along, our guide pointed up a steep slope, said it was a short cut, and that we could see all three lakes from the top. Ryan had to try it, so I went along, making Ryan follow me. Lucky that I did because, as I scrambled up the last bit, my hand went over the edge of the crater. I suppose we were really quite safe, but it was a shock to suddenly have 1,000 feet of nothing under me. After that, the lakes were a pretty anticlimax.

Jumping across a stream, and climbing a rough path, we reached a village perched on the side of another mountain. There we were shown through a hut that was reputed to have been in continual occupation for over 700 years. The wear on the wooden steps certainly supported a use of several hundred years. It was large enough to hold several families, but had no windows. Unidentified objects, hanging from the rafters, caused a little consternation as we brushed by in the gloom, giving great amusement to the much shorter Indonesians. The entrance door was graced by the carving of two breasts, outstanding beside the otherwise geometric motifs that decorated the lintel and uprights.

Ryan was the center of attention, as the Indonesians love kids, and everyone went out of their way to touch him. The ladies were in the middle of dyeing, so Ryan soon became bright red all over his arms, legs and face. He eventually became embarrassed from all the attention and from turning red and asked to leave.

Ryan (9): *This happened to me at a lot of villages. It was okay for a while, then all the touching and closeness got to be a little frightening.*

As we were stumbling back down the path, a record player (presumably spring-driven) in the last house was blaring out "Oh Carol" by Neil Sedaka. Carole bowed to all and sundry in acknowledgment, but they simply bowed back to the polite lady, and we never learned how that record got to this remote place.

Carole: *Herry took us back to his house for refreshments—fried bananas, sweet coffee and CNN. Satellite dishes can be found even in some of the most "primitive" areas. The kitchen area, separate from the main house, reminded Laurie of his house back on the farm. I was impressed with the intricately carved settee.*

Changing money was an adventure all by itself. The first bank we went to in Kupang gave us 2,700 Rupiah for $US1, with the whole transaction handled by one teller and taking less than five minutes. Another, in Ende, gave 2,500 Rupiah, wouldn't take some of my U.S. notes, as they were not new (too dirty), and then took two hours and three tellers to complete the business.

We discovered this anomaly in a lot of countries. Banks won't accept U.S. notes if there is the slightest mark on them. Some don't even like creases. They then hand out local currency that is worn, torn, and almost undecipherable. Tellers counted notes using a type of reverse, back-hand, inside-out, finger flick, that was fascinating to watch, difficult to describe, and impossible to copy.

Haggling was the order of the day for all purchases, from fruit to carvings. Most prices get inflated by several hundred percent as soon as a white face appears, which is fine by me. I like to bargain, but Carole hates it. She bought some large paw paws with the following exchange:

Seller: 3,000 Rupiah
Carole: 1,000 Rupiah
Seller: 2,000
Carole: Okay (then hands him 5,000 Rupiah and says, "Keep the change.")
Seller: (Speechless, nods head)

Somehow, I think that the point of bargaining got lost somewhere.

Carole: *Haggling was a game to me, until I realized that I was dealing with people's livelihood. I couldn't haggle over 30 cents with someone who needed it more than I did. I still paid less than two dollars for half a dozen large papaya, so we both felt we had done well.*

From Ende, we went directly to Rindja Island to see the dragons described earlier. After the free show every day at the anchorage, we decided not to go on a guided tour at the north end of the island, and not to go to Komodo Island at all. On Komodo the whole exercise was reported to be very packaged and tourist oriented, with "Dragon feeding at 10 and 4, buy the goat here, please."

Still on Rindja, we went to Lehok Ginggo, an uninhabited bay on the west coast of the island. The anchorage already held six picturesque local fishing boats, each about 30' long, with a 5' beam, supporting a 25' square bamboo fishing platform. Their engines sounded like motor-mowers with asthma. The crews of four to six people spend weeks on board, so they, and the boats, were best appreciated from up-wind. The drying fish and nets on the shore generally attracted a couple of small dragons (4 to 5-feet long) each morning. By this time, we were dragonned-out, and barely spared them a glance. Frankly, they didn't pay us much attention either.

The fishing boats all had home-made, fisherman-type anchors, attached to blue rope, wound onto huge, bow-mounted, open-drum windlasses. Their holding power has to be somewhat suspect, as one dragged into "Dolphin Spirit" in less than 15 knots of breeze, luckily with no damage to either vessel. The fishing boat motored back to its original spot, and dropped their anchor again, hopefully with an extra stone tied to it.

The anchorage was protected, with good snorkeling and great views from the brown, dry, surrounding hills. It was PL's birthday again, her 50th (was it really a year since her 49th in Suva?) and we celebrated with a beach party and bocce bowls. Carole baked and decorated her justifiably famous birthday carrot cake. Suitable presents included a funnel for use as a hearing aid, blue hair dye, a back brace, and a tube of liniment.

Ryan (16): *I wrote PL a poem which described the presents I was giving her. The only line I can remember contained the words, "Don't be a sucker" relating, of course, to the See's chocolate sucker I had managed to drag away from Mum.*

One evening, at cocktail time, we rafted up all the dinghies and drifted out to drink wine, eat popcorn, and watch the sunset. It is possible to determine grades of wonderful if you see enough sunsets. This was a 9.8, averaging the scores after deleting the highest and lowest, which may give some idea of the quality of the intense intellectual activity within the group.

As strong tidal currents race between Padar and Rindja Islands, all the navigators in the fleet did tide calculations (procedures covered the full spectrum of computer programs, tide tables, asking the locals, and guesses), to determine the correct time to leave Ginggo for the sail to Labuanbadjo, on Flores Island. Everyone's numbers agreed, so we upped anchors at 6am, and, had a five to seven knot current against us for the whole length of the pass. "Pilgrim," the smallest boat in the fleet, slept in and left an hour late. Seeing us barely out of the bay, they hugged the shore, found a reverse eddy, and shot past at dizzying speed.

Carole: *To port were fabulous mushroom-shaped rocks, some cratered and tunneled, that I gazed at for a time. I then went below to prepare lunch, reappearing in the cockpit some 30 minutes later. We were still beside those rocks!*

Once out of the pass, the current reduced to a mere two knots against us for the remainder of the seven-hour passage. We retraced our path two days later, expecting the current to help us, as we had carefully calculated the tidal time differences. Naturally, it was right on the nose again. We considered spinning around, to see if the current did too, but decided not to tempt the gods too much. However, this and other experiences did lead us to formulate the Six Indonesian Cruising Rules, herewith set out for the first time:

Rule 1: The current will always be against what you want to do, regardless of the state of the tide, time of day, or direction in which you are traveling.

Rule 2: When making passages between anchorages, regardless of time of day or direction of travel, the wind will either be non-existent, directly on the nose, or directly behind.

Rule 3: When at anchor, the wind will always be from the direction to which the anchorage is exposed, regardless of the direction it was in during the passage to the anchorage.

Rule 4: All anchorages will be at least 70-feet deep, and this depth will be achieved no more than 100 feet from the shore or reef.

Addendum: The closer you have to anchor to shore or reef, the worse will be the holding, and the stronger the onshore wind and current.

Rule 5: The narrower the channel and the darker the night, the more unlit fishing boats and nets there will be in the area.

Rule 6: The place is drop-dead gorgeous, the people are delightful, and cruising Indonesia is wonderful, so forget Rules 1 to 5, and just go.

At Labuanbadjo, the hills rise directly from the beach, and the main street, running parallel to the shore, afforded some memorably photogenic scenes. Naked kids, thatched roofed, bamboo-sided houses, chickens, dogs, satellite dishes, all backed by the blue sea and the fishing boats, made for great shots.

The two good restaurants in town were on the high side of the road, accessed by steep, crumbling sets of concrete stairs (***Carole:*** *Without guard rails, of course*). The food was excellent, the view described above, and the beer cold. The local beer, Bintang brand, came only in huge (4 glass) bottles, which cost 5,000 Rupiah ($US2). Most of the meals cost around 4,000 Rupiah; Carole, Ryan and I could have a good meal, with drinks, for less than $US10 total. Order Indonesian food, and it appeared quickly. Carole and Ryan once ordered steak, and had to wait more than an hour. We told them that they had to go find the dog, but that pleased Ryan no end, so the joke fell a little flat. Carole then refused to eat what eventually arrived.

We anchored off the island across from the town, in clear water, away from the daily ferries, and close to the snorkeling. Diesel was available and cheap at R500 per liter, so we filled up, dinghying jerry-jugs back and forth. In the morning, the pump was working, so diesel was pumped from a tank into a container, and then transferred from that container to ours by one liter jug, as a measuring device. No pump in the afternoon, so the fuel was hand-ladled into the first container, a lengthy process.

Carole: From my journal: "Plans had been made to have lunch and dinner at two restaurants (it is cheaper to eat out than to cook on board), but the Bonine (English seasickness pill) I took yesterday is still affecting me, so I bow out of both and sleep for the day. It is too hot to move. The first mosquito dined on me. Hope he didn't have striped legs, as those are the malaria carrying kind. We have soaked our sheets in Deet, and have a mosquito net over the whole cockpit, but still they get through to delicious me.

As the sun goes down, I get up and complete the housework. By the time the guys get home from dinner, the boat is sparkling, and I have drunk more than one bottle of water. They are off to bed, and I settle down to read Les Miserables. *Victor Hugo goes into such detail about irrelevant things, but I plod through and get back to Jean Valjean at last. About 10pm, I hear the roar of a freight train approaching, and about two minutes later we are hit by a gust of wind. We rock and roll for five minutes, then settle down again. A few more gusts follow. Checking from a porthole, I notice "Osprey" seems closer, so wake Laurie in case we are dragging. He checks, decides we have just swung with the tide, and goes back to sleep. I doze off.*

Ryan wakes me with a kiss and a request for breakfast. I toast the sugary bread, which is all that can be bought in Indonesia. I start baking my own again, so we can have sandwiches. The women are sharing bread baking tips in earnest now. Kneading for 15 minutes is a must and goes quickly when Ryan is kneading his loaf next to mine."

Onwards to Banta Island, a small dry-as-a-bone place, off the coast of the very large Sumbawa Island. We sailed by many villages and towns, each memorable in some way: the mosque that took up a whole island, the beach completely lined with fishing boats; the permanent fish traps that completely blocked the pass between two islands. Fishing boats of all sizes and types were everywhere, either sailing under colorful lateen sails, or hard at work, making avoiding the nets a full-time occupation. Small freight and passenger carriers were everywhere, the lifelines between the villages and towns of this island nation.

The bay on Banta was huge and protected, but we had problems finding a shallow enough place to anchor. Finally we managed, in 70 feet, just off a very pretty reef—great snorkeling. Carole loved it, as she could enter and leave the water from "Dolphin Spirit." She has no problems falling out of a dinghy, but getting back in occasionally strains our joint resources.

Carole: This is definitely grounds for divorce, even though I am almost six feet tall, and he is right.

There was another boat anchored about a mile from us, so we went across on our usual "see if there are kids on board" mission. This time there was something better, a baby monkey. It took to Ryan immediately, and wouldn't leave him. Apparently, the monkey liked only children. Ryan was in heaven, and we used a great deal of outboard motor fuel over the next couple of days.

Tammy ("Sky Bird") also visited, but when she knelt down the monkey saw himself reflected in her sunglasses, started screaming in anger, and attacked her. Even when she took her glasses off, he wouldn't calm down, to the extent of following her to the dinghy, and trying to jump at her as we pushed off. The next day, the monkey vanished, to reappear two days later, apparently having spent the entire time at the top of the mast. Worse than a kid!

Ryan (9): That monkey was so much fun. I really wanted one for myself, but of course Mum and Dad had all sorts of reasons why this was a bad idea. None were as important as the total coolness of having my own monkey, but they won.

Bima Bay, Nanganae Island, was typical of many of our overnight stops. We anchored in 50 feet, just near the reef, and off a small village which comprised six houses and a mosque. The calls to prayer woke us before sunrise, and repeated at regular intervals during the day. A black sand beach held a few gaily painted fishing boats, strolling water buffalo, and playing children. One of the boats had the name "My Livelihood" on the bow, but it never was in the water while we were there. We were startled to see a little albino girl amongst the children, and wondered about her future life.

Carole: I made my first loaf of Julia Child's French bread. Turned out nice and crusty, with good texture, considering that I didn't have the required pizza stone to bake on. Had "Sky Bird," "Marita Shan," and "Soliloquy"

INDONESIA

over for cocktails. Served the bread, rum-raisin cream cheese with poppy seeds, and curried eggplant.

A couple more day sails took us to Labuan, a small fishing village near the large city of Besar. Although we may not have been the first white faces the people had seen, they treated us that way. We had to walk through the village to get to the main road and catch a Bemo. It turned into a parade, with most of the kids following us, and most of the adults making sure they got close enough to see us, and touch Ryan. Here, and in the market we went to in Besar, Carole was touched all the time as well, but only by the women, who giggled, glanced proudly at their friends, and went away smiling. The other ladies from the fleet were left alone—they are all shorter and darker than Carole. Tall blondes are exotic in Indonesia.

The market covered several acres and was made up of hundreds of stalls and people selling produce from trays on the floor, accessed by a network of alleyways, all shadowy, with bright blades of occasional sunlight. Shoes, furniture, every spice known, electronic toys, petrol, rice, chilies, fruit, vegetables, fish (dried, salted and fresh), meat (un-refrigerated, dismal looking and smelling), cloth and clothing, kitchen utensils, satay (we had to step over the braziers it was cooking on, so dust had to be a major condiment), and unidentified things wrapped in banana leaves. Carole didn't want to leave, not because she was buying, but because of the excitement of being in such a place.

Our washing machine was having problems, so we joined the other yachties and had our laundry done in the village. Carole refused to use any of it until we rewashed it all in very hot water. The problem arose because, as we went by to go to Besar, we saw some of the clothes being rinsed in a small stream that the village children used as a toilet.

A word about Indonesian toilets. Where there are toilets, they are simply a hole in the ground with places for the user's feet on either side. The whole (I can't help myself) is generally made of plastic. Flushing is carried out by dipping water (can provided) out of an open-topped tank built-in next to the toilet. Even the occasional seat-type toilet is flushed the same way. In the villages there are no toilets. Adults and children simply wade into the sea, lift clothes, squat, stand, and go on with life. Privacy is assured, as everyone simply looks through the person. The procedure is much more sanitary than land deposits, as long as there is a reasonable tidal flow.

Sue ("Pilgrim") was the first to learn how to operate one of the local toilets, having been shown the procedure by a local man, who had no English. By unanimous vote, she was then required to repeat the lesson for everyone the next time the group encountered a local loo. We soon attracted a crowd, doubtless wondering about the sanity of these foreigners rolling on the ground laughing at a poor lady using the toilet.

The restaurants, even those in the major hotels, all have at least one hand-basin in the dining room. This seemed to me to be an excellent innovation, particularly if all you want to do is wash hands before eating, as dining rooms smell better than toilets, regardless of country.

Our anchorage was intensely fished, using the most diverse methods we have ever seen. Close to the beach, the fishermen used cast-nets, or pushed huge pyramidal frames, open base first, scooping the fish out of the pointy end as they went. Others used coconut-fiber "nets" to herd fish into a small area, where they were then scooped out. Further from shore, the more normal nets, with floats, were set from canoes. This created an interesting situation on the day we left, as every yacht was surrounded by these nets.

Carole: (from my journal) *I became the bread expert in Indonesia. It is therapeutic, slapping down the bread, then kneading it for 15 minutes, looking out the porthole and seeing South East Asia going by—majestic mountains, picturesque fishing boats, flying fish, dolphins and pilot whales. Made three loaves and some blueberry muffins today. Seemed to be the thing to do.*

Delicious lunch underway of chicken, onions and tomatoes on angel-hair pasta, spiced just right. The corn we bought at the market was hard and dry so we gave it to the fish. Watched "Lonesome Dove" video and a "10" sunset, pink and grey, reflected in a shimmering satin sea.

Carole got into the habit of tossing potato peels and onion skins out of the galley porthole as she was preparing the meals. Most of these landed on the deck, particularly if we were under way, or if any wind was blowing. It was then my job to do the clean-up.

Onwards, ever onwards, to Lombok Island. We anchored with "Marita Shan" on the north-west of the island, in Kombol Bay, in 75 feet, off a small village. Although deep, and surrounded by oyster farm floats, the bay was very calm with terrific snorkeling. Others of the fleet went to Sengigi, some eight miles south, to a windier and rollier anchorage, but off a resort area, with associated civilization.

Carole: *I desperately wanted to go to the resort anchorage, and gave Laurie little peace on the subject until the day we drove there. One look at the swaying masts was enough. It is miserable to be in a rolly anchorage, with its constant tiring motion and the clicking and clanking of items in the cupboards that never seem to be wedged tightly enough.*

INDONESIA

Our village had about 30 houses and three mosques spread around the shore of the bay. The competing calls to prayer were a daily delight. One of the callers sounded like a woman, but we never summoned up the courage, or had enough command of the language, to ask if we were right.

Several naked boys swam out, to invite us to the village, and to ask for "pens for school," a phrase which seemed to be their only English. We strolled around the houses, everyone greeting us with smiles and occasional sign language requests to have their photos taken. A passing van stopped, and we met Wayan and Heri, who became our friends, guides, transportation and translators for the next few days. This was a lucky break for us, as the village had no phones, and we were trying to work out how to get around.

The dynamic duo took us on a couple of day tours of Lombok, an island that is largely untouched by tourism, once you get away from the hotel concentration at Sengigi. We stopped to feed a troop of monkeys, who then chased us down the road, looking for more. Our first "wild" monkeys of the trip, they gave us everything. The males were huge, the babies cute and frolicking, the mothers protective, the youths inquisitive, very human in fact.

Fields (paddies) grow peanuts, soy beans and rice in three month rotations. As it was the dry season, we saw peanuts being harvested, by hand. We stopped for photos, so all the workers stopped and looked at us—an impasse. Telephoto lenses solved the problem at a later field.

We ate looking over a fresh water spring, with a swimming pool on one side, and pools, crowded with huge, multi-colored carp, on the other. Ryan just had to swim, so we bought him a swimsuit at the shop, and he had his first fresh water dip in months. Visits to a palm-sugar factory, weavers, bamboo furniture makers, potters, basket makers, and watching mud bricks being formed and fired, added to Ryan's, and our, education.

Tourism wasn't completely absent, and we did make the obligatory stop at a clothing/souvenir shop. We were the only shoppers, so the staff decided to dress Ryan up as a local Prince—pants, sash, dagger, vest and turban. He was delighted when we bought the dagger. Lombok craftsmen/women are the source of most of the goods sold to the tourists on nearby Bali. Wayan said that they keep the best on Lombok, and send the seconds to Bali. Later we did discover that the cloth, baskets, boxes and carvings were significantly cheaper in Lombok, so it was fortunate that we gave into the spiel, and bought far more than our quota.

Ryan (9): *Wayan took me to see a soccer game, and we went to his house, then back to the boat.*

As it was tobacco harvesting time, in places the road was lined with piles of leaves, either on the ground, or moving on legs or wheels. Took me right back to my youth on the farm, where we handled tobacco leaves in exactly the same way—but perhaps with smaller bundles. The smoke-free concept hadn't reached Indonesia, so tobacco was still an important crop. Bundles of leaf, with legs protruding below, began our obsession with rear-end photography. We shot leaf bundles, stick bundles, women balancing almost everything on their heads, donkeys and horses immersed in various loads, people on bicycles equally loaded, nothing was spared. After a couple of days, and many film rolls, the realization that there could be another side came to us, and we reverted to normal.

Carole: *The obsession was purely Laurie's, much derided at the time by Ryan and me. However I do admit that the wall we now have covered with these photos is both unique and exceptional.*

Over mountains we drove, through tropical jungles, and then past some of the driest, most arid land we have seen. It was in this area that the road repair gangs were at work, thirty men and women to a truck. Some dug the holes, others smashed stones with hammers, others shoveled in the resulting gravel, others gathered wood for the little fires that melted the tar. No one leaned on a shovel. Perhaps the weak were weeded out on the trips to and from the job site. Trucks seemed to be a complete mass of people, some even sitting on the cab roof. Still, they spared a hand to wave as they passed us.

At the top of the ridge on the road to Sengigi we overlooked the returning fishing fleet, with their multi-colored lateen sails. There must have been several hundred, spread to the horizon like a cloud of butterflies. Every evening we watched the little two-man canoes heading out to sea, and sat entranced at night, watching the dancing circle of lights created by their kerosene lamps on the horizon.

Ryan wanted to join them, so we tried to hire a canoe for a night, but they would take us out only in the daylight, so we settled for that. In six hours of intensive fishing, all around the islands, Ryan caught the only fish, a 4" leather-jacket, inedible. Back on "Dolphin Spirit," he tossed a line over the side, and caught dinner.

Seeking a break from the intensive touring, we had Wayan and Heri take us to the hotel complex in Sengigi to spend the day at the Sheraton Hotel beside its two-acre pool, sipping Margaritas and Pina Coladas—this may be a Moslem country, but they aren't strict enough to ban liquor to the tourists. The pool had water slides through huge carved heads, and weaved through bridges and around islands, everything dripping with vegetation.

Tiring of luxury, we hired a fishing canoe to take us to one of the nearby islands, Gili Air (Gili = Island, Air = Water), where the snorkeling is amongst the best in the world. The island accommodation and facilities were designed for back-packers, so were basic and cheap—50,000 to 60,000 Rupiah per night. We took a horse-drawn cart ride around the island, and found a use for empty plastic water bottles. The locals strap them together to form rafts, which they then use to assist in the harvest of seaweed from the reefs close to shore.

The beach was a constant parade of vendors. One eight-year-old girl won Carole's heart and sympathy, as she was staggering under a basket of pineapples and other fruit, balanced on her head. Carole bought the whole load, including the basket, not even bargaining, thank goodness. The girl ran off, and gave the money to a woman, who then lifted an even bigger basket onto her head, and off she staggered again. Carole was crushed, and went snorkeling to recover. A couple of hours later, I had to drag her out of the water, as she had become entranced by the clown fish playing peek-a-boo in the anemone arms.

Carole: *I just hung, suspended above them and didn't care if I was surrounded by hundreds of other exotic species, or even sharks.*

We sailed from Lombok and arrived in Bali on Laurie's birthday. After having such calm sails all through Indonesia, on the day I really needed one we had a bumpy passage. I couldn't go below to make Laurie's cake, or finish cleaning the boat, and we were having twelve people over that evening to celebrate. Everything did get done after we arrived, substituting brownies for a more elaborate birthday cake, and proving that I was at last relaxing my land-standards a little.

Dempassar Harbor was filthy, rat infested, and the surroundings were ugly, so perhaps that was why the rest of Bali seemed so gorgeous. The "marina" was a very shaky L-shaped, floating pier, where yachts were expected to Med-moor. The bottom was liquid mud, the holding was minimal, and all the yachts we observed had problems in even light winds. "Marita Shan" and "Dolphin Spirit" negotiated to side-tie, rafted up to each other, for the same price as two med-moors. Thus we had a little more security, although there was the ever present fear that the whole rickety contraption masquerading as a dock would just disintegrate or a rat come on board.

A rat meant Carole would have a fit; the possibility of disease and chewed electric wiring, short circuits and fires.

Somewhat expensive, the marina did provide water containing about 10% (by actual measurement) of green floating things, and wildly fluctuating power for a few hours per day. The attached building took mail, sent faxes, and provided excellent, very inexpensive drinks and meals. A large motor yacht was taking on fuel at the fuel dock, a two day process for it. "Osprey" got into a confrontation with the owner when he asked if he could interrupt to get a jerry jug filled.

We did the tourist things. Gorgeous it may be, but Bali is so tourist oriented it is sometimes hard to handle. The locals, plowing the field with oxen, asking for money to be photographed; the spot beside the road offering the perfect view of the emerald paddy fields, manned by touts demanding money before photos can be taken; the endless stalls and shops selling the second grade rejects from Lombok, at twice Lombok prices; the traffic, before which a Los Angeles freeway at peak hour seems idyllic; the wonderful Balinese dancing so packaged and presented to suit the tourist bus loads that all feeling and spirit are lost.

It was in Bali that we fully developed our "TT" (Tourist Trap) designation. Whenever possible, we have avoided TTs like the plague, requiring only one "TT" vote from any of the three of us to go into full bypass mode. For reference and use, a TT has one or more of the following attributes:

- a souvenir stand more than 50% of the size of the attraction
- a tourist bus parked outside
- a sign in English and Japanese
- items not made locally
- a paved parking area with painted car spaces (paving alone is a marginal choice)

Carole: *A monkey peed on Ryan's back in the Monkey Forest, another real tourist trap. Poor Ryan was so embarrassed. The next morning, I woke him up just to check that he had not grown a monkey tail—tickled him no end.*

The rice paddies were so picturesque I stared at them for hours. One day, we passed a reptile park, and on an impulse went in. We were just in time for the 10:30am show, which was so gruesome I closed my eyes for most of the performances. One man ate glass, another razor blades, and another had long needles shoved through his wrists, arms, neck and tongue. His companions then lit a fire on his head and fried an egg.

The stage was surrounded by a moat full of crocodiles. These were pulled out and carried around. All very bizarre, but the most bizarre was when they turned one over on his back, reached deep into a slot in his stomach and pulled out his penis. Now how many people can say they have seen a crocodile's penis? Know-it-all Ryan later asked, "How did they pull out the intestines from that crocodile?" Laurie and Ryan had pictures taken draped in pythons. I touched one, and have a picture to prove it—the tip of my fingernail is actually touching the skin

The man in charge of the cobras induced a huge king cobra to strike by tapping on the glass. All of us, Laurie included, jumped back. He did it again, and again the cobra struck, mouth open, fangs projecting, leaving a smear of venom on the glass.

We gave ourselves a present, and spent two days at the Bali Sheraton, a real extravagance. Our room had its own private entrance into the pool complex, reportedly one of the largest in the world. There were waterfalls, pools with sand beaches, some open, some secluded, all interconnected, all wonderful. Occasionally, we would dry out on our private, thatch-roofed platform, looking out over the ocean, naturally served with whatever drink or food we wanted at the lift of a finger. The two days flew by. This could become addictive, even though they raised the price on us twice during the two days we were there, because of the rapidly declining value of the Rupiah.

Ryan (9): School report extract: *Bali is a lush and tropical island in Indonesia. On the island there is a monkey forest designed for tourists, but you'd better be careful because they do pee on you.*

The rice crops and batik making are other things that are beautiful here. If you go at the time they are planting, you might be able to see the people plowing the mud in the paddies for the rice crops. The plow is pulled by two oxen, with a man steering them. Rice has to be in water while it is growing, like the mangroves. When the rice can be seen on top of the stalk, they drain the water, and wait for the ground to dry. Then they cut down the stalks, wait for them to dry, trample them, and throw them up in the air. The rice comes down, and the excess stuff blows away.

In some places it can be both as dry as the Northern Territory, and it can be as lush as the Amazon. There is a place by Kuta Beach where you get to pick out your fish or crab, they barbeque it with a sauce, and you eat it on the beach. Kuta Beach is a tourist place and therefore it has many hotels. I went surfing in the big waves. At the Sheraton Hotel in Nusa Dua we had a pool right outside our room. At the hotel they have 5,000 square meters of pool. We could just walk off our patio and we were in the pool.

There are hundreds of shops selling Batik and Ikat. At Kuta Beach people sell you Rolex watches, and a lot of other really good watches, for about ten dollars. They also sell Batik cloth, which is really pretty. They sell good shells on the beach, all sanded and pretty, shirts with "Bali" written on them, and "Rip Curl." The other things they sell are necklaces, kites and massages. Outside of the silver and gold shop, they had kites shaped like eagles and many other birds.

The marina is dirty, and the power goes off a lot, usually when I am playing a video game, and we think of the dock breaking apart and our boat floating away. The other bad thing is that planes fly over every so often. The good thing is that I had a boy named Kennedy to play with. He will be going up the Red Sea the same time as we are, so I will have company. We go ashore from the marina to fly the eagle kite Dad bought me and to look for crabs and fish.

Leaving Bali finally, we sailed to Bawan Island. There we met John and Jillian who had been sailing in Indonesia for 22 years. Their boat was so battered and travel worn we never did find out its name, and they were out of fuel, propane and money. We gave them some of each, with absolutely no expectation of repayment. Somehow a destitute boat-person is different from a land-based beggar.

Pat and I went ashore to see if there was fuel to be had. The occupants of the tiny village spoke no English, but through sign and body language we managed to arrange for a 55-gallon drum of diesel to be delivered the next morning. It came two mornings later, but it did come! The village chief then carefully siphoned some of it into a plastic bowl and filled our jerry cans with a one-liter ladle. He was going to be sure we received exactly what we had paid for. We all had a wonderful time, with an absolute and complete failure to understand a single word the other person was saying.

Carole: *Laurie has blanked out one of his more memorable errors in judgment. Walking through the town, he saw a lady selling watermelon—cut watermelon. He was the one who had warned me not ever to buy cut fruit, but he bought this, and then ate it before I could intervene. The next day, Laurie, who never gets sick, became violently ill while we were sailing, and days away from Singapore and good hospitals. My nursing and Tash's recipe for an electrolyte drink pulled him through, but it was a couple of very miserable, worrisome days.*

"Sky Bird" was in a hurry to get to Singapore and fly home, so they headed off by themselves. We arranged a radio schedule several times a day to check on their well-being, more for morale than actual safety. There was little, if anything, we could have done if they got into trouble. These were not safe waters to sail alone in at the best of times, and particularly so now, when the smoke from the huge forest fires that had been burning for over two months limited visibility considerably. Tammy had a scare one night when a boat turned in front of them, which she avoided easily, but then had to frantically swerve when the unlit barge being towed loomed up.

INDONESIA

Heading north ourselves, we had a couple of days before we entered the zone of smoke. Visibility was reduced to less than a mile, often to only a 100 yards, and we all wore coverings over mouth and nose to be able to breathe. One day we didn't even see the dull red disc of the sun. Because of the smoke, we didn't stop anywhere, just kept heading north hoping to eventually run out of it.

On October 20 we crossed the Equator and once again were in the Northern Hemisphere, where we would stay for the remainder of the voyage. The smoke was no better all the way to Nongsa Point Marina, our last Indonesian stop. A terrific marina with all the amenities, but an extremely shallow entrance (we scraped bottom at high tide); it cost only $Singapore18 ($US11) per day. Although we were in Indonesia, the marina and surrounding housing complex were built by Singaporeans, for Singaporeans, and the only Indonesians were the employees. It would be a great place to stay in smoke-free times.

Carole: Or when I didn't have a cold. I had come down with one again. A cold in Darwin and now one just before Singapore, I thought cruising was supposed to keep me healthy.

One advantage of cruising is getting to places inaccessible to most tourists, and seeing the local people at "normal" work and play. In Indonesia electricity, satellite TV, and motor vehicles, were everywhere of course, but so were wells as the sole source of water, fishing miles out at sea in tiny outrigger canoes, women crushing stones by hand for road repair, naked children playing on the beaches, the call to prayer five times per day from the mosque, the smoke from the cooking fires making sunrises events not to be missed, the markets that sold almost anything imaginable in tiny stalls, everything from pots to fish to building materials carried balanced on heads or shoulders, and people lining up for the opportunity to touch Ryan and Carole.

Carole: My journal on Indonesia began with a lament on why were we going there. Of all the places we have been, Indonesia stands out as my favorite, perhaps because it was the most exotic.

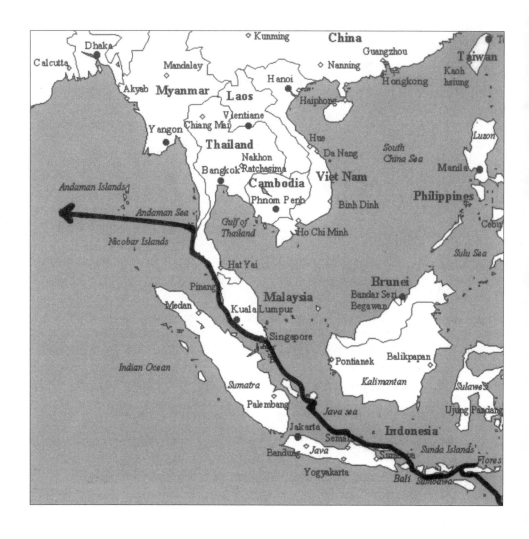

Singapore, Malaysia and Thailand
Year Two
October 23 to January 9

Crossing the Singapore Strait was dangerous at any time. The busiest and most congested water-way in the world, it boasted a two-lane, 24-hour procession of super-tankers, container-ships, freighters and lesser boats. Smoke from the forest fires was still dense, severely limiting visibility, so we lounged in the marina pool, waiting for Carole's heavy cold to get better, and for me to get up the nerve to cross. Finally deciding that, after four days of misery, she would be just as comfortable in Singapore, and I would never feel totally confident, we checked out of Indonesia (Nongsa Point Marina did all the paperwork for $S25) and headed across the Singapore Strait. Only a few miles needed to be covered, and to minimize the risk we stayed on the south side of the Strait for a while, before making a "straight across" run.

A small runabout with four men on board appeared suddenly out of the smoke. Carole's first thought was "Pirates," and mine wasn't far behind. They shouted at us to slow down, and much to Carole's distress, I did. As it turned out, they were Singapore businessmen out for a day's fishing, had become lost in the smoke, and were almost out of fuel. I gave them a couple of gallons, and they asked the direction to Singapore.

"Steer approximately 350 degrees," I told them.

"We don't have a compass. Please point." They replied.

I did, they headed off into the smoke, and we never saw them again. Then it was time for us to cross the Straits.

Carole: The lack of visibility didn't seem to slow down the big ships at all. They were in two lines, bow to stern, without seemingly enough space between them for us to get through. I would have been petrified on a perfect day.

At one stage, our radar was almost solid green with signals from ships all around us. Nothing quite grabs your attention like a multi-thousand ton supertanker looming up out of the smoke, heading straight for you. We dodged, we turned tail and ran, we dodged some more, we worried a lot, and we finally made it across.

In truth, it was heart-stoppingly terrifying. The super-tankers and cargo ships made no speed reduction concessions for the smoke, obviously relying on radar to avoid collisions, and equally obviously not caring about a little sailboat they couldn't see. Those huge bows and slab sides seemed to be everywhere we turned, and all seemed to be moving at dizzying speed. It was impossible to judge speed and distance in the smoke, as both relied on factors that were hidden from us until the last minute.

Ryan (9): *I was very disappointed that Dad wouldn't let me drag a fishing line. The big ships were cool, and I was given the job of telling Dad and Mum when they appeared on the stern.*

The view of Singapore from the Strait is not to be missed at normal times, but the smoke hid it all. We were still keyed up from the crossing near-misses when another 100 or so blips appeared on radar, all very close together. Fortunately it was an anchorage, so we had the pleasure of dodging in and around stationary supertankers, a much to be preferred situation. After that it was a breeze to avoid the fishing villages on stilts, find the channel markers, and arrive at Raffles Marina on the western side of the island.

Carole: *Laconic Laurie does it again. The fishing villages and channel markers didn't show up on radar, and we couldn't see more than a couple of hundred feet because of the smoke. The channel wound its way through extensive shallows, and Laurie had to feel our way by dead-reckoning, keeping an eagle-eye on the depth, dodging the fishing boats, and using up a lot of his luck. A "breeze" it was not.*

The Marina staff had to move the boom across the entrance to allow us in. It was there permanently to keep out fuel spills, an unfortunate by-product of the heavy ship traffic. Inside the boom the Marina was a delightful oasis of calm, with pool, restaurant and attentive staff. The great showers and daily free towels soon became addictive.

Check-in was at Singapore City. Cruisers were treated not as tourists, but the same as crew on freighters and tankers. Instead of 30-day visas, we got two weeks. Carole and Ryan had to be bonded, at $S1,600 each, to ensure they left when the boat did. The officials knew how silly this was, and laughed when I said, if all it cost me was S$3,200 to get rid of my wife and son, they could have them. Carole was not quite so amused.

Braving the ever-present smoke, we went shopping in the shopping Mecca of Singapore, and bought nothing. I guess Singapore shopping is best done from one of the hotels, being chauffeured between shops in a Rolls, as I had been in a distant past life. Once again, this story failed to amuse Carole. However, we did eat at the biggest KFC outlet in the world and, by way of balance, at the local food stalls that line many streets.

Late in October we made a hurried, three week trip to Los Angeles. As the "crew" was leaving the boat, regulations required me to specially check them out, and to obtain a letter from the captain of "Dolphin Spirit" advising immigration at the airport that they were returning to join their boat. We presented the letter on arrival back in Singapore. Immigration looked at it, ignored it, and gave us normal 30-day visitor's visas. On check-out, there was no mention of visas or bonds. Carole and Ryan therefore remained on board.

Carole: *Freeways, make-up, shoes and real clothes—ugh!*

While in California, Carole stayed with her mother in Burbank, Ryan stayed with his grandparents, Lenore and Joe, in Pacific Palisades, and I stayed in a hired car traveling between Burbank, Pacific Palisades and West Marine. Ryan went back to Marquez School, met up with all his old friends again, went trick-or-treating with his friend Riley, and generally had a wonderful time. Naturally, we didn't see most of the people we wanted to, or even get to talk to them on the phone.

Ryan (9): *Seeing my old friends again was just like I hadn't been away. Everyone was happy to see me, but no one really wanted to hear about my trip, so we just hung out as before.*

Four bags of non-essentials were taken home in another valiant attempt to clear stuff off the boat. Once again we failed dismally, returning with six bags and two boxes. The equation never seemed to work out. It was even worse this trip, as we stopped for three days in Hong Kong on the way back. Customs there took one look and waved us through. The hotel driver nearly refused to take us, but finally fitted everything in, burying us in the bags that wouldn't fit in the trunk. The hotel receptionist asked how many months we were staying, and the porters fell over themselves finding other things to do. We finally got everything to the room, and then realized we would have to do the whole thing in reverse when we left.

Carole: *Foolishly, Laurie made the flat statement that we could buy nothing big in Hong Kong. Complying, I bought small stuff—a lovely jade pendant and a gold chain. Laurie surprised me with another small item, a unique black pearl and sapphire pendant. Ryan bought a watch (a present from his Gram, my mother—lucky Ryan has three grandmothers), and Laurie bought a wide angle lens and a water-proof case for the video camera.*

It rained, but the Star Ferry from the Kowloon side to Hong Kong Island was its usual fun trip, even in the choppy seas. We took a limo to the China border and spent some time looking into China from a mountain top. Carole swore she could tell the difference, but it just looked like more hills to me. On the way back, we visited an amusement park, where we rode on one of the longest and most spectacular gondola rides ever.

Ryan (9): *In the gondola was a Chinese couple who took a lot of photographs of us. This was very strange, as it was usually us taking the photos of the locals.*

We walked through streets and markets, went to Toys-Я-Us, got lost several times, ate at little and big restaurants, and did most of the tourist things. Hong Kong certainly gave no external signs of change since the Chinese take-over, with business as usual, at least from the tourist perspective.

To protect the innocent, we will gloss over the drama of getting bags and boxes from hotel room to lobby, to car, to airport check-in. We will not dwell on the abject groveling I had to do to get the lot onto the plane without excess-baggage payments that would have made Bill Gates gasp. We will not even mention our 1am arrival in Singapore, walking through Customs with bags full of videos and books (generally prohibited imports), the need to get two taxis to the Raffles Marina, the fact that neither driver knew the way there, the brilliant way I navigated to within a mile of the marina, and then got lost. We will heap praises on the marina security staff who, at 2am, arrived with two golf carts and transported the exhausted travelers, bags and boxes, back to "Dolphin Spirit."

Ryan and I had to get new passports in Singapore, which entailed visits to the Australian and U.S. embassies. The U.S. embassy had posted a Travel Advisory, a list of countries they were suggesting U.S. citizens should stay away from. Carole was very concerned to note that all the countries we were to visit in the next few months were included. I pointed out that we had just visited several countries that were also on the list with no problems, and the day was saved.

The boat next to us at Raffles, "Spirit of Tara," from England, had 12 and 14-year old girls on board. They and their parents had been in Singapore for over a year, and before that in Indonesia for several years. Ryan spent a lot of time with them, cooking Christmas goodies (he made a wall-hanging basket out of bread dough as a present for Carole), going to Scouts, swimming in the pool, playing with their cat, and walking their dog. They were really nice to him, and included him in all they did.

Ryan (9): *Christmas in Singapore was hot and humid, but all the decorations were fake green pine trees and fake snow. In the hotels the ladies all dressed in Santa outfits with short skirts. Looked strange to me as most were Chinese. The air conditioning in hotels and shops was really cold, so I shivered when I went in.*

Night Safari, in Singapore, was an open-area nocturnal animals' zoo, which, as its name indicates, was open only at night. We took a guided tram ride, and unguided walks, to see rhinos, tigers, lions, fish otters, and dozens of other animals that come out mainly after dark. There were few fences and cages, so we got up close and personal with the animals. Pat and Tashi ("Marita Shan") were supposed to meet us there (they were at another marina on the other side of Singapore), but we/they got lost, so we missed each other. How can someone who has navigated half-way around the world get lost in a small park on a small island? Of course I am here referring to Pat.

While we were in L.A. the smoke had gone from Singapore, so we actually got to see it. We made one last foray to a nearby supermarket, a Costco clone, but bigger, fueled up, checked out, and headed north up the west coast of Malaysia, in company with "Marita Shan." Amazing how we can find each other at sea, but not on land!

The Malacca Straits have a fearsome reputation for pirates, and we hoped that traveling in company and day-hopping up the coast would minimize our exposure. A couple of nights we couldn't find a harbor, so simply moved towards land until we were in 20 or so feet of water and dropped anchor. The water was calm even if there were spectacular thunderstorms all around. "Encore," a new friend met in Bali, was hit by lightning here.

In reality, the anchoring process was a little more complicated than I stated above. Typically the depth shoaled from 70 feet to 30 feet in half a boat length. Discolored and silt-filled water precluded any visual estimate of depth, so there was always a lively radio debate between us and "Marita Shan" as to who was to be the depth sounder. We usually lost, as Pat was more patient (older) than I was.

First night out we anchored at Besar Island, off a brand new golf course and condo complex. "Windrose," last seen in Lombok, had been there for a few days taking advantage of free golf on a pristine course. Not a bad life. Breakfast in the cockpit, dinghy ashore to be met by a golf cart that whisks you to the first tee, caddies, a course that gives you views of your boat from almost every hole, and all for free.

Our first real stop was Port Klang, where we picked up a mooring at the Selangor Yacht Club. Port Klang was the biggest port in Malaysia, and the nearest to the capital, Kuala Lumpur. Entry was through the main harbor, which was huge and lined with modern container facilities. In total contrast, up the small river where we moored were local coastal boats being loaded and unloaded by hand, with lines of men carrying sacks on their shoulders.

The river water was the color of a lime soda, complete with foam, filthy, and full of unmentionable things. Fortunately, the Club provided a free water taxi, which was a relief as we didn't want to put our dinghies in. Facilities ashore were excellent, and the curries were hot (in every sense of the word), and inexpensive. Ryan enjoyed the pool. Pat and I checked into Malaysia here—Immigration, Customs and Harbor Master—all at the end of a muddy road near the train station.

We took a train (sometimes I impress even myself by the subtle way I lead into a new paragraph) to Kuala Lumpur, known simply as KL to all us seasoned travelers. It was about an hour's ride by fast, clean, modern electric commuter train. The view of KL from the observation platform at the top of a huge tower, including the two tallest buildings in the world, and skyscrapers everywhere, was, by itself, worth the trip. Sheer glass walls reflected the adjacent buildings, creating abstracts out of geometrical shapes.

Carole: *At the bottom floor of the tower was a 31 Flavors ice cream shop, so naturally Ryan had to have some. It was not good. I later reported this to a friend who is one of the honchos at 31 Flavors, and she said that each country imposes its own regulations and rules, so that tastes are always different. We made up for this disappointment by having McDonalds for lunch. They taste the same everywhere in the world.* (Laurie: Bland is bland is bland.)

Tash wanted to do some shopping, so she and Pat headed off while we continued exploring the city, planning to later meet at the train station. Taxis were few and far between, and traffic mostly jammed and stationary. Pat and Tash waited two hours for a taxi, and then sat in traffic for another hour to go some three miles. We walked to the station, so arrived much earlier than they eventually did, and caught the wrong train back.

It was a very good train system, with only two destinations, and an

SINGAPORE, MAYLASIA, AND THAILAND

excellent train indicator on the platforms. What we didn't know was that, at certain times they duplicated some trains, and didn't reflect this in the station indicator displays. Anyhow, we got on board (it was pouring rain, a real tropical downpour), and after a while commented on how different the scenery looked when we were traveling in the opposite direction, and on the fact that the stations were different too. Then the penny dropped! We caught a train back to KL, waited on the station, very nearly caught the duplicate again, and still made it back to the marina before Pat and Tash.

The entrance to the Rebak Island Marina channel on Langkowi was not apparent until we were less than 100 yards from it, a real test of nerves. We spoke on VHF to boats in the Marina, got directions, checked them at least twice, then headed straight for a rocky shore in rapidly shallowing water, with nowhere to go if the entry instructions turned out to be wrong. Just as I was about to call it quits (Carole had done so a couple of hundred yards earlier), a rock wall separated from the shore and I breathed again.

A sharp left turn took us into the channel and water less than seven feet deep (we draw 7 foot, 6 inches). Fortunately the bottom was mud, so we made like a dredge, and slithered and slurped our way through, leaving a muddy track behind. Making the turn into the slip was not easy, as pushing mud sideways with the keel forced a wider turn. Naturally I knew this was going to happen and adjusted accordingly—I wish!

Ryan (9): *The Marina was great. There were kids to play with and a pool. Two French girls about my age were on one boat and a girl and a boy were on another. We played on all the boats and in the pool. The only bad thing was that I dropped my Game Boy overboard.*

Rebak Island had excellent facilities, a very nice club house, restaurant, pool, water, electricity (240V, Australian plugs), and cheap, duty free booze. Happy Hour was 5 to 9pm with 2 for 1 drinks, very civilized, sitting in the huge armchairs looking out over the marina, palms and sea. More exciting was the free, clean, fresh water, so we washed everything, then did it again on the next day and the next, just for the sheer pleasure of it. Dragging ourselves away from the bar, pool and hose, Carole and I took the free water-taxi to the nearby town, leaving Ryan to play with the other children. We passed a huge breakwater, miles long, that enclosed just water, with no apparent towns, port facilities, or other reasons for existence. The town provided no lasting memories except for an excellent buffet lunch we stumbled on by accident.

We lounged by the pool, did minor boat maintenance, hosed "Dolphin Spirit" down daily, enjoyed happy hour, watched Ryan play and generally relaxed for five days. Thailand called, so we left, digging a new muddy track on the way out.

Ryan (9): *I didn't want to leave as I was having a great time with the kids, but I knew they were all going the same way as we were, so we would see each other again. Mum and Dad always let me have time off school, so it was a double bonus when I was with kids.*

An overnight sail took us to Ao Chalong (Chalong Bay) on Ko Phuket (Phuket Island) (pronounced Foo-ket, so don't say it fast). To check in, we went by local taxi (Tuk Tuk, pronounced Took Took), a four-wheeled vehicle with bench seats and a motor-mower engine, driven by a kamikaze trainee. We rounded corners on two wheels, passed on any side, at any time, and generally used up a lot of our nine lives. The only people who seemed to be living more dangerously were the motorcyclists, who were driving both ways on the same side of the road. Phuket, the main town, seemed to have everything, supermarket, fresh fruit and vegetable markets, meat imported from Australia and New Zealand, one-hour photo developing, and travel agents.

As I wanted Carole and Ryan to see the Grand Palace we flew to Bangkok, and booked into the Hyatt Erawan for three days. Not wanting to leave "Dolphin Spirit" at anchor, we moved her to Yacht Haven Marina, north of Ao Chalong. This was a brand new marina, with excellent docks completed and empty, and little else except a bar and restaurant ashore—the essentials, I guess. The bar served excellent margaritas.

The Hyatt Erawan had been selected for opulence, as we felt that we needed a little more decadence in our lives, and we weren't disappointed. Everything, from the huge foyer on, reeked of wealth and sophistication, so we were right at home in our Tevas and shorts—Carole insisted that we dress up for the occasion. Being so well trained, the hotel staff took us in stride, and unobtrusively, but effectively, screened us off from the real patrons.

Right next to the hotel was the Erawan Shrine, with a crowd of worshipers and dancers around it at all hours. We stopped there many times and it always provided new sights and sounds. As we were in Bangkok for only a short time, we took tours, something we generally avoid. The decision to do so was made easier by the justly infamous traffic and resultant air pollution.

The Grand Palace overwhelmed us with its golden spires and domes, ornate carvings, and the Emerald Buddha. An unexpected highlight was the river and canal tour.

Ryan (9): *The tour boat stopped at a couple of places where the canal seemed to be full of huge carp. They swam right on the surface of the muddy water so we could see them really churning up the water as the boat crew* *fed them. I liked the long-tail boats which are driven by huge engines with propellers at the end of long shafts. Steering is by moving the whole engine from side to side. They are very fast.*

To restore our self-esteem as intrepid independents, we undertook a self-organized tour through the flower market and adjacent "everything" markets. Whole streets were just flowers and there was little space left to walk through. Photographs don't register the overwhelming aromas, the ever changing colors, the movement as porters carried masses of blooms around, and the sheer sensual overload, but we made several hundred attempts.

Bangkok was full of temples, most of which forbid photography inside. On an evening walk, we actually found one that allowed photos—at least there wasn't a sign saying not to, so I did. Buddha won, as most of these bootleg photos didn't come out.

My old friend Thierry, a Frenchman who, with Angeline, his Singaporean wife, oscillates at dizzying speed between homes and offices in Singapore, Bangkok, Kuala Lumpur and Hong Kong, was in town, so took us to dinner at a restaurant built over pools full of the main course. Ryan ran round feeding everything that moved.

Ryan (9): *Dad paid the extra, so we flew Business Class back to the boat—YES!*

Kurt, PL and Katie (**Carole:** *Yes, she flew in again, avoiding the thrills PL and I were experiencing by staying on board.*) joined us for Christmas Eve dinner at the Marina restaurant. For Christmas, we sailed into the islands in Ao Phangnga, and anchored off Ko Hong. Imagine jade green water, massive vertical red and white rock walls partially covered with dark green shrubs and trees, rock spires rising sheer from the water. Add blue skies, caves, hidden lagoons, overhangs with huge stalactites and a background of similar islands. Then make allowance for the inadequacies of the writer and you begin to get the picture. Carole said it was better than her favorite, Yosemite.

Santa found the boat again, and Ryan professed himself to be pleased with every present. This year, Santa and parents went for quality, not quantity. Christmas dinner on "Marita Shan" was turkey, stuffing, ham, gravy, mashed potatoes, Carole's cranberry/mandarin orange Jell-o salad, green beans, brownies, cookies, wine and champagne.

Carole: *Tash really wanted a big traditional Christmas dinner even though it was so hot and humid. I couldn't bear to put the oven on, so instead of my* *traditional Christmas cookies I made cranberry Jell-o. This time it was able to stay with the main course as only one true Aussie was on board. It was our second tropical Christmas playing "Dashing Through The Snow" in 95-degree temperatures.*

The next day, we hired a long-tail boat to take us for a tour of the northern islands, as it was a little shallow for the captain (read Carole) to be comfortable taking "Dolphin Spirit." These boats are long and narrow and are driven by an engine which direct drives a propeller at the end of a twelve-foot-long shaft. We saw six-cylinder and V-8 car engines driving them in Bangkok, but our boat had a modest 4-cylinder engine—open exhaust of course. The whole engine/shaft/propeller combination was swiveled at the stern of the boat, and steering was by rotating everything about that point. It was fast, if noisy.

James Bond Island, featured in the film *Man With The Golden Gun*, was picturesque from a distance, but when we got closer we saw that every flat space was covered with shops selling shells, post cards and touristy things. Any beach left was covered with the boats that brought in the day trippers, mostly Japanese. Carole was in great demand to have her photo taken towering over bunches of Japanese ladies. Ryan found caves and bats.

Carole: *I have always spent the day after Christmas shopping at the 50%-off sales, buying presents and decorations for the next year. Apart from the absence of Macy's, this year was no different as I got great deals on huge shells. These were then stored on board until the following Christmas, when they flew home in our baggage to become presents.*

Our next anchorage was simply spectacular, as distinct from very spectacular. It did provide us with a unique experience however. We took the dinghy through a tricky, rock-filled entrance into a cave, which led into a tunnel, which turned a corner, so all daylight was cut off. In pitch blackness, we paddled another hundred yards or so, round another corner, and out through another cave into a hong (lagoon), completely surrounded by vertical rock walls. Fortunately we knew what to expect, and our flashlights enabled us to see the walls and the hundreds of bats hanging from the tunnel roof. Ryan called it his best day ever.

We did this exactly seven years to the minute before the 2004 tsunami hit. Had it happened then, we would have been crushed against the tunnel roof.

That night, we sat on deck and watched thousands of flying foxes (giant fruit bats) flying from their camp on the island to raid the fruit trees on Phuket Island.

SINGAPORE, MAYLASIA, AND THAILAND

Carole: *As we sat watching the sky filled with the screeching and flapping wings of the myriad flying foxes, the sea around us changed from pink to a velvety violet, to a purple blackness. The last flying fox passed as real night came and the stars came out in dazzling numbers. Laurie was sad we could no longer see the Southern Cross, but the perfect end to a perfect day made up for it.*

Off to an anchorage in Tonsai Bay on Phi Phi Don Island. The Phi Phi Islands are supposed to be the prettiest in Thailand. Unfortunately, Phi Phi Don was overrun by day trippers and ugly hotel developments, so some of the beauty had been lost. The anchorage was criss-crossed by speed boats pulling inflated "bananas" loaded with screaming tourists, by howling long-tails taking visitors on island circuits, and by huge tourist boats from Phuket that went by at 25 knots, throwing up five foot bow waves. We stayed—it was very nice before 10am and after 3pm.

Thierry and Angeline happened to be on holidays in Phi Phi Don, so we honored them by a very rare day-sail around the island. Most cruisers, and we are no exception, don't day-sail (out and back to the same anchorage the same day) by choice. It generally takes us several hours to get "Dolphin Spirit" really ready for sea, putting everything away securely, and going through the pre-passage check-lists.

We anchored in Maya Bay on neighboring Phi Phi Lee for lunch. It was a pretty place with exceptionally clear water, nice coral and fish, but all of us felt as if we had been dusted with itching powder as soon as we got in the water. It wasn't jellyfish or sealice, and even a hand dipped in the water suffered the same sensation. The tourists on the tour boats apparently thought it was one of the pleasures of swimming in Thailand.

Ryan (9): *I think it is very funny that in Thai, Phuket is pronounced Poo-ket, Phi Phi is pronounced Pee Pee, and to be polite, Thai men end most phrases with the word "Krap," pronounced as written.*

We really struggled with the Thai language. Indonesian was much easier, especially for Ryan. Perhaps it was because we spent more time there, and more time off the tourist track, where English was rarer, and the local culture and way of life more prominent. For all its spectacular scenery, the Thailand we saw, including Bangkok, was heavily tourist-oriented, and therefore basically cultureless. I don't regard shows put on for visitors, and handicrafts made for sale, as culture. It wasn't as bad as Bali, but it was getting there. It was sad to see fishermen who don't fish, but rent their boats to transport tourists. They make more money, and the fish are happier, but a whole way of life is disappearing. There has to be a middle ground somewhere.

Ryan went parasailing, towed behind a boat, and had a great time. Carole and I had heart attacks, particularly when the flyer ahead of Ryan had a mishap on landing, and Ryan had to go around several more times before making it down safely. He thought the extra time aloft was just perfect.

We would regularly dinghy to a nearby deserted beach for lunch. On the last day there, we found the sand occupied by a troop of monkeys that wouldn't let us land. Our response was to anchor just off shore and watch the show they put on for us.

New Year's Eve provided a spectacular midnight fireworks show from three points around the bay. Earlier in the evening we went to a special dinner-dance at one of the hotels.

Ryan (9): *They gave me and the other kids huge sparklers to hold. As soon as one died, I was given another. When the waiters weren't looking, I would hand my sparkler to one of the local kids who were standing outside the fence around the dining area.*

Preparing to leave for Sri Lanka, we spent five days back in Ao Chalong. Ryan was in his element as the two boats with kids on board, which we had previously met in Langkowi, had arrived. Two other boats had a mixture of boys and girls ages 7 to 17, so we hardly saw Ryan after his abbreviated school day was finished. They swam, played, and generally were kids. Boat kids often have to be miniature adults, as being kids might result in damage to the boat, or to themselves. Whilst this is good for the development of a sense of responsibility, there needs to be times when being an irresponsible kid is okay.

Jimmy's Lighthouse Restaurant was taken over for a combined birthday party and pre-passage get-together. Ryan, Carole and Tammy ("Sky Bird") all have a January 8 birthday, and Tammy's husband Steve has his on January 12. Ryan got a lot of presents from the cruisers. "Magnum Bonum" gave him a horn-handled sheath knife. We all had quite a night, making the trek back to the dinghies, at the end of a long, dark, wooden, flexible, jetty, an even more memorable experience.

As usual, we needed to get diesel, petrol (for the outboards), propane, provisions, meat, drinks, bread, fresh fruit and vegetables. We looked ahead to the next few ports to check on what was available there. For example, those who wanted hard liquor had to buy it at Langkowi, Malaysia, as it was either expensive or non-existent from there to the Mediterranean. Toilet paper was a constantly monitored item, as, in the quality and softness we wanted to continue to enjoy, it was scarce, or unavailable. Many hours of cocktail conversation were devoted to determining the correct quantity of toilet paper to have on board. And you thought we were frivolous and shallow!

At Ao Chalong, diesel was provided by a fuel barge, which tied up off our stern and passed over a long hose. Petrol came from a regular gas station ashore, propane from a shack where the proprietor had one word of English, "Tomorrow." It was there at the notified time. Robertsons, the only supermarket in Phuket, had an extensive range of local, U.S., Australian and English goods. Local markets provided excellent fruit and vegetables, and bakeries provided bread and baguettes. Meat came from a local importer of Australian and New Zealand meat, who vacuum-packed and froze our order. The big problem was money—Baht, the Thai currency. It was falling like a stone against the U.S. dollar, and everything had to be paid for in Baht. Changing too much meant leaving the country with worthless pieces of pretty paper, changing too little meant additional trips to the bank.

Before leaving Phuket, we went on an elephant safari (my birthday present to Ryan and Carole). Ryan had his own elephant to ride, while another poor beast had to carry both Carole and I. We went down the banks of streams and up hills, through the jungle and out onto a lookout over the harbor. Other than concern for the probable demise of our elephant from overwork, we had a great time. Ryan got to pull dried rubber sap from the trees and see how elastic it was.

Carole: *Elephants are my favorite animal. Before this I had seen them only in zoos, but now I rode on one, stood close to it and looked into its long eyelashed eyes.*

Check-out should have been as painless as check-in, a 60-second event. The Customs officers asked for a "fee" of 300 Baht both times. It wasn't a huge amount, so almost everyone just grinned and paid. This time a cruiser decided to argue over the amount, asking to be shown the regulation requiring it. Obligingly, the officer hauled out a volume and pointed to the page. "But it is in Thai, I can't read that," argued the cruiser, who, in the minds of the rest of us lined up behind, was rapidly rising to the top of the list of people to be hated. After more arguing, he must have taken note of the rumblings at his rear, because he offered 100 Baht. The officer countered with 200 Baht and the cruiser agreed.

"Now can I have my clearance?" he asked.

"First we search your boat," replied the officer.

The cruiser then had to pay for a taxi to transport him and two officers to his boat, watch while they systematically tore it apart for three hours (of course not putting it back together afterwards), and then pay for the taxi back to receive his clearance. Certainly it was worth the $1 he saved!

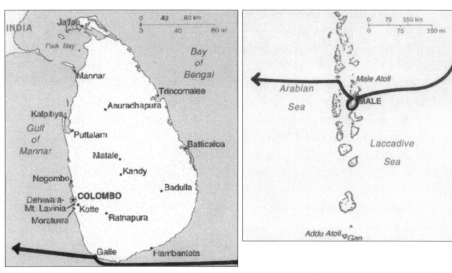

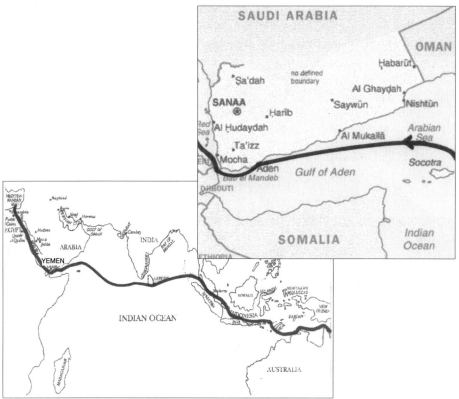

Sri Lanka, Maldives, Indian Ocean and Yemen

Year Two
January 9 to February 19

To go to Sri Lanka or not to go, that was the question. For years there had been reports of problems with the Tamil Tiger revolutionary movement, and these problems had apparently escalated. We debated, we asked, we changed our minds many times, and then went anyway.

That's a rather glib way of minimizing a very serious decision, one that could, if wrong, put us in danger, perhaps even cost us our lives. We were moving our home and our family to a country where the security situation seemed to change daily. Why take the risk; why go there at all?

The roots went right back to the original decision to go up the Red Sea and through the Suez Canal into the Mediterranean instead of around the Cape of Good Hope and into the Atlantic. That meant we went to Singapore and Thailand instead of taking the more southerly route across the Indian Ocean. In its turn, that required we pass close to the bottom of Sri Lanka on the way to the Maldives. We were in a group; there was safety in numbers; it broke an otherwise very long passage; the Maldives had little in the way of fruit and vegetables—who knows but the fruit-aholic in me may have made this the deciding reason.

I have said before that cruisers never have time to do what they want, and Thailand was a perfect example. We wanted to stay for another couple of months, but that would have meant we missed the good weather window for crossing the Indian Ocean and going up the Red Sea.

During the seven day sail from Phuket to Galle, Sri Lanka, the winds were perfect, the seas were almost flat, there were dolphins, the skies were cloudless, the stars at night magnificent. I know we cruise to get to exotic and wonderful places, but sometimes the passages to these places can be just as memorable.

From the January 10 log:

"Course 255-degrees magnetic. Winds E 15K. Caught 10-pound tuna in the middle of a school of dolphins. Tidal rips (?) at 1 to 2-mile intervals. Flying fish. Wispy clouds."

Carole: *Pointing ahead I asked, "Laurie, what's that? The water looks all jumpy."*

The so-called tidal rips were lines of bubbly water and foam with fish jumping all round, which stretched as far as we could see at right angles to our path. We had some hesitation about crossing the first, but as there was no alternative we ploughed on, recording no change in current, water temperature or color as we crossed. A swordfish leaped out of the water at one line. The lines recurred all day. We decided that they were "interesting, unexplained phenomena" and never saw anything like them again.

Between Phuket and Galle we made five mid-ocean transfers. Just out of Phuket, as reported above, Ryan caught a tuna, too big for us to eat alone, so we passed some over to "Marita Shan." I drove up behind them, with Ryan and Carole in the bow holding out the fish at the end of a pole. There was little wind, only a three-foot swell running, but the relatively simple pass still required two attempts.

Later in the passage, the fresh water pump on "Sky Bird" went down for the count, so we passed over a spare we had (which unfortunately didn't work when Steve installed it). The state of the sea and the weight of the pump were against a simple pass, so "Sky Bird" put their dinghy in the water, towed it behind them, and swooped in front of us. I had time to hang over the side and drop the pump in the dinghy. Getting the dinghy back on board was a saga in itself. "An E-ticket ride," Steve said.

Just out of Galle, we were approached by three lots of fishermen, and gave each caps and cans of coke. No dramas, calm seas, goods dropped into nets on poles, and Carole standing by with the pepper spray just in case.

We arrived outside Galle Harbor around 4am, and stooged around waiting for light and for the Sri Lanka Navy to open the net and chain they put across the harbor entrance each night (presumably to keep out Tiger frogmen and submarines). A Navy boat came out, took our crew list, decided we weren't subversive, and allowed us into the harbor.

Galle was a small harbor, with Navy boats and freighters on one side, yachts in the middle, big fishing boats on the other side, and paddle or oar-operated fishing boats with nets and lines everywhere there was a space. It was absolute chaos. What made it even worse was that we were supposed to anchor, then back up to a mooring buoy and attach a stern line to prevent swinging. Every mooring buoy had at least three yachts tied to it already, and "Dolphin Spirit," barely controllable in reverse, was no help. By some miracle, assisted by brilliant seamanship of course, we hit no one, got as set as possible, and crossed our fingers, as the bottom was sludge with the holding power of melted marshmallows.

Fishermen were chasing schools of fish that swam around with their heads out of water. Every now and then a school ran into the mooring lines, and leapt about in great confusion. We asked whether the fish had begun to swim with their heads out of the water only after the depth-charges were started, and were told that it was an ancient characteristic.

There were two types of fishermen, those who dragged nets where the schools of fish weren't, and those who chased the schools and tossed lines at them, in the hope of hooking a few. To my simple mind, it would have been a lot easier to just put a net around a school and catch them all, but then what would there be to do tomorrow?

Ryan (16): *This was one of the few places where I didn't get any local knowledge on how to fish. The fishermen didn't talk to us at all.*

Dinghying ashore, we dodged moorings, lines, nets, boats, and tied up at a small floating dock. A little later, one of our friends was standing on it when someone stepped too heavily, and flipped him into the water. I almost did the same thing when Ryan jumped onto the dock. I think he was trying to get me wet, as he had seen what happened.

Ryan (10): *I was.*

Anyhow, off to our agent, Don Windsor and Company, to fill out the Immigration, Customs and Health paperwork, get passes to allow us through the port security (several security police and a soldier who didn't look old enough to shave, but carried an AK47 automatic rifle), and clear into Sri Lanka.

Customs insisted on coming to the boat—using our dinghy—for the simple purpose of getting whatever they could scrounge or exhort. They fingered everything, and asked for everything, liquor, beer, cigarettes, books, CDs, caps, magazines. If it was movable, they wanted it. It was the worst and most blatant exhibition we have seen. The Windsors warned us about it, and said that it is so lucrative that the Customs Inspectors were rotated every six months, so that the wealth was shared around. From us they got two caps and a small bottle of whisky I had bought expressly for the purpose.

One new officer went to a yacht and returned empty handed. This so incensed his superior that he commandeered the next dinghy that came to shore, went to the offending yacht, and stayed on board until the required presents were provided. These officers have the power to stay within the law and make a cruiser's life miserable.

Carole: *Laurie usually has to stop me from giving stuff and money away to those I consider in need. I would have had the same attitude if these people hadn't been so in-your-face rude, pulling out CDs for example, and saying they were taking them. With no qualms I said an emphatic, "No!"*

That uncomfortable situation over, we were free to explore Sri Lanka. Santosh Windsor took us on a tour of Galle and the surrounding country. Part of the city is inside a huge fortress (it takes two hours to walk around the walls) and businesses seem to be divided between "inside" and "outside" the wall.

The coast was pretty, with white sand beaches, rocks, deep blue water, and the famous stick fishermen—they sit on sticks out in the sea, and dangle lines into the water. As with the harbor fishermen, it seemed an inefficient way to catch fish, but was very picturesque. Children haunted the shore nearby, asking for payment for the right to stand and watch "their father." We understand the stick positions are inherited.

A tea factory took us back to the dark ages. Tea leaves are picked by women (40 pounds per day quota—a lot of leaves!), then dried, crushed, dried again, sorted, graded and packed. Machines perform each of these tasks, but moving the tea from machine to machine is all done by hand, by women carrying bags of the stuff. They work in gloom, as light apparently causes some damage to the tea, and were paid around $US2 per day.

Carole: *Here, at the end of the 20th century, when we live in relative luxury, it took an experience like this to make me really realize that so many others work and live in such circumstances. And yet these women smiled at us as we came in.*

It sounded as if someone had hit the hull of the boat with a hammer, but without the vibration. "That's the fifth depth charge tonight," called Ryan, and went back to his reading. We became very quickly adjusted when between 16 and 60 depth-charges were dropped around us every night. It was annoying to start with, but eventually we slept through all except the ones dropped right next to the boat. Those got our attention immediately. Apparently the Navy was concerned that the Tigers would somehow penetrate the net at the harbor entrance and attack the rather tattered and forlorn Navy boat at the wharf, so they lit sticks of dynamite and tossed them around all night. Returning from dinner late one evening, we dinghied back to "Dolphin Spirit" during one of the depth-charge forays. I am quite sure it was on purpose, as two explosions occurred very close to the dinghy, smacking the soles of our feet through the inflated bottom. As we saw neither dead fish nor frogmen floating around in the mornings, we cannot report on how effective the depth charges were.

It was on another day that we gathered around, nervously looking at the bullet that had flattened the rear tire of our safari vehicle. "Not an Army bullet," said our guide authoritatively, "Must be one of the other crowd." He then set about changing the tire while we wandered about looking at the buffalo, and wondering how the bullet got in the tire.

That morning had been a 6am start (just after the last depth-charge, and just before sunrise) for us (Pat, Tash, Carole, Ryan and me) to drive to Yalu National Park to see wild elephants. Our driver told us, after we were under way, that Yalu had been closed to visitors, as the Tigers (two-legged) had attacked in that area the night before. We were directed to another Park where Tigers hadn't been seen for a couple of days. The roads were abominable, and it was debatable as to whether my back or my behind would go first during the four-hour drive. The good thing was that we got a good look at the people and their way of life as we lurched from rut to pothole.

Carole: *Almost all of the primary and secondary school children went to school dressed completely in white, skirts, shirts, pants, socks. The only color was from the ties most of the girls wore—boys didn't. They all looked absolutely immaculate, both going to, and coming home from school. Not even the children from the best of homes where I taught looked this clean, and to this day I can't wear white for more than an hour. These people did it in villages where the only water was from a central faucet, and where the houses had dirt floors.*

At the outskirts of the park we transferred to an ancient Land Rover with bench seats in the back, and rather fragile looking roll bars. Our two guides, one driving, one sitting on the roof, spoke reasonable English, but drove like maniacs. The bench seats were hard, so we probably should have been grateful that we were airborne over a lot of the bad road. In retrospect, it was only when we slowed down that we got the bullet-induced flat, so perhaps their driving so fast had a reason.

Roads through the park were dirt, narrow, and lined with thorn trees whose branches reached right into the vehicle. All of us got well scratched arms. We saw lots of monkeys, birds and buffalo, but no elephants. At one time the Land Rover couldn't make it up a hill, so we got out while the two guides threw water on the front hubs (green, slimy water, from a buffalo wallow). For whatever reason, this seemed to refresh the vehicle, and it made it up the hill the next try. Then came the flat tire, then came the drive back to our van, then came the four-hour return drive to the boat. We were so tired we heard only one depth-charge before we were asleep.

To celebrate our first wedding anniversary, we went out to dinner. The Lighthouse Hotel was the unanimous recommendation of the locals. Unlike most recommendations it was a FIND. Then open for only seven months, it sat on a cliff overlooking rocks, surf, sand, palms and wonderful sunsets.

We drove right up to the reception desk, and walked to an extraordinary staircase that spiraled up for three floors. Its banister was made up of life size copper figures that looked very Spanish Conquistadorish, cannons, muskets, and pikes. To the right on the first floor was the pool, set at the top of the cliff, with a cascade over the edge. On the left a restaurant and a patio looked out over a wonderful coastal and palms view, with frozen margaritas to match. The restaurant had a seven course fixed menu (a la carte restaurant on the third floor) for 500 Rupiah ($US8 approx.), and it was excellent. We went back twice before we left.

For the very first time, I actually saw the fabled "Green Flash" as the sun set, and I saw it again the next time we were there. I am now a believer, and it wasn't the margaritas either, because Carole saw it too, and she had drunk only one.

Ryan (16): *The Green Flash is an easily explained phenomena, with a clear scientific basis and is caused by the refraction of the sun's light, as with a rainbow. As the suns sets, we first see red, then orange, then yellow, then green. The Green Flash can be seen only over water, never over land. Circumstances do have to be right, but they have nothing to do with alcohol intake. Sometimes Dad gets a little carried away when he writes.*

On the way back from a short drive to see mask carvers in action, we happened on an elephant working at a construction site. Naturally we stopped and the elephant operators offered to give Ryan a ride (Rupiah 500). The elephant knelt down, Ryan climbed on, and off they went, with Ryan in sole control, apart from the mahout on the ground. Responding to purely voice commands, with no physical contact at all, she (I checked) stood on two legs and put her trunk in the air for a photo op, then knelt to let Ryan off. As a finale, she picked Ryan up in her trunk and carried him around. I was fiddling with cameras and looked up to see the business end of the trunk about six inches from my eyes. It looked two-miles wide.

Farewell dinner was at the Lighthouse. "Osprey," "Gigolo," "Magnum Bonum" and "Sky Bird" were heading to the northern Maldives, "Marita Shan" was coming with us to the southern Maldives, and as it turned out, we were not to see "Topaz" for nearly two years.

Galle is not a place we would come back to, but we are glad we went. The people were pleasant, the town had nothing to offend, the beaches were attractive, the Lighthouse Hotel was unique, but we had a general feeling of discomfort, more than from any other third-world country we had been to so far. Perhaps it was the nightly depth-charges.

With some relief, we upped anchor and moved over to the commercial wharf to get diesel and water. Water came through a canvas fire hose, under terrific pressure, so getting it into the tanks was a Keystone comedy. The valve operator had two words of English, "Stop" and "Go," but randomly got them mixed up. The decks received a great washing. Diesel came in drums, gravity-fed to our tanks. Fuel should always be filtered, and I luckily did so this time, as it was full of junk.

The sail to Male, capital of the Maldives, took three nights, and was comfortable and unremarkable. We learned, en route, that the Tigers had bombed a temple in Kandy, killing eleven people. Some of our friends had visited there the day before, and others were due to visit on the day of the bomb, but put it off when Lois ("Topaz") got very sick. Pat ("Ankle Deep") was a doctor, made a quick diagnosis, and decided that Lois had to be flown to Singapore for an emergency operation. She made it with less than 12 hours to spare, the surgeon later told her.

Other Galle news, heard over SSB, concerned the arrival of a solo lady sailor, who hit a rock in mid-bay and sank. Divers went down and couldn't find the yacht, but within days much of its stores and equipment was on sale around Galle.

Male is a small island, about one-mile square, with every inch covered by buildings or roads. No back yards, no gardens, no trees, no grass. It had one car for every five yards of road, plus innumerable motor bikes and bicycles. Why people needed cars, when no place was more than a ten minute walk away, was never explained.

The Maldives sit on top of the tallest mountain range in the world, with the highest spot in the whole nation just nine feet above sea level. Except for one little 50-foot area, the Male anchorage was about 150-feet deep. We circled round trying to find THE SPOT, and eventually did, after missing it on either side by feet. It was just big enough for two boats, so we fitted three.

Coast Guard came out and gave us security clearance. Apparently the perpetrators of the last coup in the country arrived by yacht, so no one was taking chances. An agent was required, so we chose the FIFO Company, a choice assisted by the fact that there were no others. However they did good work, bringing out the usual Immigration, Health and Customs officials, who were all polite and efficient. The only other requirement was for us to go to the FIFO offices and fill out a Cruising Permit application, for which we were charged $US50.

"Sky Bird" arrived. They had been heading for the Northern Maldives when the printed-circuit board on their auto-pilot failed. There is almost nothing worse than not having an auto-pilot, so they headed for the only real civilization—Male. Unfortunately, Male was renowned for its total lack of auto-pilots, and equal absence of electronic repair shops. Persistence led Steve to a teenager who repaired TV sets in his bedroom. Without a circuit diagram, or any knowledge of the board's functions, he had it working in 24 hours, and it continued working all the way up the Red Sea.

The Maldives had a currency, the Rufiah, but U.S. dollars were the normal medium of exchange. The resorts (there were 43 of them, each on its own dedicated island) took only U.S. currency, even though most of the visitors were from Europe.

"La Scala," an Australian boat, had its dinghy stolen one night, the first theft we had heard of since Tahiti, so we decided to leave civilization and moved five miles south to Laguna Resort. Finding the lagoon entrance was not easy, as it was well past the island, in the apparent middle of nowhere. We entered, dodged around reefs and coral heads, and anchored in a pretty lagoon, surrounded by coral. The island had a blinding white beach (10-minute walk around), aqua water, great snorkeling, a small but adequate pool, and expensive food and drinks.

Ryan (10): *As always, Mum was easy to find in the pool or swimming in the sea, as she was the one bobbing up and down doing her aqua-exercises. She tried to get me to bob with her—no way! I had seen how funny she looked, and would rather swim anyhow.*

As the Maldives are Moslem, strict Moslem, no alcohol can be sold or drunk in the country, except in the resorts. Even there, a Maldivian will take and deliver your drink order, but a non-Maldivian must open the bottle, and mix or pour the alcohol. We were in the month of Ramadin, when no food is eaten between sunrise and sunset. Businesses don't open until 10am, and close early (banks 9am to noon). It ended on January 31, and was followed by five days of celebration.

All the yachties met to drift-snorkel on the reef around the Resort, as it was exceptional. There were clouds of fish, moray eels swimming around, sharks, turtles, and pretty coral of all types. The current drifted us slowly along the reef, and we would cover about two miles before we started to get tired. Two of the ladies used pool floats to support them. Carole didn't want to swim with the sharks, so she drifted in the dinghy with us. The dinghy was necessary as there was no way we could have swum back.

Between snorkels, Ryan did school work by the resort pool—one lesson, one swim, one lesson, one swim. Carole taught, drank Pina Coladas, and read—one lesson, one drink, one page, one drink. I drank beer, one beer, one beer, one beer. I don't like the stuff (truly), but it was cold, wet, and available. The resort was very expensive for food and drinks—chicken curry $US25 (we paid $US0.75 for the same dish in Sri Lanka), and bottled water $US3.50 a bottle.

Ryan (10): *"Fantome Blue," a 60-foot aluminum boat, anchored next to us. Jonathan was only 6-years old, but he had lots of toys and I enjoyed playing with another kid again.*

Back in Male to provision and check-out, we had to anchor in 150 feet of water, just outside of the fish and ferry-boat harbor. Fast ferry boats were back and forth past us every few minutes, apparently desiring to give their passengers intimate views of our boat. In return, we got great photos. The barge that transported full garbage trucks to a nearby island, where the garbage was used as land fill, provided an indescribable smell, but luckily went by only twice every hour.

Because there was so little real soil in the Maldives, there was very little fruit. This lack was a sobering experience for Ryan and I, more so when we realized that this meant there would be no fruit for the passage. We had to wait a day for the water-barge to come out to fill us up. The water-maker, repaired in Bali, had cracked in the same place again, and again I had applied the same repair. It was holding, but I was not trusting it to continue.

The water-maker problem was not solved until much later, when I flew back to the U.S. and confronted the manufacturer with the offending object. Up to that time they had been steadfastly saying that this problem was impossible, it couldn't happen, and implying that I was confusing their water-maker with something else. I showed them the cracked box, and they finally agreed that such an occurrence might be possible.

The eleven-day sail to Aden, across the remainder of the Indian Ocean, was our best experience; calm seas; winds either perfectly on the beam, or absent; blue skies and plenty of fish and dolphins. Carole wasn't sick, and we had several 180 + mile days (our usual average was 140 to 160 miles). It was our second-longest ocean passage, and by far the nicest.

"Marita Shan" had left a day before "Sky Bird" and us, as we were both much faster, and they didn't want to feel they were holding us back. The perfect conditions elevated their performance too, and we didn't catch them until the ninth day, when they hove-to for an hour waiting for us. Pat's anchor-winch expired at Male and he had to haul up the 300 feet of chain and anchor by hand, and repeat that at every anchorage all the way up the Red Sea.

Carole: *I dreaded crossing the Indian Ocean. The Pacific was my ocean. I had seen it all my life and felt on intimate terms. Columbus and the Pilgrims had crossed the Atlantic, and it touched my country. The Indian Ocean was so far away and so foreign. The family in* Dolphins at Sunset *(the book about a circumnavigation which I read faithfully before we started into each new area) had experienced such a frightening crossing, and here we were on a joy ride.*

My only real fear was at night, when the white foam from our wake rushing past gave me the sensation that we were going too fast. I did find that I couldn't watch bloody movies (e.g. "Platoon") on the TV set Laurie had set up in the cockpit to while away the boredom of those watches. Always nervous on passages, I couldn't relax even on one as easy as this.

Random notes from the log:
    February 6—Ryan running a temperature of 100.8. Cough and sore throat. Carole still has her cold.
    February 7—Ryan better. Carole better. Caught 20 pound tuna and pulled in just the head. Sharks got the rest. "Marita Shan" 111 miles ahead.
    February 10—passed 62 degrees Longitude. Half way around the world. Champagne to celebrate. Caught 3-foot barracuda.

Carole: *Now we were homeward bound. Two years gone and only four or five to go.*

We added a day to the passage by making sure we came no closer than 100 miles from Socotra Island, as we had heard recent reports of pirates and other problems emanating from that place. The wind dropped, and we had 24 hours of absolute calm. We noticed little ripples on the surface, and found them to be caused by thousands of small crabs, each about three inches across the shell. We were 100 miles from the nearest land, in water at least a mile deep, so they were a real mystery.

That night, still dead calm, Carole noticed more than usual flashes of phosphorescence. I shined a flashlight over the side, and the ocean lit up. We seemed to be moving over swarms of either squid or jellyfish that lit up when a light was shined on them. The glow lasted for 30 seconds after the flashlight was switched off. Sweep an "S" we got an "S" glow that extended down for several feet. I got out the spot-light, and we could almost have read by the resultant glow. The show lasted for about 10 miles, and then the animals disappeared.

Carole: *During passages, we got into the habit of spending most of the time, day and night, in the cockpit. Two twelve-feet long padded benches, and one six-feet long, allowed plenty of room for the three of us to be comfortable, asleep and awake. From my perspective it meant that Laurie was always handy if there were problems on my watch. Of course if he were sleeping below, all I had to do was to turn around and call him through the hatch over our bed, but there was something reassuring about actually seeing him right there.*

At times, sleeping in the cockpit took some skill. In rough weather, I would hook one arm around the cockpit cover supports, then slept like a baby, knowing my death-grip would never be loosened.

There were certainly big fish around, as we averaged a snapped line a day. The breakage extended to the spinnaker pole, which cracked at the mast end as we were converting back to normal rig after sailing wing-on-wing (For the non-sailors, this is a sail combination used in following winds, with the main out one side of the boat, and the jib held out on the other, usually by the spinnaker pole.). One day out from Aden, we had dragon flies, moths and a small owl land on various parts of the boat.

The Aden, Yemen, yacht anchorage was also used by local boats. We went to bed the first night alone, and woke in the morning with our three yachts completely surrounded by thirty or so local boats, some in very intimate proximity. They were full of people and goats, both packed tightly.

That was the day when there was a huge explosion in the town, accompanied by a cloud of black smoke and hundreds of crows circling and screaming, enough to wake the dead not already quickened by the blast. We later learned that a bomb, stored for two years in the police-station safe, had exploded spontaneously. Miraculously, no one was badly hurt, but the police station was leveled.

Ryan (10): *"Look, an unexploded bomb. What will we do? I know, let's store it in the office, it will be safe there."*

After anchoring, Pat and Steve and I, the three captains (I am promoted every time we get to port, and every time a toilet stops working) went ashore to check in. The Customs office seemed to be run by the person with a souvenir stand just outside the office door. He gave us clearance in return for $US2 each, tea money, he said. When we cleared out, the stand was manned by the tea lady, who took a second $US2, signed forms we hadn't completed, and told us to fill them in after we left. They were both more interested in selling daggers and shawls. It was really very informal, and we still are not sure whether it was a real office, with real officials, but no one seemed too concerned.

Then it was off to the Immigration office, where we ran into another story. They took our passports, and then asked for $US80 per person, visa fee, in cash. We calmly pointed out that we only wanted to go ashore to provision, not to pay the national debt. They, equally calmly, pointed out that they had our passports. We eventually got a no-charge, 12-hour shore pass, as we claimed lack of funds (true) and a need to get some when we could get to a bank (false).

By this time we had met Omar, reasonable English, fiftyish, hair dyed bright orange, who became our mentor, driver, guide, interpreter and general "whatever you want I can get it wholesale" person. His Number Two was Johnny, sixtyish, who handled water, washing, and took over every time Omar was absent. Then there was young Omar, excellent English, good looking, who seemed to be at war with old Omar. Every time we went ashore, there seemed to be an ever increasing number of people who could do everything for us—for a price, of course.

After our run-in with Immigration, Omar drove us to see the Port Captain. He was a refreshing dose of professionalism, in an air-conditioned office, and speaking perfect English. Referring to the "Immigration bandits" (his words), he promised to intercede on our behalf if we ran into further problems.

The next day we went back to Immigration, as we had to get our passports back to take to the Egyptian embassy for visas. They were most upset we hadn't brought the $US560 (7 people) they were expecting. We explained that we had decided to leave the next day, as the visa cost was too high. After much discussion in Arabic, much fingering of the passports, and much movement from one office to another, they gave us back our passports, plus clearances to enable us to check out. We were not stamped into, or out of, the country, so have no record of ever having been in Yemen. At the time, getting our passports back seemed a major victory.

Omar and Johnny drove us to the Egyptian Embassy and the supermarket, both in the city of Crater. The place was dirty and rubbish strewn. Some buildings were still pockmarked with bullet holes from the recent local war. There seemed to be men everywhere standing round, with very few actually doing something. Many had automatic weapons slung over their shoulders, a few had western style gun-belts, and most had curved knives stuck through belts or sashes. One man, in a white caftan and turban, had a pager hung off his knife handle.

The women seemed to dress in three styles; no veil; veil covering the face except for an eye-slit; and veil completely covering the face, including the eyes. I have to say that the "eye-slit" ladies all seemed to have gorgeous eyes, so maybe the style has merit. The cruiser ladies had to wear long skirts and have their shoulders covered, but were spared the veil.

There were numerous beggars, some just children, and I had to forcibly restrain Carole from giving them everything we had. One lady with a baby got milk, apple juice and bread, and followed us everywhere asking for more. Eventually, I recruited Omar to chase her off, so I could turn around without tripping over her. Ryan reported that she passed her baby over to another "mother," who then approached us as a new supplicant.

The supermarket was well stocked and reasonably priced. They took payment in U.S. dollars, as did everyone we met. The bread looked and smelled good, but turned into crumbs as soon as it was touched. Around the corner, the open-air market had a good selection of fruit and vegetables, with reasonable prices and quality. The fish stalls would carve a tuna for you on request.

The best show in town was the chicken seller. His little stall was surrounded by banked cages of chickens. He would select one, pluck it, gut it, and chop it into quarters so quickly that the legs were still kicking as they were hung on hooks. I am unsure, after long and close observation, as to whether he actually killed the chicken beforehand, or left it to the procedure. A return trip to Aden will need to be made to clear up this controversy.

To refuel, we had to tie up to the Aden Bunkering Company dock, estimate the amount of diesel we needed, get a form from the Senior Bunkering Officer, take the form to the accounts office (different building), pay in U.S. dollars, take the receipt back to the SBO, wait for him to issue a chit to the Pump Operator, find the PO, get fuel, ask the PO to find the Senior Pump Operator, go with the SPO to collect a form saying how much fuel we actually got, have the form signed by some woman behind a door, and by the SBO, back to accounts to get our refund, back to the SPO to give him his "tip."

The tide was out, so the deck was about six feet below dock level. My foot slipped and I fell backwards, caught a pocket on a stanchion, hung suspended for a second or so, then smacked my head on a winch and my back on the deck. Spectators gave me a 9.8 average, deducting marks for not pointing my toes.

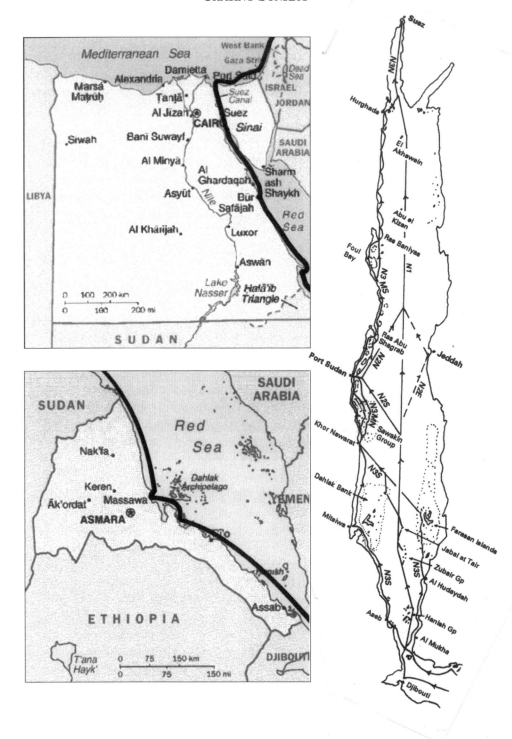

Red Sea, Eritrea, Sudan, Egypt and the Suez Canal

Year Two and Three
February 19 to April 12

The Straits of Bab el Mandeb, the southern entrance to the Red Sea, have a fearsome reputation for strong winds and rough seas. Sporadic warfare had made the islands there unsafe for landing. The tanker and freighter traffic was continuous in both directions, so we stuck to the edge of the shipping lanes and only a few times had to take evasive action. We experienced perfect south-easterly winds, sailed right through on flat seas, and kept sailing for three days. Ryan hooked and lost a 6-foot long dorado, then landed a 25-pound wahoo, a taste of the great fishing to come.

Carole: *Before we left home, there were lots of things Laurie did tell me. He did say our first passage would be the longest, there would be trade winds and big smooth swells, and if there were storms I wasn't to worry, as we would simply turn left and sail away from them. He never mentioned the Straits of Bab el Mandeb, or the dreaded "Big Red."*

Our first African stop was at Howskil Bay, Aguiz Island, about 50 miles south of Mitsawa, Eritrea. Some fishermen came by, one of whom spoke good English (remember where we were to understand how remarkable that was), and invited us to their village. The fishermen worked for the government, and a freezer boat called every five days to collect their catch.

We brought them caps and sandals, drank some very strong, sweet coffee, and were taken a mile to see the well that was their sole water supply. It was a huge hole, some 200 feet in diameter, all dug by hand.

In the rock bottom were holes filled with green/brown/murky water, some open, some covered with boards and mud to keep out the goats, whose presence was indicated by the several skeletons scattered about.

Carole: *Africa! Sitting in the cockpit drinking our sunset wine, the "Out of Africa" CD playing on the stereo, Laurie and I kept pointing out elephants, giraffes and lions to Ryan. They were all windswept acacia trees, but with a little imagination and surrendering to the atmosphere, there they were.*

A flat coral-rock island, mostly no more than five feet above sea level, covered with shells and coral and scattered acacia thorn trees, the only animals Aguiz had were the introduced goats, and millions of birds. We took the dinghy to investigate the masses of birds we could see everywhere. There were huge patches of seaweed and these were almost covered with a tremendous variety of sea birds. Others were always diving into the water. Some low cliffs were completely lined with pelicans. Every now and then, one would fall forward and splash into the sea, coming up with a fish. I think the others then shuffled sideways, as we never saw a gap in the line.

Walking across the island, we discovered many abandoned ruined houses and several graves surrounded by low stone walls. Apart from the one village, there appeared to be no other inhabitants. No water, no real soil, no vegetation other than the thorn trees and some equally prickly shrubs, so one had to wonder why there were houses at all, especially those in the middle, distant from the sea.

An official, just arrived on the freezer boat, came out to chastise us for going ashore without visas. He then forgave us, because we did it to give caps, so the real reason for his visit was probably to relieve boredom, or to demonstrate his importance to the fishermen. As we sailed out, the villagers chased us up the channel to give us fish, as thanks for the presents.

Ryan (10): *They gave us a lot of fish, including a large grouper, a small shark and a moray eel. Because of my fishing, we already had more fish than we could eat. I got a little upset, because Dad won't let me fish until we have eaten the previous catch.*

Our departure was eventful. The engine starter refused to work, so I kicked, pushed and prodded, and took credit for its eventual operation, although I didn't have the faintest idea why it began to work. In the process I knocked off a cooling water hose, so we had to switch off the engine again to replace this. The starter hesitated again, then did its job.

Carole: *After the initial problem, Laurie said we would sail all day with the engine running, as he wasn't sure he could get it started again. Sometimes he can be a real source of comfort! Ryan, doing schoolwork in the salon, heard sparks. Laurie discovered he had displaced a wire, but luckily was able to fix it with the engine going. Then came the overheating, and this time the engine had to be shut down. We were drifting a mile off shore and all I could think of was how far we were from help.*

Ignoring the official warning to get visas before touching land again, we moved to Shumma Island, about half way to Mitsawa. There we met Larry and Mary, a young couple in their mid-20s on a small sailboat, "Troubadour," who had used up all their fuel, cooking oil, kerosene and anything else remotely resembling diesel, to get to the island. They couldn't sail out because of the reef, so "Marita Shan" gave them fuel to get to Mitsawa.

Carole: *Tash steamed the fish we were given as presents and made three kinds of sauces to dip it into. I provided the artichoke-rice salad and mint brownies. Tammy made corn bread with bacon and a haystack salad. Mary told us they were just going to sail the coast of Mexico, then headed west on a whim.*

After 30 years of guerilla warfare, Eritrea separated from Ethiopia and became an independent country about 10 years before we arrived. It was the poorest country in the world, but in contrast to Aden, every place we went to was scrupulously clean, even if pockmarked with bullet holes.

On entering the Mitsawa harbor, the first landmark was Haile Selasie's old palace, partially destroyed by bombs, rockets and gunfire. We tied up at the main cargo wharf just next to a gaping hole caused by a bomb dropped too early to hit the palace. Wheat, a UN food shipment, was being unloaded from a bulk carrier, and bagged on the wharf using a machine made in England, closely attended by thousands of fat pigeons.

Port Captain and Immigration came on board and took our passports away. I was becoming less paranoid about giving our passports to people I don't know, but still got pangs about handing them over to an individual in jeans and sandals, who had no papers to prove his identity, and who went on to offer black-market money changing and laundry services.

With some trepidation therefore, we waited the requested three hours, then went to the Immigration office (turn left at the bomb crater, and go past the bullet-ridden bank building) to collect our visas. There, we watched while the senior official laboriously filled out a form for each person, then glued it onto a page of the passport, carefully spreading the Elmer's glue with his finger. He filled out a second form which I took to a lady in an office down the hall to pay the fee, in U.S. dollars.

I admit to being a little startled when, after I passed over the money, she got up, closed the door to her office, and switched off the lights. She was reasonably good looking, but even for me that was moving quickly. While I was still in a slight state of shock (fortunately speechless), she went back to her side of the desk, got out a little black-light device, and shone it on the bank notes to see if they were forgeries. I was unsure whether to be disappointed, or relieved. Visa payments were discriminatory, $US25 for U.S. citizens, $US30 for Australians and Canadians.

We moved off the wharf to an anchorage well inside the harbor, past the ruined palace. The bottom was mud and poor holding, but there was good protection from the weather, and the smell wasn't too bad.

Ryan (10): *On one dinghy trip to shore we passed a floating dead porcupine. It was all bloated and I wanted to get some quills, but Dad said no.*

A group of us hired a mini-bus, and were driven for three hours to Asmara, the capital of Eritrea. The drive over the mountains gave us precipices, cliffs, remarkable Italian bridges, camel trains, donkeys, eagles, and baboons in various combinations. The clear weather made it a photographer's paradise. Asmara was just another Italian city, stuck in the middle of an African country, with excellent cappuccino (N1.20 per cup, very sweet). The local currency was the Nafka, then being exchanged for seven Nafka per U.S. dollar at the bank, when it was open.

Deciding to dine at the Milano Restaurant, by good fortune we stumbled into a room reserved for locals. It had a wonderful ambience, with weapons and game-heads on the walls, and low tables with stools and couches, each covered with an individual baby goat-skin. Dinner was a four-foot diameter platter, lined with pancake-like sour bread, and covered with heaps of various local dishes, all meat. Correct procedure was to tear off a piece of bread and scoop up some food with it, all with the right hand of course, as the left is reserved for more intimate cleaning functions. Left-handed me had some etiquette problems.

Ryan (10): *A great meal, best ever. Most of the meat was goat, cooked in various ways. Mum kind of picked at the bread.*

The nine of us had a huge amount of food (especially since Carole and Tammy weren't eating much), beer, bottled water, cokes, coffee, local wine, all for under $US5 per person. The wine was not bad, and the coffee superb. A lady, seated on the floor next to the table, roasted the beans over a bed of coals, crushed them in a mortar, then added water that was boiling over another fire. Both fires were lit on the floor.

The drive back was a trial for Carole. At the top of the mountains, fog began pouring over the ridges, just like in San Francisco. From then on we were in dense fog, with minimal visibility, driving down a switchback road with no railings, fences, or marker posts. The problem was we had come up the road, so knew that it was edged by a 1,000-foot precipice for most of the way. Carole was sitting beside the driver, insisting that we stop, stop now, right now, so she could get out and walk the 60 kilometers back to Mitsawa. She helped him steer and brake all the way, and must have done a great job, because we made it. We should stop hiring mini-buses, because the next time we did, we finished up in jail.

Carole: *When I can see the precipice I panic, and I'm even worse when I can't, but know it is there. One happy note was passing a camel caravan swaying down the road, big ones in front, babies behind.*

Back at the dinghy, moored at the main wharf, we found it liberally covered with human excrement. I had the lovely job of cleaning it so we could get back to the boats. Another dinghy, right next to ours, was untouched. When I reported it the next day, the security officials were horrified, and we had a permanent dinghy-guard from then on. We still don't know whether it was some kind of accident, deliberate malice, kids trying to be cute, adults trying to pass some sort of message, or what. It wasn't nice at the time, and I still shudder at the smell and the tactile joy of cleaning the whole boat with a couple of tissues and two sanitary pads one of the ladies happened to have.

After several hours of scrubbing the next day, the dinghy was pronounced fit for use, so we drove to a nearby village to buy fruit and vegetables (potatoes, onions, carrots, limes, papaya, tomatoes, and green peppers). Carole and Ryan were fascinated by the camel trains, and Carole began a love affair with the camel that continues to this day.

Larry ("Troubadour") stayed on in Asmara for a few days, and the next time we saw him he was yellow and weak from contracting a version of Hepatitis. We had shots before we left the U.S., so felt reasonably secure in most places, but still took every precaution. A few weeks after we left Eritrea, war broke out again, and Asmara was bombed.

By the time we left, there were thirteen boats in the anchorage. We were in the second group of boats up the Red Sea, with probably 20 boats ahead of us and 100 behind. Our plan was to day-hop all the way up, being at anchor each day by 2pm. The reasoning behind this was simple. All anchorages are on the west side of the Red Sea, as the east is Saudi Arabia, and they frown on yacht visits. After 2pm the sun is too low to allow us to clearly see the reefs and the narrow entrances to the anchorages. We stuck with our plan, except twice, and we got busted both times.

Every morning there was a semi-formal SSB net to keep track of everyone, and to share weather information. The theory was that the weather the furthest north boats were experiencing would reach the southern boats a day or so later, and it was almost right some of the time. Cruisers were divided into the "straight up the middle and don't stop" group, and our "stop every day" proponents. We made it to Suez in about the same number of days as the other group, and in much better shape.

The three-foot-high, steep-fronted, square waves that built up when northerly winds got over 15 knots brought "Dolphin Spirit," and most other yachts, to almost a dead stop. The pounding became unbearable. Yachts tacking back and forth for a day often finished up miles south of where they started.

Radio transmission was variable, both SSB and VHF. Many times we could hear and speak by VHF (normal range 20 miles) to yachts over 100 miles away, and one memorable day to "Just Magic," a New Zealand boat over 200 miles behind us.

We stayed at Difnein Island for four days, waiting for the north wind to die down and allow us to proceed. It was an open anchorage, and the island was very flat, so we had little protection from the wind, and the swell bent around the corner causing us to roll a lot. Still, it was better than pounding into the waves.

A fishing boat came by and asked for hydraulic oil. I gave them some, and they later returned to give us two huge fish and a moray eel. These boats had up to nine men on board, with absolutely no shelter. They cooked over an open fire on the deck, and slept wrapped in some cloak or light blanket.

Most days we walked on the island. There were turtle tracks and robbed nests, and Ryan found skulls of a dolphin and a goat. One beach was totally covered for almost half-a-mile with a moving carpet of millions of hermit-crabs, which either scuttled away, or retreated into their shells as we approached. The abandoned light tower had a solid foundation, but the steel structure looked well rusted and rickety. On the edge of the sand was a large, broken, cement and brick tank, with walls that were two feet thick. A tremendous effort must have gone into building this in such a remote spot, and now it was abandoned and forgotten.

Every afternoon at around 4pm a pod of dolphins would swim by, and often we got to swim with them. One afternoon, Ryan, Pat and Steve were snorkeling a little distant from where I was in the dinghy, when suddenly I saw two huge fins in the water behind them. They couldn't hear me shouting "Shark," so I scrambled to get the outboard started and the anchor up.

The fins got closer to the swimmers as I raced towards them, only to discover a huge manta ray swimming placidly along with its wing tips surfacing. Ryan caught a lot of fish and thought the place was just great.

Khor Nawarat anchorage presented wild camels with babies, bird skeletons, a huge grey heron, nice coral and another manta ray. For some reason the water at Talla Talla Saqir Island was cool, so we snorkeled over pretty coral in wet suits. The engine starter motor gave trouble again, but we eventually got going. Marsa Esh Shiek Ibrahim was a typical hole-in-the-reef anchorage, with enough room for three or four boats, and entrance markers for a change. There was a small fishing camp on the flat, arid shore. The fishermen, using small sail/paddle boats, skimmed in and out all day.

Here I decided that, before the starter motor failed completely, I would remove it and install the spare. Let me set the scene. We were anchored between "Marita Shan" and "Sky Bird," in a hole in the reef barely big enough for the three boats to swing. Night was falling, and there are no long twilights in the tropics. To get to the engine, I had to pull up the companionway steps and most of the salon floor. Changing the starter motor took almost three hours, as nothing was easy. Eventually I got it installed, and pressed the remote starter switch mounted near the engine.

Carole: *Poor Laurie had to spend hours in all sorts of contorted positions, upside down most of the time. The starter whirred, the engine started and we all cheered wildly, congratulating ourselves on not being stranded in the wilderness. We heard the other boats calling us on the radio, but with all the noise of the engine, we thought they were calling to offer congratulations.*

Replacing the floor and stairs, I climbed into the cockpit to discover we were in trouble. Somehow the gear lever had been knocked into "forward," and using the starter switch at the engine had bypassed the safety interlock. We had dragged the anchor and driven ahead into the dark, reef-filled water. Quickly taking us out of gear, I went forward and pulled up the anchor. Guided by the lights of the other boats we turned around and re-anchored.

The morning light showed how lucky we had been. The wind direction was such that we had pointed up the only crack in the surrounding reef, which shallowed very quickly. A couple more minutes and we would have jammed into the reef. A different wind direction and we would have been on the reef. If the rudder hadn't been set straight ahead, if we had been anchored twenty feet or so to either side, if we didn't have such a big anchor to slow us down, if we hadn't heard the calls, the end would have been very different. We were certainly smiled upon that night.

Suakin, Sudan, was magical, one of our favorites, a place that few foreigners other than sailors get to see. The anchorage was past the gun emplacements on the harbor wall and then a sharp turn to port between the new Suakin and an island covered with the ruins of Old Suakin. Getting into the anchorage required that I drive within 15 feet of the island, so everyone but the captain had a close look. These ruins sparkled in sunlight and were especially romantic with the moonlight reflecting off the white coral stone.

Our agent was Abu Mohammed Hadib, known as Mohammed. The full name was important, as the competition agent was also Mohammed, full name unknown. Mohammed II was waiting on shore with Mohammed I and immediately jumped into the dinghy, refusing to leave until I threatened to get physical. He was most upset at not being the chosen one.

I became the ferryman, with my first task being to take the Port Doctor to each yacht for Health clearance. The doctor was a tiny man, who filled out all the forms himself, with little or no input from the cruisers. His only English was "Flag down," and he wouldn't leave the yacht until the Quarantine flag was on deck.

Then I had to dinghy Mohammed and everyone's passports to the Immigration office at the terminal where the ferries taking pilgrims to and from Mecca docked. Apparently the pilgrims also do significant buying in Saudi Arabia, as all the returnees were burdened with everything from beds to suitcases bursting with clothes and tied with rope. Everyone was yelling at everyone else, but Mohammed walked me to the head of the very long line, and we were ushered into the general's office, where I was given tea while a flunkey took the passports away for stamping. Very civilized!

The Suakin market was wondrous, full of camels, donkeys, men operating sewing machines, blacksmiths using hand-operated bellows, goods and people of every description. We were followed for a very long time by a robed Arab on a camel, with rifle and sword, obviously fascinated by Carole. He was there every time we turned around. Eventually he left, probably to go count his camel herd, so as to make a proper offer for Carole.

Carole: *With these romantic ruins so close to the boat I couldn't do any work and just wanted to wander through them at every opportunity. They were the second rebuild, dating from 1881 and abandoned in 1905 because the unbaked brick and coral stone used in construction started to crumble. Crumbling maybe, but the buildings looked like they were covered in silver glitter in the sun and moon light. Wild flamingos dotted the shallow water, the first we had seen. They were not pink, probably because their diet was deficient in shrimp.*

I adored the market. We were followed everywhere by a gaggle of children, mostly boys, and by men selling swords and combs. The produce was sparse—watermelon, tomatoes, eggplant, potatoes, onions, some bananas, and just five eggs. Men operated sewing machines, making caftans to order. There were cobblers, and a bakery that made the one in Tonga, with the dead pig on the oven, look sanitary. Laurie bought the flat bread that both he and Ryan gobbled up and didn't die.

Sudanese men are tall, dark and handsome, and the one following us on the camel was no exception. He was the real life Rudolph Valentino. Laurie often wonders about how many camels he would have offered for me, and if I am upset with him I suggest that he was lucky I didn't just turn around, climb up on the camel and disappear into the sunset.

Mohammed organized a visit to the Suakin Cultural Center (two rooms with old photos, camel saddles and swords), followed by a real Bedouin dinner. Under a colorful tent, seated on a rug, we watched as Mohammed roasted coffee beans and made sweet coffee, and were then introduced to the dinner, a sheep.

Ryan (10): *I watched the man slit the sheep's throat, then skin it, pull out the insides and cut off the head. He then shoved a long metal rod through the carcass and tied it in place with the sheep's guts. The whole thing was then lifted up and put over a wood fire that had burned down to coals. It took about an hour to cook. The man then used the same knife to carve off pieces of meat for us to eat. Most of the ladies, and of course Mum, ate only tomato salad.*

Through Mohammed, a group of us hired a mini-bus to take us to Port Sudan, the nearest big city, so we could post letters, make phone calls (we couldn't as it turned out), and drink the chocolate milk shakes the place was noted for—best in the Sudan—an enviable reputation, as the nearest cow was a thousand miles away. We walked to the local bus station, an open field, and found our bus hadn't come. Another was immediately appropriated, and the poor Sudanese already on board were taken off, and their baggage thrown down from the top of the bus. We protested, but were ignored, then told if we wanted to go this was the bus to use, so boarded.

The forty-mile drive was along the coast, through desert, with occasional camels, donkeys and Bedouin tent encampments. These looked dusty and desolate, far from the romantic scene of Hollywood films. We saw a freighter that had been run aground more than fifty years ago, during World War II, still standing upright and looking as if it could sail away.

Almost everyone in the city was in Arab dress, and the streets were full of people, with almost no vehicles. Naturally, we sought out the market, and wandered through, bargaining for oranges, grapefruit, tomatoes, eggs, and carrots. Ryan had a burger and THE malt for lunch at the Palace Hotel—local fare!

On the way in we had stopped at two police check-points, one just outside Suakin, the other just outside of Port Sudan. At both places our driver got out, and presumably paid some toll or fee. Returning, we stopped at the Port Sudan control, where the driver simply waited a few moments, then drove on.

We were almost back at Suakin, when two tanker-trucks bracketed our bus, and forced it to a stop off the road. Two men, one in a green uniform, the other in casual civilian clothes, got out. Green Uniform started shouting at our driver. Mohammed got out and started shouting at GU. This went on for a while, and then Plain Clothes entered the bus, came up to me and tried to take my video and still cameras.

While we were engaging in a tug of war, Mohammed said they were now saying we had been seen taking pictures of military things. I was holding on, asking who PC was. "Secret Police," said Mohammed. PC was starting to get nasty, when Carole grabbed the cameras as well. This really threw PC off his stride, particularly when Carole started to peel his fingers, one by one, off the straps. After more tugging, shouting, and general uproar, PC let go, GU got in the bus, and directed the driver to turn around and drive back to Port Sudan.

Mohammed and GU engaged in a long-term shouting match (PC didn't say a word), which didn't stop until Ryan crawled into my lap and started to cry. GU shut up as if he had been switched off, and we rode in fearful silence for the rest of the hour-long return journey. As a sort of comedy sideline, Steve went into contortions to hide his camera bag under his seat when he thought no one was looking, only to remember later that it was full of eggs, and his cameras were in plain view on another seat. We were all just a little freaked out, and not in control.

Carole: *I knew we hadn't filmed any military installations. Laurie was very strict about it because of his experiences in these countries in the past. Steve, on the other hand, had filmed a complete 360 of the anchorage, which included the gun emplacements at the entrance.*

After dropping GU off at his check-point, we continued with PC to town, where we drove into a walled compound, Military and Secret Police headquarters. Wandering around were uniforms with automatic weapons, one with two, one over each shoulder, and more Plain Clothes. PC, Mohammed and the driver disappeared inside a building, while we sat in the bus and counted guns. At least half-an-hour went by, when Mohammed reappeared and said that they wanted my video film to look at that night, but "they will return it tomorrow"—right!

I calmly (selective memory working here) explained that no, they were not getting my film, and even if they took it, they couldn't watch it, as it needed the camera, and a U.S. type TV, but I would be happy to show them anything they wanted to see, now. It was really a bit of a risk, as they could have just said that they would take both film and camera—guns talk! More discussion, and more waiting. Eventually, another PC appeared, apparently a VIP-PC, as he was accompanied by PC flunkies. I was taken off the bus, surrounded by weapons, uniforms and PCs, with the rest of the gang in the bus trying to read my expressions to see what was going on.

VIP-PC asked me to give him a film show. He looked through the last ten minutes of film twice (markets, camels, donkeys, tents, in glorious black and white through the camera viewer), then waved me and my camera back into the bus. That was a long 20 minutes for me, longer for those in the bus who could only guess what was happening.

Carole: *All kinds of thoughts were running through my head—imprisonment in a tumble-down, dirt-floored prison; wondering where Laurie and Ryan were; starving because of the cold, wormy food. In spite of this tumult, I sat calmly, as did the other cruisers, who were probably having the same thoughts. We all sat in silence, waiting. I knew that, if anyone could get us out of this predicament, Laurie could, so I was calm, nervous but calm.*

More waiting, more gun counting. Mohammed, VIP-PC and PCs reappeared and motioned me out again. After emotional farewells all round in the bus, I stepped down, to be greeted by handshakes, advised that it had all been a big mistake, and offered profound apologies. VIP-PC even smiled.

I shook hands with everyone at least twice, even two-gun, and got back into the bus for an ecstatic reunion. Then they couldn't find the driver, so we sweated a while longer. Then the bus stopped at the gate, and we started sweating again, but all they were doing was offering Ryan use of a toilet. It was protected by an almost tangible wall of smell, but I told Ryan he had to go in. Poor kid, he did as he was told, and we drove out of the gate. We eventually got back to Suakin, the one hour drive having taken five and a half hours.

It makes a great story in retrospect, but was very scary while it was happening. Carole was the heroine of the day. Her grabbing the cameras saved them, and probably the rest as well. Ryan was very brave and coped as well as the adults. If they had chosen Steve's video camera to check they would have seen pictures of the gun emplacements at the harbor entrance and we would have really been in trouble. The incident made the decision to leave Suakin easy.

Carole: *The heroine? No, Laurie. I didn't know the gravity of the situation* when I wouldn't let MY possessions be taken. The stupidity of that act, in retrospect. It could have cost us our lives. We were in Sudan!

Inside the reef north of Suakin, the calm water and perfect winds tricked us into an all-night sail. As soon as we were past the point of no return, the wind increased, swung to the north, and we pounded into the short, vertical sided Red Sea chop all the way to Khor Schinab.

Carole: *I went to bed with 20 miles to go to the anchorage, and woke up five hours later with 15 miles still to go, and poor "Dolphin Spirit" doing 0.5 knots over the ground. We could have crawled faster. The possibility of another night at sea loomed. Given all the nights we had spent at sea, this may not seem to be a big deal, but I will always choose a calm anchorage over being bounced around on a rough sail. We made it to the anchorage by early afternoon.*

This was a deeply indented anchorage with a narrow winding entrance, completely surrounded by desert and low bare hills. Ryan, Steve and I climbed one, saw more desert and bare hills, and found camel tracks and the skeleton of a fox-like animal.

Carole: *The water, mirror smooth, reflected the full moon and surrounding hills. There was absolute silence. This had happened to us only a couple of times, as it requires complete stillness and total absence of people. Even a breath of wind creates some sounds.*
We had planned to stay several days, but the calm meant that we had to head north again. No wind was better than wind from the north, and there was no assurance it would last.

The Red Sea was full of fish and dolphins. Every time we dropped a line, we got fish, big fish—tuna, dorado, barracuda and wahoo. We also lost a lot of tackle here, even though we were using 150-pound test line. One dorado that we actually got to the stern before it broke loose, had to have been over six-feet long. Ryan was in seventh heaven. We took a picture of him with almost every fish, for his future wall of fame.

Ryan (16): *Later I found out Dad actually let the big dorado go, as he couldn't face the task of subduing such a big fish, but at the time, he told me the line broke. I hooked a huge tuna, probably over 50 pounds, but all we got on board was the head, with teeth marks more than two inches apart. That shark took the tuna body in one gigantic bite.*

There was very little commercial fishing here, especially compared with the saturation we saw in Indonesia. Apparently most of the fishing boats had been confiscated by the various governments so they couldn't be used to smuggle, or as spy boats. Paranoia perhaps, but the fish were happy.

Ryan (16): *Until I came along!*

Carole: *We didn't always have fish. One day the menu read—roast leg of lamb, mint jelly, mashed potatoes and squash, with lamb sandwiches, homegrown sprouts on homemade Indian bread the next day. Another day was breaded steak, cabbage salad, beets and marinated eggplant. I don't cook this well, or this much, ashore.*

At Marsa Umbella we saw purple jellyfish and a manatee, and snorkeled over a spectacular reef. The wild camels ashore featured a lot of pregnant females and one albino male. A southerly wind blew us north, actually surfing down the waves, and we again opted to continue through the night. In the space of a couple of hours the wind fell to zero, went through 180 degrees, and blew up in our faces. Our pleasant overnight sail turned into another nightmare of head winds and pounding seas.

We decided that it was all too hard and headed for Ras Banas. Thank goodness for G.P.S. and radar, as the night was pitch black, no lights on the shore, which was only about five feet above sea level anyhow, charts that were unreliable, and no navigation aids at all. We worked our way behind the reef (which didn't show up on radar) and out of the swells, and waited for daylight to see if we were where we thought we were, and we were.

For six days the wind howled through the rigging at over 30 knots. We rapidly became full of sand and dust, but we were safely at anchor behind the reef. Several times the water-maker intake clogged with some sort of sticky jellyfish. We were at 24 degrees latitude, so well out of the tropics, and the water was cold, even without the wind chill. The flotilla built up to include "Lady Kathryn," "Osprey," "Shanty," "Tranquility," "Marita Shan," "Sky Bird," "Dolphin Spirit" and "Mimosa," a French yacht.

Ryan (10): *I helped Tash bake a birthday cake for Pat. She also taught me how to make pizza and pancakes from scratch.*

Carole: *The cake was baked in my Grandmother's favorite pan. I was heartbroken when it fell from my bag into the sea and wasn't found by a scuba search. Laurie has lost several glasses overboard, and I have lost a lot of clothing I thought I securely pegged to the line, but this was the worst loss, although saying that sounds so silly now.*

The Egyptian army visited, young chaps who really wanted just to see fresh faces I'm sure. Their outpost was a couple of huts on a sand hill, so life must have been miserable with the wind and dust. I didn't see any roads or vehicles, and there certainly was no electricity they didn't make themselves. Why they were there at all, except perhaps as a symbolic presence, I really don't know. This was a disputed area between Egypt and Sudan, so we had to guess which courtesy flag to have up, and luckily chose the right one.

We managed to get ashore, and paid a return visit to the eight soldiers and their captain. One walked the shore with us, as there were land-mines scattered around. After the soldier showed us where a land-mine had been dug up the previous day, right on the beach where we would normally walk looking for shells, I turned to see Carole carefully stepping only in my foot prints. Life in the Red Sea! Depth-charges and bullets in tires in Sri Lanka, bomb explosion in Aden, land-mines in Egypt, all certainly kept us from being bored. Ryan couldn't wait for the next challenge.

I am almost sure I got this correctly, but as we had no Arabic, and they had no English, errors could have occurred. We were explaining where we had been, and mentioned an island where we had spent a couple of days. They said (?) this island had been heavily mined and never cleared, so we were fortunate to have survived.

Being weather bound wasn't so bad. Ryan and Carole gardened, growing sprouts for wonderful sandwiches made on the bread Carole baked every day. They also learned to play Backgammon (part of Ryan's school assignments, as he was learning about Egypt, and this had been a popular game here through the ages), and held daily tournaments. Ryan's piano playing progressed well, and he moved way ahead with school work.

Carole: *Ryan and I read "Lonely Planet's" guide to Egypt, and I created a test for Ryan and the other cruisers on the Egyptian dynasties.*

I completed a lot of little jobs on the boat, and dove to free "Mimosa's" and "Tranquility's" anchors from coral-heads and boulders. Carole cooked gourmet meals every day, so life, apart from being coated in dust, was good. The coating of sand and salt that we gained set like stone and resisted cleaning for several months.

"Osprey" and "Lady Kathryn" decided to leave before the wind died, and we watched them pounding into the seas, thankful it wasn't us. Later that day "Osprey" hit a reef, but got off, losing only a golf-ball sized chunk from their keel. Rough seas make it even more difficult to spot coral.

After six days of being sand-blasted and dust-coated, the wind dropped to 15 knots so we took off. It immediately went back to 25 knots, and we pounded into head-seas all day. This meant we would reach the anchorage at Wadi Gimal after dark, and we never, never, enter a new anchorage at night by choice. I spoke on VHF with "Lady Kathryn" who had just left that anchorage, and got the way points and directions. We took a deep breath and headed in—a very scary business, even under those conditions.

To make matters more interesting, after we had threaded our way through the reefs into position, the anchor chain jammed on the way down. Here was the situation; pitch black night; 25 knots of wind; island in front of us we could see only on radar; reef all around us that we could not see by eye, or on radar; me upside down in the anchor locker trying to unsnarl chain; Carole driving, trying to stay in the one spot; Ryan calling depths; some anxiety all round.

Then I got stuck getting out of the anchor locker, lost some skin and gained some bruises. The anchor finally went down, and we had lamb chops for dinner. The wind was again blowing at 30 knots, all the way up to Suez (SSB net report), so we stayed for two days, but we were 60 miles closer to the Canal.

Carole: *It was nerve-wracking. Laurie just said, "Keep the boat in the same position, there are reefs all round us," and disappeared below to untangle the anchor chain. How do I do that, when there were no points of reference, the night was pitch black, and I had no idea if there was a current running? Was there a reef just in front of us? Behind us? I just used the compass to keep pointing in the right direction, applied power when I thought we had moved, and hoped for the best. Laurie FINALLY re-appeared and the anchor went down. Then he had the audacity to ask for dinner!*

Ryan (10): *A south-bound yacht was anchored inside the reef, and the two teenage boys on board took me to a small island the next day to run around, and shoot at targets with their bow and arrow. I was sorry they were there for only a day. I caught two huge squid with my squid jig and gave them to Tash. She let me help her stuff them.*

Southerly winds and smooth seas meant that we moved, and we went overnight to Safaga, the entry port for Egypt. Because the winds were southerly there were seas breaking over the wharf where we were supposed to go to clear Immigration and Customs, so we went straight to the anchorage off the Paradise Hotel. Naturally this was a major No-No, and got us into hot water with the authorities—again!

We (captains off four boats) caught a taxi to the Police/Immigration office, and five hours later got cleared in. In the meantime, we sat, were lectured to by everyone from a Captain to a General, sat some more, drank sweet tea and a hot fruit drink which was surprisingly good, stared at the automatic weapons all round us, wondered at the buses and trucks full of pilgrims going to and from Mecca, received more lectures, and finally were given clearances. The General said we were not being put into jail because we had visas and, "You just made a small mistake." At least we got to meet a General, and shake his hand. Do it the right way, and you get cleared in less than 30 minutes, but get to meet only privates.

The fleet built up to 12 and included "Dolphin Spirit,"(1) "Marita Shan," "Sky Bird," "Just Magic," "Encore," (2) "Mimosa," "Shanty," "Dasein," (1) "Fog City," "Gigolo," "Honey Bee," "Troubadour" and "Zandunga" (1). Children on board are shown in parenthesis. We took a mini-bus (incident free) to the tourist center of Hurguda to organize a tour for everyone to Luxor. Hurguda had a number of large hotels and probably an equal number half-built. Unfortunately, both types seemed to be equally occupied.

Ryan (10): *My friend Kennedy on "Dasein" arrived. They had a very bad trip with a lot of breakdowns and rough weather. His parents and he took a break and stayed in the hotel for a few days, and I stayed with them.*

"Dasein" was an interesting story. They and "Encore" had originally begun in one of those "Round the World in 18 Months" organized groups, but got tired of the regimentation and the need to keep moving, so peeled off in Bali, where we met them. Having a boy Ryan's age on a boat planning to go up the Red Sea at the same time as we were seemed too good to be true, and it was. We met only sporadically between Bali and the Red Sea, then they had engine problems and spent several weeks in Somalia getting them fixed. This put them well behind us, so they decided on the "straight up the middle" method and were beaten up badly, finally catching us in Safaga. Kennedy's father got sick during their Canal transit, they were on "fast-track" to get back to Florida before school started in September, so they finally left the boat in the Balearics and flew home.

A somewhat amusing anecdote (it may even be true) about one of these round-the-world sailing marathon groups involves an Australian who was on his third circumnavigation and was quietly anchored in the South Pacific somewhere (nameless for reasons which may become obvious). A yacht entered the anchorage, came over to him and said, "We are the first boat in the XYZABC Round the World Group. There are about forty boats coming in. You are in the best spot, so would you please move, as we like to be together." The Australian's response was probably anatomically impossible.

A better story, about true cruising camaraderie, happened in Safaga. A yacht, with husband and wife aboard, was hove-to in the middle of the Red Sea for two days because of high winds and an overheating motor. Carole and some of the women in our group took turns staying up to talk over SSB with the lady when she was on watch at night, as she was very concerned about their situation. She later said that this constant encouragement was what got her through the ordeal.

Four months earlier there had been an "accident" (Egyptian phrase), when more than 60 tourists were shot and killed in front of the Temple of Queen Hatshepsuf at Luxor, so there was some trepidation amongst the cruisers about going.

Carole: *There was more than some trepidation. The gunmen had not only killed the tourists, they had chased them down one-by-one and shot them. Why did it have to be us testing to see if it was an isolated incident?*

The Egyptians were also very concerned about our safety, as we were the largest group to visit Luxor since the "accident." We were taken in a convoy from Safaga to Luxor (3 hours) with trucks and jeeps full of guards at the front and rear. At the tombs and temples there were guards everywhere. Most wore uniforms, and all had automatic weapons, which unfortunately seemed to be pointed in our direction. They had this disconcerting habit of keeping their finger on the trigger at all times, which made me a little nervous as I was sure the safety was off. Ryan was quite taken with the guards on the return convoy, all in plain clothes, and who mostly had the latest Hecklers, a truly vicious looking automatic weapon, only about 18 inches long. Naturally we had to ask for a close look at one, which we got, with no problems.

Ryan (10): *We stopped halfway for something to eat, and I got to have my first camel ride. I wasn't ready for the lurch he gave in getting up, but it was really smooth when we got going. Mum thought he was a good looking camel.*

An advantage of traveling at this uncertain time was that we did not have crowds at any of the attractions, in fact, we were mostly alone. Egypt was really feeling the tourist drop off, and we were everywhere greeted, even on the streets, by cries of "Thank you for coming."

The tombs in the Valley of the Kings were better than our best expectations, and the Temples of Karnak and Luxor better still. We went to Karnak in the day, and again at night for the light show, which was worth the entire trip in itself. Karnak covers 2,000,000 square meters, with huge columns, marvelous carvings, spectacular vistas and statues. St. Peters Cathedral in Rome would fit into a small corner of this place.

In the Valley of the Kings we descended into several tombs, including that of Nefratti. It is a barren, desolate spot in the hills where all these magnificent burial places hide. Looking around, I could believe hundreds were still awaiting discovery. Paradoxically, the biggest problem in tomb excavation is caused by silt and rocks, washed into the tombs by the very infrequent flash-floods.

Carole: We hired a horse-drawn carriage and rode through the Souk (market). Men were sitting in groups by the side of the road puffing away at their water-pipes. The crowds parted to let us through, then closed in behind. Every sort of ware was being sold and even plastic buckets looked exotic in this setting. Laurie saw everything through the video camera lens, with Ryan and I pulling on him to take this, be sure to get that, and how could you have missed those old men playing Backgammon.

Ryan (10): We were supposed to sail on the Nile in a felucca, but there was no wind, so the crew had to row. I helped pull on one oar. We ran into a bunch of reeds near the shore, but got off easily. Later I made some papyrus in a papyrus factory to show how easy it was.

Our hotel room looked out over the Nile, which was the foreground to a magnificent sunset, and was wonderfully lit by the sunrise through the cooking smoke. We couldn't miss on this trip.

Carole: Not quite. I was very sick with stomach flu the night we got back to the boat, as were a number of the others. Luckily it hit after the long ride back, as I lost control over my fluid exits. The food had been so delicious for the whole trip, except for the McDonalds we had for lunch on the last day. Can't trust that exotic Scottish food. We did eat at McDonalds in each of Fiji, Australia and Singapore without problems.

Arriving at Safaga meant that we had only 200 miles of the Red Sea to go, only 200 miles and the dreaded Big Red would be behind us. That last 200 miles to Port Suez took us a long, long, five days, as we day-hopped, and waited for weather windows.

First day out, the weather caught us once again, so about midnight we decided to try for the Ras Gharib anchorage. We led the way in, a role that should have been taken by "Gigolo," the only steel boat in the fleet. There were no navigation aids, just the way points provided by the *Red Sea Pilot*, which on my charts plotted as right in the middle of the reef. Deciding to trust the *Pilot*, we gingerly felt our way in—if the movement of a blind, bouncing cork can be so described, and anchored. The morning light revealed we had dropped anchor on the reef, but were swinging over sand.

Red Sea, Eritrea, Sudan, Egypt, and the Suez Canal

Unfortunately, although better than the open sea, the anchorage was exposed to wind and waves, so we had a day and a night of rolling and pitching, bad enough to keep us from moving about inside the boat. With justification we named it "the Anchorage from Hell."

Carole: *Laurie was at the bow getting ready to drop the anchor and I was driving the boat, when I noticed two huge cockroaches crawling on the cushions. We were in a really dangerous situation and all I could concentrate on were those black horrors crawling near me. Our first cockroaches—were they mating?*

Next morning, Laurie told me to stay in bed, as I wouldn't be able to cook, or do anything else, and would only get sick, so I lay in bed for the whole time we were anchored, looking out the porthole. First I saw the sea, then the sky, then the sea, then ....

The Red Sea narrowed, and with Egypt on both sides now we had a wider choice of anchorages. One, on the east side, was completely lined with partly built, and apparently abandoned, hotels and resort complexes. At another, a soldier waved at us, and we chose to interpret this as friendliness rather than a request to come ashore. Freighter and tanker traffic increased in density.

Our agent in Port Suez called himself Prince of the Red Sea, and answered to "Prince." He met us and escorted us to a mooring. I asked Prince if we could use a credit card to pay him, and he said that he needed cash. In response, I made some weak joke, and he then said that, if we didn't have the money (approximately $US300), he would trust us to send it some time in the future. This was a first for me. We paid the cash.

Prince's eldest son was the Malta and Canada Consul. One visit to his office coincided with the day Muslims give food and gifts to the less fortunate. As we walked up the steps, we passed the usually pristine, white bathroom, and it was hard to miss the blood running down the walls and into the drain from the two sheep being slaughtered there, for later dispersal to the poor. It made perfect sense, as the drains were there, together with water for washing, but the ladies showed some reluctance towards later use of the facility.

Ryan (16): *I remember the blood, and a cage with two canaries in it. The office furniture had hairy cowhide covers.*

Carole: *Planning to have the freezer empty by the time we got to Suez, I succeeded, even if we did have to suffer several days of steak and eggs for breakfast. We did run out of potatoes, onions and fresh fruit, but had plenty of canned fruit to keep the guys happy. An empty freezer meant no food loss while we were touring Cairo and the boat was unattended.*

Chasing Sunsets

Our Cairo visit lasted two days. Carole absolutely loved riding a camel around the Pyramids and out into the desert. Ryan preferred a horse. After 30 minutes on a camel, the muscles on the insides on my thighs started screaming, and got progressively louder for the remaining 90 minutes. I was certain I would never walk again, but recovery was only a cold beer away.

Dorothy ("Gigolo") was hoisted into the air by one leg, when her camel stood up as she was mounting. Steve's ("Sky Bird") horse simply lay down on its side, pinning Steve's leg under it. They lay there, in exactly the same position as if they were in motion, just rotated 90 degrees and still. In both instances it was very difficult not to laugh, so we didn't try.

Carole: *Steve is the smallest and slimmest of us all, so the horse must have been in a bad way if it couldn't take him. I was so glad I chose a camel.*

Ryan (10): *We were standing outside our hotel waiting for a bus. Pat gave me a balloon and I burst it. Immediately we were surrounded by soldiers with guns pointed at me.*

We were allowed to climb up on only the first few tiers of the pyramids, not right to the top. Dad had to haul me up as the stones were so big. Later, Pat, Steve and I went on a tour of the inside of a pyramid. Dad didn't go as the passages were too low for him.

Carole and I sat in the hotel bar, watching Ryan swim in the pool, with the Pyramids looming overhead only a couple of hundred yards away. We saw rugs being woven, walked through another huge Souk and visited the Mohammed Ali (the original, not the pugilistic one) Mosque, which provided a panoramic view over Cairo to the Pyramids.

Cairo Museum was a must, with huge statues, Tutankhamen's stuff, mummies and other Egyptian artifacts. We did get to visit with real mummies, and we could still see what the people looked like, after 5,000 years. Sadly, we were mummied-out after two hours.

Carole: *In 1976, when the King Tut exhibit visited America, my fifth-grade class and I were among those chosen to see it. How lucky I felt to be seeing it then, even dressing my students in King Tut T-shirts for the occasion. I never dreamed that one day, in Egypt, I would be seeing it again, plus all the other treasures that didn't get to the U.S., and I could take my time without having to continually check every member of my class was accounted for and not touching anything.*

Cairo had 17 million inhabitants and horrible traffic. Traffic-control

Red Sea, Eritrea, Sudan, Egypt, and the Suez Canal

police stood on the side of the road and flicked fingers to indicate which lane was to move. Merging and crossing traffic seemed to happen through some sort of osmosis, with every driver leaning on his (no women drivers here) horn and heading for where he wanted to go, regardless. Hesitant drivers would die of old age waiting for a real space.

Prince arranged for the Suez Canal transit and threw us a farewell party, complete with cake. The pilots were delivered to the yachts by tug, and if you didn't have a carton of cigarettes for the tug crew, the big black tires used as fenders accidentally left equally big black marks on your topsides. We had a pilot for each of the two transit days, and a third one to take us two miles through Port Said. Fortunately all three were nice (a relief, as there were all sorts of horror stories around about the pilots). We gave the first a present of $US10, the second the same, but he then asked for another $5, soap, T-shirts, and cigarettes, but quite nicely. The third was the only one in uniform, and was quite offended when offered a "present."

After all the build-up, the actual Canal transit was uneventful. It is simply a ditch in the sand. All we saw from the boat was the ribbon of grey water and piles of sand on both sides. Supertankers going past about 50 feet away helped to keep us from getting too bored. The only real excitement came when our pilot was screamed at over the VHF by another pilot, because he had us cross the canal in front of a freighter, instead of behind.

Yachts were required to anchor overnight at Ismalia, about half way up, and finish the next day. We dropped off our pilot by going bow-in to a dock and holding while he stepped off. Not exactly an easy maneuver to finish the day. There had to be something in the Ismalia mud, as our anchor came up the next morning looking as if it had been dipped in acid.

Carole: *We celebrated our third cruising Easter. Ryan was now too old for the Easter Bunny to visit on his yellow jet ski, but he and I made chocolate Easter eggs from a recipe given to me by my Grandma. Ryan delivered them to the other boats anchored with us.*

We didn't stop in Port Said, just dropped the pilot off on the run and sailed through into the Mediterranean, and on to Ashkelon, Israel. We had made it up the Red Sea and through the Suez Canal, all in one piece; relatively unscathed; coated with a mixture of salt, sand and dust that looked and felt horrible; with lines so full of dirt they stood out straight; with an empty freezer (Ryan complained about two meatless days); with a lot of wonderful memories, and a determination to not do it again. It had been a great trip, with less than 10 hours of really bad weather (some boats had less than 10 hours of good weather), only one really bad anchorage, and never at sea had winds over 35 knots, or seas over five feet.

CHASING SUNSETS

Carole: *Something else Laurie didn't tell me: Six months later, in Marmaris, Turkey, over cocktails, Pat ("Marita Shan") made casual mention of the night everyone thought we had been hit by a tanker. Laurie looked a little sheepish, as he had deliberately not told us about the incident.*

It was during the first night passage at the bottom of the Red Sea, where the sea lanes for the big ships were quite narrow. "Dolphin Spirit" was between the "up" and "down" lanes, ahead of "Marita Shan" and "Sky Bird" who had chosen to sail close to shore. When ships appeared, I would move more to the middle, and the other two closer to shore. Several had passed with no problems. I always started the engine, as a precaution.

Then the next tanker blew its whistle, immediately changed course and headed directly for us. It was so close that, if we doubled back and the tanker returned to its original course, we would have had no chance, so I chose the full throttle, straight ahead option. For the longest time I stared mesmerized at the red and green running lights getting bigger and bigger, as seeing both meant the tanker was heading straight for us. Finally, the red went out and the wall of steel slid by less than 100 yards from our stern.

Israel, Jordan, Egypt and Cyprus

Year Three
April 13 to May 30

A full-moon night, nice winds and flat seas, were terrific introductions to the Mediterranean. We were approaching Israel and I was having a preparatory shower, when Ryan called down,
"Dad, the Navy wants you."
"Tell them I'll call back."
"No, Dad. You've got to come NOW!"
Quickly, I pulled on a pair of pants and ran up to the cockpit. There was a gunboat circling, with all guns pointed at us. We convinced them that we were who we were, and apologized for missing a check-in. The Israel Navy had called us when we were about 50 miles out, and we were supposed to then check-in every ten miles after that. A little later we were buzzed by a fighter jet, and a helicopter gunship sniffed around us just outside the marina. The country appeared to be just a little security-minded.

Ashkelon Marina entrance had a moving sandbar right in the middle, so getting in was nerve-wracking. We made it, but the next day a yacht got stuck, and was there for most of the day arguing with the Marina about who would pay for the large towing charge. The Marina was still under construction, but there was electricity and fresh water—water to wash off the salt and sand of the Red Sea. The security continued with two very polite policemen opening every locker as soon as we tied up. Looking for bombs, they said.

Most ports of entry allow only the captain ashore to complete formalities, but here all of us had to take a taxi to Ashod for Immigration and Customs There we found the offices closed because of Passover. Someone took pity on the forlorn looking rabble we were, and opened the offices especially for us. Back at the marina, "Zandunga" arrived and Ryan had his friend Jennifer to play with again.

Ryan (10): *This was the first time I went to check-in with Dad. I was so bored. I wandered around and picked some wildflowers for Mum.*

Surrounded by construction and large stretches of bare ground, we were constantly in a dust cloud, but apart from that the marina made an excellent base from which to explore Israel. What other marina can boast an archaeology dig right at the entrance? We checked out the new finds every day on our walk to the El Pancho restaurant, where we continued our tradition of eating local food. What is more Israeli than steak and chicken tacos?

By happy co-incidence we were witnesses to the festivities marking the 50th anniversary of the founding of the State of Israel. The three of us climbed the seawall next to the marina and went to the celebrations at the nearby town. The whole place was given over to pedestrians, dancing, outdoor entertainments, and probably the best fireworks display we have ever seen. The golden rainfall lasted and lasted.

We hired a car and drove to Jerusalem a few times, to Tel Aviv, the Dead Sea, the Sea of Galilee, Akko, Golan Heights, Nazareth, Haifa, and generally around. It was difficult to follow our normal pattern of finding things by getting lost, because the sign-posting was so good, and a wrong turn caused us to quickly run out of country. Ryan and I speculated that Israel was so small the jet fighters, which flew overhead every few minutes during the day, would hardly have time to get their wheels up before running out of air-space.

Bobbing around in the Dead Sea, we proved you really can lie back in the water and read a book, and have the photos to prove it. Carole, who never has to tread water, and floats with her shoulders out of fresh water, had trouble getting her knees wet. The water looked normal, but felt oily because of the high salt concentration. From the surrounding hills we could see that the Sea was drying up.

The ruins of Masada, covering the top of a small plateau, were accessed by cable car or several hundred steps. After some debate, we went by the cable car, as I had already had my daily exercise reading in the Dead Sea. The citizens of Masada probably chose the site as one that could be easily defended, but they had great views as well, if they ever looked past the Roman Legions that besieged them for three years. During that time, the Romans built a sloping ramp to get up to the walls, over a thousand feet above the surrounding plain. It was still there, as were the outlines of the Roman camps around the foot of the plateau. We asked ourselves how many of our modern buildings would be there 2,000 years from now.

New Jerusalem is a very pretty city, built entirely out of local stone around the Old City. We stood on the walls of David's Tower in the Old City, right where Jordanian riflemen stood only 30 years ago, to fire at the Israelis. That brought home the fragility of the political situation there and caused us to wonder about the inability of people to co-exist peacefully.

The Wailing Wall, the Stations of the Cross, and all the other renowned sites, were reached only by passing through miles of winding alleyways, completely lined with shops and stalls. There must have been several thousand, each selling seemingly identical wood carvings (olive wood, hand made, master craftsman, unique, best price, don't tell anyone what you paid because it is so cheap, special price because you are my first customer today), fake icons, and statues. We did buy olive-wood statues and beautiful Jerusalem-ware wine and champagne glasses.

Walking through without a guide meant we were almost continually lost, but then if we had been guided we would have missed so many of the sights, sounds and smells that made the experience so memorable.

Carole: Certainly the wares may have been recently made (even the antiques), but walking through gave me the feeling of being back in time. Jerusalem! I had dreamed of going there when I was a child in Bible class and now I was here, and it was better than I had imagined. I had been giving Ryan daily Bible lessons and he was seeing the places that featured so prominently. Read and then see is much to be preferred to read, wait 50 years, then see.

Laurie was not raised in a religious atmosphere and therefore some of what he has written below I find to be in poor taste.

There was a flat stone at the entrance to the Church of the Holy Sepulcher, supposedly where Jesus' body was laid after being taken down off the cross. People were kissing it, rubbing it with rosaries and pieces of cloth and generally being overtly pious. We had to line up to see Jesus' tomb, a 40-minute wait. What was once a cave has had the rock carved away all round it, so that it now stands above the floor of the church, surrounded by pink marble. Inside, instead of the plain rock that would have made the place seem real and spiritual, was one of the tackiest conglomeration of tinplate figures I have ever seen.

Ryan (10): And the candle smell was horrible.

Long-haired, black-coated and hatted Hassidic Jews were easy to identify among the groups paying homage at the Wailing Wall. Showing my crassness no doubt, I was fascinated by the power of this seemingly commonplace stone wall, and by the devotion it drew. Each person seemed to have a different method of worship. Some simply touched the wall and stood silent; others stood and bobbed their heads rapidly; others took quick steps forward and back, with and without the head bobs. At another place, these "dances" would have been ludicrous, perhaps humorous, but here they were appropriate, simply part of the overall atmosphere the Wall generated.

From the Mount of Olives was a clear view of the city, over the huge cemeteries that lie on the slopes. The graves were covered with rocks, placed there by mourners as a sign of respect. Our guide through the Garden of Gethsemane had two Masters degrees in Israel history, and was working on her third, She noted that the olive trees were only (!) 1,500 years old (core samples as proof), but that the site was somewhere in the right vicinity of the Biblical garden. We then walked past a local priest assuring a group of tourists that this particular olive tree was over 2,500 years old and was the actual one Jesus stood under. The same with the Stations of the Cross. They are in the general area, but were marked by Constantine's mother, around three hundred years after Christ, so are pretty random (our guide), are the real thing (local guide). Why be precise? Celebrate and revere the spirit, not the thing.

Ryan (10): *We stopped at a rather ordinary looking valley, and our guide said that this was the place where David slew Goliath. It was like that all through Israel. Places that don't look special have thousands of years of history, and are the sites for stories I studied in the Bible. I read the Old and New Testaments, and memorized many verses as part of my schoolwork.*

A U.S. friend had a brother who moved to Jerusalem, so I called and arranged a meeting in a local hotel.

"How will we recognize you?" I asked.

"That's easy. I have glasses and a beard and look like a Jew."

He managed to sort us out from the crowd, took us to an excellent restaurant and on an insider driving tour. One street was to be avoided on the Jewish Sabbath, as the residents throw stones at passing cars for defying the Sabbath rules.

Bethlehem, controlled by the Palestine Authority, was dangerous to drive through, so our guide drove us in her car to visit Jesus' birth site, a cave under a church. Again, tacky reigned supreme, inside and out. The church was surrounded by businesses such as the Manger Mini Market, Wise Men Souvenirs, Bright Star Hotel, and these were the ones with good taste. It is sad that such a significant and holy site has been allowed to become just another tourist trap.

I had to go to Tel Aviv, a big city with traffic problems, to get a document notarized at the U.S. Embassy, because some hide-bound U.S. institution could not conceive that my signature could be genuine unless an American consul so certified. Do not believe Embassies are there to serve their citizens. The U.S. Embassy would notarize documents only on Tuesdays between 1pm and 3.30pm, then had the gall to charge $US50 for the "service." There were two U.S. Consulates in Jerusalem, East and West. West referred everyone to East, and so was generally known to be Spook Headquarters. A roof that fairly bristled with antennae may have been an additional clue. East provided the same "service" as in Tel Aviv.

The Golan Heights, along the border with Jordan and Syria, were a place of war and tension, so we were nervous going there. When we didn't see another vehicle for more than two hours, and drove by many blown-up and burnt tanks, we got positively twitchy. What did others know that we didn't? Signs saying "Minefield, Keep Out" didn't help, nor did driving through a deserted town that had been totally destroyed by bullets and shells.

Stopping to let Ryan climb into the turret of one of the abandoned tanks, we found some of the controls still appeared to be in working order. Our first human in hours walked across the fields to join us at the tank, and we greeted him with real relief. A Canadian from the UN forces in the area, he told us not to worry too much about land-mines, as the minefields were "mostly fenced." Now wasn't that comforting?

Crusader-built Nimrod Castle sprawled across the top of a mountain, and was exactly what I imagined a castle should be. Unfortunately, imagination had to remain as my guide, as it was closing for the day when we arrived.

Nazareth also covered a mountain, but was paralyzed by a major traffic jam, so we drove around, great views, but no church visits—traffic jams do some good sometimes (**Carole:** *Laurie!*).

> Akko was an old city full of winding alleys, small shops and interesting old structures.
>
> Haifa was uninteresting at street level, but it looked pretty from the top of Mt Carmel.
>
> Cesaria had excellent Roman and Crusader ruins.
>
> Tiberius was all hotels and hills, with a great view of the Sea of Galilee.
>
> Megiddo had 25 layers of civilization on view—incredible history right there, an arm's length away. It was awesome in the true sense of the word. In the U.S. and Australia we revere anything over 100 years old!
>
> Back in Ashkelon, the young man in jeans, with a huge automatic pistol

shoved into his belt, walked into the bank and was completely ignored by everyone but me. The man ahead of me had a pistol in a holster at his side and walked through, but the supermarket security guard stopped *me*, to search my tiny hip pouch. Guns were very evident in Israel. Soldiers (male and female) on leave were everywhere, each at all times carrying an automatic rifle slung over the shoulder. When they were standing, the barrel pointed down, but when sitting it went horizontal, and had to point at someone. This was a little disconcerting in a movie theater, a restaurant, or on a bus.

Carole: *If I was a school teacher in Israel, I'd think twice before setting up field trips. First the school must get police permission. Then the accompanying parents and the teacher go to the police station and are issued automatic weapons for the day, if they don't have their own. Being in Israel gives new understanding to the term "siege mentality."*

I did find a great hairdresser and got the best cut of the trip. He introduced me to a L'Oreal hair treatment that I have been able to find only in Europe and which did wonders for my hair, now grown very long.

Mobile phones were everywhere, almost as prevalent as in Singapore and Hong Kong. A pistol on one hip and a phone on the other was dress unique to Israel. Instead of BC, Israelis use BCE—Before the Common Era—and CE for AD. English is taught in schools from Grade three or four, but we were surprised by the lack of English comprehension, particularly in the cities away from the tourist areas.

Israel was expensive, at least equivalent to U.S. prices, a real shock after the places we had been to in the past year. To compensate, fruit and vegetables were excellent and plentiful, even Jerusalem artichokes.

Ryan (10): *I learned to eat artichokes here, as Mum bought them every day. She served them with butter, or soy sauce and mayo, in salads, with curried rice and with lemon chicken. I was lucky she didn't put them in my morning cereal.*

Together with Kurt and PL ("Osprey"), we hired a van and drove through the desert for five hours to Eilat, in the very south of Israel, on the Red Sea. From there, we took a one-day, organized tour to Petra, Jordan. To do this, we had to check out of Israel, 57 shekels ($US17) per person, then check into Jordan, 44 dinars ($US66) for U.S. citizens, 22 dinars for Australians. No food or drink, including water, could be taken into Jordan, for the openly stated reason of forcing us to buy in Jordan. Our hotel had given us a boxed breakfast to eat before we got to the border. Now breakfasts are different in different countries, but did they really mean to include that carton of sour cream?

The Jordan city of Akabah is a continuation of Eilat, around the head of the Gulf. This is the city Lawrence of Arabia captured by crossing a previously impassable desert. It was the major port for Jordan, and full of trucks waiting to transport goods, as there was no railway. A large part of the port had been rented by Iraq, so they could import and export material. So much for the UN embargo. By what intrigue did we discover this nefarious information? We drove through the port area, and our guide told us! He also pointed out that Akabah was five times the size of Eilat, and had only six hotels, while Eilat had over sixty. Perhaps the Jordanian practice of charging to walk on the beaches, extra for swimming, had something to do with the dearth of tourism.

Petra, "That rose red city, half as old as time," had been haunting me for years, and finally I had the opportunity to see it. The entrance is a mile-long, narrow, winding slash in the mountains, with walls over 100 feet high, carved channels for water pipes running down both sides, and assorted statues every hundred feet or so. The city at the end of the canyon was built more than 3,000 years ago, and the first building we saw, the so-called Treasury, cut into the solid rock, showed few signs of wear. Bedouin rifle fire, in the last fifty years, had destroyed some of the statues on the fascia, but the place was still inspiring.

All the edifices carved into the rock walls were tombs. The residential and commercial city was further up the canyon, where it opened out a bit. Those buildings were built in the open, of stone blocks, and were totally destroyed by an earthquake about 700 AD. All that was left were piles of rocks. The tombs weren't damaged—build for the dead, not the living!

The Romans conquered the city about 2,000 years ago. Part of the floor of the entrance canyon is the original Roman road, built to make it easier for the chariots. The Roman stone pavement is still there, and as we walked on it, I fancied I could hear the tread of the Legions, marching off to defend or extend the Roman Empire. We saw the ruts in the stone, worn by the chariots over the centuries. One of the canyon walls had been carved into about 25 huge tombs, each about 120-feet high and 100-feet across. A Roman Emperor was so impressed with the place that he had his tomb built in Petra, in the style of the locals. His is one of the 25, but by no means the most impressive. Naturally, the Romans also built a theater, which was still standing and usable, seating 4,000, tickets on sale at your local chariot shop.

Some of the smaller tombs have been carved into rock comprised of layers of different colors. The resulting effect is of permanent multicolored striped walls and ceilings. The tourist toilets were roofless, and built into one of the tombs, so you stand/sit and stare at carvings above and around you. Made me almost forget the job in hand. Unfortunately, the door-less entrance to the Men's was so placed that the ladies were required to stare at the urinals as they mounted the stairs to their own facility.

No longer can you ride a horse up and down the canyon. As tourist numbers increased, picking a way through the piles of horse-droppings became difficult (the entrance canyon is only 15 to 20-feet wide in places) and galloping horses killed or injured too many tourists. The mobility-impaired could still take horse-carts up and down, but these moved at a sedate trot.

These days the horse-touts wait at the canyon entrance to entice you to ride the last half-mile up hill to the main entrance gates. The final scene of the Indiana Jones movie *Temple of Doom* was set in Petra. After finding the Holy Grail and killing the baddies, Indiana gallops up the canyon, out into the desert, and into the sunset. The Petra shots were real, but the canyon/desert ride isn't possible, and never was. The whole place is surrounded by more mountains, not desert.

We rode, naturally. Every horse was individually led, much to Ryan's disgust, but necessary, as the horse-leaders then rode them back down at a gallop, to catch the next tourist and maximize the number of rides. The horses were in pretty good condition, much better than the Pyramid nags, but they were the usual docile, brown, bred to carry tourists at a walk, "Omigod-not-another-one" look on the face, lot. One stood out. He was huge, silver in color, and was dancing about, kicking and biting at every horse and person that came by.

The horse people took one look at me, encumbered by two camera bags, water bottles and other bags, and decided that it was "Destroy a Tourist" time. Carole and Ryan were already mounted and off. I am always last, as I take the obligatory still and video shots, and bargain with, and pay the handlers. The chief-handler patted me on the shoulder, and said something about a special horse. I almost said thanks, when I saw three men circling the silver beast, trying to get past hoofs and teeth to untie it. All other activity stopped, as the "Don't tell me they found a sucker to ride that one" news spread like wildfire.

Probably I should have remembered my age and infirmities, said no, and walked. However, I was wearing my Akubra hat, and therefore imbued with the spirits of Crocodile Dundee and Greg Norman, so I simply smiled, waved to the hushed crowd, and climbed on board. Mounted was too refined an expression for the scramble to get me, bags, cameras, and bottles, on to a dancing, biting horse, twenty feet high, with one of those Arab saddles that doesn't have a pommel to grab. The ride after that was an anticlimax. Old Silver realized he was beaten, contented himself with only the occasional bite or kick at passing horses and people, and tried only a few times to buck me off.

At the top, I stood in the stirrups to dismount; he danced sideways; I grabbed mane, saddle, cameras; he spun around, trying to bite anything nearby (there was only me, as the handler was wisely as far away as the lead rope would allow). At this time I decided that anywhere off the horse looked great, kicked both feet free of the stirrups, slid inelegantly to the ground, and ran like hell. Chalking up victory over another tourist, Old Silver simply stood still and looked around, as if to see what all the fuss was about.

Horse business aside, Petra was one of the highlights of the trip. The area is totally devoted to tourism. The nearby new town of Petra is wall-to-wall hotels, more than 60 (one called the Cleo-Petra), with several 5-star ones overlooking the old city. We had lunch at one, and the view was great. Food wasn't bad—not quite proving the old saying "Food or view—pick one." If we ever do it again, we would stay overnight at one of the good hotels.

After Petra we had a day of rest in Eilat. This is simply a tourist town, completely built around an airport. The plane noise was deafening, and the jet blast blew sand and dust over everyone, but the locals loved it. "Where else can you walk from your house to the airport in a couple of minutes?" was the common refrain. "Where else do you have to walk a mile around an airstrip to get to the other side of the street?" was the response I was too polite to give.

The movies in Israel were in English, with Hebrew sub-titles, so we got to catch up a little on ones we had missed. All movie theatres had this interesting ritual of stopping the movie for a ten minute interval. The first time it happened to us, we thought the film had broken, as there was no warning, the film simply stopped in the middle of a scene, and the lights came on. We guessed that it was either to promote popcorn sales, or because Israeli bladders were short-fused.

To drive to St. Catherine's and Mt. Sinai, in Egypt, we had to check out of Israel, again 57 shekels each, and into Egypt, mercifully free. The first thirty miles of the drive was along the coast, lined with abandoned hotel and resort developments. Our guide insisted that they were not abandoned, just on hold, and that, within a short time, over five million Egyptians would be employed here. As all that was there was desert, crumbling masonry and sea, I found this a bit of a stretch.

St. Catherine's Monastery, picturesquely huddled at the foot of Mt. Sinai, housed 22 Greek Orthodox monks, several thousand icons, and the Burning Bush. One monk we met was from Melbourne, Australia, another from somewhere in Texas. We saw, as a special treat for Ryan and Carole, the charnel house, where the bones of previous monks were stored. Skulls were neatly stacked, remaining bones were simply tossed onto a very large pile. Head monks were better treated, with complete skeletons in wall niches. When a monk dies, he is placed behind a nearby wall, and left for three to seven years (depending on the weather) until his bones are in a suitable state for storage. Present day monks try to transfer out before death.

The Burning Bush, of Moses fame, looked like a rather dilapidated blackberry bush. No one, least of all the monks, seemed to take it seriously. The icons were something else! Two on display, dating from the 6th century, one of St. Peter, one of Jesus, were three-dimensional, lifelike, and breathtaking. They could have been painted yesterday. There were less than a hundred icons being shown, and the remainder, 4th to 15th centuries, were your usual, flat-looking, idealized representations. Each icon was reputed to be worth from several thousand to millions of dollars, so the sect wasn't penniless, but they still actively sought donations for building maintenance.

There were two choices open for the Mt. Sinai (height 2,400 meters) climb, 3,500 steps, or a path followed by 750 steps. We chose the path, and left about 4pm, so we could be at the top to see the sunset. Carole decided to read in the hotel room, and frankly, an hour into the climb, I wished I was there, too. The camel-touts hung out under the monastery walls and offered camels to take us up the path to the steps, but we macho-types declined. We met a camel and driver on the way back down after a tourist delivery. The driver took one look at me, turned around and followed us for a while, continually offering the services of his camel.

Ryan (10): *I was getting a little tired, so Dad hired the camel for me to ride. It was so cool, riding a camel up Mt. Sinai.*

I had my second wind by this time, and pressed on. The views were stunning, and every mile or so there were vendors of water, chocolates and tea. The vendors slept in their stalls, as the other popular climbing time was 2am, to catch the sunrise from the top.

The path finally ended, and the steps started. In reality, these were just large rocks, somewhat casually related to each other, rising at a 45-degree angle, or steeper, with no railings. I salute Moses, who made the climb, twice, at the age of ninety or so, and still had breath left to talk to God.

The top was a small flat place, partly occupied by a tiny church and two or three vendors, surrounded by sheer drops and wonderful views. We were in time for the sunset, and it was as claimed. The climb down was far worse than the climb up. It was rapidly getting dark, and just making it down the "steps" to the top of the path was a hair-raising exercise. How Moses did it with his arms full of tablets, God only knows.

The next day it poured rain. Remember we were in the middle of the Sinai Desert, where it spits rain every other year, and we had a tropical deluge! Driving back to Eilat, one section of the road was covered by a flash-flood. Large earth movers and trucks were everywhere, building dams and diversions to try to save a new resort complex (owned by the son of President Mubarek), which had been built right in the stream bed—where else? Water was flowing through the buildings as we drove around one of the newly flung-up dams, which also had water flowing through it.

A few miles further on, another flash-flood blocked the road. This one was right at a police/army check point, and all traffic in both directions was stopped. Here was the picture. A stream of water, some six-inches deep and fifteen-feet wide, was flowing over a paved road. All traffic was stopped about 100 yards from this stream, and people with uniforms and in plain clothes, all with AK47s, pistols and/or equivalents, were running around making sure no one got close to this lethal stream. Apparently, someone decided to stop the traffic, and now no one was prepared to take the responsibility to start it again, hence the guns and the authoritarian posing.

Our driver, egged on by us, offered to take the responsibility of crossing and was firmly rejected, with much arm waving and shouting. We stood around for an hour, peering at the pitiful dribble through the automatic weapon screen that protected it, and watching new arrivals going through the same "What's going on—you must be joking—why can't I go closer—who's in charge here—we obviously aren't in Kansas" routine we did. Eventually, on the other side, one driver decided that enough was enough, got in his car and drove through. He barely got his tires wet, but was immediately surrounded by police and army, hauled out of his car, and hustled off.

Perhaps it was the cheers and jeers of the crowd that made the officer-in-charge realize he had a problem. No longer could he say that passage wasn't possible, or safe, so he ordered the barriers down, and waved us all through. We asked about the fate of our "savior." In spite of the fact that he had shown that there were no problems, he was going to have the book thrown at him, and would, at the very least, lose his license and be fined. Egyptian Catch-22, you did good, so now we are going to let everyone do what you did, but because we were originally wrong, we are going to punish you for doing what we are now telling everyone to do.

Our Egyptian expedition marked the end of our stay in Israel. An overnight sail took us to Larnaka, Cyprus, stopping there mainly to avoid sailing for two nights to go directly to Turkey. As it turned out, we made an excellent decision, as we thoroughly enjoyed the place—they have wonderful, cheap oranges—and stayed a week.

It was our first "Med Moor" marina since Papeete. We go bow in, as we have little directional control in reverse, and find it easier to wiggle our way into the minute spaces usually allocated to us in the crowded marinas. Our 15-foot beam, plus three feet for fenders, usually caused some consternation as we pushed into the small gap between boats, and everyone shuffled sideways to make room—steel boats have real advantages here.

Coming into our Larnaka spot, I put the gear lever into reverse to slow us, and the mechanism chose that exact time to come apart, leaving us stuck in forward gear and barreling ahead. I had the presence of mind to switch off the engine, but then demonstrated my real intelligence by leaping out onto the deck to stop our 25-ton boat by grabbing a mooring post. By a miracle my arms stayed attached to my body, we didn't scrape any boats, and were stopped by riding our bow up over, and sinking, the low, wooden, floating dock, with only cosmetic damage. I was so relieved I even managed to smile at the persistent, "Is that the way you do it in Australia?" questions.

Our land-cruising was restricted to south of the Green Line that divides the Greek and Turkish parts of the Island. There was a house from where we looked out at the now ghost city of Famagusta, which was in the northern, Turkish area. If we had sailed to Turkish-held Cyprus, we would have had problems entering Greece later. Should we have braved that, then returned to southern Cyprus, the Cypriots there would have jailed us and confiscated our boat. We got the feeling that there was some ill-will around.

Cyprus has some magnificent, white-limestone seacliffs, clear blue seas, and pretty mountain scenery. This is the island where Aphrodite was born, and we went to her Baths, a cave with a small stream flowing through it.

Ryan (10): *I found small eels in the water, but couldn't catch any.*

At Polis, a small village on the coast, we stopped for lunch at an outdoor restaurant, in a street reserved for pedestrians. An old man patted Ryan on the head (a normal occurrence), then sat down at our table, and settled in for a long conversation, in broken English and signs. He said he was the President of Polis (later discreet enquiries determined that he was the Chairman of the village council). The conversation was pleasant and informative, but my underlying problem with such encounters is that, 99% of the time, the person is leading us into some sort of scam or con. This turned out to be one of the 1%, and he was genuinely sad to see us go.

Carole: *He didn't ask for money, but he did suggest we rent a room at his daughter's house and spend the night.*

One of the mountain villages was very pretty, with a different type of tourist hook. The inhabitants actually made all the stuff they sold, in their houses, right there for the visitors to see—lace, wine, glassware, pottery. What interested me was a huge grape press—a wooden beam 3-feet by 3-feet and 20-feet long, cantilevered out, with a huge wooden screw at the end to provide the pressure—beats foot stamping any day, but you lose the flavor of old socks. Some of the houses were maintained with the furnishings of 100 years ago—fireplace cooking and kerosene lamps, just like we had back on the farm I grew up on in North Queensland.

My children don't really believe that on the farm, until I was about 16-years old, we had no electricity, no phone, no running water, a 5-gallon drum for a toilet (that I had to empty when I got old and strong enough), and therefore obviously no TV, no refrigerator, no washing machine, no computers (no one did at that time), but we did have a battery-powered radio that was used only for 60 minutes per day to conserve the battery. Things have changed in one generation.

Carole: *The Mediterranean marked the break-up of our group of boats that had been together since Papeete. Sadly everyone now had different agendas. I wanted to stay and cruise the Med. This is one of the main reasons I came along. The Med! We were in the Med!*

Turkey

Year Three and Four
May 30 to April 8

Turkey surprised us. The southern coast had terrific scenery, crystal clear water, ruins at almost every anchorage, delicious, cheap food, and, as Turkish Lira was 260,000 to $US1, we could be millionaires for under $US4. It is one of the great cruising areas of the world and we had the time to savor it slowly.

An extract from one of our letters, written towards the end of our stay in Turkey, perhaps helps to describe our feelings:

We haven't been arrested, or shot at, no sand storms, no long sea crossings, just a lot of tourist stuff. As of this date, we are officially ruined-out, having walked through more old cities, seen more temples, admired more mosaic floors, tested the acoustics of more Roman theaters, climbed over more sarcophagi, and walked on more ancient streets than Alexander the Great.

Ruins list: Ephesus, Iassus, Phaselis, Termessos, Myra, Lymira, Limyra, Helicarnassas, Hierapolis, Lycia, Olympos, Telmessos, Aperlae, Aspendos, Simena, Perge, Knidos, Caunus, Antiphellos, Didyma, Asklepieion, and Teimiussa. This list excludes various Lycian rock tombs, castles (Alanya, Bodrum, to mention a couple), temples, mosques, churches, and cities and towns with integral ruins/tombs/mosaics.

We love Turkey, the people, the country, the history, and the food. A lot of Roman and Greek history has been enacted in what is now Turkey. Julius Caesar said " Veni, Vedi, Veci" in Turkey; the Gordian knot was cut here; Troy, of Helen fame, is in Turkey; St. Nicholas (Santa to you) was born here; the Virgin Mary died here; St. John preached here, as did St. Paul (letters to the Ephesians was to the people in Ephesus); and so it goes.

Cleopatra and Anthony came here to be alone. One beach is supposedly made up of sand they brought from Egypt, as they decided the local stuff was too coarse—it is now the only fine sand beach in Turkey, so there may be some truth to the story.

Did you know the following facts, which you probably never wanted to know, but now you have started to read this letter you may as well keep going and find about anyhow so you can bring them up in casual conversation and bask in the awe and admiration of your listeners, assuming that you have any once you start to quote Turkish facts:

- *The turban was banned in 1826, in favor of the fez, and the fez was banned in 1927, in favor of European style hats. At both times, many died rather than give up their head covering.*
- *The tassel on top of the fez is the representation of the single hair by which devout Moslems are effortlessly raised to Paradise by Allah.*
- *The Turkish word for scarlet, vermillion, maroon, cerise, purple, mauve and red is "fezrengi," meaning "fez colored."*
- *A Turkish anthropologist: "The origins of the fez, you say? From the penis of course. Like the English top hat, it represents the primal human instinct."*
- *In the early 1930s Turkey had its first census, and all citizens were told to stay home and occupy themselves on census day. Nine months later, a previously unknown first name—Nufus, meaning population or census—enjoyed a widespread popularity.*
- *The local bus, generally a mini-van, is called a "Dolmush," which is derived from the words "to stuff," as in peppers and vine leaves. Having made several journeys in an 18-seater carrying 38 to 40 passengers, I understand the derivation.*
- *The language may seem difficult at first, but here is a list of words you may be able to translate: telefon, otopark, kontak lens, seks, feribot, yat, polis, bira, coke, otel, taksi.*
- *Conversely, the Turkish use of English, in the tourist areas, has a charm all of its own: lamp chops, fried squit, French freud potatoes, cold drings, stew of bot, grilled red mallet, supe, bolloknese. Our Marina notes that a particular service "has to be paid in advance, after use."*
- *Road rules in Turkey are simple:*
  - *Stop lights and signs are advisory only, not mandatory.*
  - *Pass every vehicle as soon as you catch up with it, preferably on blind corners and narrow roads.*
  - *Whatever you want to do is OK, as long as you blow your horn and/or flash your lights.*
  - *Half a second before the light turns green, blow your horn.*

Turkey

— *Assume that, on every corner, there will be a car or truck coming towards you, on your side of the road, flashing its lights at you to get out of its way.*
— *Might has right—if your car is small, drive it faster to compensate. If your car is big, drive faster, to stop the small cars from passing.*
— *Lanes are for wimps.*
— *Pedestrians have no rights.*

- We counted over 200 high-rise (10 floors or greater) apartment buildings being built along the five miles of road from Antalya city to the marina. This is repeated in every city we have visited. We were told that inflation is degrading the currency so quickly that money is being put into real estate, regardless of demand.

A 240-mile sail took us from Larnaka to Antalya. All our reading didn't prepare us for the magnificent mountains that surround this city of 250,000 people. In winter, one can ski in the morning and swim in the sea in the afternoon. Setur Marina was some five miles outside the city and we liked it so much we booked in for winter. They did lots of things for cruisers, including checking in and out, and providing a free bus to Antalya every hour during the day. Wintering cruisers had a special club room (The Porthole Club) with a bar, TV, books and videos. After settling on where we were to winter, we had four-and-a-half months to explore the delights of southern Turkey.

Tekirova. Here we had our first gulet experience. A gulet is a local wooden boat, 30 to 70 feet in length, with masts and nominal sails, and a 300+HP engine, which takes tourists on day trips, or for overnighters. Every day, about 25 arrived in Tekirova at 10am and departed at 3pm. They all carried huge fishermen anchors, which they dropped at speed, either forward or reverse, then fitted into places which seemed impossible. The distinctive rattle of a gulet anchor chain soon became the signal to drop everything and stand by the fenders. Early morning and late afternoon the anchorage and shore were blissfully empty.

Carole: *Luckily "Marita Shan" had been in the anchorage for a few days, as we arrived after 10am and the place was full of gullets, with no room left to anchor. Side-tying to them, we chatted in our cockpits, watching the tourists do their rush-about tourist things. The gulets up-anchored and left us in peace, so we dinghied ashore to enjoy the deserted ruins of Phaesalis— theater, baths, temples, mosaics, arches, aqueducts, streets, and ancient Trireme harbor.*

Ryan (10): *Under a marble slab I found a tunnel, roofed with stone blocks, with a small entrance. It looked as if very few people had been in it before us. Dad and I explored with a flashlight. He let me go first. We climbed a small hill, through thick brush, and discovered more columns and stone carvings that I think hadn't been seen since the Romans left. Dad said we should call the spot Ryan's Villa.*

The rock at the point had been eroded by the sea exposing the shafts of several deep wells, probably used for water storage for the villas of the rich. On the other side was a lovely little bay still with stone piers where the Roman galleys tied up. An aqueduct, almost complete enough to carry water, ran off into the hills. Scattered around the foreshore were tombs, some partly exposed, others lying broken on the shore where erosion had dumped them.

We sat in the theatre seats as Ryan stood center stage reciting poetry, walked the streets, stepping over the ruts worn in the stone by chariot wheels, and explored the villas. In the hush and dreamy light of evening, blissfully all alone, it was so easy to slip back in time and imagine the city brought back to life. This is the magic those on tours generally miss.

Carole: *We were to return three times. On the second visit the art bug had bitten Ryan and me, and we spent most of one morning sitting on a rock sketching the aqueduct. We were very pleased with our amateurish attempts.*

Cinevez. An anchorage surrounded by steep cliffs, it was remarkable as there were no Roman ruins to be seen. However there was a small fish restaurant as possible compensation. Hiking over the ridge to the next bay, we saw our first wild goats, and thanked them for the path they had made for us to follow. The bay was almost completely filled with nets and circular fish farms.

Carole: *On the way back we picked wild thyme and rosemary. This was delicious on the inexpensive Turkish leg of lamb. Tash was by far the best cook in our group, but she thought the lamb was tough and stringy, so never bought it. I marinated it in vinegar and a variety of spices and my guys found the results tender and tasty.*

Finike. Setur had another marina here, just completed and empty. The small town provided a pleasant walk, an adequate market, and several restaurants, but not enough activities to consider wintering there, even though it was very inexpensive. Many yachts did and, based on the comments of those who lived on board, we made the right decision to go to Antalya.

Turkey

Bayindir Limani. We anchored about a mile from the city of Kas, under some Lycean tombs carved into the cliffs. The bottom was green slime with no holding, so we moved to the other arm of the bay.

Ryan had his first try at water-skiing, and got up on his third attempt. Being young and fearless is wonderful. Being somewhat smaller than Carole and I also helped, as our outboard (25-HP) was just not quite strong enough to get us to our feet.

***Ryan (10):** I started skiing on two skis, but soon moved to one. It was great fun swinging from side to side, through the wake. Dad drove, with Mum watching me and telling him when I was down. Once I fell off and Dad just kept going. He said he did it on purpose as a joke—right!*

Fethiye. The pier here was technically available to yachts, but only the foolish took a space. It was crowded with gulets, and they were very unkind to any boat in "their space" when they returned from the day's tourist run. We anchored, with the dual benefits of safety and satisfying Ryan's now insatiable desire to water ski.

The engine fuel pump chose this time to fail. With some trepidation, I took it ashore and approached a group of gulet captains to enquire about service. They called over a gentleman riding past on a bicycle, and he took it and rode off. With limited English (them) and much hand waving (me) I was able to discover that it would be back the next day. It was, and worked perfectly.

"Sky Bird," "Osprey," "Just Magic," "Tryst," and "Encore" all arrived separately, the first time we had been together since we left the Red Sea. A celebration dinner ashore was in order. It was especially nice for Ryan as "Encore" had on board a teenage boy and a girl a little older than he was.

***Ryan (10):** Jenny was cool, but she couldn't get up on water skis. We spent a lot of time playing and reading. Jeff was older, just out of high school, so he didn't hang around with us too much.*

I became an instant tourist attraction, falling into the water as I was trying to climb from the dinghy to the pier. In my defense, it was an eight-foot climb. Too bad I was in my "best" clothes, as we were on the way to the airport to pick up Carole's mother and four other relatives, including Michael, a boy Ryan's age. "Dolphin Spirit" suddenly shrank.

***Carole:** A day of disasters. For the past week I had been cleaning every nook and cranny of the boat, somewhat assisted by Laurie and Ryan, both of whom would not know real cleaning if it bit them. Now I do admit to* being a perfectionist, but there was no reason for mutiny just because the cleaning tool I insisted on was a toothbrush.

Then my beautiful black pearl necklace (the one Laurie had surprised me with in Hong Kong) went missing. I wanted to wear it and couldn't find it, with no real memory of the last time I saw it, or where. Sometimes I hide treasures in the strangest places, so Laurie turned the boat inside out with no result. I was very unhappy.

Then Ryan slipped on the steps of the car rental office, and smacked his head with a sickening thud on the stone, leaving him with a splitting headache. This was just after Laurie had performed at the pier for the tourists.

Then we picked up my mother and her first words were that, after one day in Turkey, they were tired of Kebabs, the food they were going to be eating most of the time they were with us.

Then we discovered that a bottle of Chris & Pitts Barbecue Sauce (one of my requests) had broken in my aunt's suitcase, coloring and perfuming all her new clothes. Fortunately, my trusty Australian Nappisan made them like new again the next day.

Laurie alienated everyone with his description of how to use a marine toilet, warnings on using minimal water in the showers and dire threats to follow his orders implicitly as he was the captain. Michael and Ryan didn't get along together as well as we had hoped. I saw more disasters looming large.

Boynuz Buku. The large, fjord-like bay was very sheltered, calm, and deserted, except for a small open air restaurant at the end, and a couple of other yachts. The boys went ashore and caught three eatable-size crabs and several shrimps. We ate at the restaurant, and made friends with the owner and her family (all girls). She took the boys fishing the next day, and served us their catch for dinner.

Ryan (16): *We had fun fishing in the shallow water on shore. When we got back, we saw a cockroach, a big one, that I said had flown in. Michael insisted the cockroaches couldn't fly, and wouldn't change his mind even after Dad had shown him he was wrong. Months later, he sent me an article cut from a magazine about a flightless cockroach, so I guess he still thinks he was right.*

Carole: *It was HOT and my mother and aunt didn't handle it well. The freezer couldn't produce ice-cubes fast enough. At least one of my early worries, that there wouldn't be enough hot water for all the showers needed, never materialized. Even my super-delicious eggplant stew went unappreciated.*

Turkey

Gocek. We had earlier made a dinghy run here to get fresh produce and to check out the refueling facilities and marina slips. The fuel dock was very shallow and had even shallower areas all round it, so I drove "Dolphin Spirit" in bow first, trusting to Providence (and the superb boat-handling skills of the captain) on the way out. For whatever reason, we only scraped a little.

Carole: We ate ashore, Turkish-style, seated on rugs and cushions—very uncomfortable for those of us with long legs, especially as the food service was so slow, not our usual Turkey experience .

Tomb Bay. No one was too impressed with Gocek, so we sailed off into the sunset (actually south) to the lovely Tomb Bay, where we anchored under the Lycean tombs carved into the cliffs. The surrounding mountains were all pine covered, the water a deep blue, as was the sky, and it was calm and peaceful.

Carole: In keeping with the overall theme of my mother's visit, I was stung by a bee, for the first time in my life. The men and boys climbed up to the tombs, and I stayed on board to keep cold drinks coming to my mother and aunt, and I got stung.

Ekincik Limani. This is a large bay and the weather was settled, so we were able to anchor just off the long beach. There we arranged with Aladdin, a local entrepreneur, to charter a boat for a trip up the Koycegiz River to visit the ancient ruins of Caunos. The river entrance is blocked with reeds through which a passage has to be forced, so it isn't big boat or dinghy friendly. We had heard stories of yachts being broken into while the owners were on this trip, so I stayed on board.

Carole: The first ruins we stopped at were a mile hike from the river and neither of the older ladies wanted to attempt it. Then came the famous tombs, viewed high in the hills from the restaurant where we had lunch. I was impressed though I had seen many of them before, but my guests were unmoved. Then, on the way back, the seas were quite high. I was very worried as, the previous day, my mother had demonstrated that she had lost her swimming skills, and I knew my aunt couldn't swim at all.

Marmaris. A huge marina and two miles of shoulder-to-shoulder restaurants lining the waterfront made up the total town, except for the carpet shops. The carpet vendor who broke down our impenetrable "no thank you" wall was a man with Turkish parents, who was born and raised in England, who was getting out of the carpet business, and whose opening offer was for a stack of fifty or so carpets for $US10,000. Our actual purchase was a more modest, single, silk carpet.

Carole: *At last, a place my relatives loved, with its shops and restaurants and they partied well into the night. We had gotten used to our 8pm bedtime, but were perfect hosts and stayed up with them—sometimes. Their reactions made us realize how we had changed over the years, now preferring the simple pleasures of life on board to the frenzy of the land.*

We checked out of Turkey at Marmaris, to go to Rhodes, Greece. Both governments made it as inconvenient and as expensive as possible to go from one country to the other, which was a pity. The legal method costs more than $300 for a check out of Turkey, check into Greece, check out of Greece, check back into Turkey. Checking out of Turkey was a two-hour process involving Immigration, Customs, and Customs Police, and required paying the last group an "overtime fee" of eight million lira. I asked for a receipt and was simply shown out of the office, and the fee went into a pocket.

The 20 miles to Rhodes was a calm sail. Arriving at Rhodes City, we were told the Mandraki Marina was full, so kept going south to Lindos. This is a very pretty harbor, under the shadow of a huge castle, the walls of which surround the columns of a Greek temple. Between the castle and the harbor is the town, with white houses, blue doors, fuchsia bougainvillea, and cobble streets shaded by grape vines—oh so Greek. The beach became wall-to-wall people and umbrellas from 10am to 4pm, deposited there by about fifty buses and ten gulets. From 4pm to 10am the next day, the town and the castle belonged to us, the other yachties, and the few tourists who were staying in the town's hotels.

The bottom of the well protected bay was almost completely covered with large rocks. Anchoring, with some chance of anchor retrieval, therefore required searching for the sandy spots, and dropping there. Here we saw for the first time boats going around in tight circles to create an area of smooth water inside the circle, and allow a clear view of the bottom.

Carole, Ryan and relatives took a donkey ride up the hill to the castle, while I ran up and down taking pictures. It wasn't often that I could get pictures of "Dolphin Spirit" with Carole on a donkey in the foreground, or through the columns of a Greek temple.

The visitors, Carole and Ryan, left for Athens, leaving me all alone for a few days, or so I thought. A couple of hours later, I heard the call "Dolphin Spirit" and there were Carole and Ryan in a pedal boat. Turkish Airlines had cancelled their tickets because they hadn't been confirmed some four weeks before, a U.S. travel-agent oversight.

Turkey

Carole: *Mother bid me an especially tearful farewell, as she had been hoping to have a better few days with me in the air-conditioning in Athens, and now suddenly she was off. When people leave we are sorry to see them go, but glad to be back to our favorite foursome—us and "Dolphin Spirit."*

We had fun swimming and playing in Lindos for several weeks, with occasional bus trips to Rhodes, while the wind howled at 25 to 30 knots. Dinner every night at Mavriko's, at a table they held specially for us, was followed by ice-cream at Gel Blue, a stroll through the village mercifully empty of tourists, a short dinghy ride to our boat, and time sitting on deck under the stars.

Eventually we checked out at the little police station set on the beach. I had to dive to free the anchor from under a rock (missed the sand patch on anchoring), but we eventually got away and sailed back to Marmaris, checking back into Turkey again.

Knidos. We anchored right in front of the Roman Theater, and spent two days walking the marvelous ruins of Knidos. Ryan and I crawled/walked through a long tunnel under the Temple of Aphrodite, whose 4th century BC statue (long gone) was one of the first of a naked woman. Sostratus, designer of the Pharos Lighthouse in Alexandria, one of the Seven Wonders of the Ancient World, lived here.

Being at anchor below a set of Roman ruins was really special. We sat in the cockpit, sipped wine, and speculated on life all those years ago, peopling the streets, houses, temples and theaters with Romans, and the anchorage with triremes. It really didn't take much imagination when the buildings were right there

Carole: *and you had a glass of wine in your hand.*

Bodrum. We anchored in the bay, around the corner from the marina, and under the walls of the castle. The whole shore of the bay was lined with restaurants. At one end was a huge, open air disco, with Greek columns, and a set of lights that probably could fry eggs at a mile. They, and another disco at the other end of the bay, got going around 10pm. The noise was incredible, with vibrations felt through the hull, and we were half-a-mile off shore. Someone described it as a "churning decibel hell," but even that doesn't do the cacophony justice. At 1am they set off fireworks and cranked up the volume a little, finally giving up around 5am. This happened every night, seven days a week. The natives say, "If you don't like the noise, don't come to Bodrum." We lasted two nights.

Gumusluk. There is very little tide in the Med, so this little bay has nine restaurants lined up along the shore, with tables right at the water's edge. I believe this is the first restaurant we have eaten at where our dinghy was tied to my chair.

The captain of a Turkish boat anchored near us came over and pointed out that our Turkish courtesy flag (made in Australia) was not quite correct, and gave us a new one. When we later returned to Turkey from Greece, I inadvertently put up the incorrect flag again. Almost immediately we had a visit from another captain, who also gave us a correct flag. We were impressed with the sharp eyes and with the great courtesy.

At the entrance to the bay was Rabbit Island, named after its inhabitants. We paid for the privilege of wading across the shallow sandbar at low tide to see rabbits pop in and out of burrows. The island was crowded with tourists and locals, so perhaps we missed some significant fact about the scarcity of rabbits.

One of the more enjoyable things in life is to be sitting comfortably in an anchorage, wine glass in hand, watching the evening chaos as the charter boats come in for the night. I have been a charterer many times, but that doesn't reduce my pleasure at watching others screw up royally, which brings us to the entertainment at Gumusluk.

One evening, fourteen boats of a charter flotilla arrived to tie up at three moorings, for their first night aboard. The flotilla had an employee of the charter company, who led the fleet in his own boat, and whom we nicknamed "The Admiral."

The charterers were supposed to drop anchors and back into spots around the three who got in first and took the moorings. As a general rule, everyone did okay, apart from an apparent lack of knowledge that there were throttle settings somewhere between full and idle, a lack of appreciation of what a beam-on 15-knot wind will do, and the "Omigod Mabel, which locker did he say the ropes were in" panic that struck when the Admiral told them to toss a line. The Admiral gave up on the anchoring after a couple of incidents that I should have videoed, and went round later pulling out anchors, and dropping them from his dinghy.

He was Australian, so we chatted in the evening, when he could relax. His job was quite stressful, responsible for all the boats in the fleet when they are chartered, and for their maintenance on the one day free between charters. He did, after a couple of beers, give us the fleet's VHF channel.

The next morning's departure was even more entertaining. Inside the anchorage, the wind was blowing at 10 knots, but outside was a howling 20 to 25 knots, with whitecaps to the horizon. There was no way we were leaving, but these thirteen, brave, 29 to 35-foot innocents, were.

One boat soon riveted our attention. The lady was in the cockpit gripping the wheel with a white-knuckled intensity that could be felt from where we were. The gentleman was hauling his anchor up by hand, sitting on the deck, feet braced against the pulpit. The anchor came out of the water and the shackle jammed under the bow roller. Unable to see it, he assumed that the anchor was caught on the bottom and screamed at his wife to back up, which she did, adopting the full throttle mode. I believe the damage to all four boats which became involved was mercifully slight.

The poor charterers headed out into the waves and wind. Their one-hour, "learn how to sail" lesson, obviously didn't include reefing, as all, one after the other, pointed into the wind, put up full mains and jibs, turned, and were immediately blown horizontal. You would have thought that some doubt must have entered one or two minds, after the first three or four met this fate. Perhaps they thought this was what sailing was all about.

Asim Limani. Anchored under the ruins of Iassus, capped by a Byzantine Castle, was a constant thrill. The ruins were only partly excavated, and visited by very few people, so we could get a true feel for what the place was like in its heyday. Scratching the ground we uncovered mosaics put there by the later Romans. There was a jewel-like little theater with marble seats that looked like it was still in use. We sat in the seats and looked across the water to "Dolphin Spirit."

Ryan (10): *I scraped the dirt off a flat spot below the walls of the castle and found a very pretty mosaic. I wondered if I was the first to see it since the Romans left. All around were pieces of pottery.*

The remarkable charter fleet came in one evening, with us listening to them on VHF. The Admiral told them that they were to go bow first in to the concrete dock; that they were to have the spare anchor ready to drop off the stern when he told them to; that the anchor rode had to be un-kinked and unknotted, with the bitter end attached to the boat; and that there had to be one person in the bow ready to throw him a line on the dock.

All went very well for the first half dozen, and we were getting bored. Then our faith in humanity was restored. "Drop the stern anchor now," the admiral roared. The man in the stern stood like a statue, anchor in hand, un-moving. "Drop it NOW." Still no action. "NOW, NOW—too late." This galvanized the statue, the anchor dropped, and the bow hit the dock.

Whilst the Admiral was busy, we were hearing him being called on the VHF by an increasingly more distressed charterer, who had stayed on at the luncheon anchorage. He could see a light-house ahead of him, and wanted to know on which side to pass it. I knew the area, the light was at the end of a high ridge, and I had to be restrained from telling him that to the left was land, to the right water, and he should go where the water was.

Carole: *We dinghied up to the small restaurant and tied up at our table. Laurie always asked for the small fish grilled whole. One night there were no small fish, so the owner jumped into his boat and headed out. Ten minutes later, he was back with Laurie's fish.*

We met some wonderful people at the restaurant, just by being regulars, chatting, and having Ryan along. Some of the charterers Laurie had disparaged were there, and they proved to be very nice people, thoroughly enjoying themselves.

Kusadasi. "Marita Shan" had decided to winter at the large marina here and we enjoyed a few days with them. The boat in the slip next to us caught fire. Thanks to the almost immediate actions of the marina staff, the damage to it was minimized, and we were unscathed.

We met two American yachts that had been tied up there for 10 and 15 years respectively. One said they tried to sail a few years before, but so much gear and equipment broke they haven't been out since. The other said he had a great sail across the Atlantic to get here, so obviously would get beaten up on the way back, and in any case was too firmly embedded in coffee grounds to move.

The Rankin family, friends and keepers of our cash, visited us again for a couple of weeks. We went to Ephesus, a magnificent city of ruins. There we saw the very impressive library, with its secret tunnel to the brothel ("Excuse me dear, just popping down to the library to read a scroll or two."), the stone pavement streets with grooves worn in them from the chariot wheels, the houses, the theatre, which is still used for concerts, and the communal toilet with marble seats arranged in a square so the conversation could flow.

Ryan was entranced with the toilet, so we all had to sit, emulating the slaves who warmed the seats, not the Romans who followed. The streets were wall-to-wall tourists, and we had to line up for photo-ops. A few weeks later, we returned, very early in the morning, before the bus-loads arrived, and had the place almost to ourselves.

We checked out of Turkey again and went to the island of Kos where we Med-Moored at the town wharf. The area boasts some mediocre ruins (we considered starting a ruin-rating service, as we were such experts), but was otherwise unremarkable, so we moved on to Simi Island. This was again a small, Med-Moor harbor completely surrounded by a very colorful town, seemingly rising vertically from the water. Drinking water was available on the dock, through the local water boss, who measured and charged it by the drop. A nearby restaurant gave us a guided tour of its huge wine cellar, so we could select an appropriate vintage for dinner.

Our second visit to Lindos was just as nice as the first. After the Rankins left, we stayed for another two weeks. Ryan and I climbed the hills behind the anchorage and found massive rocks that had big building blocks cut from them, some completely, others partly sawed through and abandoned. This must have been the source of the castle-wall material.

Carole: *We ate at Mavriko's almost every night, sitting at the same table and eating the same food—Laurie and Ryan, lamb shank, me, mousaka. One night, because a group of tourists had taken too long to eat, our table was occupied, so we received extensive apologies from the owner, and free drinks as compensation.*

Ryan (10): *I tried wakeboarding here for the first time and did well. My water-ski expertise really helped. Dad hired a local powerboat to pull me around. The best place in town was Gel Blue which made and sold great ice-cream. If you stand with your back to Mavriko's, then walk past the big tree in the town square and take the second street to the left, walk for a few minutes then turn left again, it is right there. Maybe one of those turns was to the right. We got lost every time we went, but always kept going until we found it.*

Fethiye (again). In case it isn't apparent, we really liked this area. "Baltic Bird" arrived with Tom, an 11-year-old boy on board, so we stayed a little longer, and decided to go to the next anchorage when they did. To fill in the time, we took the bus to Oludeniz which has a nice beach and the added attraction of paragliding to the beach from the mountain top just behind. Unfortunately they had only one vacant place, so Carole and I unselfishly gave it to Ryan.

Ryan (16): *Yeah, right! Mum was especially relieved, and even more relieved years later in Gibraltar, when we met a lady who was still recovering from a paragliding accident.*

A bus took the paragliders to the top of the mountain, where they were harnessed to the front of the person who actually operated the parachute. They then jumped off to begin the 25-minute glide to the beach. Ryan had a blast. I was below videotaping, standing at the edge of the landing area, and noted that most landings were all around the target, but not on it. When the time came for Ryan's approach, I stood on the target filming him getting closer and closer, then had to leap out of the way as they landed right in the center.

Ryan (10): *I wasn't scared at all, even when we jumped off the cliff. We stayed up a lot longer than everyone else.*

Bayindir Limani (again). Michael and Val saw our Australian flag and swam out to the boat to meet us. They were Australians who had decided to retire to Kas, as an ideal place to live, and had a very pretty house with a terrific view of the bay. We went out to dinner (French provincial) with them to celebrate our meeting, and my birthday. At the next table was a gentleman who heard our accents and introduced himself. He was the owner of the hotel in the bay where we were anchored, and invited us for breakfast there the next day. Such is the cruising life!

Michael and Val encountered major problems in getting their idyllic life to work in real-world Turkey. Officialdom reigned supreme, nothing happened when it should, and when it did it wasn't what they expected. A magnificent view can provide only so much compensation. The last we heard, they had moved back to Australia.

Ucagiz Limani, Kekova Roads, Polemos Buku. The sarcophagi lined the shore, but the water was too murky (a first in Turkey) for snorkeling. We had walked across the isthmus from Polemos to see the ruins of the ancient city and port of Aperlae, some of which were under water. Ryan and I snorkeled but saw only vague outlines. Camels and goats made the walk entertaining, at least for Ryan.

We would like to have dove on the ruins to experience an underwater city, but a special guide was required for all diving in Turkey. Unguided diving was forbidden because there are so many underwater ruins and antiquities that the Authorities wanted to preserve from damage and looting.

We dinghied to Kale Koy (ancient Simena), past rocks with stairs cut in them leading to the top of the rock, but to nothing else, past huge sarcophagi with holes smashed in their sides by ancient grave robbers, and tied up at the wharf at the foot of the stairs to the castle. Two ladies immediately attached themselves to us and were our guides up and down the very steep staircase. Carole's assistant was short and heavy and looked much older than Carole. She leapt up and down the stairs like a gazelle, a fact I was smart enough not to mention more than once. The view from the castle walls was worth the climb. Most of the surrounding islands are covered in ruins, so this must have been quite a metropolis in its hey-day.

Carole: Those stairs had no railings, glass-smooth stone surfaces, and sheer drops. Laurie was lucky I didn't just sit down and scoot my way up and down on my bottom. It was gorgeous though, and well worth the terror.

Finike. Ryan wanted to see the birth place of Santa Claus, and as we were in the vicinity we hired a car and took him there. The village of Demre contains a church with the tomb of St. Nicholas, who was in life the Bishop of Demre. Excellent frescos on the wall were somewhat faded, but worth seeing.

As we were out and about, we went on to Myra, the ancient Lycian port (St. Paul was taken there on his way to Rome) that is now several miles from the sea. The rock tombs were quite superb and there was an extraordinary, well preserved Roman theater.

Carole: We had it to ourselves, as we were there before the buses. For an hour we wandered around, through the arches, up and down the stairs and in and out of the rooms. You get such a better feeling for a place when you are alone with it. Then the buses arrived, and we were surrounded by American tourists, many of whom we interested in how we happened to be there without a guide, and with such a knowledge of the theater.

Antalya—Setur Marina. There were about 30 yachts wintering at the Marina that year. Apart from us, there were three U.S., five German, one French, two Swedish, one South African, three English yachts, with people living aboard for the winter. Many others simply went home for the winter, re-appearing around April. Ryan was the only child.

This period also marked the final breakup of our sailing group. We had been together since Papeete, had shared many adventures and become close friends. "Marita Shan" and "Sky Bird" were put up for sale in Kusadasi and Marmaris respectively; "Osprey" wintered in Marmaris and they were then to dash across the Atlantic the next year, not waiting an additional year as we planned to do; "Soliloquy" had been sold in Singapore; "Pilgrim" spent an additional year in Thailand; "Topaz" took a year in Thailand to recover from their medical problems; "Gigolo" wintered in Malta; "Encore" left the boat in Finike and went home for the winter; "Blue Ribbon" was still in Oman.

The resident yachties continued the organization called the Porthole Club—it ran every year, sponsored by the marina, using marina facilities—operated a bar every night, organized local excursions, and arranged for Turkish language lessons, aerobics and exercise classes, movie nights, concert visits, you name it and we did it. We went to a number of classical concerts, piano recitals and ballets, at the Antalya Cultural center, most for less than $US4 per person.

Carole: It was at the Porthole Club that I gave lessons in Country and Western dancing, where other cruisers gave us the benefits of their special skills, and where the marina staff taught us all Turkish. Laurie won't mention that the cruisers elected him President of the Club, and so he was in charge of most of the functions.

Chasing Sunsets

One of the organized trips was to a Turkish bath, so I went with my Swedish friends to enjoy a new experience. We were ushered into a room, men and women together, and everyone (except for one person) took off their clothes. Totally shocked, I didn't know where to look. Waiting until everyone left, I quickly got into a swim suit and followed to the next room where we were to be scrubbed down by—a man! I got back into my clothes and waited on the street. I guess the Swedish heritage I have always been so proud of has been taken over by my Puritan English side.

A free shuttlebus ran seven times per day to the center of the city and to the market. We did the trip every two or three days. The huge market was open every day, and received fresh produce every morning, as the Antalya region produces most of the fruit and vegetables for Turkey. Watching the lettuce, tomatoes, oranges, and every fruit and vegetable imaginable, arrive by every type of vehicle imaginable, from horse drawn carts, to motor scooters, to trucks, was always novel and interesting.

Carole: *As in Indonesia and many other countries, we had to bring our own egg cartons, or accept the eggs loose in a bag. U.S. markets do not have such a wide variety of fresh and flavorful fruit and vegetables. We soon sorted out which stalls to buy which products—this one for the best oranges and cherries, this for tomatoes, this for potatoes and lettuce, and this for spices. Just standing still, inhaling the smells and watching the colors of the people and the produce, was a sensual experience we got to repeat every second day.*

We learned Turkish words and phrases so we could ask for fruit and vegetables by name, instead of pointing. I cooked lots of lamb, eggplant and cucumber dishes, marinating the legs of lamb and cooking them in oven bags so they were always tender and delicious. Strawberries were huge, succulent and cheap.

Cockroaches arrived in legions. Until now I could recall seeing only two huge black ones (in the Red Sea), and now we were crawling with them. I cleaned every cupboard and storage space and still, when the light was switched on, there they were scurrying away. I got into the habit of having a can of bug spray in my hand before switching on a light. When the cold weather set in they disappeared, and I could give up my nightly "Raids." Laurie and Ryan helped kill the brutes, but laughed at my paranoia. Serve them right if I had served cockroach stew.

Ryan (10): *I worked some mornings in the marina office and practiced my Turkish. "Dolphin Spirit" was tied up just a few feet away. There was a huge sailboat owned by the marina owner at the end of our dock, but I* *wasn't allowed on board. One day the marina held a canoe race, so I entered, but fell into the water, with my new shoes on, and didn't win.*

Our days were occupied with boat repairs, Ryan's schooling, getting ready for an April departure, writing magazine articles about our travels, discussions, playing tennis on the marina court, eating, drinking, and wondering how we could ever settle down to a "real" life again.

We hired a car and drove to Marmaris and Kusadasi to see "Osprey" and "Marita Shan." The road took us through a six-mile-long tunnel, totally unmarked on the map we were using. Six miles was a long time to be underground, not seeing another car, and not really knowing where we were going. It was with some relief we saw daylight again and found a road that was marked.

Undaunted, we pressed on to sight-see at the white cliffs of Pamukkale, the ruins of Perge, Aspendos and Side, and the wonderful castle at Alanya. Snow covered mountains were only two hours by car from Antalya, so we did a lot of mountain driving. The villages away from the tourist coast all seem to continue life as in the old days—horse-drawn carts, wood fires, traditional clothes, men gathered round the gaming boards, tractors, satellite TVs, cellular phones. Carole really enjoyed the narrow, winding mountain roads! Ryan loved hearing her screams.

Carole: *Ryan and I began to draw in Finike and practiced every day after that. We sat for hours drawing the aqueduct at Phaeselis and the fronts of many Roman theaters. Every day we had to produce at least one drawing each. Some nights, I was up past midnight getting mine finished. By the time we got to Istanbul, we had graduated to water colors of the skyline. Great art it is not, but that portfolio of drawings brings back memories photos can't.*

Istanbul was a stop on our way back to California. We could look to the left from our window and see the magnificence of the Blue Mosque. To the right loomed the Aya Sophia, with just beyond it, the walls of Topkapi Palace. Our hotel, Yesil Ev, or Green House, was a converted house, painted green, right in the middle of everything we wanted to see in Istanbul. The big three mentioned above, together with the Yerebatan Saray, were all within 300 yards of the front door.

Who needed a TV (there wasn't one anyway), when the misty-blue, flood-lit, Blue Mosque filled the window. Who needed alarm clocks (you guessed it, none in the room), when the call to prayer boomed at us from at least six mosques, at first light. They seem to practice call-and-respond, or we-can-be-louder-than-you, or both, randomly. Although these were more strident than most, we have been woken by similar calls for almost two years since Indonesia, so our response was to sleepily note that it must be six o'clock, and roll over for more snooze.

Ryan (10): *My school work was mostly learning about Turkey. Before we went to each place, I had to read the appropriate section in the* Lonely Planet *guide book and make sure that we saw every important thing. I was also supposed to be the translator for my parents, but my Turkish was never very good.*

Yerebatan Saray was a place I had sort of heard of, but it isn't a prominent Istanbul tourist attraction, and it should be. A Byzantine underground water cistern, several acres in size, with the roof held up by columns taken from the various Roman temples above, it is unique and impressive. Some of the columns are upside down, all are well preserved, together with their original carvings, and seem to march unending in every direction—special lighting and classical music are thrown in. Highlights were the Medusa carvings, and the sheer size and grandeur of the place.

The Topkapi Dagger, centerpiece of the Emerald Room in the Topkapi Palace Treasury, was stunning. The three huge emeralds in the hilt almost take attention away from the scores of diamonds that cover the rest of the hilt and scabbard, each one of which even Elizabeth Taylor would gasp over. Thrown casually under the dagger were more emeralds, one bigger than my fist. In other displays, emeralds and rubies bigger than hen's eggs were common, and pearls were scattered with gay abandon. Want a snuff box—here, carve one out of this emerald, add a little gold trim, not much, but it will do! Baby's cradle—well of course it is solid gold, and we had to do something with those couple of hundred pearls, emeralds and rubies that were left over after we made the Sultan's writing set!

Perhaps the nearness of all this opulence was why Istanbul was so expensive. We had been very well fed and happy eating out on the Turkish southern coast for around 5,000,000 Turkish Lira (\$US1=TL300,000 now, as the Lira value was dropping quickly), for the three of us, including drinks. In Istanbul we averaged over TL11,000,000, with one very nice lunch knocking us back TL30,000,000. By U.S. and Australian standards, paying \$US100 for a meal for three, with drinks, is acceptable, but we have been accustomed to three years of third world expenses, and now had different standards. By Indonesian and Thailand standards, even the Turkish south coast was grossly expensive.

Carole: *The $100 meal was at the Four Seasons Hotel, built in the jail featured in* Midnight Express, *and it was a truly magnificent, gourmet buffet, in an historic setting.*

TURKEY

Back to Topkapi Palace. In the cold and the rain that dogged us all day, we toured the Harem, the one place in the Palace where a guide was mandatory, in company with a group of Spanish tourists. They complained so loudly, and at such length, about the guide speaking English (options were Turkish, English, German, with separate times for each language, clearly marked at the ticket booth), that the guide gave up on them and treated us to a personal tour.

Contrary to your (and our) immediate Pavlovian reaction concerning orgies and debauchery, the Harem was simply the private living quarters of the Sultan, his four wives, hundred or so concubines, children, eunuchs (black and white; the black fixed early and coming voluntarily; the white through capture and subsequent part removals) and servants, some 400 to 500 people in total. Apart from the Sultan's quarters and those of his mother and his heir, the place was something like a plush rabbit warren. Hollywood's Sheiks would never have found the swooning maidens, and if they did, would have been lost getting back to the horse.

The Dolmabahce Palace, replacing Topkapi, was built by the Sultans in the mid-1800s to be modern and European, and is ornate and ugly, a second-rate Versailles, with central heating. Pillars are wood, carved and painted to look like stone, and there is the usual palace rabbit warren once you get away from the formal reception rooms. Even the Harem area was dull. The Sultans also stopped wearing traditional robes and adopted a quasi-military cavalry dress, tight pants with a stripe down the leg, waist length jacket with acres of braid—very dashing, but not Sultanish. Perhaps the rain made the place more depressing than it really was, or perhaps it was the reappearance of the Spanish group that we met in Topkapi. They still hadn't got the message that Spanish was not a guide language in Turkey and were even more Latin in their denunciations of guides, Turkey, and the world in general.

Carole: I stepped into the crowded tram and, before Ryan and Laurie could enter, the doors closed and we were off. All I had was an umbrella, as Laurie was carrying all our money and passports. During our travels I never wore a watch or carried a purse.

Hoping Laurie had been shouting to get off at the next station, I did, and waited, somewhat panic-stricken, for the next tram. Sure enough, there came my heroes to rescue me. My first words were, "Laurie, I want some money now."

We made all the tourist stops, including the Grand Bazaar—a collection of several hundred shops, all selling the same for-the-tourist things, the sunset ferry ride over the Bosporus, and the Mosaic Museum (we had already uncovered our own mosaics at Iassus, so were a little blasé). There was no way we could be blasé on our last morning when we woke to see the first snowfall of the winter, with the Blue Mosque, snow covered and magnificent, rising above the white landscape.

Carole: *We were so cold in Istanbul. We were going to Los Angeles, planning to bring back our winter gear, the first time in three years it was needed. I layered, and layered, even going to the extreme of draping a thin sweater around my head, and finished up looking, and feeling, like an old peasant woman.*

We decided to take advantage of the long enforced stop in Antalya to get some work done while we were away in Los Angeles—new salon upholstery, new cockpit upholstery, re-varnished floors and everything wood, repaired sails, rejuvenated life raft, new lifelines, new bottom paint, new dinghy and hatch covers, plus a lot of minor stuff, all for a little less than the national debt. I was reminded of the fact that, in Turkey, as in most other places, you get quality workmanship only when you supervise personally. I didn't, and we got what we deserved.

On our return to Antalya from Los Angeles in February, we stayed at the Talya Hotel—4-star, center of town—until "Dolphin Spirit" got back in the water. Our expected five-day stay extended to 16 days, as three days of bad weather and Turkish Time got in the way. Luckily the hotel served great buffet breakfasts and evening meals, included in the price, so we spent the days in happy anticipation of the next feast. Our resolutions to lose weight were put behind us (I couldn't resist it) for the moment. Ryan did work out every day in the hotel gym, with me providing non-participatory supervision.

Carole: *The Talya served a huge breakfast buffet, including the standard Turkish breakfast—cucumber, olives and hard-boiled eggs. Fresh honeycomb, straight from the hive was another Talya specialty. Ryan and I soon were saying, "Today is Tuesday—lamb chop night." Desserts included tiny cakes, each beautifully and uniquely decorated. The pianist played nightly and we always waited for "Fur Elise," Ryan's and my signature tune.*

Finally everything was done to the stage where "Dolphin Spirit" could go back in the water and we could resume our real life. However, before our winter lay-up ended we wanted to make one last trip, to the Cappadocia region of central Turkey, a very special place with land formations right out of *Star Wars*, part of which was actually filmed there. Neil Armstrong used the area to practice moon landings, as the closest approximation on earth to the moon's surface. There are over 100 underground cities, some of which go down 26 levels, 365 churches and thousands of houses, all carved into the tufa rock, rocks balanced on rocks, balanced on rocks, white and pink rock waves, canyons, spires, plateaus. How could we stay away?

The 10-hour bus ride (2000 hours to 0800 hours) from Antalya to Urgup was cheap (L4 million, $US15 each way), but sheer torture, as the seats were designed for short, slim Turks, and the bus was full. There was a steward who distributed free water and cokes.

Carole: When I was a small child, my Grandmother drilled into me how unsanitary public toilets were. As a result, I had almost never, until now, used one. The exception was when I'd take the train in from Connecticut to New York City for the day. My first stop was always Trump Towers, because they had the most luxurious bathrooms. The ten hours in a bumpy bus were just too long, forcing me to break a life-time taboo, and what a place I chose to do it! A bus stop, in the middle of the night, in the center of Turkey. A hole in the floor, filled to overflowing, but I had no choice and in desperation put my feet on either side.......... Oh! Grandma!

Un-kinking after the ride, I was glad that we had splurged and booked into a 4-star hotel. We also booked a private guide. The guide—Ali, from Argeus Tours—was no extravagance, as he spoke excellent English, really made the place come alive for us, and made sure we missed nothing.

Around 3-million years ago, three volcanoes surrounding the region began eruptions that lasted for over 100,000 years, and laid down layers of lava and ash. The ash became a rock called tufa, which is relatively soft. This rock has become exposed in cliffs and spires, capped by the harder lava, and eroded into quite fantastic shapes. The local inhabitants began digging houses into the tufa some 10,000 years ago, digging the underground cities about 5,000 years ago, and being inundated by tourists about 10 years ago—mainly French and Italian. Perhaps the English and Germans, who smother the Turkish coast in summer, prefer sand and sun to culture!

The churches were built in the period 700 to 1,200 AD, utilizing caves already dug. Cappadocia became a Christian center, as it was easy to hide in the underground cities during periods of persecution. Most churches have very interesting and colorful frescos, partly destroyed or defaced by subsequent Islam invaders, as their religion forbids the showing of faces in religious settings, but with enough remaining to give an appreciation of the art.

We went down eight levels in one of the underground cities, sufficient to become completely disoriented and lost, even with electric lights and arrows to show the way. The cities were used to hide out in when invaders appeared, and were occupied for a maximum of six months at a time. Consider the engineering necessary to get fresh air circulating through 26 levels, remove human and animal wastes without leaving surface traces, provide water and food to 3,000+ inhabitants, provide light and so on. Round rock doors were still in place, ready to be rolled across passages to block invaders. Kitchens have smoke collection rooms attached, to prevent egress of any tell-tale traces. Everyone must have been about Ryan's size, as he was the only one of us who could walk about in comfort. I followed him down one tunnel, got stuck, and had to back out, as there was no room to turn around, much to the amusement of a gaggle of Japanese teenagers who were passing.

Carole: *From our hotel room in the morning, we would see the hot-air balloons rising. Laurie made reservations for the next day, and all night long I lay petrified, waiting for the 4am call to tell us the weather was right for a flight, hoping for a cancellation. Once we were up, I overcame my fear of heights, assisted greatly by the wonderful fantasy landscape we were sailing over.*

Our early morning hot air balloon ride was a hit with us all. We watched the sun rise five times, went low enough to pick apples and high enough to see for ever. It was exciting and fun, and the view simply stunning. The landscape is almost indescribable, the shapes, the colors, the canyons, the cave houses, the light, all combining to create scenery that must be unique in this world.

Ryan (11): *It was still dark when we got to the balloons and watched them light the gas burners and fill the bags with hot air. When we were in the baskets, the burners made really loud roars when the pilot used them to lift us, otherwise we drifted in silence. We landed on top of a ridge and the basket tipped over on its side.*

Carole: *On horseback we rode through the countryside, villages and towns, clattering over the cobblestones, waving to the locals, dodging the traffic and watching the birds fly over the hills, fields and vineyards. The fact that, after a two-hour ride I could barely hobble, did nothing to diminish the pleasure. Ryan's horse wanted to eat everything in sight, Laurie's wanted to fertilize every inch of the ground, but mine just ambled on. Perhaps that's why the other horses tried to kick it every time they got near!*

Turkey

Visiting a local pottery workshop, in the top levels of another underground city, Carole and Ryan worked a foot-powered pottery wheel, and turned out remarkably good looking pots. Ryan's had a hole in the bottom, which meant he wouldn't get married in the near future, but Carole's was perfect. The show rooms were also in the underground city, and formed a maze that seemed to go on forever. The complex housed some 400 artisans, but all we saw from ground level was a small house and yard.

The weekly Urgup market was a riot of people and goods. Clothes, shoes, plastic ware, toys, fruit, vegetables (cabbages half Ryan's size), fish, olives, home-made butter and cheese, honeycombs, spices and lots of things we couldn't recognize—all were for sale. There were no tourists, they were out looking at the rocks, so we strolled, chatted, took photos, smiled, waved, bowed, shook hands, fingered things, admired everything, and had a great time.

Carole: *Laurie was in his element, chatting up the locals in English, while they replied in Turkish, neither caring about the lack of verbal comprehension, because the friendship message was getting across, both ways. On the bus back to Antalya, he made friends with a Whirling Dervish, who was so sorry when he had to get off the bus and miss Laurie's next Australian story.*

It was in Turkey, that we joined the World and got an email address. Tammy signed us up, and life changed. We now sought out Internet Cafes as well as markets at every port.

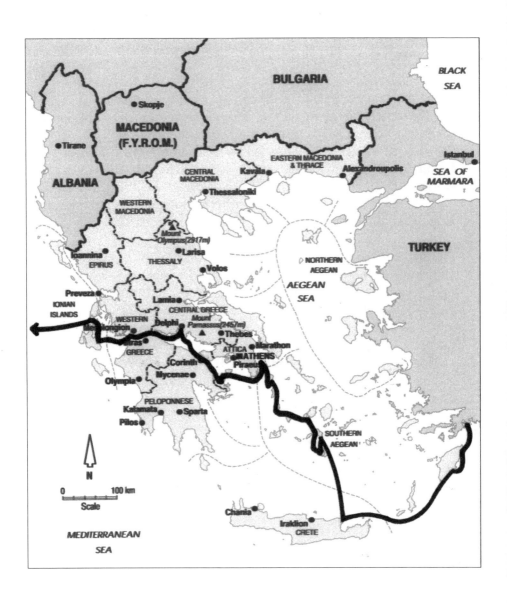

Greece

Year Four
April 8 to July 3

Greece is really a complicated place, divided as it is into four regions, the Aegean, the Mainland, the Peloponnese Peninsular and the Ionian. We visited all four, so by way of assistance to the reader, we provide a chapter summary.

Islands visited—Rhodes, Crete, Santorini, Ios, Naxos, Paros, Mykonos, Delos, Syros, Kea, Poros, Trizonia, Ithaki, Lefkada
Ruins—Malia, Gournia, Lato, Zakros, Gortys, Phaistos, Knossos, Delos, Parthenon, Temple of Poseidon, Big Epidouras, Little Epidouras, Delphi.
Castles—Lindos, Rhodes, Iraklion, Rethimnon, Chania, Livadia.
Other—Monastery of Moni Toplou, Athens, Corinth Canal, Monastery of Oy Louka.

Miscellaneous information that may be of some use to a future traveler includes:
• The commonest tree on all the Greek islands is the olive, followed by the Australian eucalyptus. We were told by a Greek, who was amazed that the Greeks in Australia hadn't spread the word, that the eucalyptus was a tree native to Greece. The logical extension of this is that the Greeks were in Australia before the Australian aboriginals arrived.
• The Rhodes "Sound and Light Show" might have been okay several years ago, before the trees grew and blocked the castle (the "light" part of the show) off from the viewing seats.
• The Athens, Parthenon "Sound and Light Show" was even worse, but the

view of the Acropolis and Parthenon in the daylight was superb. Terrible script, mediocre lighting.
• Crete in April was marvelous, wild flowers, wonderful mountains, great ruins, pretty villages, few tourists.
• Santorini was magnificent from the water, pretty villages hung on the edge of the cliffs.
• The ruins on Delos Island were interesting, in a spectacular setting, but were not up to the "OO-Ah-Gee" standard of many of the others we have visited.
• A Crete restaurant owner told us that he had "no Greek food, as the tourist season hasn't started yet." He was serious.

We untied from the dock at Setur Marina earlier than intended, and headed off for Rhodes to meet John (Carole's brother) and his wife Janet. The Turkish winds gave us a final goodbye by being right in our faces, no matter what direction we headed. We fully expected to see a yacht coming towards us, also with the wind on their nose, but it was too early in the year for others to be venturing out. We lost track of the number of "You're leaving when!" comments we got. Leaving early meant few tourists, even fewer yachts, and very windy and unsettled weather.

To make it easier for John and Janet's arrival, we went into the main harbor at Rhodes, instead of going to Lindos. Riddle: "When is a marina not a marina?" Answer; "When it is Mandraki Marina, Rhodes." No space, no water, no fuel, no showers, no toilets, sporadic electricity—you get the picture—but it is right downtown Rhodes City. We were directed to go next door, to the ferry harbor, where we tied up, nose in, between some tugs and a 95-foot sailboat.

As you might expect, there was a little excitement associated with our berthing. Med-mooring requires Carole on the bow to throw lines, me in the cockpit driving, and Ryan at the stern dropping the anchor. We had run out the stern anchor and chain in Antalya, to make sure it was free, so naturally it jammed immediately. Ryan drove the boat in circles (small harbor full of ferries, each ocean liner size) while I emptied the lazarette to get at the chain locker and free the chain. Second try saw 100 feet of chain and the stern navigation light go over the side before another jam. By then it was too late to retrieve the situation, so I just powered in, dragging the anchor, and we successfully tied up. This harbor was further from the city center, but we could get electricity.

To keep us off the rough cement dock, we had to rig another anchor and drop it with the dinghy, as the wind chose to blow at 30 to 40 knots from the stern. We also tied a line to the big yacht next door, to hold us off the tugs on the other side. Peace reigned for a day. As a prelude to future activities, let us remind you that very large ferries also anchored and tied up in this harbor, and that the 95-footer next to us was also Med-moored, stern in, with bow anchor set towards the harbor middle.

We were just sitting down to lunch, when we heard a shout from the big yacht, and "Dolphin Spirit" lurched to the side. We all ran up to the deck to see the big yacht's anchor chain nearly horizontal, then the line tying us to them snapped, immediately followed by the explosive parting of the four 2-inch lines that held them to the dock. The yacht took off like a rocket, out to the middle of the harbor, trailing lines, electrical cords (including ours), gangplanks and other bits and pieces. An incoming ferry had dropped anchor chain across the yacht's anchor, and when it moved into the dock, simply pulled the yacht with it. The ferry-boat captain never even noticed until it was all over, and then he denied that it happened, that they did it, that, if they did do it, it was their problem, that the sun came up that morning, and so on.

One of the 2-inch lines was across our bow and, before it snapped, it pulled our anchor into our bow, scoring a hole in the fiberglass. Apart from that, and the loss of some electrical fittings, we were unharmed and feeling very lucky. The big yacht lost some wood from its toe-rails, and the broken lines, but was otherwise undamaged. The captain was on board, and managed to get everything back together, hoist the anchor, and return to the dock. A brand new experience for us, and an interesting introduction to the "Year of the Anchor" as this sailing season soon became known.

The big yacht had a fifth line tied to a nearby Greek Navy vessel. This didn't break, but simply ripped out the cleat to which it was attached. The Navy personnel obviously weren't happy with this display of weakness, as they repeatedly denied that they had lost a cleat, even when presented with the very item, and the hole pointed out. Real men don't lose cleats!

We were in Rhodes for the Greek Orthodox Easter celebrations, and had ringside seats on "Osprey," which was tied up in the Mandraki Marina, right in front of the central church. Preliminaries to the main event seemed to involve exploding fireworks, at all hours of day and night. The climax came at midnight, Saturday night, with a procession from the church, more explosions, including several that had to be half sticks of TNT, and a lighting of candles by the crowd as they dispersed—a mixture of religion and anarchy.

Carole: Long ago, I had made for myself a list of things I wanted to do. One section included a cruise ship to Greece and an emerald ring. Therefore it was natural that Laurie and I would go looking for an emerald ring in Rhodes. One shop-owner showed us the most magnificent emerald, surrounded by huge diamonds, and offered it to us for $40,000. What really *blew us away were his financing terms. If we gave him post-dated checks for a total of $40,000 we could take the ring with us to the U.S. and have it appraised. If the appraisal was below $60,000 we would return the ring and cancel the checks. Unfortunately, the ring was far too big for my hands (Laurie surprised me with this comment, as he normally won't say anything negative about my appearance), so we had to pass it up.*

John and Janet arrived late at night, and being uncertain that they could find us, we stood on the street for over two hours, peering into every taxi that passed—Carole got some interesting, potentially lucrative, offers. Naturally, their plane was late, so Carole and Ryan had gone off to bed leaving me in lonely vigil before THE TAXI arrived, and of course knew exactly where to go.

Touring Rhodes city took up the next day—400 jewelry shops take a while to investigate—and allowed J&J time to unwind from their previous three weeks of strenuous cruise-ship activities (Buenos Aires to Barcelona).

One night we decided to see the Rhodes Castle "Sound and Light" show. After buying the tickets and walking the several hundred yards to the seats, we discovered that there were only two others there. The show would not start without 10 people in the audience. We offered to buy the necessary three tickets, but were told that the count was people, not tickets.

In desperation, John and I took to the streets, stopping everyone that passed, begging them to come in. We have missed our calling as ticket-touts, as we very quickly rounded up the necessary "volunteers."

Perhaps several years ago the show was worth the visit. Now, the trees had grown tall and totally blocked the castle (the "Light" segment) from view, making the extremely boring "Sound" even duller. Luckily, our volunteers had a sense of humor, so John and I lived.

You can't visit Rhodes without going to Lindos. As the wind would have made it a rough trip on "Dolphin Spirit," Carole and the Js went by bus.

Carole: *Naturally we went to Mavriko's for lunch. We hadn't been there for almost six months and I was so surprised to be immediately recognized without my usual male entourage, and given apologies that MY table was taken.*

The Wells all reported a flat, calm ocean and anchorage, so off we went in DS the next day. Of course we had strong winds and rough seas all the way to Lindos, with waves marching straight into the anchorage when we got there.

Carole: *I made a delicious breakfast of French toast before we left. No sooner had I given that up to the rough seas, when my brother, seeing how gracefully I had done it, gave his breakfast to Poseidon as well. That trip was one of the roughest of the whole voyage. Janet asked if it was always like this. The normal two hour passage lasted over five.*

Sitting in the anchorage was "Freya," last seen in Antalya. Seeing us come in, they assumed the sailing was okay, so left, only to be back the next morning after a terrible night at sea.

The next day was calm, but we decided that continuation of harmonious family relationships required an extended stay at anchor in Lindos, rather than the proposed trip to Crete. This gave us time to rent a car and drive around Rhodes. A sandbar at the very south of the island where the Aegean Sea was on one side (rough), and the Mediterranean on the other (smooth) deserved the visit. At a place in the interior mountains called Seven Springs (we saw only three) Ryan and I walked through a small tunnel (five-foot diameter at best—I was an hour straightening up again) leading, under a hill, from the river to a lake.

Ryan (11): *It was long, dark and wet, and I enjoyed it so much, that we went back through again, possibly some sort of a record?*

Close to Lindos was an avenue of huge eucalyptus trees, and, half way along, we found the Koala Hotel. It was still closed for winter, and no amount of peering up into the trees found any koalas, so I decided to spare the others by not telling my litany of "falling koala" jokes. For those fortunate enough not to have been told these "jokes," and who wish to spend half-a-day in misery, simply find an Australian and ask.

The Js were great guests and we were sorry to see them go. Lindos was a terrific place to spend time, regardless of the reason, so after they left, we stayed on a few more days to prove that we didn't do it just for them—in total, we were there three times for more than five weeks stay.

Eventually the wind died down to acceptable levels, so we hauled up the anchor and headed off for an overnight sail to Crete. Fantastic! For the first time in many months, we actually sailed. Then, as expected, the wind died, and we motored on, arriving at Agios Nickolaus at 3am. It was so calm that, after we had switched off, we drifted only a mile in the next four hours while we waited for sunrise. Getting no response on the radio from the marina, we entered and tied up, just as the 30-knot winds started up again. Sailing in the Med is a lottery.

As it turned out, the marina office was open only from 9am to 1pm, Monday to Friday, the fees were expensive, the water drinkable, but not free, the power reliable, but extremely expensive, and there was one temporary shower/toilet for the whole place. It was the only marina in Crete however, and the only place where I was happy to leave the boat and go land-cruising.

The Greek Islands generally are a nightmare for cruisers, with mostly bad to poor anchorages, roaring northerly meltimi winds every afternoon, tiny harbors with rough quays, and few marinas. Visit by ferry, as the islands are beautiful, but sail in Turkey, which is equally pretty, and much more yacht-friendly.

We had read that the best time to visit Crete was in spring, and so we decided to see it all, renting a car and driving more than 1,000 miles on the island roads. The spring wild flowers were all out, mainly yellow and white, with occasional splashes of red. Crete is very mountainous, and the higher spots were still snow-capped. Many of the roads were lined with, and overhung by, bushes and trees loaded with flowers. Even the eucalyptus trees that were everywhere were in flower. Made me quite revoltingly nostalgic.

The road from Agios Nickolaus to Iraklion, the major city, was a "four-lane highway," and an excellent road by any criteria. Most of the others were paved, two lane, and well signposted. When the road came to a village, it simply wound its way through, twisting around houses, and down alley ways, without disturbing the original village. Of necessity then, the road became one lane, or less, made even narrower by the fact that the villagers simply ignored its presence, parking cars, holding conversations on their front door steps (now a part of the highway), and generally going about their normal business. This was quite fascinating for us in the almost total absence of other traffic, but must be chaos during the tourist season.

Crete is the home of the Minoan civilization, the earliest in Greece, and we tried to visit every ruined city on the island—the passage from Turkey to Greece had allowed us to recover from the ruinitus we had contracted there. Minoans had a lot in common with present day home buyers—position was everything—so most of their cities were placed on hills, near the sea, with spectacular views. Only one—Malia—is on a plain.

Ryan (11): (from his trip report) *Ancient Gournia was an important Minoan site. The ruins date from 1551 to 1450 BC. It is a network of streets and staircases.*

The monastery of Moni Toplou looks like a fortress, not a monastery. The place was ravaged by the Knights of St. John and the Turks. Monks poured boiling oil on intruders from a hole, just above the doorway, and I stood under it.

The Lassithi Plateau is laid out like a huge patchwork quilt. Vast expanses of pear and apple orchids plus many almond trees cover the plateau, which has been farmed since Minoan times. The many windmills that dot the place are used to pump water, and at restaurants, to attract tourists.

The goddess Rhea hid the new-born Zeus from his father, an offspring gobbler, in Dikteon Cave. It later became a place of cult worship. We walked through it to see the stalactites and stalagmites.

Just outside of Rethymno is the 16th century monastery of Moni Arkadiou. It is of Venetian baroque architecture. Turks attacked with 2,000 troops and everyone was killed by an abbot who lit gunpowder and blew them all up except for one girl, a baby, who survived by being blown into a tree.

Gournia was our favorite site, as it was a real working city, not just a palace with outbuildings, like Knossos. Knossos is the most visited place in Crete, as it contains some magnificent frescos, and has been partly restored so you can get a feel for what it must have been like. The Minoans had flush toilets (that of the Queen can be inspected, in all its splendor), sewerage systems, skylights for air and light, and a lot of the amenities of modern cities. All this over 5,000 years ago, when the English and most of the Europeans were painting their faces blue and living in mud huts.

The wonderful Anthropological Museum in Iraklion has over 20 rooms, each dealing, in sequence, with a period of Crete's history. The first room, the earliest period, contains cups, bowls, jewelry and other items that are startlingly modern looking, so clearly the civilization must have been in full swing for some time before this. Weapons (swords, spears, and daggers) did not appear until about 3,000 years ago, and no one seems to know why.

Highlights were a magnificent bull's head, carved from a single green stone, with gold horns; a delicate crystal vase that somehow survived the ages intact; the partly restored Knossos frescos, particularly that of acrobats leaping over a bull; a gold pendant of two bees and a honeycomb; and the perfect teeth on two adult skeletons. As an aside for the dentists among us, all the teeth were there, both upper and lower sets, and there seemed to be no cavities and no fillings, just perfect, white, straight teeth. Perhaps the Minoans, to take a break from inventing toilets, discovered fluoride.

Eventually, as we were driving through magnificent mountains, along a road lined with wonderful wild flowers and past exotic Minoan ruins, with Ryan reading in the back seat, and Carole and I discussing the finer points of salad making, we realized that it was time to move on.

It was an overnight sail, north to Santorini, so naturally the wind came from that direction, but we were able to motor-sail into it. In fact, we were making such good time that I tried to slow down so we would arrive at dawn. The wind chose that moment to swing round to the south, and we picked up a northerly current (or were being towed by a whale), so we shot past Santorini at 3am, and went on to Ios. The Greek Islands are generally less than 20 miles apart and look very alike (except for Santorini). How many variations can you have of dry, brown hills, blue sea, and white, square houses with blue shutters, blue doors, and a red geranium plant?

After a day of rest, we sailed back to Santorini, the crater of a volcano that exploded around 3,000 years ago, with the houses (pastel as well as white here) encrusted on the rim. We stooged around for a while, couldn't find a place to anchor or moor, dodged four cruise ships, drifted under the prettiest encrustation while we lunched, took innumerable photos, and went back to Ios.

Carole: *But I wanted to see it from the land! Santorini was one of the places Laurie promised to take me if I would sail with him. So what if there were no suitable anchorages or marinas. He promised! He suffered, boy did he suffer.*

The local Town Constabulary ran us out of the harbor at the main town of Ios. Our choice became either the town wharf, or around the corner. We have a particular dislike of crowded, shallow, rough, expensive, town wharves, so chose to go round the corner, and rolled and rolled and rolled all night—probably the worst night we have spent at anchor, apart from the "Anchorage from Hell" in the Red Sea.

As soon as it was light we headed for Naxos, the regulation 20 miles away. We followed a ferry in (ocean-liner size), watched as its props and bow thrusters made the anchored yachts heave and bounce, and decided that this was no place for us, so on to Paros, only six miles further.

Naoussa Bay, Paros, was huge, open to the north, but with a secondary bay just inside the entrance that offered north protection. We headed there, and anchored in a terrific spot, just off a beach inhabited by nude male-female couples and nude male groups. Made going ashore quite a trial, as we were never quite sure where to walk, or look. Do you say "hello" as you step over a nude woman, or just smile and proceed on your way? Thank the Lord for sunglasses! How do you handle having to pass through a group of nude men applauding another, equally bare, dancing for them? Life in the Greek Islands can be complicated!

To pry me away from my binoculars, we rented a car and drove around Paros—pretty, interesting, and over in less than an hour. So we went around again, found an Internet Cafe, ate lunch, drove around again and generally used up the day gainfully. Back at the anchorage we got a huge surprise, as there was "Marita Shan." We had last been anchored with them in Turkey, twelve months ago. As MS was being sold in Turkey, Pat and Tashi decided to do a quick fling through the Greek Islands before becoming land-locked.

We had a great reunion. Then three Australian yachts, and a New Zealander arrived, all of them having come up the Red Sea with us and MS. Quite a co-incidence, as everyone was sailing independently.

The winds blew 30+ knots from the north for a couple of days, then swung to the south (have we mentioned that the Greek Islands are a terrible place to sail in? Can we mention it again?), so we moved to the other end of the bay, near the town. Late in the afternoon, a particularly vicious gust plucked "Marita Shan's" anchor out, and away they went.

In the hustle of getting them re-anchored, we didn't immediately notice that a charter yacht, just beyond MS, had taken off as well. No one was on board, so I took our dinghy, and with Ryan, and a Frenchman off another yacht, went to see what could be done. The yacht was locked up, so we couldn't start the engine, but pushed it with the dinghy to keep it off a rocky island, and then let out enough anchor chain to allow the anchor to catch again. The wind was blowing 40 to 50 knots, so we had a terrible time getting back against it to "Dolphin Spirit" and a very anxious Carole.

A few hours later, the winds died down, and a local fishing boat went out to the yacht, just as the charterers reappeared. They hailed the fishermen as saviors, and heaped rewards on their heads. Naturally the fishermen had no objection to this, and we had sufficient reward from our knowledge of a good deed well done—yeah, right!

Finally the bloody winds dropped, "Marita Shan" left for Turkey, never to be seen by us again, and we headed for Mykonos—20 miles away. Mykonos Harbor is to be avoided, so we anchored a couple of miles south in Ornos Bay, which actually had a sand bottom, not covered by weed. As you may gather, we were less than thrilled by Greek anchorages, but this one was pretty and safe, although open to the south.

It was much frequented by charter yachts, so we anchored well off the beach, in about the middle, to be away from their anchoring antics. Charter yachts clustered around the first to anchor, regardless of available space, and appeared to have minimal knowledge of the concept of "scope" (the amount of anchor chain or line let out in relation to the water depth). Actually, there was a practical reason for the clustering close to shore. Most of the charter yachts had at least eight people on board, many had 10 or 12, mostly all male, mostly German or Austrian. Their dinghies held two people dry, three wet, with outboards that provided a top speed of a couple of knots, so dinner ashore meant a lot of trips.

The next episode in the Year of the Anchor Saga. First the Rhodes thrill, then the Paros debacle, now Ornos. Just as we were about to dinghy to shore late one morning, we noticed a charter catamaran attempting to anchor in front of us, so decided to wait, as the Meltimi were doing their usual 25 knots. Sure enough, the cat came back—on us!

They saw they were too close, so pulled their anchor up to just off the bottom and motored across in front of us, in spite of my impassioned screams and pointing at our anchor chain. Of course, their anchor caught our chain. "Drop your anchor and go back," I advised them calmly, in the Pavarotti voice I assume on such occasions. Naturally they pulled up the anchor even further and powered forward. This swung their stern into our bow and, amongst other damage, broke their lifelines.

One of the broken wire ends caught Carole on the inside of her elbow, punctured a vein, and left her spurting blood everywhere. Ryan was racing to move our dinghy to save it from being run over, and I was trying to prevent major damage to "Dolphin Spirit," so poor Carole was left to spurt alone. After the initial pint or so, the bleeding slowed, and she went below, leaving a trail of huge blood drops behind.

I finally made the people realize that they had to release anchor chain, and got them tied up to us. By then most of the damage had been done, and all that was left was the hard work of getting their anchor untangled from our chain. The charterers had no clue, so I hauled and juggled lines and chains and eventually got things separated. Then the damn fools wanted to drop the anchor where they were, tied up to DS. Carole, by then non-spurting, managed to restrain me, as I was ready to strangle all and sundry. I piled their chain and anchor on their deck and untied them from us. They promptly backed into our stern and almost sank our dinghy. For once, I was almost speechless, reduced to screaming, "Forward, forward," in an almost falsetto croak.

All this took approximately an hour. Carole had a group of eleven punctures and a neat bruise inside her elbow, and would have had some difficulty in convincing authorities she wasn't a heroin addict. Ryan was quite wonderful, running, on his own initiative, to get the engine ready to start when it looked as if our anchor had been pulled out, helping Carole staunch her bleeding, and getting the dinghy out of the way. We shudder to think what would have happened had we left the boat earlier, and not been aboard to sort things out. The charterers were worse than useless, as virtually everything they did made matters worse. At one stage, I was straddled across both bows, hauling on their anchor chain, when the woman driver decided, for some obscure reason, to drive the cat forward. I nearly lost a hand and various other important anatomical parts before my bellows penetrated, and she stopped. At least she did something—none of the others did anything except stare.

Mykonos, basically a brown, barren island, is relieved by white buildings with blue shutters and doors and, if not red geraniums, beautiful bougainvillea. The town is charming, in a touristy/contrived way, and hugely expensive, even by Greek standards of ripping off the tourists. We did an hour's E-mail at the local Internet Cafe and were charged over $US50. The most we had ever paid before was $US6. The local promotion boasts of more discos and restaurants than the rest of the Greek Islands combined, and goes on to claim that Mykonos is the most beautiful island in the world. Sadly, the promotion works, and everyone goes to Mykonos—once. It is by far the least pretty of the Greek Islands we have seen.

As only light winds were forecast one day (I was paranoid about leaving the boat at anchor in the Greek Islands), we took the ferry to Delos to see the ruins. The ancient city must have been huge, as we saw only a fraction of the place in the three hours we were there. The view from the top seats of the theater, across blue seas and islands, had to have distracted the play-goers from the action on stage below. We must be getting close to being ruined-out again, as we were not as enthusiastic about the place as it deserved. Even the museum with its phallic exhibits didn't even get the usual response from Ryan. The 30-knot winds that came up may have had something to do with it (**B**loody **G**reek **I**sland **W**eather).

My oldest kids, Jenny and Philip, and Philip's new girl-friend Lilia, arrived by ferry from Athens. By then the 40-knot winds (BGIW) had died a little, so they could enjoy the anchorage. We hired scooters and motored around the island, with the only casualty being Jenny's knee when a stone wall leapt into the middle of the road and hit her. The poor scooter that carried Carole and I started blowing huge clouds of black smoke, then refused to go up a hill, but performed very well on the downhill return trip.

We motor-sailed to Syros (winds nil, then 30-knots on the nose—BGIW), a pretty little anchorage. The four youngsters set out one morning to climb a mountain that loomed over the bay. I was exhausted watching through binoculars, and Carole prostrated herself just thinking about it. Then it was on to Kythnos. BGIW struck again—we were heading west, so the wind turned to westerly, and we couldn't go to the anchorage we wanted. Jenny and I made an executive decision (everyone else was asleep as it was around 11am, repeat am), and we went to Kea instead. As soon as we were committed to this, the wind became northerly, our new course (BGIW).

Kavia Bay, Kea, is somewhat reminiscent of Twin Harbors, Catalina Island. That likeness was reinforced the next day (Sunday) when 49 powerboats from Athens (26 miles away) arrived and snuggled up to us. They ranged in size from 50 to 150-feet, and there were a lot of 30 to 40-footers as well, but those were too small to count. Luckily, the wind blew lightly and constantly from the one direction, as the normal anchoring procedure was to power in, drop a few feet of chain, throw fenders over the side, and open the beer. We actually kept a few feet clear around us by glowering at each new arrival, and gesturing at them in what must be universally recognized sign language. Carole and I refused to leave the boat, so the kids (they just love that term) went to see the famous Kea lion by themselves.

It was a bit ego-deflating for us, after having mostly been the biggest boat around, to get to the Mediterranean and be somewhat smaller than a dinghy. A 300-foot (100-meter) sailboat takes some getting used to, while a 300-foot powerboat is awesome. On most of the biggies, the uniformed crew of 20 or more were usually pleasant (a lot of Australians and New Zealanders), but we found some difficulty in wandering up to owners/charterers, and inviting them over for drinks—nowhere for the helicopter to land, you see.

A chance conversation with a nearby powerboat changed our set in marshmallow plans, and we went to Olympic Marina at Lavrion, on the Greek mainland, a new marina, with excellent facilities. We needed a secure place to leave the boat to visit Athens. The marinas near Athens have a terrible reputation, and the clincher was the assurance that Olympic was only an hour by road from Athens. That it may be, if you have a car and live on the outskirts of Athens. By bus it was $153^1/_4$ minutes of excruciating torture, as we developed intimate relations with every small village, on and off the road, and then sat in Athens traffic. Greeks are normal size people, as are the Turks, so why do both design their buses for midgets?

The bus dropped us off somewhere in Athens, at a spot totally undecorated by street signs or names. "Acropolis?" we asked. "Go there, catch train, three stations," we were told. "There" turned out to be not quite "there," but we eventually found the underground train station. The ticket booth was on the platform itself, and there were some "do-it-yourself" ticket stamping machines scattered about. As no one checked us either going into the station, or out at our destination, one has to wonder how the system pays for itself, given the greediness of the Greeks above ground.

We found the Acropolis and staggered up to the gate. A cafe was selling frozen lemon and orange drinks, so we bought six. "D1500 ($US5)," said the vendor—each! He enjoyed our slack-jawed amazement. It was the same price to enter the Acropolis area, and they wouldn't let us in until we had finished the drinks. Anyway, the Acropolis was very grand, and the view of Athens made the city look quite picturesque, instead of the crowded, dirty place it really is.

Someone had told Jenny that the "Sound and Light" show was not to be missed, so we dined and waited for the 9:30 pm start. In the fading daylight, the Sound & Light seats provided a wonderful view of the Acropolis, but, unfortunately, neither the sound nor the lights were even a close approach to "ho-hum." How anyone can take such a setting, make it totally boring, and then claim credit for the disaster, is beyond me.

I had the acumen and foresight to reserve two taxis for the return trip, and, surprise, surprise, they were waiting for us (***Carole:*** *Of course they were. Laurie had promised them an arm and a leg.*). In retrospect, even the bus torture may have been better, as the taxis gave us one of history's scariest rides. Our driver spent his time constantly talking on his two-way radio, when he wasn't on his mobile phone, doing 120 to 140 kph, and advising us, in excellent English, that this was, "one of the most dangerous roads in all Greece, and two people have been killed here, just today."

Laundry done, water tanks filled, batteries charged and more peanut butter bought, we headed off in an absolute dead calm (BGIW), past the Temple of Poseidon imposing on a bluff, and on to Poros Island. We hired cars and drove to Epidouras to see the huge ancient Greek theatre there. It was in a great state of preservation, but we have seen others that were more beautiful, others in prettier settings and others that seemed to breathe history.

The sun was up at 6:30am, and set after 8:30pm, with darkness coming around 9:30pm. This complicated our life no end. When darkness disappeared at 6am and reappeared at 7pm, we could safely begin cocktail time at 5pm, in the sure knowledge that drinking time was only long enough for a couple of glasses of wine. Now the start time was just too ingrained to change, so we regularly ran out of wine, having drunk on, waiting for darkness to signal a stop.

Jenny, Philip, Ryan and Lilia caught a ferry to Athens, then another to Santorini. Carole and I were somewhat at a loss to know what to do with ourselves, having the boat with no one else on board for the first time in years. We found something!

Jenny and Ryan returned to us. Philip stayed on to propose to Lilia on a balcony overlooking the island (romantic isn't he, wonder where he gets it from?), and then flew directly back to L.A. An American boat "Elena" anchored near us. We had seen them last, almost exactly 12 months ago, in Fethiye. Their 11-year-old grand-daughter was on board, so we sailed with them for the next week, giving Ryan a friend to play with and his first Harry Potter book to read.

The Corinth Canal is one of the three "must sail" canals in the world. Some three miles long, about 50-feet wide, with vertical walls 200 to 300-feet high, and spanned by several bridges, it cuts across the narrowest part of the Peloponnese Peninsular and connects the Aegean to the Ionian. When we tied up at the receiving wharf there was a low bridge just in front of us for vehicle traffic. We paid our $US125 transit fee and waited for the East-bound convoy to arrive. There is no way two boats, even small ones, could pass safely. I was idly watching the traffic bridge when it started to sink. At first I thought that I was seeing things, having expected the bridge to rise, swing, or open, but never did I think it would go down to allow the ships to pass.

Ryan (11): *I wondered why the bridges weren't fitted with nets to catch fish on the way up. It's what I would have done.*

The operators allowed two navy vessels to go, then our group of yachts, with "Dolphin Spirit" in the lead. Carole and Jenny photographed and filmed the rock walls, the bridges high above us and the boats behind in various combinations, but still couldn't fully capture the unique experience.

The operators of the traffic bridge at the other end waited until we were close, then dropped it, but maintained the red light until we were less than 100 feet away, when it changed to green. I had conceded defeat and begun to turn, and had to get back on course, so I guess they won that game of scare-the-yacht.

The ancient city of Corinth was just to the left as we exited, so left we turned and wound through a very shallow channel, in a very extensive even shallower area, to get to the City docks. Luckily there was a space at the entrance to side-tie to the harbor wall, as water under the keel ran out. We ploughed a turn, and then a channel, through the soft mud to get out the next day.

Itea was reported to have a marina where it was supposed to be safe to leave the boat to go to Delphi. It may be a marina some day, but the docks were in place, and that was all we needed. The ruins at Delphi have an outstanding setting in the mountains—those Priestesses must have been real-estate agents on the side. We didn't want to leave, not a normal reaction for the seen-it-all Panes.

Carole: *The athletic arena had been partially restored, so I ran on the track, recording the best time ever in the "un-fit female sailor" category.*

The Monastery of Ossoiy Louka contains some of Greece's best frescos in a building that is "a symphony of marble and mosaics"— actually it did look good. Carole almost got us thrown out when she tried to film one of the Brothers consulting with his parishioners. (***Carole:*** *Consulting! They were drinking wine.*) Once again the monastery was sited with a magnificent view, for inspirational purposes.

Then it was on to Livadia, where we lunched overlooking the Spring of Lethe, a well known historical place—look it up in your Funk and Wagnel. We sat on a bridge and watched women washing clothes in the stream below.

We may be giving some readers the impression that we were having a bad time in Greece—not true. To be sure, the Aegean anchorages were not good, the winds too strong, the prices too high, the people not friendly, and the scenery spectacularly boring (blue water, white houses, blue doors, red geraniums), but we rose above it, and enjoyed ourselves. Actually, the really good bit was about to begin.

Having tearfully abandoned Jenny to the goodwill of a Greek taxi driver (***Ryan [11]:*** *That wasn't part of the good bit*), we were visited by the Itea Port Police, who invited us to come to their office, at our convenience. They had guns, so in accordance with our principle of absolute compliance when faced with overwhelming odds, I was at their office before they returned. We were relieved of several thousand drachma for the privilege of staying at a free marina with no facilities. One grins, pays, and goes on with life.

Our next stop was the lovely little island of Trizonia; no cars, no fees, no Port Police, just a very protected, free marina, clear water and tranquility—hard to believe we were in Greece! A big car-ferry arrived loaded with about 15 cement-mixer trucks. The village had apparently decided to have a road, so they poured a concrete one, about half-a-mile long, in a day. The car ferry had to make two trips, and the whole village was walking up and down on concrete the next day. What's next, the token car?

The yachtie hangout was Lizzie's Yacht Club, a restaurant/bar perched on the hillside above the harbor. Lizzie, an English lady, was no longer there, having departed somewhat mysteriously (Hey, there has to be something new and different to talk about over cocktails), leaving her daughter in charge. An English couple, living on a yacht in the marina, were cook and waitress, or cook and waiter, or other combinations that suited the occasion. The menu was therefore somewhat of a chancy thing, but the view was great, and the drinks cold.

The Drymna Hotel, the only one in town, was attempting to break the Lizzie lock on yachts, and gave everyone a color brochure extolling the hotel's virtues and facilities. These included internet access, so I was there in a flash. The owners (brothers) wouldn't let me use the computer until after 10pm, because it was too expensive before that. I offered to pay, whatever the cost (it turned out to be $US10 per hour), but the owners were adamant that they couldn't let anyone be that crazy. The hotel also did laundry, fed into the machine by one of the brothers. Our last load was delivered to the boat at 11pm, because of owner overload—they were also the cooks, barmen, receptionists and cashiers.

Old friends from the Red Sea, "Lady Kathryn" (Australian), "Idunn" (U.S.) and "Espace" (New Zealand) showed up. We exchanged books—Carole got "Angela's Ashes" and "Under the Tuscan Sun," so was thrilled—drank cocktails on each other's boats, and generally caught up with past doings. The nights at Lizzie's grew to be long and loud, making the goat track back to the boats steeper and narrower than it really was.

After walking around the island, finding a beach covered in plastic debris, getting lost in the thorn bushes (the last time I will follow a New Zealander), and taking some great photos, we finally succumbed to the call of the West.

Mesolongian is up a canal, through a salt marsh. The canal is lined with fishermen's houses on stilts, accessible only by boat. We tied up at the quay, across the road from the town's disco, which was preparing for a big night, a swimsuit parade. We had a ringside seat, with absolutely nothing between us and 2,000,000,000 watts of amplifier power.

It was fun to see the 8 to 10-year-old girls who were opening the parade, rolling up with their mothers, and practicing on the catwalks. Show-biz mothers are the same, world over, and so are the kids. Some showed up powdered, painted and frizzed to perfection, others looked almost normal. Some stalked the catwalks, others strolled. Some did the circuit once, others too often to count. All were 10 going on 30. Ryan and I slept, lulled by the vibrating hull, but Carole couldn't enter that Zen state. When we pulled out at 6am, the last dancers were leaving, and Carole slept the entire trip to Vathi, capital of Ithaca Island, home of the legendary Odysseus, Homer's hero.

At the end of a fiord-like bay, Vathi is a very pretty, pastel-colored, town. We anchored off to one side, with the houses all round us, rising up into the hills, very like Simi, in the Aegean. Apart from the twice daily appearance of a huge ferry that played chicken with us, and some very high winds, the anchorage was secure and calm, even in the above-mentioned gales, and we had it mostly to ourselves. The other yachts tried to tie up to the town quay, about half-a-mile from us. There were so many of them that they were often two or three deep. Still they seemed to prefer the smell and wash and noise, with the doubtful benefit of paying for the night, and the facility of being able to crawl over other boats to get to shore. We dinghied casually up to our restaurant of choice, tied up next to our table, ate and drank, then indulged in an after-dinner stroll, past the chaos of tangled lines and anchors and the sound of grinding fiberglass, before returning to our peaceful abode. As the King of Siam was wont to say, "Is a puzzlement."

The Ionian Sea islands were much greener and nicer than those in the Aegean, and there were pastel-colored houses! For some reason, except for Corfu, they were much less touristed. Perhaps that was why the people seemed nicer too. Onwards, past Onasis' private island ("Gigolo" anchored there and were immediately asked to leave.), to Tranquil Bay, opposite Nidri town, on Levkas Island. Our friends from Trizonia were there together with "Sea Bird" (Australia), "Honey Bee" (Australia), "La Scala" (Australia) and "Just Magic" (New Zealand), who all came up the Red Sea with us.

Nidri is one of the "yachtiest" places we have been to, as it is totally oriented to sea-borne tourists. A major charter fleet is based there, and all the shop keepers assume you are either on your own boat, or chartering. The super-yachts seem to stay away, being more prevalent in the "in" Aegean, rather than the "nicer" Ionian.

Somewhat bizarrely, internet access was at the local Hard Rock Cafe. Any garbled E-mails people got during that period can be totally blamed on sound volume. Ryan met Tom, an 11-year old English boy, and had a great few days swimming, fishing and playing around. School was mostly suspended for both of them.

"Trilogy" invited us over to see their two rare cockatoos. These huge birds had taken over, and largely destroyed, the entire salon area of a lovely Mason 43. I almost cried when I saw it. Their proud owners were pleased to report that the birds snuggle under the covers with them every morning, pull nose hairs as a wake-up, live to be over 100-years old, cannot be left alone for more than a few hours, and cannot be left with other people or they will pine and die. Therefore their owners had not been off the boat for more than a few hours for the past three years, and looked forward to a lifetime of sleeping every night with a bird! At least children leave home, eventually.

As we were now some six weeks behind our self-imposed schedule (Barcelona by November), and theoretically had only two days left in our three-month Greek visa, we decided to forgo the delights of Corfu, and head straight to Italy from Levkas.

Until now we have had to check into, and out of, every country we have visited. In fact, we usually weren't allowed into a country until we could prove that we left the last one properly. Moving back and forth between Turkey and Greece was the same. We now tried to check out of Greece to go to Italy. Because of potential VAT (tax) problems, we wanted proof that we left Greece. The EU charges VAT on non-EU boats that have been in the EU for more than 6 months of a year. A far as we knew, only France was enforcing this, but we were being cautious.

The sole Customs official in Nidri told us to get lost, he wasn't interested, so we took a taxi to the head office in Levkas town. Same story, but, egged on by Carole from the rear, I stood my ground. Reluctantly, the official took our Greek cruising permit, stamped it, and directed us to more offices for the other two stamps. Port Authority stamped, and charged us one day port fees for the privilege, even though our boat wasn't there. The police stamped the form, but flatly refused to stamp passports. In desperation, I said we were heading for Malta, which is not in the EU.

"Oh, yes it is," they said.

"Oh, no it's not," said I.

Guess who won? Back to Customs for the third stamp, and they took all the papers and waved us away. At the end of the day, we were down taxi fares and port fees, and up exactly zero by way of proof we had left Greece.

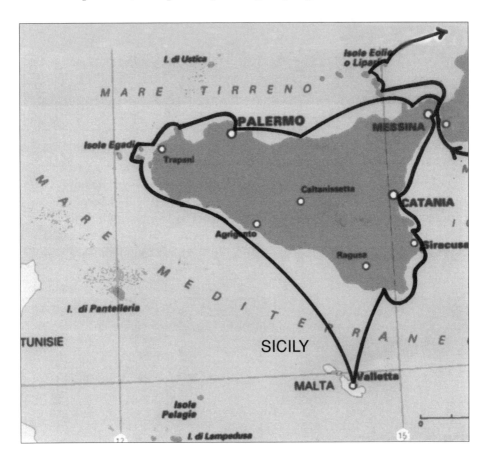

Sicily and Malta

Year Four
July 4 to August 23

"Where do we go to see the fireworks?" asked Carole. We had just motor-sailed for 36 hours to Rocella Ionica, on the east coast of the toe of Italy, arriving on the Fourth of July. As a result I was a little tired, so perhaps my reply was somewhat overstated. That night, perfectly framed in the harbor entrance, we saw one of the best fireworks displays ever. We have no idea what the local occasion was, so to maintain the peace were perfectly happy to accept Carole's suggestion that they had been provided to welcome Ryan and her to Italy.

Carole: During the overnight passage to Italy, I was on watch and was so thrilled to hear some U.S. Navy ships calling each other on Channel 16, the International hailing channel. That pleasure turned to revulsion as the callers proceeded to try to top each other in using the filthiest possible words. I wanted to tell them to get off the air, but Laurie (I woke him up of course) convinced me to let it go.

The local Coast Guard rolled up to ask us to fill in a form, and to tell us to move off our comfortable wall to a berth farther in. I pointed out that we were too long and too deep to do this, we would be gone in the morning, and wouldn't he like to stamp our pretty passports. Consigning us, and our passports, to some private hell, the official consulted long and hard with his superiors, and finally decided we could stay where we were, no charge, as we weren't where we should be. We loved his logic, even though our passports remained stamp-less, and we now had no record of entering Italy.

Rounding the toe, we headed up the Straits of Messina to Messina, in Sicily.

Ryan (11): *Since the Red Sea, fish had been few and far between, so I was thrilled when we saw a huge swordfish basking on the surface, and later a very big sunfish. Sunfish are the ugliest fish in the world, as they are big and grey and don't even look alive.*

The locals have very specialized boats for catching swordfish. The hull is about 20-feet long, with a 50-foot mast topped by a crow's nest for the captain, and a catwalk projecting some 60 feet in front of the bow. The whole thing is held together by a network of wires. The captain spots a fish, and a crew member spears it from the catwalk, before the poor beast even knows a boat is near. The boats are usable in calm weather only, so perhaps the odds are evened a little.

Messina was our introduction to the expensive Italian marina—there is no other kind. Lira 165,000 per night ($US1=L1,800), including electricity and undrinkable water, with the floating pontoons and boats (including us) bounding about in the wakes of the 250 ferry passes every day.

Carole: *One of Messina's claims to fame is its clock tower, with several sets of mechanical figures that perform on the quarter, half, and full hour, providing the hour is 6pm. The ice cream shop gave us free whipped cream on our gelato when they heard we had sailed from the U.S. (our first sailing-related freebie in all the years we had been sailing). For our first Italian restaurant meal, we chose one on the waterfront, so naturally I had to try the Pasta Marinara. I love fish, but not fishy tasting fish, and this dish had very fishy fish. Laurie, the perfect gentleman, exchanged meals with me, and seemed to enjoy it.*

The fabled Straits of Messina whirlpools were absent, but we did strike fierce currents (against us, why ask?) which set up little waves and swirls, and moved "Dolphin Spirit" about like a floating chip. The ferries, cargo ships and aircraft carriers that were all trying to funnel through the less than a mile wide strait at the Northern end were more of a challenge. Passing Scylla on our starboard and skirting Charybdis on the port (read your *Odyssey*), we got through, turned left, and headed along the north coast of Sicily.

Ryan (11): *The engine stopped. Dad was very embarrassed and had to admit he had read the fuel tank levels incorrectly, and had not switched tanks. We were about a mile off shore, in 30 feet of water, so while Dad was bleeding the fuel lines Mum and I got ready to drop anchor, in case there were problems. Mum then asked Dad about fuel every day we were sailing.*

SICILY AND MALTA

Increasing winds demanded a safe harbor, so we went to Portorosa marina—L204,000 per night, but we could drink the water. Essentially a failed real estate development, in the middle of nowhere, the marina was unique in that we had to dinghy around, as there were no roads.

Ryan (11): *One pedestrian bridge was very low, so I jumped out of the dinghy just as it went under, ran across and jumped back into the dinghy as it appeared on the other side—very James Bond.*

So we could leave early the next morning, we fueled, and stayed overnight at the fuel dock, with zero to six inches of water under the keel. Mud bottom luckily, so we didn't bounce.

Carole: *Laurie wanted to change the engine oil, so Ryan and I spent the day on a nearby beach. A lot of people were there and the beach would have been lovely but for all the plastic bags floating in the sea. Ryan and I decided on a "Clean the Beach" campaign and spent hours pulling bags out of the waves and taking them to the trash bins. The more we collected, the more that seemed to wash in. The currents must act as collectors at that spot. However, every bag got there because someone didn't dispose of it properly. The only garbage that ever went over the side of "Dolphin Spirit" was bio-degradable, such a peels and food scraps.*

That is absolutely correct except for one thing—Carole's used barf-bags went overboard as well. On a long sea passage, such as the 19 days across the Pacific, garbage became a real problem for the eco-minded such as us. In mid-ocean we did squash cans and throw them over, but never discarded plastic or glass. (***Ryan (11):*** *I helped by putting messages in the wine bottles and setting them afloat.*) In spite of this, the mound of garbage bags on the stern grew to alarming proportions.

Cefalu was our next stop and again the Year Of The Anchor continued to hold sway. We were anchored in the harbor when the wind increased, and we started dragging towards the rocks. As I was pulling up the anchor, I discovered the reason. Through some mental aberration, I had let out only 60 feet of chain, instead of 120 feet. As the chain is clearly marked, I had no excuse or explanation, other than YOTA syndrome.

A spot at the dock then became available, so we pulled up anchor again to move to it—rather, we tried to pull up the anchor, as the anchor winch chose this time to cease functioning (YOTA again). As partial atonement for my previous error, I had to haul in the 150 feet of chain and 110-pound anchor by hand. A gear in the anchor-winch gearbox had magically lost all of its teeth.

Cefalu is a lovely spot, but it is a small fishing village, expanded to a tourist town, and the likelihood of a machine shop to make a new gear was remote. Hope springs eternal, so I set off, stripped gear in hand, to talk to the local fishermen. Although anchor winches were conspicuous on the fishing boats by their complete absence, I had no problem getting the message across, and they had similar ease in relaying, "Cefalu, tourists only, go to Palermo."

Off to town we went, to hire a car. The first rental place (there were only two in the town) was out of cars for three days, so we made a reservation, and headed for the second. He was also carless (it turned out that they both drew cars from the same garage, having none of their own), but had some English, so we chatted. I asked about getting a new gear (hire cars, cars, gearbox, gears, the connection was obvious). The guy said he had a friend who might help, and made a phone call.

Half-an-hour later a scooter arrived, the friend listened to the problem (arms waving, pointing, broken English, broken Italian, diagrams scribbled on paper), I climbed onto the back of the scooter, and off we roared to see the part I had left on "Dolphin Spirit." The friend took a look at the gear, motioned me back onto the scooter, and off we roared again to the local fishermen's co-operative. Escorted to a person completely hidden behind a beard and a solid wall of fish odor, I went into my now familiar song-and-dance routine. The beard took the stripped gear and told me to come back at 6pm the next day. I spent the night wondering how to get a gear made if the original vanished.

At 3:30pm the next day there was a knock on the hull. On the dock was the beard, complete with newly made gear. I very nearly kissed him. All our concepts of angels have been revised to include beards and fishy smells. Total cost was 100,000 lira, or approximately $US50. Ryan and I assembled the gearbox and winch (the part fitted perfectly), and, with Carole's assistance, struggled to bolt it back in position. Carole and Ryan tried to kill me by dropping the unit on my head, but I foiled them, as they underestimated the thickness of my skull.

We will gloss over the fact that, when moving into the quay, I let a line dangle over the side and wrapped it round the prop. As there was no fee, and we were very secure, we decided to land-cruise Sicily from there. Every evening the quay was crowded with people strolling and fishing. The in-thing seemed to be to drive your scooter, girl-friend behind, to the end of the quay, gaze around, rev the engine a couple of time, point at something, then roar off. We were fascinated by the whole families on scooters, Dad driving, one child standing between his legs, Mum behind, with a second child wedged between her and Dad, no helmets of course. Given the price of petrol, more than $US4 per gallon, scooters were understandable.

Ryan (11): *I watched a one-armed man catching octopi with a lure, and made a copy of it out of a plastic bag and a treble hook. Almost immediately, I caught a large octopus. Dad took photos and videos galore, and I gave the octopus to one of the locals, who wasn't having luck with his lure.*

Cefalu harbor is under the shadow of a mountain topped by a wonderful-looking castle. The road to the castle was too steep for me, so Ryan had to make do with distant admiration. Old Cefalu town skirts around the edge of the mountain, houses rising straight from the seacliff rocks. The three and four-storey houses, on both sides of the narrow, winding, cobblestone streets, complete with tiny, colorfully draped balconies, washing, ladies chatting, gentlemen sitting in groups pondering the world's problems, and tiny shops, made for hours of contented strolling.

On the other side of the mountain was a long, sand beach, covered with beach umbrellas. Each section of the beach was controlled by an entrepreneur, who rented the umbrellas and chairs, and charged us to sit on the sand. We actually went swimming, as the water had warmed. Ryan used his body board, but the waves were mere ripples. Carole did her patented bobbing up and down exercises. Dining on a balcony overlooking the beach and the setting sun, all three of us saw the green flash, the first since Sri Lanka.

Ryan (11): *I liked the cathedral with its two pyramid-shaped bell towers and the massive mosaic of Christ just inside the apse.*

The hire car took us south, across the island, to Agrigento and the Valley of Temples. Actually, the five temples were lined up along a ridge, but we guessed that "Ridge of Temples" didn't sound quite so good. At the museum, we were asked for our country of origin before they calculated the entry fee. A highlight was a twenty-foot-tall statue, one of an original line of twelve. On the way to Agrigento for lunch, we became totally lost in the tiny streets, all completely lined with parked cars. Grabbing the first parking space (we blocked a street waiting for someone to leave), we discovered that we were near the city center and the best restaurant. Once again, we found virtue in getting lost. Some of our best moments have come from this, by now well developed attribute of our land travels.

As part of our quest to see every temple in Europe, we headed for the temples at Selinunte, only two of them this time. One was standing—ho hum—the other was a magnificent pile of broken columns, that Ryan and I enjoyed scrambling all over. Carole, seeing snakes and scorpions under every piece of marble, was a little more circumspect. Driving home via

Marsala, we had to buy some of the famous local wine. Undrinkable, it made good spaghetti sauce.

We rested from ancient temples, and went to see the not quite so ancient, gilded wall-mosaics in the cathedral at Monreale. They were quite outstanding, depicting complete *Bible* stories, and even the "seen-it-all" Ryan was impressed. He was the one who discovered the coin-in-the-slot-on-for-a-minute lighting, and just had to keep feeding in coins until he had examined every mosaic.

The square in front of the cathedral featured a fountain, with water (not common), and decorated ponies pulling even more-decorated carts. Locals charged us to park in the streets around the cathedral, and looked after our car. We didn't try to see what would happen if we didn't pay. Had coffee (me) and sweet rolls (Carole and Ryan) standing at the coffee shop bar. The place had a three-tier price list, take-away, standing, and sitting, in rising order.

Back to temples, this time at Segesta, where there was a single, still-standing temple, half way up a small mountain, and a wonderful amphitheatre right at the top. A bus went to the top, so we took that, and marveled at the ancients' desire for entertainment. The walk up would have been bad enough, but the walk down, after a night of culture and wine, would have been frightening. Although the views from the theater were absolutely stunning, one questions the commercial acumen of the builders. We guessed that "if you build it they will come" was not a new saying. We walked down, at Carole's insistence, and were rewarded by great views of the temple. (***Ryan (11):*** *I took the shortcuts and got to the bottom first.*)

Up the side of a tall mountain again, on a winding, skinny road (***Carole:*** *Just a regular white-knuckler.*), to the walled town of Erice, which had great promotion, but was somewhat disappointing. Just another walled town on top of another mountain with more stone buildings, and a square full of restaurants and souvenir shops. We must have been getting jaded, as the bus loads of tourists seemed to be enjoying it.

Templed-out at last, we headed for Piazza Amerina to see the Villa Romani di Casale mosaics. A large Roman villa that was buried by a mud slide and only recently uncovered, it has every room floored by colorful mosaics which are mostly complete. After being entranced by the few square feet of mosaics we saw at other places, the thousands of square feet here were breath-taking.

Ryan (11): *One mosaic shows women doing athletics, wearing what are believed to be the world's first bikinis.*

Walkways had been built along the top of the room walls to allow us close-up, unimpeded views. The central corridor of the house was some 200-feet long and 15-feet wide, giving an idea of size and the amount of mosaics to be seen. We found it difficult to imagine the work that went into the creation of it all, the laying out, the selection of colored stone chips, the placement of each chip individually, and the inevitable, "Julius, I've changed my mind. The hunting scene would look better in the other room!"

Reluctantly, it was time to move on to Marina Villa Igea, at Palermo—L150,000 per night plus water (undrinkable), and electricity—in an absolutely grotty part of the city. We took the bus to Palermo city center, and made two discoveries—the bus was free, and it didn't go there. The free buses went in circles, and the trick was to know when to get off to catch the next. It took us two tries to get it right. The bus drivers were too intent on horn blowing and Fiat chasing to help.

Carole: *Of course, we took a horse and carriage ride through the romantic city and saw the Palermo Opera House, featured in the movie* Godfather III.

To gain additional "kulcha," we watched *The Ten Commandments* in Egypt, *Helen of Troy* in Turkey, *Zorba* in Crete, the *Godfather* trilogy in Sicily, and were all set for *The Maltese Falcon* in Malta and *Fall of the Roman Empire* in Rome. A pity none had any relevance to the named country or city.

I was really spooked by the unique Cappucine Catacombs. We walked down a long tunnel to a maze of underground caverns completely lined with bodies, standing, lying on shelves, and seated in family groups. The earliest was a monk who died in 1500, and the latest was a three-year-old girl who was placed there in 1923. She was the scariest, as she exhibited no sign of death or decay. With pink, plump cheeks, perfect skin and hair, she could have been sleeping. All the bodies were dressed in sack-cloth or period clothes, some rags, others well preserved. Many still had all their skin and hair, just mummified. Facial expressions ranged from peaceful to screaming horror. After half an hour of this, I wanted out, but Ryan and Carole were made of sterner stuff, so we walked every corridor. Not to be missed. Not to be repeated.

Carole: *Having Laurie freaked out was a new experience, as he is generally so calm. We almost had to drag him into the area which was mostly children. I didn't mind skeletons from the 1500s; it was the ones from the recent past that were too close for comfort.*

Ryan (11): *It was creepy and I had a stomach ache when we left, but no nightmares.*

The weather was bad, so we were forced to stay in Palermo for several days. It really had been a bad-weather summer. We walked along the waterfront to the main Palermo harbor, where there was a yacht basin. It was easy to find. The water was the color of old pea-soup and the smell reached out and pounded you. Overnight there would save the cost of paint-stripping.

Ryan (11): (School Report) *The Quattro Canti (Four corners) is the busy intersection of Via Vittorio Emanuele and Via Marqueda, and is the oldest part of Palermo. Each corner of the intersection has its own 12th Century fountain and statue. La Mortorana is the most famous church with many Byzantine mosaics. I preferred the Chiesa di San Matteo, a Baroque church with a richly decorated interior and many statues. One statue looked weird, with a neon halo. Another, seen in the proper light, seems to be crying, with two tears down one side of her face, and one tear down the other.*

Eventually, we untied and went to Capo lo Vito, on the north-west corner of Sicily. Under the shadow of a huge red cliff, with lovely, pale green water, palm trees and sand, it was quite "south-sea-ish." As we anchored close to the beach, every day we were surrounded by a flotilla of paddle boats, which entertained us probably as much as we did them. We swam, ate pizza and pasta, watched the full moon rise over the mountain, and relaxed after the exertions of the past couple of weeks.

Ryan (11): *Every day the wind blew a lot of beach balls and floats past us, so I was busy collecting them with the dinghy. Dad said there was no way we could find the owners.*

The Egadi Islands, off the west coast of Sicily, were reported to be very nice, so we went. None of the recommended anchorages were suitable, and we were heading back to Sicily, round the south of Favignana Island, when we spotted boats tucked in under a small island. Investigating, we discovered a delightful place, really protected, very pretty, and not on any chart. We stayed three days. Ryan and I explored the small island and found lots of seagull bodies and bones. On the larger island we discovered several anti-aircraft gun emplacements and pill-boxes, all connected by concrete tunnels. Imagine looking out over that view, and seeing only someone to shoot at.

We decided to head straight for Malta, an overnight sail. There was no wind and solid fog for almost the whole day. Radar going and fog horn sounding, we ploughed on. Almost as bad as the Indonesian smoke, but we could breathe. It cleared about half way across the strait, allowing us to make an easy landfall at Valletta harbor, after a Carole trip—no wind, flat seas. The approaches were congested with cargo vessels, so we had to do some ducking and weaving. Entering below the huge walls of the city was an enthralling experience.

Ryan (11)*: I had been studying about Brunelleschi Domes, and there was one, atop the walls overlooking us.*

Calling Valletta Harbor Control, we were directed to the Customs dock. This was almost full of permanently moored local boats, with the small space left occupied by fishermen, and no officials in sight. Valletta Control, a little testily, told us to tie up and go find the Customs people, so we headed in. The fishermen waited until the last possible moment to pull in their lines, but I was more interested in the rocks that were passing, seemingly inches away, as we were forced to come in parallel to the very end of the dock. Carole had to toss the bow-line over the top of a fisherman, who cast his line out the instant we seemed to stop moving forward—dedication!

The Customs office was, in fact, close by. The officer, who insisted on filling out the forms himself, was constantly distracted by phone calls. He eventually threw the phone, with some force, across the desk, and completed the forms without further interruption. I asked Immigration to please stamp our passports. "No," he said. "Please," I begged. The official hauled out a sheaf of forms and said that, if we wanted a stamp, all had to be filled out now, and on departure. "You really don't want to stamp the passports," said I. "What was your first clue?" said he. No record of leaving Greece, entering Italy, leaving Italy, or entering Malta, the list grows.

Back on the dock the local agent for another yacht presented himself to me. We needed refrigeration repairs, parts, new dock lines, hire car, duty-free drinks, duty-free fuel, and so on—he organized it all. One of his men even drove us to the supermarket, waited while we shopped, helped us pack, and transported us back, all at no charge. Most Maltese speak English, or at least understand it. Ryan was relieved that he didn't have to learn a new language.

Malta had a great bus service. The yellow buses, most with rear fins, non-synchromesh (crash) gearboxes, and other 60's decorations, were fast, regular, cheap, and ran all over the island. The drivers ranged from uncommunicative to surly, and seemed to delight in passing potential passengers, or making them run. We used the buses every day, 20 cents a person to anywhere.

Our friends, John and Lois ("Topaz") were in Malta having their boat repaired after going through a saga no one could have invented. You may remember that Lois had to be airlifted out of Sri Lanka for an emergency operation in Singapore. John and his brother took "Topaz" back to Thailand and Lois joined John there to recuperate.

They decided to have the boat hauled out for repair and maintenance while they were waiting. John (well over 70), forgot the lifelines had been removed, stepped backwards and fell more than 15 feet from the deck to the concrete floor, breaking a great number of his bones. He was wired together in the local hospital. Lois forwarded X-rays back to their U.S. doctor, and his opinion was that John would recover well, but that the techniques used were ones he hadn't seen for a very long time.

While John was in hospital, the work on "Topaz" was completed and the boat re-launched. The travel-lift gently deposited her in the water, and "Topaz" kept going down, and down, and down. A quick re-hoist prevented total inundation, and it was discovered that all the through-hulls had been left open and unconnected to hoses.

With Lois, John and "Topaz" all well and rested, they set out the next year to go up the Red Sea. On the way to Oman, the drive shaft to the propeller snapped on a calm day, and they had to be towed the last mile into port. A quick repair, and they were off again, but the delay had put them well behind their cruiser group.

In southern Eritrea they went aground on a sandbar, but managed to get off. Unfortunately the sand had blocked the cooling water intake for the engine so it stopped, and they were too close to the shore to prevent being driven by wind and waves onto the beach. Thanks to the SSB cruiser net they were able to let others know their plight, and through one cruiser's satellite phone were able to contact their insurance company.

Getting a towboat to assist them was a saga in itself, even with the insurance company paying all the costs. One came, decided it was too hard, and left. John and Lois were flown out by helicopter to Mitsawa to try to organize another. That task accomplished, they then spent three days getting back to "Topaz" by 4-wheel drive over non-existent roads.

The second tug hauled them off—for $US90,000 payable in advance—and towed them to Mitsawa. There they were loaded onto the deck of an Italian freighter, for transport to Malta. The tow from the anchorage to the freighter was too fast, so "Topaz" began, swinging uncontrollably and hit four boats.

This provides just the bare bones of a story that involved more intrigue than a James Bond movie, midnight phone calls, and more stress than any person needs. When we caught up with them in Malta, "Topaz" was back in the water, and there were only 70 items left on John's to-do list. I would have said "Enough" long ago. A year later we heard that they had safely crossed the Atlantic and were home in Connecticut. Well done!

We dined with them at the local Tex-Mex restaurant, just across from the TGI Friday franchise. Both restaurants had excellent margaritas, the first we have found in the Med. Tex-Mex won out with great ribs, in huge portions. Even Ryan could eat only one of the two slabs that made up each serving, so we always had ribs the next day on the boat.

The Co-Cathedral of St. John was in the center of Valletta. Its entire floor was made up of gorgeous, marble, 17th century grave-stones, all in brilliant color. Around the walls were chapels, each dedicated to one of the divisions of the Knights of St. John, who ruled Malta for many years. A highlight was the huge painting by Caravaggio of the beheading of John the Baptist. Luminous and wonderfully detailed, it alone made the trip to Malta worthwhile, especially as it had just been restored to its original magnificence. The museum attached to the cathedral contained many tapestries, illuminated hymnals, and the robes of Popes and Grand Masters of the Knights of St. John. We tried to give Ryan an appreciation for the years of effort that must have gone into the hand-working of each of these items.

Ryan (11): *Some of the paintings looked as if they stuck out of the walls because of the clever use of shadow. I really liked the gravestones that made up the floor but was struck by the thought that they moved the graves, but not the bodies.*

The "Malta Experience" made the history of the island come to life through a multi-media show with an excellent script. Ryan asked to go back and see it again. Our follow-up walk through the huge fortifications was made more relevant by what we had just seen. Valletta is completely surrounded by huge walls, and cars are banned from the streets. Although very English, the place follows Mediterranean hours, with shops, banks and offices closing between 1pm and 4pm, and restaurants mostly opening around 8:30pm. Every night we saw families promenading until 11pm, children included. We stopped to watch ballroom dancing under the stars at one of the cafes. Mostly older couples, all the dancers were very graceful.

Carole: *At the crosswalks, cars stopped as soon as they saw a pedestrian approaching. I always hesitated, as I couldn't believe they really meant it.*

Swimming beaches around Valletta were, with very few exceptions, just flat shelves of sandstone. There were channels and rooms, carved into the rock sometime in prehistory, which now extended out under the water. The practical Maltese have added ladders, and turned some into miniature pools. Covered with mostly English tourists, all turning bright pink in the 100-degree sun (we had 100-plus for five days in a row—"Never had weather like this before!"), the rocks were a spectacle.

The "Festa" season was in full swing. For a month, every village decorates its local church, and indulges in two or three days of feasts, processions and fireworks. There were fireworks somewhere on the island every night. We took an organized tour to one village. The sky show was nice, but the highlight was the ground display, with spirals, spinners, and all manner of colors and shapes. The church, dedicated to St. Lawrence, and featuring many statues of that special person, was brilliantly lit outside, and splendidly decorated inside. The grave, serene, awe-inspiring, wise, and truly magnificent features of St. Lawrence dominated all, unexpectedly for so modest and self-effacing a Saint.

Ryan (11): *Of all the Saints we could have visited, why did we pick this one? For days Dad insisted on being called "Santo Lorenzo."*

We hired a car for a couple of days to see Malta's megalithic temples, the oldest free-standing buildings in the world. Heading for the first site, we followed the signs, until we came to some pointing back the way we had come. Turning round, we followed those until we got back to the first set, again pointing behind us. After doing this a couple of times, we parked and asked a local. Just around the corner and up the street, so we walked. Sure enough, there was a sign, pointing up a street. It was obscured by a "Do Not Enter" sign, so we could be forgiven for passing it. The actual entrance to the temple site was a completely unmarked doorway in a featureless wall. Engrossed in a phone call to his wife/girlfriend/stock broker, the guard kept us standing for five minutes before taking our money. We were somehow getting the impression that Malta was not big on tourists, although they are the country's major income source.

Ryan (11): *From the south side of the island, on a tall hill, we could see the north side clearly. Most of the countryside was covered in rocks and rubble and was not pretty. Libya gave Malta a million trees a few years before, but most died, or were cut down by vandals.*

Our next stop was a cave, noted for its layers of hippopotamus, elephant, deer, bear and wolf bones. We almost passed by, as its presence was suggested only by a tiny, faded sign, and a parking space for three small cars—no tourist buses welcome obviously. The cave, and the display of bones, were well worth the visit. Understandably perhaps, we had the place to ourselves. Onwards we went, into the unknown, as we seemed to be able to find only roads which were single lane or less, and were not marked on our somewhat rudimentary road map. Malta is a small island, so working on the premise that the land was to drive on, and the sea to look at, we eventually arrived at the next temple site.

These temples were really wonderful. Built before Stonehenge, with great views over the sea, the walls, doorways, rooms and altars are almost eerie in their permanence. Proving that idiocy knows no boundaries, some vandals had recently sprayed graffiti all over one of the temples, and the porous rock made it impossible to remove.

Ryan (11): *I had to crouch down to squeeze through some secret doorways, so the builders must have been tiny.*

People had gathered at one of the temples, the highest spot in Malta, to see the eclipse of the sun. We retired to a nearby cafe, sat in the shade sipping cool drinks, and watched the event on TV. At the parking lot, we found that the attendant had spread a sun shade across our windscreen, and that has to be a world first!

Mdina (the marina was Msida) is an old walled town that has banned cars, and so attracted tourists. The cathedral floor was a miniature version of that in the Valletta cathedral, and the entrance was protected by cannon. We put Ryan in the stocks (really) and pelted him with rotten fruit (in our minds only), before touring the dungeons and their waxwork displays of torture through Malta's history. Be Catholic, and on the side of the person with the biggest army, or be hurt, was the message. The Spanish Inquisition was very active.

Driving through a town, we saw an Australian flag flying, so naturally I had to stop. The owner of the house and his wife had lived in Australia for many years (he was in Air-Sea Rescue), and we were invited in for a drink. The next night, both appeared at the marina, so we had more drinks on DS. Apparently they fly the Australian flag for only a couple of days a year, and we were the first ever to call in.

Eventually, all the work on the boat was completed, and we left, only to be turned back by headwinds and rough seas. After 25,000 miles, this was our first such experience. Customs didn't want to know we were back, as we had already checked out—no documentation of course. We waited a couple of days and Bingo!—Carole conditions again for the 60 miles to Porto Palo, at the south-east corner of Sicily. After an overnight at this rather uninteresting spot, we moved on to Syracuse, a very special place.

The old city, on Ortega Island, was a marvelous hodge-podge of narrow streets, churches, old buildings, squares with fountains, and twisting alleyways. The Duomo (main church) was built on the foundations of a Greek Temple to Athena, and used the columns from that temple to support the walls and roof. This gave the church a unique look, inside and out—stained glass Christian windows supported by pagan columns!

A short walk took us to the Greek and Roman theaters, both carved out of the solid rock, another first for us. (A re-read of this chapter discovered at least five other statements that could have been labeled as "firsts." We apologize for this lapse on our part, as there should have been a lot more.) A large cave, shaped like an ear, added to the uniqueness of the site.

We anchored out in the huge harbor instead of going into the city quay, as there seemed to be a surge there all the time. In the evenings, the quay was solid with strollers, and about a hundred stalls selling everything from purses to African statues. We met up with "Old Glory," who we had last seen in Cyprus, and had the usual catch-up chat and drink.

Next stop, Catania, at a basic marina tucked into the back of a dilapidated, but busy, port. Two boats away was an American catamaran, with Michael and Swanee on board. They were delighted to speak English again, and we arranged to go together by train around Mt. Etna. It was an interesting trip, stopping at every station, with Mt. Etna smoking from two craters, lava flows everywhere, and houses, walls, and churches built from lava—your basic black-on-black countryside. One town, where we stopped for a couple of hours, didn't have a restaurant, so we made do with gelato ice cream for lunch.

Sailing this coast was made more difficult by the permanently set tuna nets that often extended a couple of miles out to sea. Designed to lead the tuna schools into a non-return labyrinth of nets, they do much the same with unwary yachts. Usually marked by a flag at the outer edge, the trick was to see the flag, which may be a mile out to sea from us. The government takes a very dim view of any damage done to nets, as do the very testy fishermen.

Taormina was a pretty anchorage under cliffs that supported the town. Only about a thousand feet straight above us, the town was a several-mile trip away by a very winding, narrow road. "Old Glory" was there with some Spanish friends on board, including two boys and a girl, all about Ryan's age. We didn't see him for two days. Ryan works long hours, seven days a week, so he can take such days off and not lose out on his education.

Carole: *They introduced Ryan to "black foot" smoked ham ("smoked in trees in Spain") and it was an instant hit at $200 per leg. Later, in Spain, we surprised him with a leg as a silly stocking-stuffer at Christmas.*

Through the Straits of Messina again, this time almost spun through 180 degrees by a current eddy, and on to the Aeolian Islands, which include Vulcano and Stromboli. Approaching the Vulcano anchorage, we had to dodge three hydrofoils and a huge ferry, before finding it was full. The bottom shelved up from 200 feet to 50 feet in about two boat lengths, and there was a strong, rotten-eggs smell from the three volcanoes on the island. We moved on to Liprari Island—same story, without the smell. After much circling, we found a possible spot, anchored in 60 feet, and swung from 30 to 150 feet, depending on wind direction. The winds were relatively light, so the night was comfortable enough, but we didn't leave the boat.

With some relief, as the bottom seemed to be anchor-eating rock, we got the anchor up the next morning and headed for Stromboli. This famous volcano last erupted in 1992, and we sailed past the mile-wide, black slab of lava running from summit to sea, that was the result. The two towns (original population 5,000, present 500) were perched at either end of the island, on old lava flows. While the last few eruptions have sent lava elsewhere, we completely understood the population decrease. Passing Stromboli completed our circumnavigation of Sicily, and left only Mt. Vesuvius to complete our volcano-run.

Italy
Year Four
August 24 to October 29

A thunderstorm of truly awesome magnitude struck the west coast of Italy, including Agropoli. Lightning, torrential rain, and winds of up to 70 knots buffeted the area for over two hours. It seemed, at first, to be your normal, every-day thunderstorm, which performed the usual pyrotechnics, then grumbled off into the distance. Carole and Ryan were watching the vanishing display, and I was in bed, when wind, rain, and lightning seemed to arrive all at once. Within seconds, the wind was roaring at over 60 knots, luckily almost directly on our bow, and the rain was almost horizontal.

I had to go on deck to check our situation, and the rain drops hurt, forcing me to back into the wind to protect my eyes. The foresail on the 120-footer near us came loose at the top, and was explosively cracking every second. Our wind generator was putting out enough power to light New York. Jibs on two other yachts came loose and shredded, adding to the noise and confusion.

"Dolphin Spirit" rode through it all like the lady she is, and we sustained no damage, other than loss of sleep and some bruising on my back from the rain. We did expect the floating dock to which we were attached to break loose, but it held. The weather forecast was for winds of 10 to 15 knots, decreasing. Italian weather forecasts are as accurate as those of every other country.

That morning, a very tattered and torn sailboat limped in. He had been at sea, and swore that the winds reached more than 90 knots. Certainly they had been strong enough to strip all his canvas off the boat, and turn his dinghy into a glider, never to be seen again. Luckily he was close to land, so the wind-generated waves were small.

Another thunderstorm accompanied by 40-knot winds struck two days later at 9am. While daylight was preferable to dark, and 40 knots to 70, the crew was becoming a little tired of the weather, and demanded some decent stuff for a few days at least. I was able to intercede with those in charge, and good weather resulted.

The Agropoli marina was notable, not only for its storms, but because each dock was run by a separate person, and had a different name. Theoretically therefore, it was possible to check each out, bargain with the operators, and make an informed selection before tying up. In practice, we entered the harbor, saw the docks with people waving at us, and picked the one that seemed easiest to get into and out of. Having therefore lost a lot of negotiating power, I discussed prices with the operator, and decided I was just too tired to look elsewhere.

YOTA struck again one night, twice! About 8pm, a sailboat, attempting to come in next to us, got its keel caught on our mooring line, and I spent a wonderful half hour sorting that out. At 1am, a 150-foot power yacht came in behind and tied up at right-angles to us. Somehow, their mooring line tangled with ours, and we woke to the sound of complaining lines, as the yacht attempted to tear us loose from the dock, or break us in half, whichever came first. That little fracas wasn't resolved for a couple of hours. Luckily, the winds had moderated.

The next morning, I decided to repair the holes in our inflatable dinghy floor—I found seven pinholes. Careless, perhaps because of lack of sleep, I was unscrewing the valve when the rush of air blew it out of my fingers and over the side, six feet away. Donning scuba gear, with little hope as the bottom was soft mud, I headed down. There was the valve, sitting on a piece of rope, poised delicately above the bottomless slime.

Carole: *Forget YOTA, forget thunderstorms, to see and experience Italy was one of the main reasons I had sailed so far. Rome—your seven hills; Venice—your sinking city; Genoa—Columbus sailed from you. The streets, the fountains, the churches, the restaurants, the romance—Italy, I am here!*

Because of the weather, we decided to land-cruise from Agropoli rather than further north, so we went by taxi to Paestum, and by train to Pompeii. Paestum is reputed to be the best Greek temple site in Italy with three huge, very impressive temples, roofless but with all pillars standing, original and un-restored. The whole area, temples and ruins of the town, was surrounded by a magnificent wall and guard towers. How everything survived earthquakes, volcanoes and World War II, is simply amazing. Half the place can't be excavated because modern houses and a main road have been built over it.

ITALY

Ryan (11): *It was really strange; to see the best Greek temples you go to Italy; to see the best Roman ruins, you go to Turkey.*

Pompeii has been the subject of countless books and films, so there is little for us to add. For four hours we walked constantly, saw all the highlights, and about half of the ruins. The fabled erotic murals in the brothel are small, high up a wall, and faded. They look much better on postcards. Throughout the city, red was the dominant mural color, and it seemed that there were only three interior decorators, given the repetitive nature of the decorations. Mt. Vesuvius loomed in the background, but we didn't take the trip to the top.

Ryan (11): *Seeing the bodies preserved in ash made me realize how quickly the eruption must have happened. There was writing on one wall that was supposed to be an ancient political slogan. Maybe it was just the graffiti of the time.*

A lot of land-cruising in Italy taught us the secret of survival on Italian roads. It was very close to the Turkish rule:
"Do anything you want to, as long as you blow your horn and flash your lights if moving, and put on your emergency flashing lights if stationary."
Driving in Italy was made very simple by the excellent road sign systems and road maps. On the maps, blue roads are freeways, red are first class, and yellow and white are the lesser quality roads. Scenic roads have a green shading. Signs are also consistent, country wide. Directions to freeways are green, to first class roads, blue, and to other classes, white. Therefore, to get to a blue road, you follow the green signs, and to get to a red road, follow the blue signs—what could be simpler. Most of the scenic roads are yellow or white, so to get to a green road, follow the white signs. Local sights, such as temples, are indicated by brown signs. Do not be color-blind driving in Italy.

Ryan (11): *Dad drove and Mum was the navigator. That sounds OK, but Mum needs glasses to read and she can never find them. When she looks down in a car, she gets car-sick. She also gets so involved in the passing scenery that she is not "proactive" as Dad says. I could have taken over, but was too smart to offer.*

Every town and city, regardless of size, had white signs directing us to the city center ("Centro" with a symbol of a bulls-eye of concentric circles beside it), the main cathedral ("Duomo" with a church symbol), the port

("Porto") and so on. These started at the outskirts, and repeated at every turn or intersection. Driving into a strange city was therefore very simple—just follow the white signs. Actually there was no other choice, as street names were conspicuous by their absence, or invisible to any driver without telescopic vision.

Our maps did not show the small towns that the road signs directed us to. A blue sign, showing a major town, would be followed, at the next intersection, by a white sign showing a village. Every intersection was a round-about (traffic circle), so I simply drove in circles for the several minutes necessary for Carole to find her reading glasses, unfold the map, find the correct section, determine that the town wasn't marked, and "discuss" which exit was the correct one. The distance to the next sign was fraught with tension and recrimination. Round-abouts do make it easy to make a U-turn.

A minor problem was, in many cases, we were required to choose a lane before we saw the appropriate sign. In one extreme instance, part of the road went up-hill, the rest down-hill, with the sign directing us up-hill situated on the down-hill road, a hundred yards past the split and around a corner. This was easily solved by simply reversing back to the intersection, because we were in Italy and therefore could do anything, provided we did it with confidence, determination, and flashing lights.

The only crises were caused by tourists in hire cars who obeyed the rules of the road. They even stopped for pedestrians crossing the road at designated crossings! Every Italian knows that the pedestrian is required to make the first move, and then only when there is a reasonable chance of weaving across without relying on the drivers to do more than slightly slow down.

Except at major intersections, traffic lights appeared to be advisory, not obligatory, for cars and trucks. Motor scooters and bikes totally ignored them. Double and triple parking was normal and accepted, provided that the vehicle's emergency lights were flashing. This was particularly applicable on very narrow, one-way streets, with "No Parking" signs on both sides. Motor scooters may be parked on any sidewalk, provided that they are positioned so as to require pedestrians to walk on the roadway. Any sidewalk, not covered with scooters, may be used as a car park. The system worked flawlessly.

French roads were not as well marked as those in Italy, but the same basic traffic and parking rules still applied. In a city, the French seem to think that, once they had provided the initial signs to get us started in the right direction, little further was required. This introduced us to the Friendly French Driver (FFD). Every time we were slow away from the lights, or slowed at an intersection to see if there was some semblance of a directional indication, several FFDs immediately began to provide assistance by flashing lights, blowing horns, shouting, and waving hands. Unfortunately, probably because of the physical constraints imposed by small cars, the finger pointing out the direction for us to go moved in an upward direction, so they were of little help.

One road hazard appeared to be unique to Italy. We were driving towards Pisa, along a country road lined with trees, when I saw, in the shade of one tree, a lovely, tall, slim, black lady, dressed in thigh length black boots, tiny red miniskirt, yellow tank top, no bra, perfectly coiffed hair, perfect make up, including false eye lashes, with ear rings, bracelets and handbag to match. Of course I didn't get many details, as we were driving quickly. Carole and Ryan missed her, and thought that I was dreaming, or fulfilling fantasies, or both, when two more ladies appeared and waved to us.

To cut a long story short (there has to be a first time), we saw these ladies on almost every tree-lined road that was reasonably close to a city. They were all black, all gorgeous, and all startlingly dressed. From the luxury cars we occasionally saw parked behind them, business must have been good, but the question was, where was it conducted?

We left Agropoli, feeling that YOTA was releasing its grip. Not quite so, as later events will demonstrate. The dedicated reader will recall that "Dolphin Spirit" is not an easy boat to drive in reverse, so we go bow-in to the docks, and get marina dinghies to assist us out when space is tight. Agropoli had no dinghies, but all the problems were to our right, and DS always goes left in reverse—need we say more! A brilliant recovery from me saw us out of the harbor with only superficial damage, heading for the Isle of Capri.

Capri is a "must visit" spot—by ferry. The winds made untenable the anchorage at Marina Picolo on the south side, so we reluctantly went to Marina Grande on the north, knowing that we would probably have to sell the boat to pay the marina fees—reported to be over $US200 per night (no towels, no TV, no maid service). Thankfully, the docks seemed to be full as we approached, and no one answered our radio calls. The entrance was narrow, filled by constant ferry and powerboat traffic, with little room to maneuver inside, so we looked, and then departed for Mergallina Marina, near Naples. Squalls chased us all the way across the Bay of Naples.

A call to the marina got an immediate response, in perfect English, advising us that the Authorities had closed the place down. Later detective work determined that the marina owners hadn't paid the right people the right money (remember that this was Italy). I scrambled for charts and cruising guides as it was getting late in the day, and we headed for Port Miseno.

Things do happen for the best. Instead of paying through the nose in

Capri, or standing guard all night in a Naples marina, we anchored in a lovely, protected bay, under sandstone cliffs pierced by caves and tunnels. One tunnel had to be man-made, and went 600 feet right through the point to the sea on the other side. Naturally, we ran it in the dinghy several times, at Ryan's insistence. A huge thunderstorm during the night produced wonderful fireworks, but only 25 knots of wind. After the terrifying winds at Agropoli, we treated each thunderstorm with great respect.

Mediterranean marinas and harbors are always full of yachts during July, August and September, so it was a great relief when we got to Ventotine Island to see that, in the well protected harbor, the limited anchoring space was full, but the sea wall was empty and inviting. We side-tied and relaxed.

The yacht/ferry harbor is under a very pretty, old village, and next to a small harbor carved out of the solid rock by ancient Romans. They even carved storage places into the cliffs for their boats. Some were still in use as stores, while others held shops and restaurants. The Roman harbor itself was used by small boats and the brave yachts which negotiated the 20-foot wide entrance, followed by a right-angle turn into a 100-foot wide harbor, crisscrossed with mooring lines.

Entering yachts gradually filled the sea wall space, with me running around taking lines and generally helping them tie up. That way I made myself look good, and ensured no one got too close to "Dolphin Spirit." Eventually, with a good buffer zone established fore and aft, Carole and I set off to explore the quaint village and the Roman harbor, leaving Ryan on board to play video games.

From the top of the wall separating the two harbors, I looked back to see a newly-arrived charter yacht getting very close to "Dolphin Spirit." I started back, and broke into a run when the yacht pulled up to DS, and men boarded. By the time I arrived, the yacht was securely tied to DS, with Ryan really upset. He had tried to stop them, but they just pushed him aside. I have a very short fuse for anything that affects DS, and an even shorter one when Ryan is involved.

The charter had six German men on board, two of whom were still on DS. These were treated to a calm (under the circumstances) "Get off my boat, NOW!" and I went to cast off the lines. "But we always do this" protested one of them, from the safety of his own cockpit. I could have pointed out that what they had done was the equivalent of walking into a stranger's house, uninvited, pushing a kid off the sofa, and sitting down in front of the TV, but contented myself with casting off the lines. Some discussion in German followed, obviously not terribly complimentary, but eventually they started their engine, and moved off to a space on the wall which they could have gone to in the first place. Ventotine was a picturesque village, mostly vertical, mostly restaurants, and well worth the visit

ITALY

we made to it after I could be trusted to speak coherently.

Reports painted a wonderful picture of Ponza Island, so we aimed the pointy end of DS in what Navigator Me laughingly calls "the right direction." It really is a great feeling when, out of an empty ocean, a little island appears, when it is supposed to, right where it is supposed to be. We anchored in crystal clear water, in a bay just to the north of Ponza Harbor, with the place all to ourselves. Five minutes in the dinghy took us into Ponza Harbor and town, into dirty water, with yachts everywhere, bouncing in the ferry washes. The herd instinct is hard to understand sometimes.

For the first time in months, all of us went swimming and snorkeling around the boat and the nearby rocks. It was terrific, until Ryan got stung on the face and neck by a jellyfish—the first time in four years. Although we treated him immediately, the pain and welts lasted for hours. Two days later, there was still a mark on his neck that looked like a vampire bite. In spite of this, it was a really lovely place, so we decided to stay for a few days. Our bay, and Ponza Harbor, were on the south of the island, but at this time of year, the winds were invariably from the north, so we were perfectly calm and secure.

Naturally, the weather had to change. One morning a southerly breeze sprang up and gradually increased until the waves coming into our bay made life very uncomfortable. Up came the anchor, and we joined the stream of yachts leaving Ponza. The good thing was that we were heading north to Nettuno, near Anzio, so had a great sail.

An hour or so out of Nettuno, a huge thunderstorm appeared between us and the coast. I reasoned with the worried Carole that, as the wind was from the south and the thunderstorm was to the north of us, there would be no problem. The subsequent sequence of events went something like this—

Wind stopped

Thunderstorm hit with pouring rain, thunder, lightning

Wind blew 30 knots from the north

Wind stopped

Rain, thunder, lightning stopped

Wind blew 10 knots from the south

—all in ten minutes. Thankfully, Carole didn't have the time or energy to berate me. Mediterranean weather was so wonderfully predictably unpredictable.

Although Nettuno is a very picturesque town, we went there because it has a protected, secure marina, and it is only 45 minutes by train from Rome. A couple of other boats we know went to the free anchorage at nearby Anzio. One went aground at the entrance, and both had uncomfortable, rolly days. Sometimes, you get what you pay for.

A word about guide books. We now own more than should be legal, mainly those published by Lonely Planet—Australian and therefore definitely the best. Each book deals specifically with one region, and therefore adjectives like "best," "wonderful" and "must see" have to be properly interpreted. This doesn't mean that we were getting jaded, but it does mean that we didn't run off to a place or sight, just because the guide book says that it is worth seeing. We thoroughly enjoyed walking through quaint winding streets, looking at, and through, old churches. It's just that we now looked at a scene which, in past days, would have sent us into a photographing frenzy, mentally compared it with others, enjoyed it, and moved on. Which brings us to Nettuno, wonderfully picturesque and photogenic if taken alone, but only a 5 on the DSPP 10 scale (Dolphin Spirit Picturesque and Photogenic).

The trains to Rome were uncrowded, fast, on time, and inexpensive. Wandering accordion players added to the ambience. The only negative was the need to select seats where the windows weren't totally obscured by graffiti. Just outside Rome, the train passed by a long, ancient aqueduct that looked wonderful (DSPP 7), but wasn't mentioned in any of our books, probably because there was no easy way to it for the tourist buses.

Rome's central station, Termini, is a short walk from everything we wanted to see, but a map was necessary. Heading, that first day, for the Vatican, we got lost (with a map) and ended up at the Victor Emmanuel Memorial and the Coliseum. Getting lost in Rome was no fun, as we always finished up somewhere great and well known, instead of discovering something new. Half of Rome was covered with scaffolding, as they cleaned up and repaired in preparation for the year 2000 influx of pilgrims and tourists. This meant that the street names were missing, or obscured.

Carole: *Disaster started our first Rome visit. You know the dream. We have all had it. There you are in the middle of a crowd—naked. Mine came true in Rome. Slacks are acceptable wear in most places, but this was Rome. I had carefully chosen my outfit and ironed (my first use of the iron in three years) the lovely dark dress I would wear, in case we were given a Papal audience.*

Laurie was always asking why I wear a slip in such hot weather, so this day I decided not to wear one. On the train, I noted, with horror that, in certain lighting conditions, the dress material was transparent. Walking down the streets in lock-step, sandwiched between Ryan and Laurie, became uncomfortable, and attracted more attention than the dress. Lingerie shops were few, and all catered only to the petite. In desperation, I bought a length of black silk, found a bathroom, and wrapped the silk around me like a sarong.

ITALY

The Roman propriety and decorum were preserved, the Pope missed a great opportunity, and we could all relax.

We did all the tourist stuff—Vatican, Coliseum, Spanish Steps, Victor Emmanuel, Trevi Fountain, Pantheon. For all of us, the undoubted highlight was the restored Sistine Chapel ceiling. The only way to get to it was through the Vatican museum, seemingly miles and miles of paintings, statues, painted ceilings, frescos and friezes, which blurred somewhat after a while. The Sistine Chapel, right at the end, jolted us back. There were chairs to sit on around the walls, and recorded announcements advising that photos and videos weren't allowed. Everyone, including us (blush), videoed on. Did you know that several wall panels were painted by Raphael, and gorgeous they were too?

Outside of that, Ryan's favorite was the Pantheon, Carole's was Trevi, and mine was secretly filming a congregation of Bishops from above them in St. Peter's dome, before a guard caught on. They were spectacular swirls of red, purple, green and white. Copies will be made available at a reasonable (considering the source, subject, and expenses incurred in getting there) price. We all threw coins into Trevi Fountain, over the shoulder, of course. The first was to ensure a return to Rome, the second to grant a wish, the others as insurance, in case the first two didn't work. Trevi had just been cleaned, and was quite magnificent. We walked, we gawked (Australian for staring like a stunned mullet), we ate, we drank wine, we drank wine, we drank wine, and we finally saw all of Rome we could absorb.

My father was born in Northern Italy and migrated to Australia with his family when he was just 12-years old. I was raised in a town where Italian was spoken more commonly than English (I certainly learned to swear in Italian before I could speak English properly). My grandparents constantly spoke of "the old country" with nostalgia, but with no desire to return. When they retired, my parents went to Italy for a protracted visit, meeting all of Dad's relatives. I spent two weeks doing the same thing in 1963.

Now that Dad was gone, I had really mixed feelings about visiting his home town again and seeing the relatives. Most had died in the 30 years since my visit, and the new generation had never met the Australian branch. The closest relatives lived in Ladispoli, a seaside town north of Rome, so we made the Riva de Traiano Marina our next base. It was huge, protected, and relatively inexpensive, for Italy. Anchoring wasn't an option, as there were no protected spots within 50 miles.

The region is noted for its Etruscan Tombs, so we headed for the closest site in a rented car. Three-thousand-year-old paintings on the walls of some 30 underground tombs were still bright and clear, leaving us wondering what was still to be found in the 1,000 or so remaining to be uncovered on the hillside.

Chasing Sunsets

Ladispoli is the closest seaside resort to Rome, and my relatives were the biggest show in town when I saw them in 1963. You couldn't get onto the beach without passing through their Colombia Bar and paying them for the privilege. Want food, coffee and entertainment—their Gran Bar Nazionale, one street back, was the place to go. Forty years later, Ladispoli had grown, but Colombia still controlled the biggest and best beach, the Gran Bar still dispensed food and drink, and the family (note the lower case f) still owned both, and more besides.

Only one person I met on my first visit was still alive, the grand-daughter of my grand-father's sister. The ones who had passed on did leave large families, and we soon needed family trees, hastily drawn on napkins, to keep track of everyone we met. Napkins were used because Colombia was also a restaurant, where we were required to eat at least once a day, at least four courses with wine, for a week. New relatives seemed to appear every meal. It was a wonderful time. Conversation was conducted, with much hand and arm waving, in my Italglish, with Italian, and some English, on their side. We communicated very well, we think! Who knows what was actually said, but it didn't really matter.

Georgio, an architect, took time off from his current project on the Grand Canal in Venice to take us to another nearby Etruscan necropolis. This one comprised massive, above-ground, stone tombs. The site Director took us around personally, describing everything in machine-gun Italian, which I, recognizing one word in ten, managed to follow—mostly. It took us three hours to see just the best of the tombs, situated along the top of a ridge. We looked across a valley to the next ridge, and were told that all we could see was "solid tombs," as yet unexcavated. There must be thousands and thousands.

Ryan (11): *I spent the night with Georgio and Mara and went fishing with them the next day. I caught the only fish of the day, cooked and served that night at Colombia. I hadn't spent a night away from my parents for a long time, and it was a strange feeling not to have them close, and to sleep on a bed that wasn't moving.*

We drove to Sienna, and then to Cortona, to try to find the house described in the book *Under the Tuscan Sun.* Carole and I had both read it and Carole had cooked many delicious meals based on its recipes. There were many villas that could have been it, so we were sure one was right.

YOTA had another fling. A thunderstorm with very strong winds had us hitting the dock, so we started the motor to help me take up the lines. An underwater mooring had come loose and wrapped around the prop. After telling the marina people about it, I said that I was going to dive and free the prop. From their reaction, you would think I had suggested rape and pillage. Their own diver appeared two days later, took two hours to suit up and prepare, and 30 seconds to remove the line.

Carole: *We agonized (I agonized) over what to give the family as a thank-you gift when we left. Food was not an option as they owned a restaurant. We drove for hours looking for a flower shop, then a couple of blocks from the restaurant came on a man selling huge bouquets from the back of his truck. It was the right thing to do. Every lady was so thrilled. Then they insisted on filling our freezer with pizza, delicious, thin crust, the best in Italy.*

After a farewell family breakfast of 24-hour eggs on DS, we tore ourselves away and headed north again. Cala Galera was a huge marina, and by the time we had walked from our boat to the marina office, we were too exhausted to walk the additional three miles to the nearest town. All the Italian marinas north of Rome were full of local yachts and powerboats year-round. We could have anchored just outside the entrance, but were getting thunderstorm jitters by this stage.

The anchorage at Portoferrario, Elba, was very protected. We anchored a little away from the other yachts, and were therefore close to the ferry path. They were never a danger or a problem, but the first couple of times these ocean-liner-sized boats bore down on us were somewhat heart-stopping. We did get to see at close range the huge murals—whales, fish, mermaids, cartoon characters—that decorated their sides. The town surrounding the yacht harbor was very pretty, with castles and old buildings—the run-of-the-mill, DSPP 6 place. We were glad not to be in the harbor, as tangled anchor chains were the norm, and basically unavoidable when boats tie up to a semi-circular quay.

Elba was where Napoleon was sent after his first defeat, and where he is supposed to have created the full-sentence palindrome—"Able was I ere I saw Elba." The "Napoleon slept here," or equivalent, signs were everywhere, but we really enjoyed the place for a couple of days. Saw an Australian flag in the anchorage, and went over to say hello to "Emmanuel," (John and Susie), who we had last met in Nidri, Greece. Susie was blind, and had to be one of the bravest people we know. The bay filled on weekends, with small and large sailboats, racing and just sailing around. We dinghied through the action for our thrill of the day.

I celebrated another birthday here. Carole and Ryan gave me a miniature globe, with the countries made out of pretty stones, ground smooth.

Wind from astern, so we motor-sailed to Viareggio. We were supposed to go a long way past the entrance, as a sandbar extends out beyond the breakwater. The chop and dirty water didn't allow us to see the bottom, or color changes, so we took a chance and headed across, clearing the sand with six inches under the keel according to the depth sounder.

Carole: What's this "we took a chance?" I don't take chances and would still be looking for the entrance.

Filling with fuel at the fuel dock, we learned that the two marinas in the harbor were full. As there was space on the wall of the canal that led up into the city, we tied there. "Emmanuel" arrived a couple of hours later. Apart from being pinned to the wall by the wind, it was free and calm, so very acceptable. As it was a Saturday afternoon, everyone in the city paraded up and down the wall, stopping to peer down at us (a very high wall), point at the flag, make comments, and stroll on.

The next morning, two Port Police resplendent in white uniforms, and a plain clothes person came along to tell us to move to another spot on the wall, further up the canal. We always comply immediately with polite official requests, and with impolite ones, if the requestor is armed. These were polite, and armed. We are some 55-feet long, bow anchor to stern anchor, and draw 7 feet, 6 inches. The canal was less than 60-feet wide and 8 feet, 6 inches deep in the middle, with a sloping rock wall on one side and the tall concrete wall on the other. The space for us was between a 30-foot sailboat and a 70-foot powerboat. Reversing into it wasn't an option, so we headed in, and had to spin "Dolphin Spirit" around in the canal. An extra coat of paint would have been scraped off, but we made it. The applause from the awestruck crowd on the wall was thunderous.

Carole: Of course I didn't hear the applause. My heart had stopped when we began the turn.

Viareggio was simply a two mile strip of restaurants along the beach that runs north of the harbor, and three companies (Bennetti and Perini Navi being two of them) which make huge power yachts. The local service facilities were therefore slanted towards the mega-business—finding a $100,000 chandelier, or a $10,000 silk-covered lounge, was no problem. It was, however, a very pleasant town and made a good base from which to see Pisa and the surrounding mountains. Internet access was through a place called "The Hacker." We were buzzed through the door, just like a bank, so we wondered a little about its real purpose, but access is access!

Took a day trip to Pisa to see the tower, now held up by cables and lead weights. There used to be a perfect spot where you could stand with upraised hand, and the photo would look like you were supporting the tower. Now it is inside a fence, but the lawn was green. Into the mountains we drove, got lost, but found the coast again, using the old seaman's trick of heading towards the setting sun. We arrived back at the boat to find chaos!

Viareggio Harbor is well protected, but contains a design fault. Seas, of any reasonable size, suck water out of the harbor and cause a tremendous surge. As the canal wall was so high, our mooring lines went over the sharp concrete edge, and all five had parted, as DS bounced up and down. Luckily, "Emmanuel" was there, and John ran between our boat and theirs, replacing lines on both boats as they snapped.

The next day, I went to the Port Police and begged for help. The Officer in Charge turned out to be the plainclothes man of the first day. He found us a temporary spot further into the harbor, and then persuaded one of the yards to make a place for us in an inner lagoon. We later found that he had used the "but they have a child on board" ploy—Ryan can be useful sometimes. Just goes to prove that the policy of being polite and responsive with officials always pays, but have a child back-up. The lagoon was dirty, but very calm and protected, and we had unlimited water and electricity. We needed to drop a stern anchor, so, naturally (YOTA Rules) the anchor winch ceased to work when the time came to pull it up again.

Feeling secure, we took a day trip to Verona to see Ryan's grandparents, who were there on holidays.

Ryan (11): *I had just finished "Romeo and Juliet" and it was interesting to see a city that was the basis for some of Shakespeare's plays. However, I believe he never visited the place. The apartment where Grampa and Granma were staying had a piano, so I played "Fur Elise" for them, the first time they had heard me on the piano.*

Following that success, we set off for a longer trip through the Dolomites and to Venice, Ravenna, San Marino, and Florence. We started the day warm on the coast, and then drove through two snowstorms in the high passes. The scenery was simply stunning. As a bonus, we saw ski-jump practice on a snowless ski jump—gravity doesn't seem to work for those jumpers. The fashionable resort of Cortina, high in the Dolomites, was happy to provide us with accommodation in one of the very few hotels that were open in the off-season.

Venice was sort of a let-down. Carole wanted to stay in a hotel on the Grand Canal, but those reasonably priced ones (oxymoron?) were full, so we stayed on Lido Island, across the lagoon from St. Marks. The lagoon seemed to be in constant motion, with launches, car and people ferries, cargo boats and assorted craft everywhere. The water was dirty, a match for the grey sky. There was a yacht "marina" near St. Marks, but it seemed to have little protection, and the yachts were bounced around by the constant wakes.

Carole: **In retrospect, Laurie should have been proactive and asked his cousin Georgio to find us a great, inexpensive hotel.**

We ferried across, getting out right at St. Marks Square, which was partially under water as it was high tide. Making our way around water and pigeons, we queued on the walkways to get into the cathedral. The water was inside there, too. A pretty outside, but the interior was not up to our high standards. The square is surrounded by restaurants, whose tables extend well into the open space. They compensate for being partially submerged by each having a string orchestra playing, and waiters in tuxedos. We snacked at one, noting the "reasonable" prices on the menu board, and were somewhat shocked by the $US6 coke, and the $US12 wilted cheese pizza slice. I protested, and was sniffed at by the waiter, who informed me, in perfect English, that we had to pay extra (translation, double) for table service. The orchestra was nice.

We did love walking over and along the canals. Did you know Venice has more miles of streets than it has of canals? Some of the original gondola landings at the old palazzos are now well under water, but we tried to imagine Lucretia, and her temporary friends, being rowed up to them. Carole window-shopped for glass, but the only thing she wanted was a little larger than DS (or seemed to be), so, although I immediately whipped out the credit card, she decided against it.

As part of his schooling, Ryan had learned about the wonderful mosaics of Justinian and Theodora at Ravenna, so we drove there, taking a detour to the Republic of San Marino. A city on the top of a mountain, it declared independence from the various Italian kingdoms many centuries ago, and has been overlooked ever since, except by the tourists.

Carole: **All my life I studied, reading about things I would probably never see. And here was Ryan, read about it one day, go see it the next. How will he adjust to regular schooling and life ashore?**

The coastal drive was flat and boring, but we soon woke up after arrival in Ravenna. Following the "Hotel" signs dumped us into a pedestrian mall, and under the stern gaze of a very solid, lady policeperson. I flashed my sheepish "Gee officer, I'm just a stranger here" grin, apologized in my best Italglish, and kicked Ryan in the shins so that his eyes teared up. Something worked, because she put away her ticket book, and led us out. The mosaics, on the walls and ceilings of two churches, were unique and well worth any drama.

Florence was for us the green and white cathedral (DSPP 9 outside, 5 inside), with its Brunelleschi Dome, the statue of David (the real one, not the many copies around the city) and the Uffizi Gallery.

David is simply magnificent. How, from a block of marble, can anyone carve an arm where the skin looks translucent, and you can trace the veins beneath it. Unlike the Pieta, in the Vatican, which was hidden behind glass, we got up close and personal with David.

The Uffizi was a sensory overload after about four hours. We had the opportunity to go through it again, a couple of days later, but, because of the long lines, chose the less exciting alternative of walking the city. Working on our normal "we have a map, but this street looks interesting" mode of getting lost, we stumbled on the pretty church of St. Croce, which has an exceptional interior. Right next to it was a very nice restaurant, so who needed the Uffizi?

In between all the above, we drove to Sienna, and learned the origin of the "You can't get there from here" phrase. The Doumo was right there, we could see it. The road sign said "Duomo," but the road was blocked, and the detour sign also said "Duomo," so off we went. The detour signs changed to real signs, which we followed religiously (you can say that when you are looking for a church), and which led, you guessed it, to the original road. We did this three times, then asked. A very helpful man took us right to the original road again. We parked. We walked. We found it. Seinna is a wonderful place for walking and gawking, but forget driving.

By accident (lost again), we visited the walled city of Lucca. The old walls are huge, and virtually intact. Continuing our day of fortunate errors, we drove up into the mountains behind Lucca and found superb scenery. On the map, the distances looked short, but failed to advise that the roads are all S-bends, stacked one on top of the other. We ran out of daylight, so I had either to drive at one-mile-per-hour, or put up with Carole screaming at every corner. Do you know how long such a drive gets to be? Believe it or not, we got stuck behind a slower car. This person almost completely stopped at every corner, hugging the center of the road so there was no chance to pass. I was biting pieces out of the steering wheel before we finally squeezed through.

We waved a final goodbye to the lovely ladies beside the road, dug our anchor out of very gooey and sticky mud, and pointed north. Genoa is not a nice place for yachts, so we headed for Rapello, and the next-door-to-each-other marinas of Lavagna and Chiavari. Both are huge, the first was full, but we talked our way into the second—my Italglish does work sometimes. For once, our hard-won expertise deserted us (note how Helmsman

Me adroitly shares solo blame), and we had to make two attempts to get into the usual foot-wide space allocated to us.

The "get to Barcelona" bug had bit, so we soon found ourselves in the San Remo marina, and very pleasantly surprised. We had plenty of space, the fees were less than half of what we had expected, and the town was just across the street. An instant decision to stay for a while was made, and ratified by all hands—the bug bite wasn't deep apparently. One thing we had come to value in our present lifestyle was the flexibility it gave to plans.

The car hire firms had another good day, and we headed east towards Genoa. From the hills around, it looked big and smoggy, so we turned north to find my Dad's birthplace of Pontestura, on the banks of the Po River. Progress has seemingly bypassed this little town that Dad left some 70 years before. We found the church where he was choir boy and bell ringer, but couldn't find his old house. I asked some old men on a corner if there were any Pane's around. After some discussion, which involved stopping a couple of passing cars, the nearly unanimous decision was reached that there was probably one, somewhere outside of town, that it was useless to ask the police anything, and (I am almost sure of this) that Carole could put her feet under their tables at any time.

Deciding not to take advantage of this offer, we drove onwards to France, as a bulge of that country cuts across the direct road to San Remo. The only way of telling we were in France, after we had passed the sign saying "France," was the abrupt deterioration in the road surface. Even the restaurants advertised pizza and pasta. Autumn leaves made the winding mountainous road (Carole is calmer in daylight) delightful, and we were quite sorry to come out of it and back to the flat coast of Italy.

We had bypassed Portofino by boat, so now we drove back to it, again dodging around Genoa. Right at the end of a little peninsular, and surrounding a tiny harbor, the town is lovely. I was very glad we hadn't taken DS there, as the harbor bottom was rock, the space limited, and the depth variable, to say the least.

Desiring some exposure to the other rich and famous, we drove to Nice and Monte Carlo, right through the closing stages of the San Remo Rally. Apparently a policeman got it wrong, and waved us onto a road, and into a tunnel where two rally cars came screaming towards us, mostly sideways. We escaped, shaken but unscathed, to enter the traffic jam known as Monaco. Any population census there has to include the people in cars, as it took a lifetime to drive the couple of miles along the waterfront, and this was in the off-season. I remembered driving up to the front of the Monte Carlo Casino in 1963, being moved on by a wonderful white uniform, and driving away. This time, an inch of forward progress was worthy of a cheer.

By contrast, the four-lane road along the beach at Nice was almost as empty as the sand. It looks a lot better with Bridgette Bardot driving a convertible along it. Not finding her, we decided to head back. Some hundred traffic lights later, we finally agreed that there was no place to make a left turn into the other lanes, so turned right, then right again onto a parallel road. Now we were going in the correct direction, but were back in the traffic. Any rich and famous who put up with this, at any time of the year, obviously weren't worth meeting, so we left them all hanging and returned to the sanity of DS.

Carole: *We watched videos, played games, and at last finished a puzzle I had given Laurie for the first birthday he'd had when we were together. While we were doing the puzzle, Ryan gave us one of the laughs of the trip. He began talking about "Naked Gun," the video we had just seen. "Wasn't it funny," he said, "when they (Priscilla Presley and Leslie Nielsen) came out wearing something Italian?" He was referring to the head-to-toe condoms they had on to practice safe sex.*

Three times we shopped, cooked, stored, lashed down, and prepared for the two-day crossing of the Golfe de Lyon to Barcelona, and three times the weather blew up and stopped us. We started to look seriously at wintering in San Remo, but on the fourth try the weather gods smiled, and we had a great, calm trip. Ryan caught a tuna, his first fish in months.

The only other excitement came from the French Navy. A gunboat cruised up, and ordered us to turn left and head out for some 20 miles, "for your safety," then shadowed us for an hour to make sure we complied. They certainly watch closely, as almost exactly 20 miles from when we turned, the Navy was back on the radio to tell us we could return to course. Listening to the radio chat, we worked out that the Navy was shooting at things in that area. Sure enough, that night, the horizon was seemingly continuous gun flashes and booms. We fantasized they were clearing up the terminal traffic jam in Monaco in the only possible way.

We dodged tuna nets, some five miles off shore, reached Barcelona just before dawn, and hove-to. Losing patience soon after daylight, we headed in to the harbor, following a huge cruiseliner, with an even bigger container ship closing in from behind. The liner went left, we went right, to find out that its left turn was a prelude to a complete U-turn, to park on the right. A 180 and several 360s from us later, the way was clear, and we proceeded to our winter home at Marina Port Vell.

Chasing Sunsets

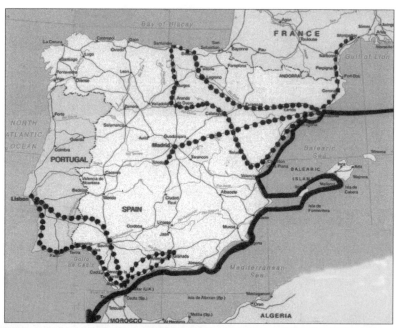

Spain and France
Year Four and Five
October 29 to June 13

Carole: *American tourists we met in hotels or at ruins "ahhhhd" at our journey, and "ahhhhd" even more when they heard that we would be living in Barcelona for seven months.*

Within minutes of our arrival, we were invited to cocktails on one yacht and to a birthday party on another, both that night. It was shaping up to be a great lay-over, and the actuality exceeded the promise.

There were almost 100 live-aboard cruising boats wintering at Port Vell that year. 35 English, 19 American, 7 Canadian, 9 Australian and 4 New Zealand yachts were amongst them. Two were from Switzerland, and there was a token Spaniard. The people off European boats generally go back to their houses for the winter, and return when the cruising season starts. In the marina therefore, English was almost the only language we heard.

Ryan (11): *A boat from Iceland had a boy my age on board and we spent a lot of time together. He and his parents were very different from most of the other cruisers I knew. They had a relaxed attitude toward school for one thing, and normally went to bed at 2am and got up at 1pm.*

Barcelona is the city of Gaudi, the architect and builder, who was unique in style and vision. From the soaring towers of the still unfinished Sagrada Familia Cathedral to the almost grotesque squattiness (couldn't think of a better word) of his apartment buildings, the "no square corners, no straight lines, dripping melted stone" look of a Gaudi design is unmistakable. He put color and shape together in ways that are either the result of genius or of nightmares. Wintering in his city was just perfect in almost every respect.

Marina Port Vell, surrounded by the buildings of the absorbing old city of Barceloneta, is under the shadow of the statue of Columbus. Within 200 yards of us were the markets for fruit, vegetables, fish and meat, the supermarket, a great bread shop, the chicken lady, one-hour photo shop, several money changers, banks and ATM machines, pharmacies, laundry, flower shop, hardware, chandlery, Museum de Catalana, and 20 or more restaurants.

Within half a mile, was an Imax theater, shopping mall, huge aquarium, the bottom of La Rambla (the most famous street in Spain), the Post Office, a magnificent cathedral, several wonderful churches, statues, squares, the Picasso Museum, the absolutely out-of-this-world spectacular Palau de la Musica Catalana, travel agents, shops of all kinds and descriptions, and countless restaurants. It was impossible to walk a block without seeing something that, in other cities, would have the tourist buses lined up for miles. In Barcelona, it had to be really spectacular to rate a glance.

Carole: *My almost daily trip to the chicken lady was a much anticipated delight. She had no English, so I would practice my Spanish each time, and she would try valiantly not to laugh. It was fascinating to watch her dissect a chicken, boning some parts, skinning others. Every bit had a specific use and she patiently told me on each visit what to do with them. My refusal to take the head and feet left her shaking her head about how I could be passing up such delicacies. She always packaged the chicken in three parcels, the bones and skin and assorted other remnants for use to make stock, the thin breast fillets for sauté, and the remaining pieces for stews and casseroles.*

The port area, including Port Vell and that part of the city alongside the beach running north from us, was completely redone for the 1992 Olympics. Though the Metro and bus services were cheap and efficient, to be more mobile we bought folding bikes. By a strange co-incidence, Barcelona was set up for bike riders, with miles and miles of dedicated bike paths along the beaches and through the city. Our folding bikes, with tiny wheels, topped by tall people, ensured that we were stared at wherever we went. The 16-screen cinema complex at the Olympic Village showed only English-language films. The bikes could probably have found their own way there by the time we left.

Walk up La Rambla and you step on a Miro mosaic. Look to the right at the imposing square, Placa Real, with its central fountain and Gaudi designed street lamps. Keep going, and there is the Gothic quarter with its magnificent churches, streets and buildings. Work your way back and go right and you find the Palau Nacional and its fountains. At night, when these change color and shape in time to music, they truly earn their name of Font Magica. Along almost every narrow, winding street, are ornate balconies, flowers, statues in niches, decorated bridges between buildings, fountains, and ornate doors.

Many days we just rambled, in no particular direction, certain to find something of interest and never disappointed. Midday we would select a restaurant for the always available Menu del Dias, fixed price (cheap), three-course lunch, wine included. All were good, some terrific. For those we made sure we returned. Passing on the location of such places to the other cruisers was a requirement. Our custom of finding a great restaurant, and then going so often we became part of the establishment, didn't work here. There were just too many fantastic ones, with new discoveries around every corner.

Also in circulation were the names of the best Tapas bars, as eating/drinking there was one of the better ways to spend an evening. For hungry cruisers accustomed to eating as the sun set, Tapas bars provided the only way to eat before the restaurants opened at 8:30pm, or later. Many a night we were the only ones in a restaurant before the regular diners started to arrive around 11pm.

Barcelona helped by turning on wonderful weather, with only a few cloudy, rainy days, and one snow shower. We all did catch the cold/flu that swept Europe, and it stuck to us for about four weeks. As soon as we settle on land, the land-based bugs and viruses grab hold.

Carole: *Ryan had been learning Spanish since the day we set sail. At long last we thought all those lessons were going to pay off. In Barcelona however, the language is Catalan. Luckily, all signs were in both Spanish and Catalan, and we could always find someone to understand us.*

Carole and Ryan employed a Spanish tutor, so were chatting away fluently to the locals. Ryan, in particular, was a hit with the market stall holders, mostly older ladies, who praised his Spanish to the skies. I, on the other hand, got no respect for my Spanglish.

Barcelona was a great base from which to tour Europe. Our first foray was a four-week car trip through France. Our time-share could be traded for places in France and we built our trip around what accommodation was available. It was planned as a week in the Alps, a week in the Loire Valley, a week in Paris, and a week getting back to Barcelona. Surprisingly, given our background of changing plans, it worked out that way, almost.

On a rare overcast day, we left Barcelona. Then the rain started, and developed into a real downpour as we headed north along the coast to France. Right through the Pyrenees and to Nimes it beat down, once heavily enough to force us to pull over. That night, snug in our "New Hotel La Bamba" (great French name), we saw on the TV news that floods in the area we passed through had killed 27 people. Over the years we have been cruising, we have discovered that it does not pay to follow us. We leave Indonesia, and that country's economy collapses, and there are riots. We leave Sri Lanka and rebel bombs go off everywhere. We leave Eritrea, and the war with Ethiopia starts up again. We leave Sudan, and the U.S. bombs the place. We leave Turkey, and they have huge earthquakes. And so it goes.

Carole: We crossed into France just as the French vocalist Patricia Kass was singing that great French song "La Vie en Rosa" on our car CD player. Our first meal, at a roadside stop, shocked us at how expensive food would be in France. However, even in this place, the honey-mustard salad dressing was superb, with a taste I have never been able to find outside of France, or been able to replicate.

Nimes stays in our mind for the Roman amphitheater, now used for bull fights (We were in France, but close to the Spanish border, so I suppose a little culture spilled over.), and for our first real French dining experience (truck stops don't count), which made me very sick. Carole and Ryan had delicious food, but I would try the fish soup, and fish in puff pastry, so probably deserved my fate.

I did manage to get out of the bathroom by morning and, exhibiting magnificent resilience, drove us to La Ponte du Gard, a wonderful, three-story Roman aqueduct. Ryan had studied about it previously, and had pictures of it in his *What Your 5th Grader Needs to Know,* so it was a great experience to see the reality. Restoration work was done around 1800 (the year, not the time of day) and you can find the workmen's signature hammers and chisels carved into stones. Some of the graffiti was dated in the 1700s. Back in those days, the vandals satisfied themselves with names and dates, unlike the wall-filling atrocities of today.

Our time-share was the Diamonte Apartment at Villard de Lans, a small town in the Alps, about 20 miles from Grenoble. The rain stopped and the skies cleared as we drove into the foothills. Based on our usual practice of taking the least-traveled road, we left the highway and wound our way into the mountains on a one-lane goat track, with views to die for (*Carole: Laurie occasionally has a poor choice of phrase, given my absolute belief that any road less than four lanes and not horizontal is a potential death trap.*). The roadway had been gouged out of the cliffs, and we drove under an overhang of rock—actually there was rock on three sides, and a sheer drop to the valley floor on the other. Carole was, of course, completely relaxed about this, helped by Ryan and I pointing out that we were 75% protected by solid rock.

Villard de Lans is a pretty little town, surrounded by the snow-topped Alps. Our apartment overlooked the houses and the surrounding slopes and green valleys. It was blue skies and balmy weather, so we made the most of it, walking, driving all around, and eating on our balcony just enjoying the food and the view.

Carole*: Ryan and I got into the habit of walking to the village each morning to buy warm, fresh, croissants for breakfast. Sitting out on our balcony, we munched, and began to relax from our stress-filled cruising life. Ryan put the exercise room, sauna, steam room, and heated indoor pool to good use. I'd fall asleep at night with French tapes playing on my headset.*

Laurie had developed an abscess at the base of one tooth and was absolutely miserable with the pain. We found a dentist in the village who gave Laurie antibiotics that reduced the infection and the pain and allowed us to finish the trip with Laurie in relative comfort. Any testiness his writing exhibits during this period is therefore explained.

Grenoble is actually three cities, spread along both sides of a river, with the usual French signs to help you get around. This means that they start you off very well, then assume that you know all the twists and turns from there. We got lost, and re-discovered most of the Alps before His Lordship (me) would deign to ask directions. As might be expected, we were about as far away from the art museum (the only reason to go to Grenoble) as we could get and still be in France. After all of that, the museum exhibits and paintings had to be wonderful, but they weren't. One Picasso, one Monet (both second-rate), and a lot of "wanna-bes" don't make a museum.

One afternoon we noticed some white flakes falling from the sky. With great excitement, we rushed out onto the balcony, trying to catch one of them before they went away. Three days later, when the snow stopped, the balcony was filled, and the cars in the parking lot were small humps in the white blanket. It was fascinating to watch the countryside turn from green to white, and realize that the green wouldn't be seen again for at least four months.

Ryan (11)*: On our balcony, I made small snow-people, then larger ones, then giant ones, as the days passed and the snow continued to fall. Some I tried to make into birds and animals such as a duck and a penguin. Mum* *helped; Dad just commented and took the usual pictures. We went for a walk one day and I stepped off the cleared path and almost disappeared into soft snow. It was great.*

The snow was still coming down, undiminished, all through the night before we were due to leave, but stopped by morning. Ryan and I found the car (not an easy task to remember whether we were the third or fourth bump in the snow), and dug it out from under about five feet of snow. The engine started immediately, the heater worked, the general opinion of the locals was that the road to Grenoble would be mostly clear, so we took off. The car had front-wheel drive, a real asset without chains, as the small streets we had to use were all down hill, snow covering an ice base, and scary. When we reached it, the main road had been plowed clear (one lane), so we did very well, actually getting up to 5 MPH between snow flurries.

Past Grenoble, the highway was clear, although snow was still falling. Through Lyons and on to Clemont Ferrari we sailed. Beyond Clemont, the road became two tracks through the snow-banks, the sky got dark, and the snow came down harder. Visions of spending the night in the car, buried in the snow, made it a very easy decision to turn around and spend the night in that very French "Best Western" hotel in Clemont.

It was a good decision, as we would otherwise have passed through some very pretty countryside in the dark. Lunch, the next day, was in an isolated building surrounded by forests and fields. Its only advertisement was several cars parked nearby. Warmth from a blazing fire; old-world charm; great vegetable soup; fresh, crusty bread; good solid local red wine; what more can one ask for on a snowy day in the middle of the French Massif?

Just outside Potiers was Futurescope, an amusement park dedicated to all types of visual experiences, mainly film and video. They had IMAX, 3-D, multiple screen, 360-degree moving chairs, audience participation, virtual reality, and other variations, each in its own pavilion. We were given a personal computer to produce commentary in English (ten other languages were available) when pointed at a screen. We participated in taste and smell tests, all electronic, and were told we were abnormal. The buildings were extraordinary in design and presentation. As the park was almost empty, we could go from place to place without waiting in lines. Perhaps the cold, the wind, the freezing wind, and the threat of snow were factors.

The snow finally stopped when we got to Tours. Continuing our policy of staying at the Frenchest of hotels, we checked in at the Holiday Inn, next to the train station.

Spain and France

Ryan (11): *Mum and I went to see the new "Star Wars" movie in French. I sort of followed the plot by looking at the action, but talking to Mum, you would have thought we saw different movies. The next day we had to get laundry done and I got a haircut from a French lady in a very shiny hairdressing salon. I was the only customer and it felt very strange as everything around was for women.*

Carole: *It was the Beaujolais Nouveau season, so we drank a lot of that great wine. While our laundry was being done at a local Laundromat, we explored a visit-worthy nearby church, and ate at a real dump of a place that had the best "Country Salad"—lettuce, tomatoes, potatoes, sausage, with that wonderful honey/mustard dressing.*

Tours was our base for touring the Loire Valley Chateaux. We saw Langeais, Saumer, Montrumer, Azay-le-Rideau, Villandry, Chenonceau, Chaumont, Cheverny and Chambord. All, in some way, were worth a visit, even if only to walk through the gardens, or in the grounds. If you could choose to visit only a couple, we would suggest Chenonceau for its unique setting, spanning a river, Villandry for its wonderful gardens, and Chambord for its size and myriad towers on the roof. Cheverny has a unique "game room," where the walls and ceiling are covered with antlered deer heads, and tusked pigs heads. All were marked with the hunter's name and the date of execution. It was like being inside an inside-out porcupine. The chateau was still a hunting center, and maintained a pack of over 100 hounds. We spent much more time with the dogs than in or around the chateau.

The biggest problem with the Loire chateaus is not their lovely settings in the delightful countryside. Nor is it their architecture or furnishings, which range from very nice to just okay. It is their nearness to the absolutely gigantic, wonderfully ornate, and magnificently furnished château/palaces at Fontainebleau and Versailles, near Paris.

If you can see only one cathedral in France, forget Notre Dame, go to Chartres. The stained glass windows there are probably the best in Europe, and that really means the world. Our English guide likened taking a one-hour tour to reading the first page of an encyclopedia. He has been guiding people through, and talking and writing about the Cathedral since 1958, and clearly recalled my previous visit around 1963.

Carole: *"The bloody Australian's back," I heard him mutter, after a typical Laurie question.*

In Medieval times, very few could read, so the windows told the Bible stories in pictures. Unlike most of the cathedrals and churches in Europe, including Notre Dame, where the stained glass has fallen victim to one of the many wars that have ravaged the place, Chartres glass is the original, and has been cleaned only.

Leon's Lodge, the next time-share and our Paris base, was a half-hour train ride from the center of the city, and ten minutes by car from Disneyland where the train station was. It is a very rebuilt, old chateau/country house, in the middle of a golf course. Our apartment had stone walls, three floors, and was very comfortable for the short periods we spent in it over the week. Carole had been looking forward to seeing Paris, and had planned very full days.

Paris has been described to death in books, movies and traveler's tales, so we will add little to its demise here. We saw it all, Notre Dame, Eiffel Tower, Champs Elise, Invalids, Sacre Coeur, Montmartre, Place de la Concorde, Arc de Triomphe, the Louvre, Musee D'Orsay, Picasso Museum, Sainte Chappell, Bois de Boulogne, to mention only the well known. We walked, we took the Metro, we rode a funicular, we even took a boat ride up the Seine. Mona Lisa was enigmatic, Picasso undecipherable, Sainte Chappell awe-inspiring, Eiffel's Tower huge and brown, Notre Dame minus the Hunchback, Napoleon's Tomb grandiose, the Panes exhausted. Some things do stay in the mind for various reasons:

- The crowd of Asian men in business suits, jostling to have their picture taken individually in front of the Venus de Milo statue in the Louvre.
- The saxophone player who entertained us on the Metro one day, and the man with the portable amplifier who harangued the carriage in some staccato language, then stood to attention and saluted as we left.
- The way the mosquito-net draped trees lining the Champs Elise became fairy tale pretty at night.
- The high, pure tones of the singer in Notre Dame, giving feeling and meaning to the stone walls, statues, and stained glass.
- The seediness of Montmartre and the Moulin Rouge by daylight.
- The paintings of Monet, Renoir, Gauguin, Van Gogh, Manet and Whistler in the Musee D'Orsay. Spectacularly converted from a train station, the central hall is magnificent.
- Being overwhelmed by the Louvre. For example, a huge room full of huge paintings by David, each deserving its own wall, was too overpowering to be in for long. Burnout came after about four hours, as we tried to see it all.
- Heresy! The paintings that surround the Mona Lisa and cover the other walls of the room, are more interesting than the Mona Lisa.

(**Carole:** *So one Cretin in our party says, but not the other two, who study, and appreciate, great art!*)

SPAIN AND FRANCE

Carole: *Ryan stood perfectly still and stared at the Mona Lisa for about ten minutes. I wish I would have asked what he was thinking. He said he had no idea so much time had passed.*

After visiting the museum which traces his art from the beginning, we have discovered Picasso's secret. The early Picasso was a real artist, and he actually did paint people with eyes and breasts in the right numbers and places. After becoming famous, we believe he simply tried to see what he could get away with. How else can you explain a paper table napkin with a couple of rips in it, being described as serious art? If Ryan had, in kindergarten, stuck a couple of pieces of tatty cardboard together and called it a violin, we would have said very nice, and tossed it away, not hung it in a museum and called it genius. We have to believe that Picasso set out to test the gullibility of the pretentious, and found no limit to it.

Ryan (11): *Mum took me to Disneyland while Dad read in the apartment. It seemed much smaller than Disneyland in Los Angeles, but had many of the same rides. My favorite was a new attraction "Honey I Shrunk the Kids." It was in 3D and phantom mice ran around our feet. Mum thought they were real and she was really afraid when she saw the snake on the screen. Her feet went right up on the seat. It was gross when the dog sneezed on us at the end. On the way out there were free video games. The best part of the day was when the Pirates of the Caribbean ride broke down and we were stranded inside for over an hour.*

The only part of the golf course that we used was the driving range. Ryan took his father's detailed instructions for a short while, then declared his own technique to be better. He actually started to hit a golf ball at age three, just like Tiger Woods. If we had pursued it, perhaps Panther Pane would have been ready to take over from Tiger in a few years time. Oh well, money and fame aren't everything.

Fontainebleau was on the way into Paris, and Versailles on the way out, so we dropped in to visit both. Fontainebleau is dedicated to Napoleon, Versailles to Louis XIV. Both are huge, surrounded by parks and gardens, and filled with ornate statues, paintings, furniture and tapestries. Napoleon apparently liked simple things, so the bedroom he preferred (he had a choice of several) is only three times the size of an average house, with the gold plating held to a minimum. Louis had no such inhibitions. His bedroom is huge, and a ladder is needed to get up to the bed. The size was necessary, as the wakening of the King was a ritual attended by many Lords and dignitaries, who each had tasks such as putting on the King's pants, spooning the King's breakfast into him, and wiping the King's bottom after he had been on the chamber pot—one person brought it in, another took it out.

Ryan (11): *I would prefer the bringing in job, thank you.*

The grounds around Versailles are extensive, and covered with forests, lakes, statues, fountains and walks. Guns were going off in the forests while we were there—hunting season for something, we guess. In keeping with our reputation, a wind-storm hit France after we left, and most of the thousands of trees we saw in Versailles were blown down, and the stained glass in St. Chapelle damaged.

Back down the Loire Valley we drove, seeing again, in passing, all the lovely chateaus we saw on the way to Paris. From Angers to Bordeaux was some delightful countryside, with hills, towns, forests, churches, fields, and farmhouses scattered around in very pleasing ways. The local landscape designer did very well here. A feature was the man with gun and dog, who we saw everywhere, walking in the fields and along the road.

We didn't drink the wine, so Bordeaux was memorable only for the huge fountain, surrounded by rearing animals, half rampant horse (the front), half fish. Not a terribly practical mix on land or water, but perfect as part of a fountain. Carole has always wanted to parade along the shore at fashionable Biarritz, so we went. Keep them happy and well fed, and they won't turn on you, is always a good policy.

Being winter, Biarritz was deserted, so deserted that we had a problem finding a place for lunch. Finally discovering a sandwich shop, we ate on a rocky headland, with beach on one side and fishing harbor on the other, entertained by surfers. It is a very pretty place with some huge hotels. Should you go there in the summer season, do not drive. The streets are narrow, winding, and "you can't get there from here" was perfected in Biarritz.

If all else fails, when in southern France "keep your back to the Atlantic, Pyrenees on the right," will get you pointed towards the Mediterranean. By using that technique, and the lesser known, but effective, "it's too late to turn now," we got out of Biarritz, and headed east. Tarbes had no hotels that we could find—a city of at least 100,000 people, and no hotels—so we drove the extra miles to Lourdes. A pilgrimage center has to have hotels, doesn't it? Apparently Lourdes water works miracles only in the summer, and all of the hotels were closed, except for one. So were the restaurants, and we celebrated our last night in France by eating once again at that quaint Scottish restaurant, McDonalds.

Entering Barcelona from the north, in peak hour (several hours) traffic, should not be attempted at the end of a long day's drive. By using modifications of the Biarritz techniques, and adding the universal "go with the flow," we found the Marina and "Dolphin Spirit," with only minor damage to family harmony.

The abscessed tooth I developed in France blew up again. The Marina directed me to a very pretty, English-speaking dentist, who fixed me up. Bruce Edwards, our long-time Los Angeles dentist and friend, was consulted by phone and E-mail during the process. I wasn't going to let even a pretty face dig holes in me without a second opinion, but did alienate Bruce a little by describing the new dentist as "younger, prettier, cheaper, and using better perfume." Bruce had the last laugh, as it turned out she performed the root-canal work on the wrong tooth.

The Port Vell Marina provided free cable TV—CNN, Sky News, BBC World, CNBC, and Eurosport in English, one French, one German, and many Spanish channels. We were therefore able to keep up with the news in the U.S. and around the world, and it wasn't a pretty picture. Ignorance was much to be preferred. No TV or newspapers over the past years spared us Monica Lewinsky, politics, wars, natural disasters, Monica, politics, and Monica. The downside was that we didn't understand most of the current jokes.

With other boats ("Miss Texas," "Horizons," "Gigolo") we drove north to see the Guggenheim Museum in Bilbao, braving the threat of Basque violence. Clad in titanium, and looking, as someone said, "like the end result of a train colliding with an ocean liner," the Guggenheim is a memorable building, with inside architecture matching the exterior. The permanent exhibitions are devoted to modern art, not appreciated by me, as I fail to see merit in huge pieces of canvas painted entirely in black or yellow.

Carole: *He really is a Philistine, you know!*

Carole, the author of the above, lives by the following credos:
   Everything in a museum is worthy of note.
   Each item in an art gallery needs ten minutes of individual attention.
   Lawyers are the salt of the earth.
   Politicians are honest.
   Policemen are always right.
   Food is calorie free if someone else ordered it.
She should know by now that you don't mess with the writer!

Back to the Guggenheim. The exhibition of motorcycles was, by itself, worth the trip. Tracing their development over the years, there were about 100 examples which we walked around, over and under. Arguably art, the display certainly was interesting.

Carole: *A large showing of Andy Warhol material seemed to be following* us around. *The exhibition had been in Florence when we were there, and we had gone to see it then as well. Strange to be in Europe looking at an American icon's work.*

We drove along the Atlantic coast to the tiny town of Santillana del Mar, where we stayed the night at a Parador. Paradors are hotels made from converted castles, manors and convents. Not cheap, but in what modern hotel can you step out of your room into a huge open area, decorated with old paintings, armor, trophies and tapestries, which may not be authentic but which certainly seemed to be.

The little town was virtually car free, and a delightful stroll. Inside the tiny church an organ was playing and the atmosphere was suitably ecclesiastical, but signs everywhere warned against taking photos or videos. The only other downside was, for the first time in Spain, we felt unwanted by the locals. Perhaps they were too involved in milking the cows and shoveling manure (it was that time of day), as this was a "real" town, not one tarted up for the tourists.

The faithful reader will have noted that, over the years, we have visited a tremendous number of castles, ruins, cathedrals and churches. To properly understand what we saw, we had to become familiar with a large number of technical terms. As a bonus therefore, we will pass on the ones we found most useful—castley-thing, ruiney-thing, churchey-thing, and perhaps the most effective, castley-ruiney-thing. Try hard, and you too can become expert like us.

We hopped on the train and went for a day trip, some 50 miles to the wonderful Benedictine Monesir de Montserrat, one of Catalana's most important shrines, perched half way up Montserrat, a mountain made up of weird rock pillars. Even stranger, the rocks are limestone, pebbles and sand, once well below the ocean.

The cable car from the train station to the monastery wasn't operating, so we took the bus up the very winding road. As always it was a thrill being with Carole on such journeys, but it was worth it, as even Carole agreed when she could be persuaded to open her eyes again. Pilgrims still come from all over the world to venerate the Black Virgin, a 12th-century wooden statue of Mary and Jesus. We lined up for a look, then stood in the back of the basilica to hear the justly famous Montserrat Boy's Choir.

The Museu de Montserrat was a jewel. The paintings by El Greco, Monet, Degas and Picasso were outstanding (far superior to those in Grenoble for example). Where else can you look at such paintings and an Egyptian mummy without leaving the building? We could have spent the whole day there, way past our usual four-hour museum burnout.

The Funicular de Saint Joan took us further up the mountain, and we then wandered along one of the many paths that wind to the top. The rock pillars that have been named, "pregnant woman," "mummy," "elephant" and "death's head," perhaps give some idea of the diversity in weather-worn shapes.

Needing another break from the hectic life in Barcelona, we went by train with Gary and Dorothy ("Gigolo") to Madrid, and then on to Toledo. We found Madrid to be just another big city with an impressive Bull Ring and a great steak restaurant where "Bull's Balls" were served on the day a bull lost. We weren't prepared to learn what was served if the Matador lost.

Toledo we fell in love with. Set in a valley inside a semicircle of the Rio Tajo, it is Arab-inspired churches, bell towers and arches, twisting cobblestone lanes and alleys, extraordinarily decorated patios, a great Gothic cathedral, with the Alcazar looming over it all. We followed the El Greco trail—well actually we cheated and went straight to the Iglesia de Santo Tome to see his masterpiece "The Burial of the Count of Orgaz." I think El Greco is great, but he has a strange sense of proportion.

What really indelibly stamped Toledo in our memory was where we stayed. Parador Nacional Conde de Orgaz sat on top of a cliff across the river from, and well above Toledo. All rooms had balconies overlooking the city. Watching the sunset provide a subtly shifting, gorgeous light across the city was simply breath-taking. The sunrise was almost as grand.

Being in the heart of Toledo blade country, we went shopping for swords and daggers, for Ryan of course. We did buy a sword, but the fun was in wielding all the different blades and imagining the history behind each shape. Toledo is also famous for its black and gold plate jewelry. We visited the factory and bought.

That's what was so great about Barcelona. The city itself was fascinating and visiting the surrounding country was a full-time occupation.

Chasing Sunsets

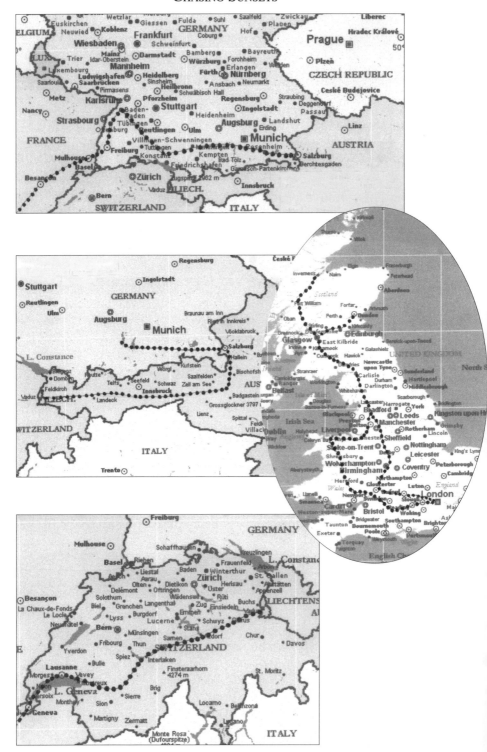

Great Britain, Austria, Germany and Switzerland

**Year Four and Five
October 29 to June 13**

Yet, we were still real cruisers. To prove it, our October to June schedule went something like:

>Dolphin Spirit—2 weeks
>France—3 weeks
>Dolphin Spirit—7 weeks
>Madrid and Toledo—5 days
>Dolphin Spirit—3 days
>Los Angeles—3 weeks
>Dolphin Spirit—1 week
>England, Scotland, Wales—2 weeks
>Dolphin Spirit—1 week
>Germany, Austria, Switzerland—3 weeks
>Dolphin Spirit—3 weeks

The New Millennium
We celebrated entry into the new millennium in Barcelona. To ensure good luck, tradition requires that you eat 12 grapes, one at a time, while the clock is chiming midnight. Together with Gary and Dorothy we devoured the grapes (all of us got it right) and then watched the fireworks amid the seething crowd in Cataluna Square. That we should start every new century in Barcelona was the unanimous decision.

Back at "Dolphin Spirit" we switched on our computers with some trepidation, and were re-assured by the familiar green glow, and the correct date and time. Guess Y2K gremlins didn't make it to Barcelona. On the morning of January 1, all the cruisers in the Marina met on the beach to enjoy coffee and rolls and watch the first sunrise of the new century. It felt different, even if it was just the regular event.

Travels with an EPIRB

Carole: Having the EPIRB (Electronic Position Indicating Rescue Beacon, I think) on board was not only a real safety feature, but it made me feel secure. I knew that if we got into real trouble, either by flicking a switch or letting the unit get wet, we would broadcast our exact position to the world, rescue would begin, and all we would have to do is hang on until they arrived.

About two years before we set out, our old-style EPIRB battery died, so I bought a new Alden 406 EPIRB. The old EPIRB had to be inverted to be activated, so I pulled the battery apart from the top and stored the lot carefully upright in a locker. About 18 months passed. Carole and I were peacefully asleep in "Dolphin Spirit" at its Marina del Rey slip, when we were rudely awakened by the thump of boots on the deck and blinding lights all around. Scrambling into clothes, on deck I found a detachment of heavily armed Coast Guard officers, a helicopter overhead and a cutter just off our stern.

Apparently the old EPIRB had fallen from its secure place and the long-dead battery found just enough power to broadcast and be picked up by a commercial flight passing overhead. The offending instrument never emitted another peep, even when pushed and prodded by the officers.

We were reminded of this occurrence when the 406 EPIRB needed a new battery, so we called Alden, in the U.S., to find out where to get one. Alden no longer provided service, but advised that the battery had to be changed by professionals, and in the U.S.! As the main use for an EPIRB is on ocean passages, Alden obviously expects users to make round trips. Luckily, we had Philip's wedding to attend, so the EPIRB traveled to L.A. with its antenna jauntily sticking out of Carole's back-pack. Alden advised that it was okay to carry on board, and we passed through security in Barcelona and London without a question.

When asked for a service center in Los Angeles, Alden advised there was only one, so we tracked it down with some difficulty. Then we found there were several service outlets in Marina del Rey, about a mile away. Obviously, you have to ask the right question, remembering that "Los Angeles" comprises over 90 cities, only one of which is Los Angeles.

Batteries renewed, and ensconced in my carry-on, the EPIRB created real consternation with the L.A. airport security (long before 9/11). It was yellow and had batteries, and no one could understand its use. Eventually security referred us to British Airlines, who, in turn, referred us to the captain of our plane. An airline official had to carry the offending device to the departure gate. The captain was very nice (he knew what an EPIRB was), but kept it, so the EPIRB traveled to London on its own seat in the cockpit. A pleasant result was an invitation to the cockpit during the flight, where we were rewarded with the sight of two planes passing under us, just skimming the tops of the clouds, leaving a wake behind.

Carole: The flight attendant wouldn't believe Laurie when he said we had an invitation to the cockpit. "No one gets invited to the cockpit, not even me," she sniffed, implying, but not saying, "Especially you low-lives in Economy Class." Laurie was insistent so she went away, to return somewhat chastened and escort us up.

In London we took possession again, and moved to transit security. Again consternation, even though they had taken no notice on the outward journey. This time the supervisor, when called, took one look and said "EPIRB, no problems," and we were through.

As a side show, the L.A. security saw a couple of bottles of benign cleaner in my bag when they were looking at the EPIRB. Although clearly marked as non-harmful, they also were marked with the skull-and-crossbones warning that, if many gallons were swallowed, a doctor should be called. That was enough for security, and they were confiscated. In London, another bottle, passed by L.A., was confiscated by the security there. In both places, we asked if the bottles could be given to a person not traveling, and were told no! All confiscated items are destroyed. Would that have happened to the EPIRB, too?

Los Angeles
Philip married Lilia. The groom was handsome and nervous, the bride lovely and serene. Lilia's parents did a wonderful job of organizing, and we did nothing but enjoy the ride. Ryan and I wore real clothes (tuxedos) for the first time in years. Jenny and Brad traveled up from Brisbane to check out what to do for their August wedding.

We didn't see Ryan for the whole time we were in L.A. First he was with his Grandparents, then with Philip and Lilia. Jenny dressed him for the wedding, and did a great job of creating a young (not small) sophisticate. For the record, he was then almost 5'9." We kept missing him in crowds, because we looked too low.

Hire Cars
It was not possible to hire a car in continental Europe that could then be driven in England. Apparently the insurance companies think that the

change in side-of-road is too much for people to handle. We rang the Budget Car Rental U.S. number and hired cars, for Barcelona and London pickup, for about half of the price we could negotiate locally with the same company.

Manual transmission was the order of the day. Automatics were significantly more expensive, if they were available. We were upgraded to a diesel engine for the Europe trip, and saved a lot of money, as diesel was a much cheaper fuel than petrol, and available at all service stations.

Maps and Roads

Where practical, we take "the road less traveled," particularly if it is marked in green on the map. These green roads are supposed to indicate "picturesque" scenery, and seldom have we been disappointed. Most are secondary, or tertiary, and although sealed, are narrow and less well signposted. The advantage was that we could stop anywhere and take photos or gawk, without worrying about other vehicles. The disadvantage was that getting lost became an occupational hazard.

Driver—Navigator Relationships

Marriage, a strong marriage, is a requirement. Casual relationships, even long standing ones, will not stand the strain.

England, Scotland, Wales

After checking planes, trains and automobiles, we flew to Heathrow and picked up the car we rented through a U.S. telephone number. Ryan wanted us to take the Lotus Elan sports car, while he rode the Harley Davidson (both for rent at Heathrow Budget) but had to settle for the staid sedan we eventually got. The U.S. booking was in the computer, but at a higher price than quoted over the phone when I made the reservation. The staff accepted our numbers readily, but the computer rejected them. Unable therefore to print a contract, they finally resorted to hand-writing one, and dealing with the computer later. When we returned the car, the computer was still upset, and once again refused to have anything to do with us. Back to pen and paper.

While living in Connecticut, in another life, Carole made friends with an English couple. They lived in Bolton, so we spent a couple of days with them on our way to Scotland. Rosalie was a great cook, who regaled us with proper tea and English scones on our arrival. Martin, her History Professor husband, provided us with a signed copy of his book on Napoleon. Their backyard garden was very English and pretty, with the only disappointment being the absence of the promised frog in the pond.

Wintering in Antalya, we had met a couple from Scotland, who were on the same dock as us, and they had invited us to stay in their manor complete with beehives, near Inverness. Mike and Celia ("Freya") were very gracious when we showed up, perhaps because we brought great weather.

Their house was a gorgeous, grey-stone two-storey, set in the woods above a golf course. Ryan spent many happy, muddy hours riding a bike through the trees. Mike and I played a "game" of golf, and we took a lovely walk around a nearby loch. Once again we were treated to superb meals, including Carole's first try at black pudding. It was her last, almost literally, when the contents were explained to her.

Carole: *Blood and guts are a great description for a battle, not for the sausage sitting on my plate.*

Ryan was most disappointed that we traveled the length of Loch Ness, with no monster in sight. His disillusionment increased when we spent the night at Duck Bay Hotel, on the shore of Loch Lomond, and there were only swans in the bay.

Ryan (12): (from his trip report) *Driving directly up to Loch Ness we saw fertile pasture lands and beautiful scenery. In almost constant rain, with only a few patches of sunshine, we made our way past the dark waters of the lochs. Loch Ness is up to 754-feet deep. The tale of the Loch Ness Monster began in the eighth century when a monk spotted it from the window of the monastery. Since then many sightings have been reported. It is said to be nocturnal and one theory says there is a tunnel which leads to a cave under the surrounding mountains, where Nessie spends the days.*

One serious expedition used submarines, helicopters and very sophisticated sonar equipment to try to track down the legendary beast. They got a picture of a great mass and a fin. Today it is still a mystery. Not seeing it, I lost hope that it might exist, but that doesn't mean it doesn't.

The Lake District was suitably misty and romantic, as befits the region beloved by English poets. Our hotel, on the shores of Lake Windermere, fitted right into the atmosphere. The "Lucky Ducks" cafe sold duck food, right beside a sign that forbad feeding the ducks. At least there were ducks!

Carole: *"Lucky Ducks" is the name of my brother's powerboat, so naturally we had to go to the cafe. He has named his dinghy "Rubber Ducky" and his electric run-about "Duffy Duck." Over sunset cocktails one day, Laurie and I named his kayak "Cold Duck" and his sailing dinghy "Donald Duck."*

Chasing Sunsets

A capricious decision to see Wales saw us make a sudden right turn, and drive along that country's north coast. It was easy to spot the border, as road signs became bilingual (English and Gaelic). From the north-west corner, we cut diagonally through the rugged, snow-covered mountains of Snowdonia. A fish and chips lunch, perched on a cliff overlooking a lot of the region, with many newborn lambs all marked with red and green paint, provided a memorable break from driving.

Mike (an English lawyer) and his wife Linda, had become friends when they spent a few years in L.A. during one of my previous lives. We stayed in Mike's flat in Cheltenham, allowing Ryan to resume his friendship with their son Greg as if they had not been apart for almost six years (half their lives). From this base we explored the lovely Cotswold's, especially the villages of Burton-on-the-Water and Upper and Lower Slaughter, Stonehenge, and Carole's ancestral home of Wells. Burton has, at the back of an inn, a miniature of the village, wherein the miniature of the inn has a miniature of the miniature minature. The Slaughters were marvelously pretty.

I had wandered in amongst the Stonehenge stones during my 1963 visit, but now everyone must stay on a fenced perimeter road, and listen to a recorded commentary—excellent, and free with the entry fee. This is still one of the world's awe-inspiring sights, particularly on a cloudy, rainy day.

We searched the city of Wells for evidence of Carole's background. The Wells family cathedral was worth a visit, even if you weren't a relative. A clock inside the Cathedral started figures moving high on the walls to mark the hours. Cornish pasties and meat pies (Carole and Ryan thought they knew the contents.) for lunch were enjoyed overlooking the countryside, a nicely romantic picnic.

Great Britain is at its best in spring. Flowers, mostly daffodils, and lambs were everywhere. To overcome the traffic hazard we often became through stopping the car and leaping out to try to touch every lamb, we went to a farm set up for the tourist. There we saw lambs being born, rubbed a calf's nose and cuddled everything that moved. Carole soon switched her devotion from lambs to calves, as they have nicer noses.

England and Wales are criss-crossed by canals. We stopped several times to inspect the very colorful "Narrow Boats" which are only six feet wide, but can be up to 60-feet in length. We had long planned that our next adventure would be an extended cruise on the English canals, but had no idea of the variety of boats available.

Returning the car to Heathrow, we tubed to London, staying at the Washington Mayfair Hotel, right across Green Park from Buck House, as we, the in-crowd, call Buckingham Palace. A visit to the musical "Les Miserables" was Ryan's first, Carole's and my fourth. We did all the tourist things, Westminster Abbey, Big Ben, Number 10 Downing Street, Horse

Guards, Trafalgar Square, Madame Taussard's Wax Works (lines were so long we didn't go in), Thames boat ride, Natural History Museum (not to be missed), and Piccadilly Circus

If you can get past the hotels with half-star accommodations and six-star prices, London is a wonderful city to visit. When I lived there in the early 60s, one cold, sleety, winter's day I curled up with a guide book and heater and calculated that I could visit one attraction every morning, and another every afternoon, and not repeat myself for six months.

Germany, Austria, Switzerland
Trip Notes:
We used the Guides:
Austria Lonely Planet
Switzerland Michelin Green Guide. For traveling quickly through a country, this was better than Lonely Planet.
Germany, Austria, Switzerland by Rick Steves. A real find. Gives a three-week trip through the countries, with all the down and dirty information a traveler needs. We followed the book almost religiously, and there seemed to be at least two or three others, in every hotel, that were doing the same. He does other European countries similarly.

Black Forest—Freiburg to Baden-Baden via Hinterzarten, Furtwangen, Triberg, Hornberg, Gutach, Hausach, Schiltach and Freudenstadt. Picture-book pretty, and well worth the day of meandering, stop-start driving we gave it. Yellow flowers covered most fields, and lined the roads. Each corner seemed to open up another must-stop-and-appreciate vista.

We got lost trying to find our hotel in Freiberg on our first day in Germany. The petrol station attendant was no help—imagine, a German who didn't speak English—but we were rescued by the car in line behind us, who not only knew where it was, but led us there. As a bonus, she directed us to the local beer hall, a huge open-air establishment near the University. There we sipped beer and coke, ate delicious blueberry cobbler and watched the never-ending parade of bicyclists.

The Clock Museum in Furtwangen was a surprise treat. In the middle of cuckoo-clock land, it provided an impressive history of clocks, with hundreds of working examples of all sizes and shapes. Only one clock had the right time, others were set to chime, cuckoo, ring, peal, at regular intervals, so they could all be enjoyed.

Carole: *There really are wild cuckoos that sounded just like the clocks. I heard them. Who knew?*

Baden-Baden. A great town to be in, even if we didn't visit one of the famous bath houses. The Roman-Irish Bath had been in operation for 120 years, was clothes-free, mixed sex, and required at least two hours to complete the entire ritual. Much to Ryan's disappointment, the minimum age was 14. "Graceful nudity" was a descriptive term used for the establishment, so Carole and I decided not to test their tolerance. The Caracalla Therme was newer, allowed swim suits, and featured "water spanking."

Spurning such sybaritic pleasures, we chose to play miniature golf on grass, an excellent innovation even in the rain which drove me to shelter, and Ryan and Carole to sodden pars and birdies. Purple wisteria draped a lot of the buildings, adding to the charm. The church steeple, just outside our hotel windows, boomed out the quarter hours, but thankfully stopped at 10pm.

Carole: Every hotel we stayed at was really clean. I loved the white lace curtains and the white blankets wrapped in white sheets that seemed to be on every bed in Germany, and the wonderfully soft, white duvets that were used in Switzerland and Austria. We are converts. At long last, hotels where we knew the blankets were as clean as the sheets. All that white—I felt sanitized.

Luxembourg. We were collecting countries, and so spent a few minutes looking out over the gorge that split the city, and the bridge spanning it. As the parking lot was full, and in any case required Luxembourg money to operate the ticket machines, we kept the car circulating, while taking turns to get out and look.

Castles on the Rhine. Our hotel room in the old town of Bacharach (the correct, guttural pronunciation of which was totally beyond our powers) had modern fittings, but was in a building at least 500-years old. Next door was the 700-year old restaurant where we ate after a day of cruising on a boat up and down the Rhine.

Ryan (12): Dad said I needed to get an appreciation of what was happening in the world when the restaurant was built, 200 years before Columbus sailed. I did a computer search and found that, in 1300:
- *the Crusades were in full swing*
- *Marco Polo wrote his* Travels
- *Tarot cards appeared in Europe*
- *The Mongolians invented lemonade*
- *The Ottoman Empire was founded*
- *The martyrdom of St. James the Mangled was first celebrated*

Great Britain, Austria, Germany, and Switzerland

- *The first Ordnance Officer was appointed in the British Military, to look after battering rams and catapults.*

The Rhine was not a river for the faint-of-heart sailor. Two-way barge traffic was constant, the smallest we saw being some 80-feet long. Often two were rafted together, head-to-tail. The current on the straight, wide stretches was strong enough to give the channel buoys bow waves, and on one bend required the use of tugs to get the noses of the barges around. "Dolphin Spirit" can stay in salt water.

The Romantic Road. Wurzburg, Bad Mergentheim, Rothenburg, Dinkelsbuhl, Augsburg, Fussen. "Bad" means "Spa," and in no way indicates the moral or odor status of the town, much to Ryan's disgust. Rothenburg is Germany's best preserved medieval city, and was touristy to the max. We walked along the top of the city wall and found steps leading up a tower. Eight panting flights later we reached the top, and were asked for money before we were allowed to look at the view. The amount was exorbitant, but just not exorbitant enough to drive us down without looking—clever. The Road countryside was pretty, and became even more so near Fussen.

Neuschwanstein Castle. This is the original Fantasyland castle, built by "Mad" King Ludwig. The outside has been deservedly celebrated, and we enjoyed it from the high Mary's Bridge, spanning a gorge that framed the castle, with green fields below it, and snow-covered mountains beyond. Only 16 of the 67 rooms were finished before Ludwig mysteriously died, to the monetary relief of his kingdom. One room (3rd floor) was made into an artificial cave. Ludwig's bedroom had a secret door to a room containing the toilet, but the room was so small that he couldn't sit with the door closed. The carved wood decorations were excellent; the paintings, mostly of scenes from famous operas and of swans, third rate; the tour of the interior rushed and expensive.

Salzburg. In a fit of madness—no other explanation comes close—I booked us on a half-day "Sound of Music" tour. It took us to wondrous things; the gazebo built for a scene in the film, then moved to be closer to the bus route; a drive past a wall that was around a house (invisible) where other scenes had been filmed; the end of a street which contained the house (invisible) that the real Maria bought in later life, and other similar exotica.

No Austrian will admit to having seen the film, as it is an almost total fabrication—the real-life Trapps tried to have it stopped—so there is only one souvenir store selling SOM stuff, and, you guessed right, we went there. The church, where the wedding scene was filmed, we actually went to. Thank God no one in the bus (all Americans) sang along with the soundtrack music we were regaled with for most of the tour. The only highlight was an off-track stop at a snowless luge, which Ryan and I rode. We managed to avoid going off the track on the corners, but others weren't so skilled.

By way of spreading the pain, here is some information that should, we hope, spoil any future viewings of the film:

> The mountain top where Maria sings "The Hills are Alive," then hears the convent bells and runs back, is more than 20 miles from the convent.
>
> The mountain the Trapp family climbs to freedom from the Germans, actually leads into Germany.
>
> The wedding scene was started in Salzburg Cathedral, but the authorities stopped the filming there because they objected to Nazi flags hung outside.
>
> The real Trapps "escaped" the Germans by the clever ruse of going to the station, buying tickets, and getting on a train, in broad daylight.

Reeling from SOM surfeit, we reverted to our normal "self tour" mode, and found Salzburg. The water in the Salzach River was so cold we felt the change in air temperature as we walked over the bridge to the Old City. Carole was hard to drag away from the shop that sold only painted egg shells. The statue of Mozart, in Mozart Platz, was feminine-looking and green; the fountain in Residenz Platz very Italian; the Cathedral okay as far as cathedrals go; the cemetery at St. Peter's unique with its flower-plot graves and in the fact that no entrance fee was charged; the streets suitably narrow, cobbled and quaint.

We stayed at Pension Bergland, in a huge room. Internet access was offered, and the owner was ex-merchant marine, who had a boat on one of the lakes, built model ships, and was interesting to talk to (if you are into boating!). Within easy walking distance of everything, the place was good value.

Ryan (12): *Waking up, after I banged my head on the window over my head, wasn't easy. Breakfast was cereal, bread and hot chocolate. The* Sound of Music *bus had a horrible sound system and they didn't give us time to eat.*

On the way to Vienna, farmers stood along the side of the road with their milk jugs, waiting for the tanker truck to come. Stopping to take a picture at a place that overlooked several lakes, we saw an old wooden structure with a ramp that extended out over the water. I think it was for practicing trick ski jumps in summer.

We ran into some of the hardest rain I have ever seen and had to stop when it turned into hail. One group of waterfalls we saw was really cool because they joined together in one place, then suddenly split apart again.

Vienna (Wein). We walked over the brown Danube, took trams around the city center, did a tour of the Opera, ate schnitzel, indulged in the infamous Sacher torte (a chocoholics fantasy), visited the cathedral by day and floodlit night, and went everywhere by metro. The Treasury in the Hofburg Palace was magnificent, equal to the Topkapi Palace in Istanbul. The fiddle-playing, gold statue of Strauss was a little much, given he was color blind and couldn't tell blue (Danube?) from brown. The Rathaus was photogenic, the Lipizzaner Stables closed, and general strolling around very entertaining. We didn't waltz.

Carole: Men! We were in one of THE romantic cities, with it oozing out of every wall, wafted on every breeze and captured in every sound. Waltzing wasn't needed to absorb the atmosphere, just walking hand-in-hand down the street was enough—wait a minute, a waltz would have made it perfect.

Ryan (12): I lost my favorite "No Fear" hat here. Dad made me take it off when we toured the Opera House and I left it in one of the rooms. We went back and searched, but it was gone.

Hallstatt (south of Salzburg). We spent only an hour or so here, but are coming back to stay at least a week. It was tiny, perched on the side of a mountain, on the shore of a lake, with a waterfall right through the middle of the town, and it was jewel-like. Stumbling on these marvels is what makes our method of random traveling so great.

Liechtenstein. The capital, Vaduz, is the whole country. Without the pretensions of Luxembourg, it happily accepts everyone's money. We drove through (country 44), stopping only to buy the sticker that allowed us to drive on the Swiss freeways. I am still not sure that we didn't park in Switzerland to do this.

Grindelwald. This is why visitors flock to Switzerland. We sat on the balcony of our room, confronted by an arc of mountains, the Wetterhorn, the Eiger (north face), the Monch and the Jungfrau. The green slopes leading up to these snow-streaked behemoths were dotted with trees and huts. Cowbells rang quietly in the distance. Just watching the clouds playing with the tip of Jungfrau was enthralling.

Murren. Coffee came as the Eiger passed the window. Rolls came with the Monch, and scrambled eggs arrived with the Jungfrau. We were breakfasting in the rotating restaurant, at 10,000 feet, on top of the Schiltorn. No restaurant has a better view, and the food was good too.

Getting there was a wonderful experience in itself. We drove to Stechelberg, where several waterfalls plunge over the cliffs, and took a cable car to Murren, a small town at a mere 5,400-foot altitude. Access is by cable-car or rack-rail only, so the town was vehicle free. Hotel Alpenruh was the only one open, as the season hadn't started, but the rooms were comfortable, and the food good. Our room looked across the valley to more cliffs, and at least six waterfalls. As the sunshine hit the slopes above them, the instant melt increased their volume dramatically. Magnificent then, they must be awesome during the thaw.

Two more cable cars took us to the top of Schiltorn, and the restaurant. The morning was clear as crystal and the views were superb. Later we watched the clouds roll in, eventually surrounding us in grey mist. We went back down to the half-way station, and were below the clouds, with magnificent views again. The only ones smart enough, we had the place to ourselves.

Murren provided access to walks of every description. We wandered through forests, over streams and small waterfalls, beside and through fields of flowers, mostly by ourselves, and always with the snow-covered Alps looming over and around us.

The Return. We wanted to spend a day or so in Zermatt, to see the Matterhorn, but the passes were still closed so we headed for Geneva. Travel fatigue, or mountain-withdrawal symptoms, struck. We couldn't find a hotel that we could afford without selling Ryan, so we kept driving around the north shore of the lake, and eventually found a very pretty place that could be financed by body-parts sales. That was enough. We decided to head for Barcelona the next day, stopping in Geneva only long enough to photograph the water jet in the lake.

Spain, Gibraltar and Portugal
Year Five
June 13 to December 16

There is no truth in the rumor that you can't sail in the Mediterranean—you can, but you just can't get to where you want to go. Another rumor has it that there are two types of powerboats in the Med, those with sails, and those without.

Both segue into the mistaken attitude among most non-cruisers, and some cruisers as well, that cruising is about sailing. Certainly sailing is a required, perhaps essential, part of it, but only a part. Cruising is about being in a place long enough to get to know how the locals live, and meet and become friends with them. Cruising is about saying, "I wonder what ....looks like?" and going there. Cruising is poking around in places most tourists don't go to. Cruising is about going to places inundated with tourists and enjoying them because they can be savored in small bites instead of having to be gulped. The average long-term cruiser is attached to land in some way for 90% of the time, sailing only for 10%.

What also brought all this to mind was our stay in Barcelona for seven months. "Dolphin Spirit's" propeller was a huge ball of marine growth until Ryan and I cleaned it. Some of the large mullet-like fish that swam around the boat were on a first name basis, and began bringing their children (born since we arrived) over to be introduced. The local shop-keepers started putting our order together as soon as we walked through the door.

For those who need to know, the boat projects that had to be completed in the three weeks before sailing totaled 75, and included replacing the hot-water heater, varnishing, gel-coat waxing, installing a new fuel filter, rebuilding a toilet, changing all interior lights to halogen bulbs, greasing the winches, changing the hull and engine zincs, and so it goes.

Why leave so much to the last minute did I hear someone ask? Because we were so busy traveling, reading, eating, enjoying Barcelona, and undertaking other similar pursuits, minor matters like boat maintenance and repair were put off to the future. Actually, I did protest, but was overruled by the Commissar Arranging Recreation Or Leisure Engagements (CAROLE).

Carole: *The real truth is that Lazy And Useless Retired Ineffective Escapee (LAURIE) preferred to read, even though Capable And Reliable Overworked Lively Energizer (CAROLE) constantly reminded him.*

We had watched the leaves on the trees that lined La Rambla wither and fall, and then return in brilliant green. Ryan had his portrait drawn in charcoal by a local artist. We had walked every street, eaten the Menu del Dia at every restaurant, seen every sight and found many more unrecognized by the tourist guides. Carole and I sat less than 20 feet from Jose Carreras during his 30th Anniversary home-coming concert in the Palau de la Musica Catalana. There was nothing left but to leave.

Of perhaps more significance, this marked the last time we were given bread, a whole tomato and several whole cloves of garlic to start a meal. Slice the bread, slice the tomato, slice or crush the garlic (I slice, Carole crushes, she is wrong) and put the result together in proportions to suit taste. There is no better way to begin a meal.

Carole and the chicken lady had an emotional parting, we folded up the bicycles into their storage bags, decided that some of the remaining jobs could be finished en route, and the rest really didn't need doing, provisioned, stored and tore ourselves away from the dock. "Dolphin Spirit" was moving again for the first time in seven months, which meant that the Captain and crew had to remember how to run the boat.

Carole: *I had no problem remembering my always asked before-sailing question, "Are you sure it is the right thing to leave today?" and added another, "Please, can't we stay longer?"*

Our departure from Barcelona had its little grab-your-attention moments. The entrance to the harbor, and the coast for about 10 miles south, were an almost solid mass of debris, planks, trees, and whatever else the recent heavy rains had flushed out. We had to find, and then weave through open channels in the mess, as plowing through was not an option for anything but an ice-breaker.

That extended what was to be a short first-day warm-up to Tarragona into a full-day marathon. The entrance to the harbor was well camouflaged, and complicated by the fact that the Cruising Guide photo of the place was printed backwards. Tarragona was a new, virtually empty marina, so we side-tied—we never Med-moor if we don't have to. As is common in Spain, the marina was surrounded by restaurants and bars. This one had a bar featuring Country & Western dancing, so Carole had to go, and was soon amazing the locals.

Carole: In Spain, a Country and Western bar and line dancing! I was doing the exact steps to the same tunes as in California. Laurie did the two-step with me a couple of times, then spent most of the evening watching the show. I taught one of the standard dances and had a hoe-down time.

The obligatory cathedral, to which we paid the obligatory visit, suprised us with tapestries covering all the walls. Houses had been built using the Roman walls as foundations, but an attempt had been made to preserve the Roman Amphitheatre. We gave Ryan a treat (he has been so good following us through all the churches and ruins) and took the train to the nearby Port Aventura theme park, which featured the longest, fastest, twistiest roller-coaster in Europe. Ryan and I braved the hour-and-a-half long queue for it, while Carole sat in comfort and watched a Chinese circus.

On the way to Valencia, we crossed the Prime Meridian for the first time; both G.P.S.s lost satellites for several hours; the stern anchor winch motor burnt out; one of the bilge pumps destroyed a valve; and that was how I celebrated Father's Day.

The Valencia marina was a long way from the city, but the local Club Nautico did allow visitors to use their facilities and pool. This was very welcome, as most European Yacht Clubs won't allow non-members, even members of other Clubs, to darken their doors. Some relented, if we could prove we were a member of a "prestigious" club, definition variable. Valencia cathedral (number 138 this trip) featured a wall of paintings as the main altar. Mass was being sung very melodically as we visited.

At Gandia, the closest port on mainland Spain to Ibiza, we bicycled to the town, some two miles away, for a look at the local church and palace. The church was ugly outside, but "nice" inside, and the palace could be seen only by guided tour at 11am and 6pm, all three rooms of it! We decided not to wait. The marina water was undrinkable, so we bicycled to town two more times for bottled water—cheap if you don't value time and energy expended to get it.

Carole: We needed the exercise. Ryan and I went walking one evening and were amazed to see it was still light at 10pm. We had never experienced the combined effects of daylight saving and long twilights.

A comfortable, overnight motor saw us hanging about outside the San Antonio, Ibiza, harbor waiting for sunrise.

Carole: *I was on watch and saw the light of a ship directly in front of us. Nothing showed on the radar, but I changed direction anyway. It was still directly in front, so I made an even more radical move. Still the boat was there, right in front of us. In a panic, I woke Laurie, who stuck his head up through the companionway, grunted, "It's the moon rising," and went back to bed. Totally embarrassed, I do have to point out this was the first time on our trip we were heading east. The moon always rose over our stern.*

We chose to anchor inside the huge breakwater, just off the marina. The water was clear enough for Ryan to swim, but too cold for the oldies. High-rises surrounded the harbor, and the foreshore was solid restaurants, souvenir shops and English tourists. The short fuel dock had rocks at one end and a ferry wharf at the other, so when we had filled we found it impossible to leave, with the wind holding us in.

In my defense, the wind wasn't blowing when we tied up, and the 15 or so knots that sprang up held us tightly to the dock. After some fruitless moves, I asked a local fishing boat, waiting to get in for fuel, if he would tow us off. He agreed, then obviously decided that major speed would be needed, so took off. The line held, and his stern almost went under water before our inertia was overcome and we started to move.

Carole: *This was one of the few places where Laurie didn't use our Baja filter to clean the gunk and water out of the fuel. He certainly was to pay for that later, both in effort and from my told-you-sos.*

Guarded by a rock that looked amazingly like a statue of Queen Victoria, Cala Binarris, Ibiza, was a delightful anchorage, perhaps because there was no tourist development. We had room to pull Ryan around on his surfboard behind the dinghy. He mastered standing up last year, and we were wondering how the new, longer and larger Ryan would go—no problem. Fishing gave us only two tiny, but colorful and spiny suicides.

We had reserved space in a marina at Palma, Mallorca, as we were planning on a two week stay. Med-mooring, with 20 knots of wind up the stern, I managed to hit the solid concrete dock and take a chip out of the bow.

Ryan was booked into Scuba School and he became certified after a five-day course, which included four sea dives and one dive as part of a normal dive-boat trip. There were only two in his class, which was a real advantage. We were very proud of him.

The stern anchor-winch motor proved to be irreparable, and couldn't be removed from the gearbox, so we had to buy a complete new winch. The chandlery said that they searched all of Europe, and found only one, in France, which was available on four-week delivery. We gave up and resigned ourselves to a hole in the deck. I visited another shop that sold mainly paint, and was telling the story to a yachtie, when the shop owner intervened. To cut a long story short, the new winch arrived the next day.

Our euphoria was a little dampened by the fact that our anchor chain was to U.S. standard, which did not fit the gypsies of winches anywhere else, so we had to buy new chain too. (Different voltage, different TV standard, different mobile-phone frequencies, different paper size, different chain size—when will the U.S. join the rest of the world, or vice versa?)

The engine-driven refrigeration system was not working again, and the local expert diagnosed the problem—a faulty clutch—but had no idea how to fix it, and no parts anyhow.

Palma cathedral was huge, and loomed over the city and harbor, particularly impressive when it was flood-lit at night. Inside was illuminated by stained glass, including an exceptional geometric-patterned rose window.

There was an excellent seven-mile-long bike path, that ran almost completely around the harbor. We tried to pedal it twice a day. The doctor who tested Ryan before his scuba school said he was out of shape, and I knew I was, so we got up at 7am every day and went riding.

Ryan (12): *I couldn't believe I was out of shape. I ride my bike at every marina, swim at every anchorage, water ski and fish. Anyhow, it didn't stop me getting certified.*

We hired a car and drove around the island for a couple of days. Some of the mountain scenery on the west coast was dramatic, with cliffs, valleys, spires and crashing waves. On the east coast, the Coves del Drac (Caves of the Dragon) had imaginatively lit stalagmites and stalactites. At the conclusion of the tour, we were seated on the shore of a subterranean lake and entertained with classical music, played by musicians floating past on a mirror smooth surface, lit only by candles in the boats.

I have repeated the following story many times, and it still sounds as unreal as it was on the day it happened. Just behind us in the marina was the fuel and arrival dock. The wind was less than 10 knots, and the long dock was almost empty, but the 35-foot powerboat made three tries, utilizing its two engines and bow thruster to the full, before it finally came along side. Fender hanging from one gloved hand, boat hook in the other, the lady leapt ashore, and stood, poised. The driver climbed down from the fly-bridge, went inside and sat on a settee. Not a line was in sight.

As the boat began to blow slowly away from the dock, under the still poised lady's watchful eyes, a man from the fuel pump came to help and, straining to hold the boat in, asked for a dock line. This seemed to create a problem. The driver, having done his job of bringing in the boat, wasn't moving from the settee, and the lady had both hands full. Struggling on board, she rummaged in a locker, handed the poor Samaritan what looked like a tangled ball of large twine, and once again picked up fender and boat hook. We did notice later, that she had exchanged gloves and attachments for a glass of wine, and the driver had moved from settee to stern chair.

My daughter Jenny's wedding was looming in the near future, and this forced us to abandon Menorca without a visit. Deciding we had seen all we wanted to of Mallorca, we headed south for Ibiza again. We SAILED for a couple of hours, before the wind increased suddenly and split a mainsail seam. Not content with that, it swung round to 40 knots, right on the nose, and made the remainder of the trip unpleasant. The Med has the most unpredictable weather. Isobars, so far apart that they were not even on the same chart, produced 40 knots of wind!

The forecast for that night was thunderstorms and north-west Force 7 winds. For once *they* were right. The wind blew from the NW for two straight days at over 30 knots. Cala San Vicente was open to the SW only, but somehow, in the teeth of the wind, a southerly swell worked its way in. Thank goodness there a nude beach to distract us.

All three Ibiza marinas were full, and we needed a place where we could get the main down and repaired. Santa Eulalia marina finally allowed us in when I pleaded, begged, played the Australian card, the child on board card, and generally annoyed the hell out of them.

I took the main to Ibiza by taxi, where a sail-maker repaired it immediately, and charged $US17! The taxi driver quoted 2,500 pesetas for a one-way trip. When the sail-maker decided to do an immediate repair, I asked the driver to wait, and drive me and the sail back. The wait was about an hour, and as we were driving back, I suggested that the total fare should be 5,000 pesetas. "Too much," was the immediate reply, "3,000 is enough."

Espalmador Island, a couple of miles south-east of Ibiza, had more than 100 boats in the anchorage, so we had to anchor a long way off shore. The wind was still nasty, and the 120-foot powerboat next to us dragged. I was screaming and yelling at the people on board (from the deck and over the VHF), but they ignored me. Eventually, the professional captain appeared on deck, took notice of me, and answered my VHF call. Immediately the boat turned into an ant-heap, with people running in all directions.

After re-anchoring, the captain came over and thanked us, followed later by the owner, who gave us a bottle of wine.

The anchorage cleared out the next morning, which gave us space to move to within 100 yards of the beach. The ferry bringing sun worshipers from Ibiza simply plowed its bow into the beach, let down a ramp and off-loaded. Getting off was a symphony of bellowing engines, black smoke and churned sand.

We walked over the shallow pass between Espalmador and Formantera Islands and liked that island so much we up anchored and moved. Gorgeous, clear water, over sparkling sand, in front of a long white sand beach, it was the closest thing to the South Pacific we have seen in the Med. Even the more than 200 boats anchored there were spread out enough to be acceptable.

Ryan (12): *The water was so clear that, when swimming around the boat, I saw a towel on the bottom, thought it was one of ours, and dove for it. It was brand new and huge, embroidered with a boat's name, and it became mine after a search of the anchorage couldn't find the boat .*

Formantera was the nudist capital of the Balearics. We were definitely overdressed, but adjusted our mental attitude, and didn't mind a bit. Ryan stepped over and around nude people with far more aplomb than that exhibited by Carole and me.

Carole: *Now I wouldn't call Laurie a Peeping Tom, but as we walked along this beach, he tried to film everyone inconspicuously, sort of swinging the camera at his side, as if it were switched off. He was rewarded with lots of footage of sand, and precious few bodies. There certainly is nothing left for Ryan to learn about anatomy, or about how it deteriorates with age. While young people were there in the hundreds, men and women my age were plentiful. What were they thinking?*

The shoreline was decorated with stones, driftwood, cordage and nets, arranged in "artistic" ways. One edifice was so huge, and had been added to by so many people, that it had a name and a permanent collection plate for donations towards its upkeep.

On a charter sailboat next to us was an Australian, with his German wife, on holidays from their home in Indonesia. Where else but in an anchorage would such people be met?

We bicycled to the town, past the salt lake, for groceries. On the return trip Carole hit a patch of loose sand and made a spectacular flight over the handlebars. Fortunately there was more damage to ego than to body, but she limped for a few days.

Ryan (12): *I really didn't want to leave, but the parental units had other plans and we headed for mainland Spain again and the marina in Moraira.*

The bull bellowed as it plunged into the water, the crowd cheered, and the young man in white bowed in acknowledgement. Side-tied to the breakwater in the marina in Moraira, Spain, we were just across the water from the bull-ring, also in the marina. It was a small bull-ring, built with one side open to the water, but a bull-ring in a marina was certainly different, and definitely Spanish. The fiesta was on when we were there, and the ring was used nightly. Young men and young bulls were in the ring together. The object was to have a bull charge, and lure it so that it ran off the end into the water. There were fishing boats standing by to guide the wet bull to a ramp, where it was able to climb back into the ring. The young men who fell in fended for themselves.

A German architect living in Moraira, who we had met in Kusadasi, Turkey, joined us for dinner at an excellent, small restaurant we never would have found without his local knowledge. He gave us a tour of the house he had designed and built, hung off a hillside above the harbor. The innovations he had included quite astounded us and changed our perceptions of how a house should work. Unfortunately, to implement many requires a house on a hill overlooking a Spanish coastline. This last sentence is my protection against Carole's asking me to add them to our house today.

The huge marina at Alicantee was selected as the best spot to leave the boat in Carole's tender care, while Ryan and I flew to Australia for Jenny's wedding. Everything was close, security was 24-hour, and there was excellent protection from the weather.

Carole: *The marina was really upscale, and I was not too nervous about being left alone on "Dolphin Spirit" for the very first time, left alone with the responsibility of looking after Laurie's baby.*

Laurie and Ryan left, and I began a wonderful routine of riding my bike early in the morning, walking to town later for fresh fruit and vegetables for lunch and dinner. Laurie and I had been on Weight Watchers for several months and we were very happy with the results. In the afternoon, I'd walk back to town to shop. My main interest was finding music that had the lyrics written out in Spanish, so Ryan could learn the songs. I bought a few Julio Inglesia, a wonderful Placido Domingo and "Les Miserables"—my favorite. I spent my evenings listening to these and reading.

All went well for a week and then my bike riding was spoiled by a surly policewoman, who stopped me from riding on an empty footpath at 7am and sent me out into the traffic on the street. That afternoon, I heard silence when there should have been the sound of the refrigeration I had to run for an hour every day. That sort of silence is really loud. I had forgotten to check the refrigerator temperature, a job Laurie had drilled me in the importance of, time and time again, and the refrigeration had stopped. The temperature gauge was at -15, and Laurie had told me never to let it go below -10. I had broken the refrigeration!

I knew it was after midnight in Australia, but I called Laurie anyhow, hoping to be told I hadn't ruined a $1,000 compressor. He was calm, and I spent the rest of the week with no refrigeration.

Alicante to Gatwick 4 hours, Gatwick to Heathrow by bus 1.5 hours, Heathrow waiting 9 hours, Heathrow to Singapore 12 hours, Singapore 1 hour, Singapore to Brisbane 8 hours, with arrival at 4:50am. Reunions with all the family, including my mother, who, 90 that year, still exhibited mental prowess that put us all to shame. The bride was gorgeous, the groom nervous, the organ loud—in fact a normal wedding, except that everything went smoothly, the food was excellent, and the speeches were short. Ryan was an usher, and had to read a passage during the ceremony, both tasks he performed with aplomb. We have yet to learn where he learned to dance the way he does, but he certainly out-Travoltaed everyone one else on the dance floor. All too soon, it was a reverse of the outward journey, with full planes, and me again jammed in a seat suitable only for a growth-retarded six-year old.

Carole: *I was still upset and concerned about the refrigeration, but Laurie did his usual magic and had it all operating again, only a couple of hours after he got back. On top of all that, he brought me onion powder, and Nappisan.*

We anchored inside the huge Torrevieja break-water (the swimming beach for the city was also inside it). Next to us was the wharf used for bulk-loading salt into ships. Getting up the anchor the next day was difficult, as we had hooked a very old, rusted, fisherman-style anchor. Perhaps Columbus left it there, as this was his departure port.

Cartagena had a very small, rickety marina, around which was being built a cruise ship terminal and new marina. Some day it will be quite something. The town was also being refurbished for tourism, with walkways, statues and fountains under construction everywhere. The workmen far outnumbered the tourists, who were mainly us.

Leaving Cartagena, we actually sailed for an hour or so before the winds moved into their usual position, right on the nose. The wind and seas came up even more, so we decided to head for Garucha. We were turned away by the marina there, and the nearby anchorage had six-foot waves through it, so we headed off again. At this time, the engine chose to stop, as the fuel filter had filled with water. Luckily, I had fitted a parallel filter, so the engine was soon going again. Unfortunately, the last crank of the starter that got it going also jammed the starter somehow, and it burnt out, filling the boat with smoke. Night was falling, and it was rough and windy. I waited for the engine to cool, then changed the starter, head down in the bilges for over two hours, and got us motoring again.

Carole: *No, no, no, no, NO! That is not exactly what happened, Laurie! Yes, we were motoring along. Yes, the engine suddenly stopped. You did not say, there we were in the Middle of the Med, with night falling and us without an engine! Remember when you didn't use the Baja filter? That was the cause of the problem.*

Now we had to SAIL! The wind was coming from the wrong direction. The sea was bouncy. We had to TACK! TACK? A cruising boat! Every time we had to TACK it was a problem, as our staysail prevents the jib from crossing easily, so we had to partially furl the jib. Figuring out just how much to roll in and when, in the dark, with a by now very rough sea...........it was harrowing. We sailed toward shore for an hour; we sailed toward the shipping lane for another hour. We were still looking at the same spot of land! We had hardly moved forward!

Then my dear, tired husband went down below to take out the burned-out starter motor and put in the one that had gone out on us in the Red Sea, and later repaired in Turkey—in Turkey, which ruined our varnishing job—in Turkey where our bottom had been poorly painted. Would this starter work? Ryan went to bed. I sat quietly on watch in the cockpit, telling myself that we had been in worse straits in the South Pacific (remember Nuie?) and the Red Sea (remember when we last changed the starter?). Laurie, with his head in the diesel-smelling bilges, had to hold the starter (an item that took two people to get off the boat), remove it, and replace it with the other one. At midnight, Laurie came up to the cockpit, pressed the starter button, and we were under power once more.

A pleasant, short hop turned into a long over-nighter to Almerimar, the only place we could enter under the conditions. People come to the Med for sailing holidays? Almerimar was a huge, huge marina that was part of an apartment development. There we found an Englishman, who confirmed the refrigeration clutch diagnosis, and found a shop that had the required parts IN STOCK. An Australian boat had a young girl on board who took a liking to Ryan, so he went with them horseback riding, and surfing.

The Alhambra, that jewel of Moorish architecture in Granada, was only a two-hour drive from Almerimar, so off we went. As it turned out, others wanted to see it too, and all Alhambra tickets were sold out for that day, and the next. One advantage of cruising is that delays like this can be taken in stride, boat jobs can be done, wine can be drunk, and visits to other boats can be made while we waited the arrival of our reservation day.

Even if the wait had been traumatic instead of pleasant, it would have been worth it. We had read all the descriptions, but nothing could have prepared us for the wonderful combinations of ponds, fountains, flowers, trees and shrubs that made up the gardens and for the breathtaking decorations that covered every wall. Some seemed to be created of air, so intricate and open were the carvings. Even the view across the city was magnificent.

The driest place in Europe is Cabo de Gata, the cape that gave us so much trouble to sail around. A huge nature reserve, inhabited during the season by thousands of flamingos, but now by only a paltry hundred or so, welcomed us as we drove by. Dragging Carole to within 200 feet of the top of the impressive cliffs, we ate a picnic lunch in the dirt (no grass or vegetation).

Again the changeable Med weather forced an overnight sail on us. As planned, we had a pleasant morning sail to Herradura, where we anchored in clear water, under cliffs speckled with quite spectacular houses. Ryan tried a swim, but the water was too cold even for him. The wind shifted, exposing us to the waves, so off we headed again. As soon as we were well underway, it naturally shifted again to a head wind, and we punched into it all night.

Estepona and Duquesa marinas were only some five miles apart, but the latter seemed to be easier to enter under the conditions. The problem with a lot of Spanish marinas was that they silt up at the entrance. We had often entered with inches under the keel and fingers and toes crossed. Carole almost manages to levitate at such times.

The winds kept us in the marina, in sight of Gibraltar, for three days before relenting, and giving us absolute calm and mirror seas for the last 15 miles around Europa Point and into Gibraltar. The Queensway Quay Marina was relatively cheap, power was from card-operated meters, water was desalinated, and therefore pure and expensive. The marina was also a long way from the airport noise that enveloped the only anchorage, which was right next to the flight path.

All Gibraltar was within a 10-minute walk from where we were. The city was somewhat seedy and run-down, and very English with Spanish undertones. There may be some truth in the story that the word "gibberish" comes from the sounds that GIBraltans make when they speak SpanISH very quickly, as almost all do. Spain was still trying to take Gibraltar back, and so the crossing, by car, from Gibraltar to Spain, could take from one to three hours, depending on whether Spanish Customs decided to search every third car, or every car. No one was quite sure what they were looking for, and no one cared, as the reason for the search was acknowledged, by all concerned, to be pure harassment.

Gibraltar may as well be an island, a thousand miles from other civilization. During the French blockade of the Channel ports just before we arrived, trucks didn't come, so the shelves in the supermarkets emptied. We ordered a stove from England, an easy two-day drive away, which took two weeks to arrive, even though it was not affected by the blockade. Then it arrived on a Friday afternoon, and Customs closed at 2:30pm, so it couldn't be cleared until Monday, except that Monday was a holiday, so Tuesday became the earliest we could clear.

It turned out that Gibraltar had a neat (for the local freight companies) concept whereby if we paid the freight to Gibraltar from the source, the interpretation was that we paid only to the border. The Gibraltar freight company then charged us from the border to their bonded store, a bonded store charge, and a local delivery charge to our address. They also charged for clearing through Customs. One of our friends was charged $75 for taking a small life raft off a truck and two paces (actual measurement) into store, because it contained flares, which the trucking company classed as dangerous materials even though they were totally enclosed in the life-raft container.

All of the above meant that Gibraltar was an expensive place for food and labor. Get boat work done in Spain at half the price and better quality. However we did manage to get the new stove, a Navtex weather system, and a new starter motor for the engine, at prices we were happy with, but only after a lot of searching, telephoning and haggling. I did all the installations. "Dolphin Spirit" seemed to be being replaced piece by piece.

Carole: *Our new stove had a broiler, so I got rid of the toaster-oven—one thing less on board.*

We toured the Rock by taxi; we went up it by cable car; we walked down it; we walked around it. We met the famous monkeys, which looked just like overfed monkeys. There was nothing else to do. The only swimming area, Catalan Bay, had icy water, and a beach which was a mixture of equal parts of sand, cigarette butts, and garbage. Europa Point, the "End of Europe" was an arid wasteland. For kicks, we could walk or drive across the international airport runway. To get to Spain we had to do this, as the runway cuts right across the peninsula.

The locals love the place. In a recent referendum, 98% voted not to become part of Spain. On Gibraltar Day, everyone—and we do mean everyone—dressed in red and white and paraded through streets all hung with red and white banners.

To avoid feeling Rock-bound, we braved the Spanish Inquisition (aka Spanish Customs) and drove to Ronda, a delightful mediaeval city, where bullfighting in its present form originated. To the "Oles" of the appreciative crowd (two), we visited the Ring and strutted on the sand floor, swirling Veroniques with our capes. The attached museum was one of the best of its kind, with colorful "Suits of Light," old photos, posters, paintings and mounted bulls' heads. If the bull wins he gets to be steak anyhow, but if he has killed a famous bullfighter, his head (the bull's) gets to be in the museum.

Given the size of the clothes, the matadors must have been tiny men. The records seem to indicate only one female bullfighter, and she appears to have been larger than most of the men. We have been very hesitant about seeing a bullfight, and so far have managed to avoid a live one, being satisfied with the TV broadcasts, with Carole closing her eyes even then.

Seville was worth the visit, but wasn't as interesting as we had expected. The cathedral was memorable because of the ramp that spiraled up the inside of the towers, instead of the usual steps. Mediaeval handicap-access? Steps are easier, both up and down. The tendency on the ramp was to accelerate when walking down, a tendency Ryan happily gave in to. We took the "Bus Touristico" city tour which mostly covered the pavilions of the two World Fairs which have been held there. No orange trees.

Driving to Lisbon, we called in at Evora, Portugal, because our guide book called it an "architectural gem," but for us its main attraction was a chapel built entirely out of human bones and skulls. The several thousand skeletons used in its construction were taken from the local cemetery when it became overcrowded. Pious bowing of the head was necessary to avoid the open socket stare and bared-teeth grins that were everywhere when we looked up. As a decorative touch, on one wall there was a full skeleton, complete with desiccated flesh and tattered clothes. The feet and hands had fallen off, a detail for those who require really accurate reporting.

We had decided to drive to Lisbon, as we had no time to sail there, and Evora was simply an accidental stop. As we have often noted, many of our most memorable times and places have come to us by accident, because we are never afraid to get lost (because we always get lost?) and because we take "the road less traveled." Rather than try to gain great philosophical insight from this, we accept it and continue the practice.

Did you know that cork trees are a dull pink when the bark is first taken off? We drove through forests of them, and past areas piled high with the half-cylinders of stripped bark. A lone, huge, black bull (Ferdinand?) stood posed on the top of a hill. On other hills, windmills waved giant arms waiting for Don Quixote.

From the south, Lisbon was accessed by two bridges, and dominated by a huge statue of Christ with outstretched arms embracing the city. The bridge we chose was very Golden Gate-ish in shape and color, but appeared to be longer and taller.

Employing our usual technique of getting lost, going around roundabouts several times while deciding on an exit, retracing our route from the next round-about when our decision was obviously wrong and starting again, we finally arrived close to city center. The Sheraton Hotel was the tallest building we could see so we homed in on it, and got a room. Our system worked again! We were perfectly situated, right next to a Metro station, and within three Metro stops of every major sight in Lisbon. The bonus was drinks at sunset in the top-floor bar, with planes approaching the airport at eye level.

Walking through the old ruined castle, we followed guitar music and found the source, a young man playing under an olive tree in a deserted courtyard. His playing sounded so perfect, so fluid, so Spanish/Portuguese, we listened for a long time, then bought one of his CDs.

The steep slope of the hill below the castle was completely covered with closely packed houses. We followed the narrow, switch-back streets down to the waterfront, wondering how people could live there, with the only level place being the floor of their house. The sidewalk, when there was space for one, was often a set of stairs, because of the steepness.

Carole: *Driving back to Gibraltar, non-stop, because we couldn't find a hotel room, I had to keep Laurie awake, so we sang all the songs we had ever known. Ryan fell asleep very soon, perhaps a protective reflex, and Laurie and I warbled on into the night.*

"Whisper," a 75-foot sailboat, had arrived from the U.S. while we were traveling. To facilitate their passage, they had a number of 15-gallon fuel drums on deck. In return for some assistance with their electrical equipment, they gave us 13 of them With everything full, we then had 445 gallons of diesel, enough to motor across the Atlantic, if necessary.

Carole: *Provisioning for the Atlantic crossing was easy, as the supermarkets were well stocked, though expensive. I found items we hadn't seen in years, and really bought a lot. Later I was very sorry because with all these goodies on board, I gained back some of the weight I had so proudly taken off.*

Preparation of "crossing food" had become a tradition (supersti-

tion?) with us. The pre-prepared dishes always had to include red-cabbage salad, even if the passage was only one or two nights. It had worked for us in the past, and there was no way we would take chances. Laurie likened it to the African tribe that always held pre-dawn ceremonies so that the sun would rise—perhaps useless, but who wanted to take the chance if they stopped?

Chasing Sunsets

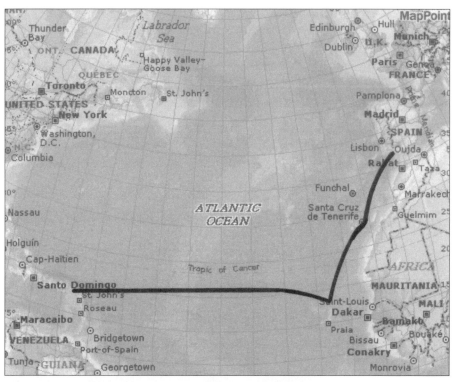

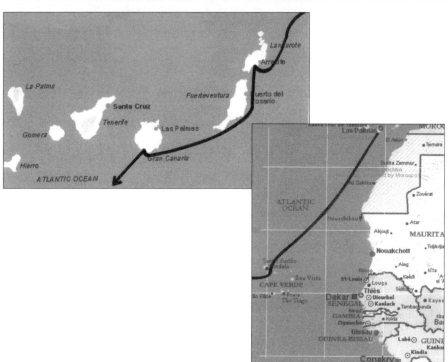

Canary Islands, Cape Verde Islands and the Atlantic

Year Five
September 24 to December 16

Passage meals cooked, we were ready to go, and then had to wait for another week, held in place by contrary winds. The Straits of Gibraltar are notoriously difficult for yachts to get through. Conventional wisdom required that we left with an easterly wind, three hours after high tide, which we did, and had opposing currents for the length of the Straits. The little twist was that we were supposed to sail within half a mile of the shore, but we didn't like the looks of the waves, rocks and cliffs.

Carole: *Tea, scones and raspberry jam were served as we passed the Pillars of Hercules—a fitting farewell to the very English Gibraltar.*

Through the Straits, we turned left across the shipping lanes and blew down to Lanzarotte Island in three-and-a-half days, with following winds, calm seas, starry nights and deep-blue seas, a magic sail.

Carole: *A little bird met us some 200 miles from shore. It stayed a few hours, then left. We chose to think it was a canary, even though the color was more brown than yellow.*

Ryan (12): *I hooked a very big marlin. It jumped a few times, then headed straight down. We ran out of line, so I tried to stop the run, but in the unequal struggle the line broke.*

Carole: *Gary and Dorothy ("Gigolo") had been on Lanzarotte for a week* *and over the radio had extolled the wonders of this fabulous island. As we got closer, all I could see was brown and black, with no vegetation at all. Gary had sounded so serious, but it was obviously just one of the elaborate jokes for which he was famous.*

Lanzarotte, one of the Canary Islands Group, is about 60-kilometers long and 20 wide. It looks like a barren chunk of lava, because it is a barren chunk of lava. It was also one of the most delightful islands we have visited in spite of the almost total lack of vegetation.

Carole: *Gary was right! The island was fabulous, and I soon began calling it the Designer Island. The sparse vegetation seemed to be mostly artistically placed fuchsia bougainvillea. The roads were lined with white-painted rocks. Almost every intersection was dominated by a creation that rotated, swayed or moved in some fashion with the wind. A restaurant and observation deck was so built into the landscape that even the parking lot was camouflaged.*

We arrived on Laurie's birthday. Gary and Dorothy took us to dinner at an old castle that had been converted into a restaurant. It deserved a return visit, but we found so many other lovely places that we never got back to it.

Dorothy distinguished herself by asking, in Spanish, for a table for us. The waiter manfully tried not to fall-about laughing, as what she had really said was, "I am a table please."

Returning to the marina that night, we hosted a get-together on "Dolphin Spirit." Many of our friends from Barcelona were there as well as others we had met over the years, now all drawn together getting set to cross the Atlantic. For the occasion, we covered the cockpit cushions in the new covers we had bought in Turkey and which coordinated with the salon cushions. In less than a week, I noticed they were fading from the sun, and in a month they looked years old and were soon discarded.

We stayed for four weeks and could have (should have?) stayed longer. Carole was correct about the Designer Island, as almost every aspect of it was influenced by Cesar Manrique, the famous artist, sculptor and designer. His house was built in five adjoining lava bubbles beneath a wild lava flow, and rivaled any above-ground mansion. He designed all the huge mobiles at the road intersections, and most of the public buildings. The whole island is imprinted with Manrique's vision of art as a seamless part of the landscape.

Hiring a car, we drove over the island, time and time again, discovering something new each circuit. At the volcano park we ate food cooked before our eyes over a volcanic vent. We saw blind shrimp in a pool at one end of a long volcanic tube. At the other end, we followed our guide almost a mile down the tube until it opened out into a space where we sat entranced as the soft notes of a cello preceded the artist's approach, and the concert we had come to hear, half a mile below the surface of the island.

Ryan: *On another time when we were on a guided tour of the volcanic pipe, our guide stopped at a ledge and asked us to look over at a pool of water below, lit by some faint lights. He asked us to conduct a physics experiment to determine how far the pool was below us by dropping a rock and measuring the time until we heard the splash. The pool seemed to be a very long way down, but was actually only a foot below the ledge, so the girl who dropped the stone got splashed.*

A cactus garden sounds like an oxymoron, but the one designed by Manrique contained 10,000 plants, almost 2,000 varieties, and was a visual delight, both overall and in the detail of the myriad shapes and colors. After putting off visiting it for weeks, we found it almost impossible to leave, so compromised by buying several small cacti for the boat.

On the southern part of the island was the only true beach, accessed by a rutted, unpaved road, mined with large rocks. Lanzarotte tourists are mainly English, who come to the Canaries for the sun. Large numbers prefer to do this unencumbered by clothing, and so it was on this beach. We sat in the shade of the rocks watching those pale bodies turn scarlet. One lady must have weighed almost 400 pounds and was in so many folds and pleats she may as well have been fully clothed. Others could have graced *Playboy*.

Ryan was now tired of hooking marlin only to have them break gear because we didn't have adequate rods and reels, so he got an early Christmas present of a marlin-ready rod, reel and line. We had fun researching, then buying, in the surprisingly extensive fishing gear shops.

We dined at colorful seafood restaurants, never hesitating to try a different one, and it paid dividends. All of the Canary's marinas were fully booked because of the various rallies leaving from there—the ARC (Atlantic Rally for Cruisers) with 250 boats, a French rally to Brazil with 100 boats and a third that no one seemed to know too much about, except, presumably, the participants.

Puerto Mogan, on the south coast of Gran Canaria Island was the place to be. They also were full and told us to try again in December, long after we had planned to be in the Caribbean. One day we were driving to visit the blind crabs, and stopped for lunch at a seaside restaurant. The Irish waiter overheard our discussion about marinas, and mentioned he had a friend in Puerto Mogan, who might help. He rang the friend, and we had a place the next day—it's not what you know.......!

Having an actual reservation forced us to leave Lanzarotte, but not before we had completed a wine tour. The island had a flourishing wine industry. Each vine was grown in its individual semi-circle gouged out of the lava, and surrounded by a wall of lava rocks. These pockmarked the mountain slopes. There was no apparent irrigation, and every grape was obviously picked by hand, as the vines grew along the ground, not on trellises. They were mainly red wines, with sweet, not so sweet, and drinkable, as the main presentations. Many wineries did not have labels, identifying the bottles by means of tags around the necks. The drinkables were good, and worth buying for the wine desert of the Atlantic ahead of us.

Puerto Mogan was a fishing village which still retained its charm, even though overlaid with a tourist resort. It was an excellent base from which to tour the island. The main city, Las Palmas, had all the problems of a big city, and none of the advantages. We drove past the Las Palmas marina three times before we could find an exit off the freeway to get down to it.

Carole: *Our stated purpose in visiting was to see friends in the marina, but mine was really to shop again at El Corte Ingles, a Spanish department store that has it all, including a gourmet shop where we buy special chocolate twigs. I had frequented the shop in Barcelona, and assure you that no visit to Spain is complete unless you shop there.*

The helpful friend who found the berth for us was Irish, and operated a waterfront restaurant that featured bacon, eggs, baked beans, tomatoes and toast for breakfast. To show our gratitude, we forced ourselves to breakfast there almost every day—sacrifices need to be made. The chandlery was owned by an American (a surprise, as we had come to believe that the Canaries were populated solely by English, Irish and Germans), who organized a Halloween party for charity. Held under a marquee in an olive grove, it featured a stage show by the "Blues Brothers," and a huge cannon that shot soap bubbles which covered the surrounding area to a depth of over six feet. Luckily, the cannon was started late in the evening, as everyone who dived in, including Ryan, emerged looking like a snowman, and soaking wet. Ryan couldn't be dragged away.

The mountainous interior was reminiscent of the Grand Canyon. We stopped at a roadside stand, perched on the edge of a cliff with a superb view, and had the best fresh fruit juice. Mogan was a small town, in the hills above Puerto Mogan, and notable only for having a decent supermarket, and an approach road lined with giant furniture. There were beds, tables, chairs, a sewing machine, kettle, candle, and other miscellanea. Not a sign was around to explain why these creations were there—perhaps an early example of "build it and they will come" thinking.

Carole: We passed a nursery. I had started a garden in Barcelona—basil, cilantro, parsley and dill, and now added some large cacti and poinsettias. In Lanzarotte we had bought a lot of small cacti, so now we were a floating greenhouse, just before setting off across the rolly Atlantic. What was I thinking?

On the road to Las Palmas, we passed a Go-Kart track, so took Ryan in for a spin. First sight was scary, as the karts were blurring around the track at over 80 mph, not a place for Ryan. Further investigation discovered a second track where speeds were only 50 mph, but where Ryan could actually rent a modified kart and go around by himself between races. He was somewhat disappointed at the reduced speed.

Carole: For the Atlantic, the last long passage of our circumnavigation, all the provisions were highly organized. Of course the usual pre-passage cooking was done and frozen, but I had also put together everything necessary for each meal. For instance, all I had to do was grab the bag marked "Coffee Cake" and everything I needed was there, pre-measured—just add eggs and water.

The long range weather forecast predicted five days of light winds and calm seas, so we headed off to the Cape Verde Islands, the next leg of our Atlantic crossing. "Gigolo" decided to sail also, even though Gary was persistent in complaining that he wanted more wind. Never ask for something—you might get it! The first two days were perfect, and then Gary got his wish.

Carole: I was only a little seasick. We had dolphins with us for such a long time, even a mother and calf. A few hundred miles off shore, a pigeon chose to lodge with us for a night and got the royal bread and water treatment. He sat right next to me as I did my watch, nodding his head in response to my attempts at conversation. Then the third day hit with 12-foot waves on our beam and 30-knot winds. Food changed from Julia Child, to passing around the Tupperware, to only fruit.

We have perfect storage for all our plates (I designed it) and lost only one to breakage while at sea, and that was on our first passage. Ryan was seated at the salon table eating, when a wave smacked us sideways. The spaghetti-filled plate flew across the cabin. On most passages now we use large soup cups we can easily grip.

The weather forecasts continued to predict 15 to 20 knots from the north-east, while we got 30 to 40 knots from the east and quite nasty seas. Wind and seas were from almost behind us, so it could have been a lot worse. Even so, "Gigolo" broke their boom, and others in the group of 20 boats doing the Verde run had torn sails, broken chain-plates, autopilot failure, and other damage. The engine alternator stopped working, our only apparent damage.

One of the single-handed, round the world, Vendee Challenge yachts passed us as if we were standing still. He had every sail up, and was bouncing from wave top to wave top. We chatted on radio with the Frenchman sailing it (who turned out to be the eventual winner of the race). He noted that his weather information, costing the race organizers many thousands of dollars, was just as incorrect as ours.

The entrance to Grand Harbor, Mindelo, San Vincente Island, Cape Verde Islands, has a local "wind acceleration zone" where bullets of 50 knots are common. One hit us just as we were taking in the sails. "Dolphin Spirit" heeled right over, sinking the rail, and causing Carole to scream and me to swear as I struggled to regain control, because we were too close to shore to just let things run. Then the wind was back to normal again, just as suddenly.

After all that, the harbor was very protected, in that the water was calm, but the wind whistled through for the first week, at 30 to 35 knots, day and night. Even with the wind, it was a relief to be in calm water.

We were besieged by the boat-boys as soon as we anchored, and selected Elvis (yes, he is alive and living in Cape Verde), who had rudimentary English. The boat-boys were licensed by the government, and were essential to visiting cruisers. They looked after dinghies ashore, translated from the Portuguese (there is almost no English spoken here), got laundry done, and found the necessary services we needed.

I showed Elvis the alternator, and off we headed in a taxi to see the "mechanic"—every boat-boy seems to have at least one. Just away from the waterfront, paved streets are replaced by narrow, twisting, hilly, dirt roads, with no names. After much winding and bumping, we arrived at a closed wooden door in a wall—there really is no better description. An old lady, sitting in a nearby doorway, was interviewed, and off we went again, to another door, which apparently was the mechanic's home. He was in residence, and, after some time, joined the taxi safari back to his workshop, the first door. Seemingly full of piles of old alternators and starter motors, mostly in pieces, it did not engender a feeling of confidence.

Never rely on first impressions in a third-world country. The "mechanic" was thoroughly competent and professional, in spite of working conditions that would turn a U.S. technician white and running to his Union. Elvis and

I were sent off to buy two bearings. One was standard, and was easily sourced from a bearing shop which was all computers and parts books, a clone of any in the world. Outside, it looked like a disaster area, probably because it seemed to be in one.

The second bearing was special, unique to that alternator. We visited every bearing and spare-part house on the island, to no avail. May all designers who use non-standard parts rot in hell trying to find them! At the end, I bought a small, second-hand alternator from the mechanic, fitted it, and we were mobile again.

All the above took about three days. In the meantime, life went on. The fruit and vegetable market had some supplies, but the produce looked tired compared with that at the wonderful markets in Spain and Italy. Carole visited only once, as she wasn't prepared to sort through the piles, and was bothered by the flies and the smell.

Carole: *The carrots were pale and gnarly. The constant wind howling through the rigging was deafening and exhausting. Ashore was very like being back in an African country (perhaps because it was an African country).*

Great bread at the bread shop—it actually lasted almost the full two weeks to the Caribbean. The supermarket had all the necessary staples. We didn't use the local butcher, although others did with varying results. Drinking water was available ashore, at the "Yacht Club" that had no other facilities, and at the "marina," a small, wrecked, aground, steel freighter, that took about 12 yachts, med-moored, along its side.

Ryan had boys his age to be with—three on an American boat. The father was a marine biologist, from Woodshole, Massachusetts, who was doing a whale survey for a year. Ryan got to go out with them, as they searched with sonar and listening devices. They also crowded into the back of a pickup a couple of times, for a bumpy ride to a nearby surfing beach.

On shore, the local boys were a little more boisterous—seemingly divided into two groups—those who went to school, in uniforms, and those who hung round on the street. The street group had toy guns, which they pointed at the visitors, and demanded money. I usually ignore such requests, so the boys moved to phase two. Luckily, I managed to grab the hand before it could get any money out of my pocket, but the young lad simply backed off a couple of paces, and stood waiting for another chance. The group followed us down the street for a long way, before giving up. This was Carole's first trip ashore and she decided she had seen enough. We have been in much worse places than this, but after more than two years in Europe, she just wasn't ready for the third-world scene again.

Carole: *The children were the main reason I didn't like going ashore. I have worked with kids all my life, and love being with them, but these were un-nerving in their absolute fixation on extracting money, either by way of gifts, or by stealing. Constantly pointing toy guns at us, they just would not go away. Usually I am a sucker for kids, handing out small gifts and money, but not at the point of a gun.*

Finally, we were ready to brave the Atlantic—fourteen days to Martinique. A group of about ten boats ("Sir Swagman," "Baghera," "Sunshine," "Capers," "Aqui Ahora," "Sound of Music" and "Dolphin Spirit," from Australia, "Just Magic" from New Zealand, "Gigolo" from the U.S., and a couple of English boats to add balance) all decided to leave together. We had provisioned, Carole had cooked meals and made salads (including the "lucky" red-cabbage salad) for the entire trip. Everything was tied down and stored away. I was making my final, pre-departure checks, when I found water in the engine oil.

With tears running down her cheeks, a disbelieving Carole watched all our friends leave, while I worked feverishly to remove the oil cooler, the most probable source of the contamination. Ashore, Elvis was not around, so I engaged Umberto, who spoke reasonable English, but was notoriously (even for a Cape Verde boat-boy) unreliable. Off we went in a taxi to find his mechanic, who wasn't findable. The taxi driver took over, and stopped a man in the street, who turned out to be the "number-one mechanic" in the islands.

He climbed into the taxi, was brought up to date with the problem, agreed to pressure test the cooler for leaks, and the augmented safari headed off into the labyrinth of hilly "streets" again. We stopped at another door in a wall, which opened into a small room containing a lathe. What was needed was a screw-on plug for one oil inlet, and a screw-on plug with attached tube for the other, so air pressure could be applied. This was apparently explained to the lathe operator, who then began to saw off lengths of steel concrete reinforcing rod.

The advantage of getting things done in a third-world country is that the technicians have learned how to keep things working, and make do with equipment and materials that would never be considered in "more developed" places. Two hours later, we had the two plugs, machined from the rod, and the mechanic disappeared to perform the tests. The next day, after some considerable effort, and more "streets" than I care to remember, the mechanic was found again, and pronounced the cooler to be leak free.

The next possible culprit was the head gasket. We carried a spare, and the mechanic was adamant that he could do the work. He and his young apprentice came to the boat, and began to pull the engine apart. Neither had

English, and Umberto had demonstrated that his reputation was earned by not showing up, so I was a little disconcerted when the mechanic asked to be taken ashore, leaving all the work to the apprentice. This young lad showed, over the following three days, that he was one of the better mechanics I have ever seen. He was quick, knew precisely what he was doing, had the right tools, and checked all his work before proceeding to the next step.

The head was removed, and was taken ashore for cleaning. Off went the taxi safari—with Umberto, who had reappeared—to the local engineering school, where the professor agreed to have the head machined flat as a class project. The school had the only equipment on the Island large enough to do the job.

Then I was advised that a couple of the small rubber grommets around the valve stems had been damaged in removal, so we headed off again into the wilds of the city. No store or junk yard—we tried them all—had such parts. Finally, we came to a road that was partially covered with dismembered machinery and vehicles, and stopped beside a group gathered to watch a truck being welded.

After some discussion amongst the group, Umberto was directed to a nearby house. More discussion with the lady who answered the door led to a man appearing through another door. Now the discussion became animated. Umberto reported that, no, the man didn't have any such parts, but yes he did, and wanted them for himself. I advised Umberto that he was to consider money as no object, and get the parts. This ploy worked, and the eight small parts were transferred into my eager hands, in return for more than eight large bills—actually about $US20 in total. The assembled crowd, who had deserted the welding to watch the negotiations, was suitably impressed with the stupidity of the gringo, and the taxi roared off in a cloud of dust.

The following day, Umberto was missing again, so I re-engaged Elvis, who had no knowledge of the mechanic that we were using, or of where things were being done, as they weren't his mechanics. I didn't know names, but managed to guide the taxi through the "streets" to get the machined head, and deliver it to the apprentice. I have to say that I was inordinately proud of this navigating feat, performed without G.P.S., sextant or chart.

Eventually, the engine was assembled again. The apprentice, who apparently was unaware that his master had tested, and passed, the oil cooler, decided to perform his own tests. No overnight pressure tests for this lad. We went ashore to the service station, filled the cooler with water, and blew air into it—bubbles everywhere. The oil cooler was the culprit after all! The head gasket didn't need changing! We could have left five days ago!

The oil cooler was in two parts, one for engine oil, and one for gearbox oil. The apprentice suggested using the gearbox side for the engine, and not cooling the gearbox oil at all. This probably would have worked as a last resort, but I was adamant that we try to find a second cooler to put in series with the old. For the non-technical, that means setting them up, one after the other, in line. Taxi safari headed off again. Several hours and many discussions with very assorted people later, found Elvis and me under a wooden boat, in conversation with a man hammering on a propeller. He seemed to understand, and roared off on a motor bike. Minutes later, he reappeared clutching a rusty, old oil cooler, which not only was not leaking, but had oil connections that fitted our hoses. Elvis was very ashamed to report that the man was asking the equivalent of $US80 for the cooler, and totally shocked when I paid.

So the saga ended. We had a rebuilt engine that ran better than it had ever done, for a total expenditure of less than $US300, including machining, valve grind, parts, labor and the new (old) oil cooler. The six day delay put us far behind our friends, and we had eaten a lot of Carole's prepared food.

Carole: *For those six days, Laurie was fully occupied, but I had nothing to do but worry. What would we do if we couldn't get the engine fixed? Each day as our friends sailed further and further away my confidence sank further and further. Until the day the engine was finally repaired we had no idea how many days or weeks our voyage would be delayed.*

We had crossed the Pacific alone, but that was when we were cruising novices and didn't know better. I worried about Laurie's safety ashore, all alone. I worried about whether the repairs would last for the crossing and of course there was the worry of something I wasn't worrying about.

All along the way I had taken each sector as it came. I can make it to the Marquesas, but will I go on? Okay to Australia. Okay to Israel. Then I was fine for two years in Europe to Gibraltar but I wasn't promising anything more. Now I had made it to the Cape Verdes and the sail here had been gruesome. We were in trouble.

The QE2 was in port and I could have said, "Thanks for the ride, but it is time for me to get out of here." Looking back, it surprises me that I didn't even consider such an action.

With all the fuel we were carrying above and below deck, our strategy for the Atlantic crossing was to get across as fast as possible, averaging over 7 knots, by using motor and sail, so it was ironic that we had engine problems. (***Carole:*** *Was it because we had 13 jugs?*) To jump ahead, we crossed in 12 days, averaging over 7 knots, so the deck jugs did their job.

The actual crossing really wasn't too bad (***Carole:*** *Says who?*). For the first week we had light winds so alternated between sailing and motor sailing. The swells were from the north or north-east, just behind our beam, so we rolled—boy, did we roll! Nothing we did could stop it. Even the required wing-on-wing sail configuration didn't help. As explained before, that is a set up with the mainsail held out on one side of the boat and the jib held out with a pole on the other, used when the wind is from behind. The rig looks terribly pretty sailing into the sunset.

Ryan (12): *I was now old enough to stand watches by myself, so I asked for the 4am to 6am watch. Dad thinks it is the worst watch, but I had a good time with my TV and video games, undisturbed by parents. Of course, I had to keep looking about for other vessels every 10 minutes, and check the sails, course, wind speed and direction. After a couple of days, Dad stopped checking on me every few minutes, but Mum's head kept popping up asking me if I was awake.*

Carole: *Thank you, Ryan. He would go to bed right after dinner, which I tried to serve around 6pm so he could get eight hours of sleep before his watch. I'd try to extend my watch to midnight so Laurie would get some sleep, too. If anything happened we would be really dependent on Laurie to fix it, so I tried to make sure he was well rested. I slept very well during daylight hours.*

Because of Ryan and Carole, I managed to get reasonable sleep every night. We saw no ships after the first day, many dolphins, no whales, an Australian yacht "Gondwana" we had last met in Barcelona, millions of flying fish, and a lot of water.

Ryan (12): *I caught only two small dorado, but I do claim a world record of ocean-to-stomach in eight minutes flat. Dad helped by cleaning the fish, having the BBQ ready, and cooking the fillets. On the first day of using my new rod and reel I hooked a marlin that was big enough to slow the boat and did a beautiful dance across the water before it spat out the lure. The worst day was six hook-ups, no landings.*

Carole: *To relieve the boredom—believe us, long ocean passages are mostly boring—I continued the gift-a-day program Jeanne Lamar had introduced on the passage from Fiji to Australia.. After lunch each day, Ryan got to unwrap a small present—actually some quite big ones, as I get a little carried away where Ryan is concerned (candy, video, video game, fishing lure).*

Celebrations for reaching half-way across the Atlantic were just over, when the engine died.

Carole: It was midnight, on my watch. The engine, which had been purring prettily, just stopped.

Jumping into action, I found nothing. Fuel was being delivered, everything was in order, it just wouldn't start. Half an hour of muttering into my beard (two-day growth), and tearing my hair, must have had some effect, as the engine then started, just as inexplicably as it stopped. I am a genius at fixing things!

Carole: Tensely but patiently sitting in the cockpit every time something needed fixing, I mostly kept myself from asking, "Can you fix it?" "How much longer?" "Are we there yet?" Laurie never volunteers information, so I get quieter and quieter, worrying to the max. (Laurie: What does she want, the thing fixed, or a stream of reports? In any case, how do you get quieter if you are quiet to start with?) *After several such incidents, I explained to Laurie that he needed so say, "No worries mate, she'll be apples." and other such Australianisms, followed by regular, "just 20 minutes more," reports and I would be happy.*

Laurie neglects to mention THE LEAK. The bilge pump kept operating, so Laurie searched for a leak, and found that water was pouring in around the drive shaft. He stopped it, but it began spurting again immediately we restarted the engine. This time his repair was permanent, but Ryan and I made sure we checked constantly. Laurie expressed a lack of concern, but I am sure he was equally diligent at checking, just more sneaky.

Ryan (12): That day, during English lessons, I read an appropriate sentence about the uselessness of a leaky boat.

Carole: Three beautiful egrets rode with us for two days. Leaping dolphins and flying fish were everywhere. The magnificent star show at night was augmented by so many shooting-stars. The constant rolling never became bearable.

That was it by way of incident, until we had less than 200 miles to go, one-and-a-bit days.

Carole: After the engine incident, I was just waiting for the next happening, and was so relieved to wake on that last day, knowing we had less than 24 hours left at sea. Then the squalls hit.

Canary Islands, Cape Verde Islands, and the Atlantic

The nice weather disappeared and we had squalls all day and night. The first was a real surprise, with over 50 knots of wind, blinding rain, and huge seas, but was past in 30 minutes. We were not without a squall, over us, or coming at us, for the next 24 hours. Fortunately, most were in the 30 to 40-knot range, with only two more baddies, and only one that lasted for 90 minutes. In between squalls, the wind dropped to almost zero. If you want to know what your socks feel like during the wash cycle, try being becalmed in confused, post-squall seas. We motored to keep up our speed, but mainly to have some control over our motion.

Carole: *To this day, Laurie and I argue over the presence or absence of danger during this time. We do agree that it was EXCITING, in retrospect! Ryan had just finished his watch and he and I were about to bake a coffee cake when the first squall hit. We were reefed down in preparation, but certainly didn't expect 50 knots. "Dolphin Spirit" heeled over—further than I can ever remember—and sank the rail. Rain poured down, and Ryan remarked that the sea "looks like giant grey sand dunes." I was certain that we would have a knock-down, but Laurie altered course, we straightened and then the wind died. Then the next squall hit, and the next, and the next, eight in all. No coffee-cake that day.*

Carole insisted that, during squalls, we wear safety harnesses, as the 50 knotters really heeled us over. There was no danger, but it made her feel more comfortable, and so the macho-men went along with her request. Ryan and I always wore harnesses when we went on deck, as one of our rules was that no one left the cockpit without being hooked on. The chances of finding a person overboard, in large seas, are vanishingly close to zero.

During the lull, we wanted to motor, but to Carole's horror, the engine wouldn't start. I discovered that the starter motor holding bolts had loosened, and one had fallen into the bilge. For 45 minutes I wrestled with finding and fitting a new bolt, bouncing around, upside-down. The bolt that was missing was one of those that can be placed and tightened in 15 seconds, if you have the right bolt, a special tool, two assistants, the flexibility of a contortionist, and the ability to ignore pain.

Carole: *I sat in the cockpit, calculating the number of days it would take to make port without the motor, and valiantly refraining from asking Ryan and Laurie for progress reports. Eventually, it was done, the engine started, and I resumed breathing.*

Remembering I was on watch, I looked around and noticed that a mainsail seam had split for about two feet. We therefore had to reef the main to past the split, to prevent further damage. It was just beyond our triple-reef point.

At that moment, Ryan looked forward, and asked what the gunk all over the deck was. I had stored on the deck a drum of used oil-water from the many oil changes I had to perform in Cape Verde. Unable to get rid of it before we left, I tied it up, and forgot it. The drum had fallen on its side, outlet down of course, in such a position that the cap touched a projection. Each time the boat rolled, this projection moved the cap a fraction, and eventually opened it. The movement had to open, not tighten, the cap so as to preserve the fundamental truth of Murphy's Law.

I was hosing the oil off the bouncing deck, using one hand for the hose, one hand for the broom, and the other to steady myself (wearing safety harness of course), when Ryan noticed that the engine temperature had shot up, and so shut the engine down immediately. I dropped everything and slid below to check. There were no water leaks, and everything seemed normal.

For some reason, later blamed on tiredness, stupidity, and sheer brain-deadisity, I decided to check on the water level in the engine radiator. Ignoring all my experience, and the huge signs warning to never, NEVER, under any circumstances, remove the cap when the engine is hot, I proceeded to place a folded towel over the cap, and turn it slowly.

As everyone with a car knows, a radiator cap has two catches, to prevent what then happened from happening. The radiator erupted in a fountain of boiling water, catching me on the forearm and face, and splashing Ryan's face as well. It didn't feel too bad at the time, so I simply poured a bottle of cold water over my face and arm, and took the opportunity to refill the radiator. The engine started, and the temperature stayed, rock steady, at normal, never to rise further. The gremlin had been appeased.

Carole: *Laurie, who never complains, must have been really hurting, as he started taking pain pills. He coated his arm and face with Aloe and wrapped ice around his arm. That night, while I was on watch, the wind direction changed, and the main, held in place by a preventer, back-winded. Laurie had to go on deck to release it. I broke down, a combination of the day's events, and my active imagination. If he fell overboard, in the dark, with those huge seas, we would never find him. Only after he has spent a long time calming and comforting me would I let him leave the cockpit, and then blinded him continually with a flashlight.*

After that, the arrival in Martinique was an anti-climax. We got under the lee of the island around midnight, into CALM water, and sat around waiting for daylight. It was a Saturday, so the marina office opened late, and then asked us to stooge around for a few hours while they freed a slip. Frankly, we didn't care. The water was CALM (repetitive, we know, but after 12 days of rolling, CALM water was a novelty to be savored), and the scenery was gorgeous.

Marina Marin was at the head of Culdesac Marin, a huge bay, surrounded by tree-covered hills, with anchorages everywhere amongst the shoals and reefs. The little town of Marin straggled up the hill, but all activity centered around the yachts. St. Anne, another small town, was at the entrance to the bay, and many yachts anchored off it, even though all the services were in Marin.

Carole: *Ryan's face was fine as he received only a light splash. Laurie didn't go to a doctor for his arm, which turned black and all the skin peeled off. Thanks probably to the antibiotics he started taking immediately, it healed completely in 2 weeks, with no scarring. He prefers to regard it as a result of a combination of superb constitution, great genes, healthy lifestyle, and a body system that told the mind, "See, you screw up, but I fix it." In any event, we were all very relieved.*

Chasing Sunsets

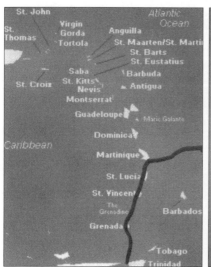
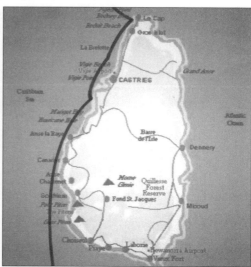
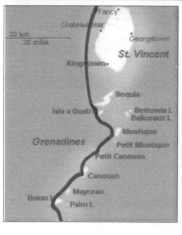
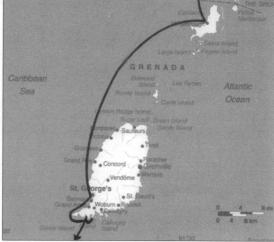
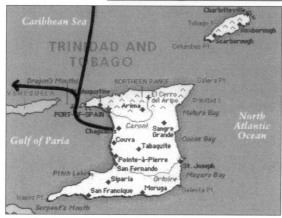

Martinique to Trinidad

Year Five and Six
December 17 to July 3

Certain readers may have been somewhat appalled at what they perceive to be the continual series of crises and disasters we have experienced over recent months. Let us hasten to reassure everyone that we have actually been enjoying ourselves.

Carole: *Laurie sometimes gets a little carried away with reporting problems—consider some of his descriptions as the written equivalent of the Italian waving his arms when speaking. On the other hand, I treat every incident nonchalantly.*

We were once again in "drop the anchor, drop your clothes" territory. There is no doubt that we have seen more male genitalia waving in the breeze than has a locker room attendant at the YMCA. The phenomena appears to be nationality related, the Germans clearly points ahead, with the French hard on their heels, and the Swedes hanging behind. On the female side, the figures are very similar at the bottom end, while topless honors bounce between French and Germans.

The sign said "No Showering On The Dock" and we wondered about its meaning and relevance. As we were sitting sipping wine in the cockpit, the man on the boat across from us came out onto the stern, a whole dock-width from us, took off his clothes and showered. The lady then appeared and did the same, but she had to wash and dry her hair as well. Yes, they were German—he certainly wasn't Jewish—and each had had their appendix removed by micro-surgery.

Martinique

We stayed in just the one spot, Marin Marina, instead of anchoring out, as we needed to have some work done on "Dolphin Spirit," and Ryan's grandparents were joining us for Christmas. Martinique is very French, and therefore has both the good and the bad associated with that. The bad relates to the extraordinarily high cost of almost everything, and to the overlay of French arrogance and bad manners (Sorry if that is offensive, and we hasten to say that some of our best friends are French.). The good was that the shops and chandleries were well stocked and extensive, service facilities were excellent, the women were beautiful, I got to practice my appalling French again, the roads were well maintained, and the restaurants were excellent. Ryan loved the local "Mango Bay" at the marina, as they featured "all you can eat" ribs, and he tried several times to put them out of business.

Ryan (12): *Those ribs were really great, but the truth is that Dad ordered just the regular, and I ordered the all-you-can-eat, and gave him a lot. They were not as good as the Tex Mex ribs in Malta, but I managed two slabs every sitting.*

We reserved Christmas dinner at "Indigo," and showed up on Christmas Day only to be told that Christmas dinner had been held on Christmas Eve, as every fool knows. The restaurant owner even flipped us off!

Our favorite restaurant was Moroccan, and we visited it every time we had a car. They prepared all food "with love and seven vegetables." We found it through our usual serendipity of looking for something else. Ryan's grandmother had read about a restaurant, so we went there to find it closed until the evening. In some wondrous way, we got to speak to the owners, who were heading off to lunch at the Moroccan restaurant, and invited us along. They provided the introductions, we became instant VIPs and regular customers, but unfortunately never visited our benefactors' restaurant to eat.

Although technically the dry season, it rained—tropical downpours—almost every day, but only for short periods. Driving with Ryan's grandparents through the rain forest during one such deluge, with torrents of brown water bounding down the low cliffs on each side of the road, and minimal visibility, was very like being in a huge waterfall. Naturally, been-there-done-that me was simply transported back to the farm in North Queensland, where it really came down, making the present rain mere mist in comparison, or so I informed everyone endlessly.

Carole: *If the cruisers were to give us a third wedding, it would have to be at The Plantation. An old sugar plantation/factory, with some restored build-*

ings, including a lovely little church, all set under huge trees, it was so romantic. While we were there for dinner, a wedding was in progress and we just had to see the bride, radiant in a white dress, carrying red roses. Another building had been converted into the restaurant, cunningly leaving areas open to the sky, so that when it rained (and it did) the downpour was all around the tables.

Ryan (12): *Again I had to take off my hat—my new special "No Fear" hat—and again I left it behind and never saw it again. I have to be allowed to keep my hat on everywhere.*

The better drives in Martinique are in the north around Mt. Pele. Saint Pierre, the city that was destroyed when that volcano erupted in 1902, hasn't really recovered since. What amazed us was that the rain forest had completely covered the lava and ash in only 100 years—the power of a good rainfall.

Thanks to the service facilities and supplies, we installed a new alternator on the main engine, repaired and rewired the gen set, sewed up every seam on the mainsail, repaired the boom, added gas to the refrigeration system, bought a new coffee pot, and generally got "Dolphin Spirit" shipshape again. I get nervous waiting for something to go wrong when everything is working properly, and am much happier when there is a small thing still to fix. (**Carole:** *How about our metal ice tray that has sprung a leak, Laurie?*)

Ryan (12): *For Christmas, my grandparents gave me a wakeboard and I quickly became an expert. Jumping the wake and the occasional wave was easy, but mid-air spins saw me crashing a lot.*

"Magnum Bonum" caught up with us here. They had gone around the south of Africa, across the Atlantic to Brazil, then up to the Caribbean. Two days out of Brazil they were hit by a major storm, rolled over and dismasted. We can only imagine the chaos that followed, as Sylvja and Egon were very reticent about it. Towed into port by the Brazilian Navy, they spent many months getting re-rigged and ready to sail again. Now they were moving on as if nothing had happened.

Carole: *I persisted asking questions, as I wanted to be prepared in case it ever happened to us. During the third day of hurricane force winds, Egon saw a giant wave approaching and had time only to wrap his arms around the steering column. The boat rolled and was back up again in less than 30 seconds. Silvja saw the wave coming from below, braced herself, but hit her head.*

A huge bottle of ketchup broke, coating the inside of the boat with ketchup and glass. The mast snapped and had to be cut free, a very difficult job on a plunging, bucking boat. The Navy decided not to charge them for the towing, but because of where they were, and their finances, they were only able to replace the original aluminum mast with a shorter, wooden one.

Finally tiring of the baguettes, ice cream, rain, and being in a marina, we checked out. Customs and Immigration (same officer) were in the marina, so the procedure was simple, even though he spoke no English. I was happy to get back into the check-in/check-out mode that was missing in all the Mediterranean countries—made me feel important and useful.

St. Lucia

From St. Lucia to Grenada, the currency was Eastern Caribbean (EC) dollars, with a fixed exchange rate of $US1=$EC2.67. As U.S. dollars were accepted everywhere, and prices were simply quoted in dollars, it was essential to find out which dollar. On credit card statements we made sure to write EC before the amount. Horror stories, some even true, abounded about people who forgot these precautions.

The sail from Marin to Rodney Bay, St. Lucia, took about four hours, a very nice beam reach in relatively smooth seas. We decided to stay in the marina for a few days as a base for land tours. It was situated inside a lagoon, with a dredged channel to the sea, so was very calm and protected. The facilities were excellent and it was quite a change to be in an English speaking country again. We found ourselves translating in our heads from English to English, before speaking. Actually, the St. Lucian accent, local terms, and the speech cadence, often required such a translation.

A major shock was the cost of everything. Martinique was bad enough, but there was a choice between quality items. St. Lucia was very third-world and expensive—at least equal to U.S. prices. We couldn't see how the locals could afford to live there. In Martinique, we used phone cards, and a $US12 card gave us about 45 minutes of talking to the U.S. or Australia. The St. Lucia $US12 phone card lasted exactly three minutes. To rent a car, we had to purchase a driving permit for $US30, and then pay $US75 per day for the car. This gave us a small Japanese Jeep-equivalent, recommended because of the state of the roads.

Carole: *The Rodney Bay supermarkets were well stocked with many U.S. products and brands that we hadn't seen for years, like sour cream, Jell-o, and frozen waffles. The fruit and vegetable markets in Martinique and St. Lucia compared badly with those in Spain and other parts of Europe. Pro-*

duce was poor quality, and very expensive. Staple Caribbean items such as pineapples, mangos and paw paws were more costly than in the U.S., when we could find them.

Road names and signposts were notable by their scarcity. For a country that is totally dependent on tourism, St. Lucia certainly works to hide its attractions. To drive from Rodney Bay to the southern part of the island, and the major scenic attractions, required passage through Castries, the capital. The car rental lady said that we would get lost if we didn't follow her precise directions. We did. We got lost. Making the return trip later that day, we discovered it had been necessary to turn off an apparently major road into an alley, which actually was the main road in spite of being less than a car width and unpaved for a few hundred yards.

Getting lost continued to provide real advantages. The roads were very narrow and rough, so sedate travel was necessary, giving time to exchange pleasantries with the locals, smile, wave, help with the washing, and mind the baby. We also traveled through some lovely mountain scenery we would have missed, because we wouldn't have taken the roads we did unless forced to.

Ryan (13): *Wrecked and rusting cars were every hundred yards or so along every road. Some had trees and shrubs growing in and through them. Although the roads are bad, they didn't seem horrible enough to create that scale of damage. Dad thought there has to be a custom of breakdown equals abandon, but that seemed silly to me.*

Finally, we got through Castries and headed south, stopping at Marigot Bay to check it out as a possible anchorage. The sand spit at the entrance to the bay was where the original "Dr. Doolittle" (Rex Harrison) was filmed. We took the ferry across the entrance, and breakfasted at the Marigot Bay Resort, an up-market establishment. The order was their standard "English Breakfast"—scrambled eggs, bacon (for me), sausage (for Carole), fried tomato and toast. The order came with bacon for both, no tomato, and the bread toasted on only one side. When we advised the waitress, she said the kitchen was busy, nothing was exchanged, and we were charged full price. There didn't seem to be any point in noting that the menu said "scrambled eggs, not "scrambled half an egg," which was what we got—probably because the kitchen was too busy to crack more than one!

In spite of that, we decided it would be the perfect romantic anchorage to wait for the arrival of Phil and Lilia, then nine-months married, but still honeymooners.

On the way out, we stopped at an intersection and were approached by a young man offering a hand of bananas. When we declined to buy, he asked for a lift to Soufriere, about an hour away. I must have been caught at an off moment, because I agreed. The young man was very pleasant, and it was only when, about half-an-hour later, I asked exactly where he wanted to go, he told us he was a guide, and didn't want a lift but to peddle his services. I was then very clear that no money would be forthcoming, and the guy left peacefully, if silently.

As good as the banana ploy was, the young man with a portable VHF radio who waved us down was better. Hand-held radio equals automatically registering authority symbol, so I stopped. Another guide offering services, and the radio was a plastic fake. Good thinking though!

Carole: *It poured rain of course, but today I welcomed it. Through the downpour we spotted the roadside stand where young men usually stood with snakes to wrap around the brave tourists. Because of the rain, they were not operating. Ryan was devastated, I was ecstatic, and didn't attempt to hide it.*

High in the hills, looking out over the Pitons and the anchorage between them, we lunched at the Ladera Resort restaurant, which has one of the magnificent views in the Caribbean,. The food was good, too. Recommended as a place to stay and spend a few expensive days.

A tiny nondescript sign said "Rain Forest," pointing off down a narrow road. We had driven by it before without noticing, but this time Eagle-Eyes Ryan spotted it, after we had passed. Backing up wasn't a problem, traffic-wise, as there wasn't any, so we were soon cruising along down a switchback road into a gorge. Passing another vehicle wasn't an option, unless we wanted to do it vertically, so as usual Carole was totally relaxed about the whole thing. Luckily I heal quickly. The forest and the views were worth the agony.

Finally the road leveled out and passed a hand-lettered sign, "Waterfall." Feeling the need for a walk, we bought the $EC15 tickets and headed into the jungle. Talk about hiding good things away. The path was magnificently maintained by the family that ran it, with solid steps and bridges where necessary. The carefully arranged and tended native flora was superb, much better than that in the botanical gardens we had earlier visited. The waterfall, the tallest in St. Lucia, was photogenic. There were rustic seats strategically placed, and it didn't rate a mention in our tour guides.

Friday Night Jump-Up at nearby Gros Islet was a tourist "must do," so we went. Maybe we had the wrong idea and/or were too early, but street stands selling spirits and beer, BBQ chicken and fish burning on all sides, and ten-foot-tall loudspeakers melting our brains with canned trash, was not what we expected. On the way back to the marina we passed a local steel-drum band practicing, and watched and listened for a very enjoyable half hour. Amazing the melodies that can be coached out of a steel can.

Ryan (13): *"Jazz Time" arrived with my friend Jack on board, so we spent a lot of time together. "Moondance" with two more boys also arrived, so Mum and Dad saw even less of me. It was great to hang out again.*

We had last seen "Jazz Time" in Gibraltar, and they had just crossed the Atlantic on a fast track back to the U.S. and home. Jumping ahead, we later heard that, during their homeward passage from St Lucia to Martinique, their mast broke in 30-knot winds when a stay parted. Better then than during the Atlantic crossing.

Our old Australian friends "Lady Kathryn" anchored nearby, so we celebrated with dinner ashore at the local Mexican restaurant. Six of us ordered fajitas, on sizzling platters, which arrived on cold plates, as the kitchen had run out of sizzling platters—there were only two other patrons, and they were eating tacos. Debating the absence of plate logistics occupied considerable time during dinner that otherwise might have been wasted on pointless subjects.

Catching the local bus to Castries, we wandered about the town and eventually found the cathedral. The plain outside made the very colorful inside paintings even more dramatic. After waiting out the obligatory daily downpour, we searched for the restaurants mentioned in the guide book. All were out of business. We did find the local market, an impressive building filled with stalls selling souvenirs. There were the usual piles of junk, but some nice baskets, very similar to the superb Tongan baskets, local dolls, and some other respectable trinkets. The fruit and vegetable market just beyond was reasonably stocked, but the real find was hidden in an alley behind the market building—a string of food stalls. The attraction was that they were full of locals, so we picked one, sat, the large female operator proceeded to tell us what we were going to eat—callaloo soup, chicken, lamb, rotis—and had a great meal at no great cost.

Moving out of the marina, we anchored in Rodney Bay, near Pigeon Island, notable for its lack of the bird, probably because it was named after a man.

Ryan (13): *I could be dragged around on my wakeboard and take the dinghy into the marina to see my friends.*

Carole: *I prefer to be at an anchorage surrounded by the blue sea rather than side by side with other boats in a marina, unless...*

Crash and rattle of chain catapulted us out of bed at 7am. "Wind Surf," a cruise ship with sails, had dropped its anchor no more than 20 feet off our stern. They were so close that, when pulling up anchor the next afternoon, they had to employ their bow thruster to keep away from us. Even then, their bowsprit passed over our stern, and I felt obliged to call them on VHF and ask if we should move. The answer was a brusque "Negative." Any other answer would have meant that they were at fault. Others in the anchorage were certain we had been hit.

Carole: *At the time we were anchored close to "Morning Glory," Rupert Murdoch's old $50 million plaything we had last seen at Lizard Island, Australia, and "Mirabella II," a $US68,000 per week plus food, drink and fuel, sailboat. Poor "Dolphin Spirit" looked like a dinghy between them. The captain and crew on "Mirabella" were Australian, and they were between charters, so we were invited on board for a tour and drinks. Not bad for one of the cheaper "big boats"—prices go up to over $US350,000 per week, plus, plus, plus. I could handle a few days of telling the cook what to prepare.*

To restore perspective, a Swedish boat that had just crossed the Atlantic in five weeks and a day, sculled in. The young couple on board managed to fit into a length of 14 feet, a beam of less than 4 feet, and survived with water storage of 110 liters (around 25 gallons). The mast was 6-feet high. Carole wanted to congratulate them and bring them some baked goodies. I was less than impressed, as I regard this sort of exploit as craziness, not bravery.

Climbing to the top of Pigeon Island, we inspected Fort Rodney, where the English Admiral of the same name held the French from Martinique at bay. Some of his cannon were still there, and we could see where cannons, powder and stores were hauled up the cliffs during the fighting. Ryan discovered a path down for us, then left to climb higher. Although not exactly requiring pitons and ropes, the slope he led us to was somewhat vertical, and covered with loose stones and gravel. I did get Carole down, without a fall, but at a severe cost to my mental and physical health. Luckily, the restaurant on the beach at the bottom had a great view, and excellent pina coladas, so peace was restored.

Carole: *By coincidence, I was taking Ryan through my almost 40-year-old "Westward Movement" college history notes the next day, and found reference to Admiral Rodney. Back in my college days, I would have loved to see into the future and know that one day I would be seeing so much of what I was studying. It wasn't until I was almost 50 that I even had a passport.*

Migrating south to Marigot Bay, we anchored just off the ferry pier to await the arrival of my son and daughter-in-law. Boat-boys sold bread, fruit, clothing, baskets and trinkets without much competition, as there was only one, expensive market ashore. Competition between them was such that some waited to meet us miles out to sea, and others grabbed hold of our hull before our anchor hit bottom. They were surly, and continually fought amongst themselves, screaming for extended periods while holding onto our hull.

Carole: Bananas hanging from the stern arch are so tropical looking, and I wanted a bunch hanging there for Philip and Lilia's arrival. There are over 100 bananas in a bunch, but we figured, with Philip and Lilia to help, plus a few yachties, we would get rid of them all before they rotted. One of the boat-boys was paddling round on a surfboard had bunches for sale. Laurie had watched him wash the bananas on shore (getting rid of all tarantulas, cockroaches and geckos) and asked him to bring a stalk in two-days time, the day before Philip and Lilia arrived.

The next day, Laurie, seeing the surfboard, reminded the fellow. Unfortunately, it was not the same fellow, so we ended up with two huge stalks of bananas hanging on the stern, plus several large hands we were given as a bonus by both sellers to tide us over until the others ripened. Every ten minutes or so the ferry went past our stern loaded with tourists, all of whom had to photograph and film "the Australian banana boat." We became the most photographed boat in St. Lucia. Undaunted, Laurie kept repeating that we were trying to corner the banana market, and asking if anyone wanted to buy some.

We now had over 250 bananas, and everyone made a solemn promise to eat their 10-banana-per-day ration. Unfortunately, instead of beginning to ripen immediately, the bunches stayed green until two days before Philip and Lilia left—we even suffered bananaless days—and then all ripened immediately the day after they left.

Thanks to my computer recipe file, we now have new words to the Paul Simon song, "Fifty Ways to Eat a Banana." We had banana bread (a dozen kinds including chocolate chip banana, cinnamon banana and marble banana), banana cake, banana muffins, banana fritters, bananas with sour cream and coconut, frozen chocolate bananas dipped in chopped nuts, banana crunch (with a baked peanut butter cookie topping), curried chicken with bananas, banana fritters, banana daiquiris, chocolate banana malts (5 bananas per malt), banana pancakes, and, of course, banana shrimp (thanks Bubba).

The three of us and a few cruising friends went through 250 bananas in less than two weeks, and were very pleased with ourselves that we had to throw away only a few disgusting brown ones. Of course, our clothes wouldn't fit any more, but we didn't waste any food.

The rain-shower-a-day weather persisted, with winds ensuring that our wind generator kept the batteries topped up. In between squalls, we snorkeled, swam, watched the local artist carving birds out of coconuts (bought several for later use as presents), did schoolwork, boat maintenance, read, dozed, ate rotis, drank wine, cooked, watched for ripe bananas, and fended off boat-boys—life as normal on "Dolphin Spirit."

Marketing and promotion lesson: Bar A offers Happy Hour from 5 to 7, selected drinks only, chicken wing snacks at $EC15 per plate. Bar B offers Happy Hour from 5 to when you go home, any drink you want, chicken wings at $EC1 per plate. Bar B is crowded every night, Bar A is empty. Both are over the water, with their own dinghy dock and equally great views. Bar A reacts by advertising, via the boat boys, putting in writing its deficiencies vis-à-vis Bar B, and stays empty. Guess it must be a Caribbean thing.

Philip and Lilia ensconced and decompressed, we checked out and headed off for a night at a mooring between the Pitons. The Pitons are two steep-sided, vegetation-covered, conical mountains, reputed to be one of most magnificent of Caribbean sights. The Hilton Hotel behind the beach was attractive, but seemed practically empty. A boat-boy came out to invite us to eat at "Bang," a restaurant started by an eccentric English Lord, which looked like the aftermath of a hurricane, and may have been. We checked with the Park Rangers, were told that fishing was allowed, so Philip and Ryan proceed to catch about six, very eatable denizens of the deep.

St. Vincent and the Grenadines

The boat-boys in St. Vincent were so bad yachts were advised to avoid the island completely. Apparently they countered this drop in business by becoming more aggressive and carrying guns. We believed what we heard, bypassed St. Vincent, and went directly to Admiralty Bay (Port Elizabeth) in Bequia.

Apparently everyone else must have done the same, as the place was crowded with charter and real boats. Permanent moorings filled a lot of the available area, so we anchored off Princess Margaret Beach, renamed from Tony Gibbons Beach when the "Royal Foot" touched it. The beach was picture perfect; palm trees, rocks, golden sands, azure water, the works. The kids could swim to shore, the water was clean and clear, but we rolled and rolled and rolled, thanks to a northerly swell that bent around the headland far more than normal wave mechanics (Physics 101) would seem to allow.

A move to the center of the Bay, into the howling 30-knot winds we had been partially protected from, saw us drag anchor in slow motion. We were in 20 feet of water, with our 105-pound CQR anchor and 180 feet of chain out. For the nautically-challenged, that is a lot of chain for the water depth. From when we anchored around 10am until evening, we were immobile, while all around us others "plowed the north forty." Then I thought I could detect a slow movement, so we kept anchor watch all night. Move backwards we did, but imperceptibly, and without any danger of hitting others, so we just watched and waited. Then, at first light, the anchor chain gave a little shake, and we were off backwards, at speed.

In five years of cruising and anchoring in all depths, and on all types of bottoms, this was only our third dragging experience. We moved back to PM Beach and forward a couple of hundred feet, to find that we were almost out of the swell, out of the wind, and solidly anchored in lovely sand. Location, location, location!

Perhaps now would be a good time to explain how we have anchored hundreds of times without divorce or murder (justifiable homicide?) following inevitably. We did begin along that path, with yells and screams as the norm. Then I bought two-way radio headsets, but they were unusable in any sort of wind. Finally we settled on the procedure that has been tried and proven over the years, and is the envy of the cruising community. Carole drove the boat, Ryan called the depths and kept a general lookout, and I stood in the bow directing and dropping. As we closed in on an anchorage, we would all confer, deciding on the approximate place to drop. I then moved to the bow and directed Carole with a set of six simple hand signals, which covered every eventuality. It was simple, dignified, mostly silent, and placed full blame for any problems squarely on the man in the bow.

A political rally brought in four ferry loads of red-shirted followers from St. Vincent and we were regaled by speeches all day. Philip and Lilia left on one of the returning ferries, plane to Puerto Rico, change to Chicago, change to LA. Not an easy place to get to, the Caribbean.

Ryan (13): *I soon cheered up after Philip and Lilia left, when I found a new friend on one of the boats. Josh was a couple of weeks older than I was and we had a good time. A second boy, Douglas, on another boat, also about the same age, plus assorted girls on still other boats made me very happy. Josh and his family were permanently in Bequia, as his father looked after other people's boats.*

Had drinks aboard "Cowrie Dancer," an Australian boat with another boy, Jack (8). They had been the only Australian boat in the ARC (Atlantic Rally for Cruisers, where you pay for the privilege of fighting your way out of Las Palmas at the same time as 250 other yachts, then sailing across the Atlantic all alone). Entering because they like to race, they won their division.

The fruit and vegetable market in Port Elizabeth was run by Rastafarians, even more unwashed and dreadlocked than most. They all pressed around, pushing examples of their wares into our faces, and grabbing our arms and clothing. Carole took this once, never to return. On my next visit, I simply stood and told them, over and over, to give me space. Eventually I got it, and went around selecting what I wanted from the various stalls. The Rasti "leader" came up to me at the end, and said that I was welcome back, as I spread my business around all the vendors, and that I would get all the space I needed on the next visit. As I walked out, they were clustered around the next victim, pushing and shoving.

On subsequent forays I became quite friendly with one of the younger Rastis. One day he asked, "You are so calm and cool. What do you smoke?"

Bequia was totally oriented towards visiting yachts. Laundry (pick up and delivery at the boat), restaurants, taxis and supermarkets were all contactable by VHF radio. Water and diesel were delivered directly to the boats by barge. Boat-boys—nice, well behaved—brought bread, lobster, fish.

Eagle Taxis took us on a three-hour tour of the island (it isn't big), including visits to the turtle sanctuary, the pottery maker and painter, and the highest point, where we could see all the islands we would be visiting over the next two months—a hectic sailing schedule for us obviously. We actually could have walked around faster, as the taxi had to laboriously negotiate some of the worst roads we have ever been on.

I needed a haircut. Mr. Eagle Taxi had a friend who did haircuts, and put him on standby, waiting for the radio call. We called, and then embarked on a fruitless search for said friend. It was probably just as well, as every male was either dread-locked or shaven-headed. Eventually the haircut was given by a French lady who, with her husband, ran a sail loft. She was good, and did note that local barbers use razors, not scissors, commending me on my lucky escape.

Another Australian friend, "Flashdance II," arrived. Their daughter was to be married on board, just off Princess Margaret beach, after the necessary three-day residence in the country. The swell calmed down and the sky was clear and blue just for the ceremony, held on "Flashdance's" bow under a fruit arch. I ferried father and bride from shore to yacht, with them standing in the bows of our dinghy as the Wedding March echoed over the anchorage. We learned that the minister worked as a school teacher until 3pm, marries at 4, then becomes a professional fisherman at 5.

Southward to Mustique, holiday home to the rich and famous (Princess Margaret, Mick Jagger, David Bowie are so advertised). We were not allowed to anchor, but had to take a mooring. What they didn't tell us was that we had to have assistance to attach our lines. We lost two boat-hooks before we gave in and launched the dinghy, with Ryan acting as boat-boy.

Some quite magnificent looking residences nestled in the hills around the anchorage, but it was obvious ashore that the heady days were past. We walked along the rather poor beach, and across the island to a great beach, protected by warning signs, "No Swimming, Dangerous Currents, You Will Die." Pounding Atlantic waves, golden sand backed by sand dunes, windswept trees, the place was worth the visit—the rest of the island, well................

Our first Caribbean, wild animal encounter happened on the walk back. Carole ahead, yelled and pointed. Ryan and I rushed up just in time to save her from a tortoise that was crossing the road. The shell, head, and legs, were beautifully marked in yellow. Forewarned, we proceeded in echelon formation in case of further encounters. Point-man me flushed out an orange-marked specimen, lurking in ambush under a bush. There may have been others, but our heightened state of awareness obviously prevented further attacks.

The place to eat and drink ashore is Basil's. The waiters were rude, but the margaritas good. Despairing of ever getting a bill, I went to the desk and was handed one showing "2 Tom Collins." I returned it. There was a discussion with our waiter, and I got the bill back, unchanged. Again I returned it, and again I got it back. Finally, the manager arrived, and in tones normally used to deal with a retarded child, advised that the prices for Tom Collins and margaritas were the same, as everyone knows, so would I please pay, get out, and leave the place to respectable people.

Canouan was our next island on the southward trek, with anchorage in the pretty Charleston Bay. We tucked up in a corner behind a reef to get out of the swell. Snorkeling on the reef, Ryan and I found it full of juvenile lobsters peering at us from every crevice. Larger ones lurked in the deeper caves. Resisting the temptation—the place was a reserve—we had pizzas ashore at the Tamarind Beach Hotel.

That night, the swell found us again, and got worse in the morning, so we headed for the Tobago Cays, the "Jewel of the Grenadines." We cautiously negotiated a coral strewn entrance to find that 64 boats shared the anchorage with us, surrounded by a huge reef, and in the circle of four islands.

Carole: *Laurie at his laconic best. It was a very winding passage, with only small, well spaced markers to keep us off the reefs and rocks. Yes, the water was clear, the sun was in the right place for good visibility, and we really didn't need the markers to see the channel, but I was nervous and think everyone else should be also.*

Boat-boys zoomed around offering the usual bread, ice, lobsters, and fish. There were no permanent residents, and it was quite cool to sit watching the sun rise over Africa, the nearest land to the East. The beaches had lovely, fine, white sand, the water was clear and every color from deep blue to pale green, the fish life excellent, but the coral was poor (perhaps a result of Hurricane Lenny the previous year). We snorkeled, swam, cleaned the bottom of the boat, walked the islands, and thoroughly enjoyed the Caribbean as it was supposed to be. On each island, an entrepreneur had set up business, selling drinks and nick-knacks during the day, and offering fish and lobster BBQs on the beach at night.

Dedicated readers will know that one of our preferred entertainments in the evening is to sit in the cockpit, wine glasses in hand, and watch the charter-boats anchor. The Cays, being charter-boat heaven, provided particularly rich enjoyment, as long as the charter-boats stayed away from DS. It was a real boat, German, that gave us the year's best line. They had anchored right on top of us, and when I indicated that we would hit, responded, "Don't worry, we will put out fenders."

"Bamsen" a Hallberg-Rassy 62 that we had last seen next to us in Puerto Mogan, Gran Canaria, anchored in front of us. Christoph Rassy and family were on board, remembered us from the Canaries, and invited us over for drinks. Very interesting to see yachts from the perspective of the builder. They were great hosts and put up with all my questions and comments. Carole, of Swedish decent, using the Swedish learned at her grandmother's knee, endeared herself to them, and has been invited to visit whenever in Sweden. Remarkable what just two words will achieve.

Carole: *It was so amazing to me that no Swede on "Bamsen" or "Magnum Bonum" could understand my Swedish. Perhaps it was my dialect, applied to the half dozen words passed down from my great grandmother..*

Finally running out of fresh stuff, we motored the three miles to Clifton, Union Island, anchoring just behind the reef that provides the only protection. The small town straggled along between the airport and the shore. It boasted two internet places, one charging $EC46 per hour, the other $EC20 per hour. A string of small stalls provided the fruit and vegetables, with reasonable selection and price. I usually did the buying, as I seem to charm the selling ladies into selecting the better pieces, doing price deals, and giving away free samples. Carole still hates to haggle. Three quite large supermarkets were well stocked—pretzels at last!

We lunched at the Anchorage Yacht Club, overlooking its shark pool, as it was simpler than dragging Carole and Ryan away from the sharks and barracudas. Carole, who leaps from the water every time a shark thought enters her brain, stood only feet away from sharks being fed and charging about. (***Ryan [13]:*** *I told Mum they were only lemon sharks and that was why she wasn't scared.*) That evening we saw one of the better sunsets of the trip—superb red, white and blue. Word descriptions are inadequate, so wait to see the video, coming to your screens soon.

Moving round the island to Chatham Bay was one of our better decisions. Definitely the nicest island anchorage we had been to so far in the Caribbean. Only a fisherman's shack disturbed the lovely beach. The couple on a nearby charter boat turned out to be Dana and Martha, last met on their boat "Sarah Jane" at Hamilton Island, Australia, in three years before. Completing their circumnavigation, obviously much faster than we did, they had been on land for almost a year and this was their first charter since returning.

At one end of the beach, Shark Attack (the man) held a nightly BBQ; lobster, fish, salad, bread for $US25; fish, salad, bread for $US15. The one we went to, with Dana and Martha, was also attended by an Italian charter boat group (off one of those $68,000 per week yachts), who provided quite wonderful wine. A local trio, guitar, drum/vocal, empty bottle, entertained us very enjoyably. Once again we heard the Caribbean anthem, "Every Ting is Gonna be All Right."

Shark Attack came round three times one day, first to deliver bread, then to borrow an onion, lastly to ask for a drink of water. Maybe he was lonely. The flat waters were a perfect place for Ryan's wakeboard, and he usually managed two runs a day. Snorkeling was good for fish, as the whole bay seemed to swarm with them. Pelicans and other seabirds dived all round the boat. Surprisingly few yachts came in during the days we were there.

Heading back to Clifton to check out, we tried to go clockwise around the island, but struck winds and seas on the nose. Being the intrepid sailors that we are, we turned around and went counterclockwise—you guessed it, wind and seas on the nose in that direction, too.

Immigration and Customs were at the airport, a 200-yard walk. I peered into the Custom's office, but it was empty, so I hung around taking occasional looks. Finally a gentleman sitting on a nearby bench, apparently tiring of his private game, stood up and advised that he was the Custom's officer. It was all very pleasant and relaxed.

Grenada

It was Dodge City at the time of the Earps, a single street lined with old wooden buildings. Then we blinked at the dazzling reflection off the water, and it became Hillsborough, Cariacou, our check in point for Grenada. Customs filled in forms and asked for a donation to the local hospital; Port Captain charged port fees and solicited donations to the church; Immigration stamped passports and asked for a donation to the boys' cricket team. Australia had just thrashed the West Indies at cricket, and they were looking to rebuild from the ground up.

The market stalls were all under cover, except for one. When I asked its lady vendor why there were fish eyes in the pile of tomatoes, she pointed at the overhead tree, where birds perch and drop beak-loads. Not wishing to make further discoveries, we moved to the inside stalls.

A nice place to visit for a day, but the forecast was for north-westerly swells, last recorded when Columbus visited, so we moved around to the slightly more protected Tyrell Bay. The forecast swells arrived, together with equally rare south-east winds, a happy combination, as we therefore only pitched a little, instead of rolling.

Tyrell Bay township was there only because yachts visit. The waterfront was lined with restaurants, an Internet place, dive shop, supermarkets and bars. Unfortunately, Hurricane Lenny seemed to have destroyed the waterfront road, and it has never been replaced properly. In the harbor was the trimaran floating workshop of Dominique, who welded all metals and fixed all things—our ice trays were finally repaired. It also housed his wife, who did massage, a combination which made for a unique sign "Massage and Welding." A nearby catamaran was a floating bar, happy hour all day long.

The dusty road over the hill towards Hillsborough, led to the lovely beach opposite Sandy Island. Although it was a possible anchorage in settled weather, the swells and wind had forced us to go on to Tyrell, and we had to content ourselves with looking from the shore. The goats, pigs, cows and chickens, which were everywhere, made this a very pleasant rural stroll.

The entrance to the lagoon anchorage at St. Georges, Grenada, was really confusing, with a veritable rash of red buoys and nary a green. There is little point in telling how we handled it, as we were obviously wrong, scraping over the shoal by the sheer good luck of high tide, with less than six inches under the keel. Anchoring in mud, only slightly thicker than the water over it, was an additional to-be-missed experience. We put up with the smell and the pollution for two nights, then headed for the clean water and beautiful scenery of Mt. Hartman Bay.

In retrospect, Grenada was the best of the islands we visited in the Caribbean. We hired a car and drove all around it, by now accustomed to the Caribbean system of "find the attraction if you can." We were looking for an abandoned airfield with two old Russian planes on it, had given up and were heading for another place, when we drove onto the strip. The planes were there, derelict and overgrown with vegetation, but crawl-into-and-around worthy. Hailing our new system, we left the airfield and tried to find it again, therefore driving directly to the beach we really wanted to go to.

The northern beaches were delightful, empty, palm-fringed and backed by red cliffs. One had a rock reef about 30 feet out, forming a calm, mile-long pool. Not a tourist or tourist development in sight—for how long we wonder? The central highlands were cool, jungle covered and spectacular. We walked to a series of waterfalls, passing hundreds of nutmeg trees, many with the fruit littering the ground. Grenada is the world source for nutmeg, so we went to visit a nutmeg factory, owned by the local monopoly—growers sell to it, island-wide, or don't sell at all.

The workers, all women, reminding us of the tea factories in Sri Lanka, were paid on performance, and seemed very subdued, compared with the friendliness we met elsewhere in the island. Perhaps mindless, boring, repetitious jobs have that effect. All parts of the fruit are used, the outer case to make jams and jellies, the nut covering becomes mace, and the nut itself, of course, is the nutmeg. The Grenada rum-punch comes with a liberal shake of nutmeg powder on top. Nutmeg is an ingredient in most island dishes. After a while, we missed it if it wasn't there.

A nice touch—the Nutmeg Restaurant in downtown St. Georges provided a free taxi to and from the anchorage. From Mt. Hartman Bay it was about a twenty-minute drive, so the convenience was much appreciated, as the chicken rotis were not to be missed. It became our nightly haunt.

We did go to the main fruit and vegetable market, but the stall-holders seem determined to rip off all pale-faces, and quality wasn't great. The government run co-op was better, but with less choice. Best of all, for price, quality, quantity and variety, were the two huge supermarkets only a few miles away. Carole was thrilled with the abundance of American brands.

Close by the supermarkets was Grand Anse, a lovely, long beach, lined with the better of the hotels and restaurants. We breakfasted at one with tables set in the sand. Carole then went for a walk and found a visiting Canadian family with a son Ryan's age. Unfortunately their holidays were at their end, but Ryan and the lad had a happy couple of days together.

Ryan (13): *The father was using a cast net, and taught me how to throw it to make the complete circle needed to catch fish. You put the net on your shoulder and arm, hold some of the weights in the other hand, pivot and throw. It was not easy.*

Carole: *We were ready to sail to Tobago when we met the family, so stayed a few more days. As it happened those days meant contrary winds blew up and we didn't get to Tobago, but what's another island compared with play time?*

Getting in and out of Hartman was a little tricky, so we went next door to Prickly Bay, an even prettier place, with a wide open entrance. The prevalent north-easterly winds instantly became south-easterly—guess the direction of Tobago—so we forced ourselves to spend another couple of weeks in Prickly.

There we met John and Melodye, on "Second Millennium," who had, for three years, run the Caribbean Safety and Security Net, on SSB at 8:15 every morning, entirely at their own expense. Cruisers call in from all over the Caribbean with reports of thefts, navigation and other problems and information on anchorages. Overdue or missing boats are tracked, and often found within a day.

We eventually decided to see Tobago by 747, at another time, and sailed to Trinidad. It seemed like a good idea at the time, along the lines of booking a round-trip ticket on the "Titanic" or moving to Guadalcanal to get away from World War II. We would take "Dolphin Spirit" to Trinidad to get her bottom scraped and painted, her varnish renewed, and her canvas and upholstery freshened up. Carole would head off for a few weeks R&R in Los Angeles, while Ryan and I completed the rather long list of minor repair and maintenance jobs, lolling beside a hotel pool to recuperate between tasks. The observant reader will by now have a glimmer of an idea that all did not quite go according to plan. Do not, however, be under the misapprehension that all was doom and gloom.

Firstly we had a delightful sail from Grenada to Trinidad. Secondly, we found Trinidad, arriving right in the middle of the Dragon's Mouth, as the entrance is whimsically named. Thirdly, we really enjoyed Trinidad.

The Crew's Inn marina design was a little strange, being a combination of Med-moor and side tie. The side pontoons only come out half way, so our stern was held in place by lines to two posts. The marina had no dinghy, so the entering yacht was required to maneuver in, the crew toss bow lines to the waiting throng, then race to the stern to lasso the two posts before the bow grinds away on the concrete dock. We performed magnificently!

The newly appointed manager of the boat yard was an Australian, an ex-professional cricket player from Perth. The person he replaced apparently created considerable ill-will. It's interesting to see how rumors spread and become facts. We were strongly warned by several boats not to go to Crew's Inn as they drop boats on haul-out. Fact—they have never dropped a boat, nor has any other yard. The story started when a boat on the hard at the nearby Peakes Boatyard fell over and dominoed two others.

Crews Inn had a huge covered work space, an ex-bauxite storage shed, but DS's mast was just one foot too high to fit in. Haul-out was very professional, with a diver to ensure that the slings were correctly placed so as not to tear off or crush any vital parts. "Dolphin Spirit" looked so small and vulnerable on dry land, especially when suspended inside a 250-ton travel lift.

Carole caught her plane, and Ryan and I settled in our room, all according to plan. The varnish contract had been bid and agreed, with interior work to proceed at the same time as the bottom painting, so would be finished just as we re-floated, leaving the topsides to be varnished in the water. Settee cushions were delivered to the upholsterer, with completion set for two weeks. Everything would be over in three weeks, leaving Ryan and I a week to finish other jobs and clean up the boat before Carole's return.

Enter the weather. In violation of all accepted norms, it rained almost every day, so bottom painting took four weeks not two. That was just as well, as the interior varnishing took four weeks also. While the work was acceptable, the attention to detail and clean-up was so poor that we canceled the topside work. In addition, a worker stole some weird stuff—a knife of mine, a brass spray nozzle from a deck hose, and some Turkish money, a canceled library card, and Ryan's Scuba card from an old wallet of his. The wallet, which was discarded on the bunk, was how we noticed the losses.

Because of the rain and the interior and exterior work, Ryan and I couldn't get access to the boat, so most of our jobs didn't get done. Instead of finishing in two weeks, the upholsterer didn't start work for four weeks. The boat got back into the water on a Friday.

Carole*: I arrived on Saturday, to complete chaos instead of the newness I had expected—no salon cushions, the salon table away being varnished, dust from the pre-varnish sanding everywhere. Then the refrigeration quit, and the weather, hot and humid, didn't help. When, a week later, we got the cushions back, they didn't fit. A new refrigeration system, a thorough boat cleaning, a cunning cushion rearrangement and the return of the table resolved the crisis, though it seemed much more end-of-worldish at the time.*

As we've said, we really enjoyed our stay in Trinidad. Before Carole left (BCL), we hired a car and drove to the north coast to see the leatherback turtles coming ashore to lay eggs. These are huge beasts, some seven feet long and weighing over 1,000 pounds. We stayed the night at a local inn on the beach and were rewarded by about 150 turtles coming ashore under a full moon, with several still on the beach in the morning, providing some great daylight photos and video.

Carole: *Late in the afternoon, as we sat sipping wine under the palms, we could see the occasional head pop up just beyond the breaking waves. Not until dark, with the moonlight glistening on their broad backs, did one huge turtle after another begin to slowly lumber up the beach.*

Seeing these gigantic animals heaving themselves ashore through the silvery waves was an almost unworldly experience. It got even better as they sprayed sand everywhere during the preliminary nest excavation stage, then delicately and precisely, one rear flipper at a time, dug the egg chamber. One poor lady had half a flipper missing, making the resultant hole somewhat irregular. She would never have finished, or laid her eggs, because it was not perfect, so the guide had to help her. Then it was marvellous to see the hundred or so eggs come popping out, all soft and rubbery. Laying over, sand spraying started again as the nest was filled in, and an attempt made to disguise exactly where it was. A little difficult really, with tracks that could have been made by a fair-sized tractor leading to and from the site.

Although there were "rangers" on the beach, they were just locals who made money guiding the visitors. We were not allowed on the beach after 6pm without a guide and without paying a fee. Daylight hours were open access. No attempt was made to systematically tag or count the turtles, as there was no money available for this. It does seem a little strange that an endangered species, which provides one of the few real tourist attractions to Trinidad, is treated so cavalierly.

The beach accommodation was excellent. The beds were all covered with mosquito nets, a novelty to Carole and Ryan. We dined and breakfasted at their restaurant and were treated to probably the best cooking in Trinidad. Ryan made friends with Jason, the cook, a nephew of the owner, who supplemented his income by selling postcards of his turtle photos.

After Carole's return (ACR) we went back to see the baby turtles hatching. Making friends with the locals certainly helped, as we were taken to three nests that were boiling with babies, all in daylight, resulting in a guaranteed rise in Kodak stock. We got to help carry the little turtles closer to the water so that the circling vultures (ugly black birds in the hundreds) remained unfed. A rudimentary effort was made to count the babies, but with up to fifty nests a night hatching and only a couple of "guides," not much could be done.

Ryan (13): *I had learned in Australia, when we went to watch the turtles come ashore at Mon Repos Beach, near Bundaberg, that the baby turtles need to travel most of the journey from nest to water by themselves, so as to be properly imprinted with the location. We pointed the ones going the wrong way in the right direction.*

Driving east, then north, introduced us to a unique Trini feature. We were proceeding along a rather crowded, convoluted, two-lane road, peppered with traffic lights and constricted by parked vehicles, when we came upon a broad, four-lane, magnificent highway that headed off right where we wanted to go. Elated, we swung onto it, and zoomed along in comfort and virtual isolation. After a while, a vague sort of unease set in. Why were the only other vehicles on the road the occasional Maxi-Taxi? The unease grew, so we got off and asked about the road. Yes, all 30 miles of it went to where we wanted to go, but use was restricted to Maxi-Taxis and government vehicles. The other 99.99% of the vehicles had to put up with the old two-lane horror.

Another BCL trip was to Caroni Swamp to see the thousands of scarlet ibis flying in to their night roosting trees. They were magnificent, flying close overhead with the afternoon sun blazing off their scarlet feathers. Unfortunately for us, but fortunately for the ibis, boats were not allowed closer than half-a-mile from the roosts. Still, seeing the green trees sprout thousands of red flowers was amazing. We did get up close and personal with a small boa and a tree porcupine, and the boat ride through miles of mangrove channels was a delight in itself.

To keep my hand in, I did some free marketing consulting work for a couple of local companies. The standard of assistance they were previously getting must have been abysmal, as they expressed a very high regard for my work. I was glad to see that my old expertise hadn't atrophied too much, and we were treated to lunch and dinner at excellent local restaurants we would never have known about, or visited.

We decided, at the last minute of course, that we would get a new dinghy, so as to provide a better platform for towing Ryan on skis and wakeboard. At over six foot, albeit skinny, he was a fair load. I walked to the local (only) dinghy showroom to find that they opened only by appointment.

The next day we had hired a car to do provisioning, so I drove to head office to make an appointment. Yes, they had a suitable dinghy in stock. No, they wouldn't take the old dinghy as trade, as it is illegal for cruisers to sell anything in Trinidad, and a trade-in is regarded as a sale. This must restrict new dinghy sales to locals (negligible) and to cruisers without dinghies or with dinghies suitable only for scrap (marginally over negligible). No wonder the showroom was never open. In passing, I asked when I could take delivery, if I paid immediately. "Only five or six working days, because it is in stock," was the response. Apparently sales to cruisers are duty free, so two signatures have to be obtained from Customs, and this takes five-plus days. The weather was good, we were ready to go, so we decided to wait until Venezuela for a new dinghy.

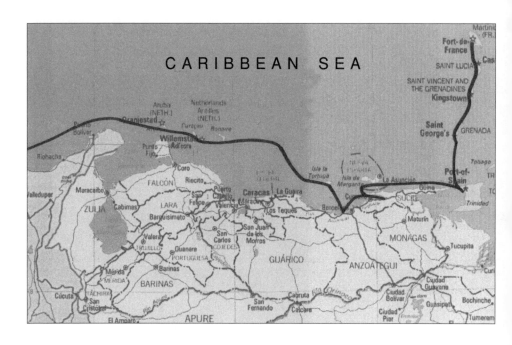

Venezuela
Year Six
July 4 to September 9

The solo cruiser woke to the sound of footsteps on his deck. Grabbing his automatic rifle, he opened fire. The people on deck did the same, and there was an exchange of shots for several minutes. During a lull, the invaders announced themselves to be Venezuelan Coast Guard, and promptly arrested the cruiser for shooting at them. In spite of the dozens of rounds fired, no one was injured.

This incident happened off the Venezuelan coast, in an area with a reputation for pirates. We had avoided pirates in the Malacca Straits and around Socrota Island, so wanted to continue the good luck run. "Bolero," (dinghy name "Ravel") and "Ciris" were two Dutch boats heading for Venezuela, and we teamed up with them for security.

The check-out from Trinidad had its small problems. Apparently Carole was supposed to check-in with the Immigration in Chagauramas the next day after her arrival and check-in by Immigration at the airport. By not doing so (it said in the fine print of the stamp in her passport) she had been illegally in Trinidad for weeks and was therefore subject to a fine and deportation. The fine was $US10 approximately, and we were leaving anyhow, so it wasn't a big deal after all.

An overnight sail took us to Los Testigos Islands. Inhabited by only a few fishermen and by a contingent of the Venezuelan Coast Guard, the islands were a real relief after the crowds and dirty water of Chagauramas We checked in with the Coast Guard and they allowed us to stay for two days, then came on board for a very thorough equipment and safety check.

Ryan and I scrambled over a huge sand hill to the other side of the island and a wonderful, deserted beach that was also a nesting ground for leatherback turtles. We found the body of one that had died some time ago and a piece of driftwood that looked just like a dragon.

Carole: I was persuaded to make the climb the next day—it really was a steep, loose sand slope—and posed for many pictures to record this historic event.

The lizard life was fantastic, ranging from little grey tail/yellow body ones to a couple of huge, five-foot-long, black iguanas that we were very pleased to see run away. The snorkeling gave us several lobsters and some nice fish.

We sailed to Margarita Island and anchored with the crowd of yachts off Porlomar. The entrance to the anchorage was blocked by several nets, in circles, clearly defined by the thousands of pelicans that lined them and filled them. Presumably the net circles contained fish, as the pelicans were continually diving, but the numbers of birds would seem to leave little for the fishermen. We entered by driving between two circles. A later visit by dinghy discovered several lines between the nets, so we must have been saved by our full keel. The pelicans were a major entertainment. They flew in long lines, dipping and rising in concert.

Carole: Laurie and I, under the influence of sunset cocktails, awarded points to each group for neatness of line, co-ordination, complexity of maneuvers and general beakiness. Perhaps getting score cards printed was a little extreme.

Juan was the check-in/out agent to use. He spoke excellent English and French (as did his mother, who seemed to be the driving force behind the operation), had the only real dinghy dock, with security guard, Internet access, free bus to shopping, U.S. telephone, telephone cards and other necessary cruiser requirements. Margarita was a duty-free island, so some things were cheap and the shopping trip was quite a production. After completing shopping, we lined up and had our goods boxed and numbered. They then went by separate truck to Juan's place, where we claimed them.

Diesel came to us by boat, hand-pumped from drums to our tank. It was clean and less than $US0.45 per gallon after all that. The boat driver was extremely proud of the fact that he had 21 children, expressing his pride through a series of hand, arm and pelvic movements, that left no doubt as to his opinion of his virility. Son (number unknown) sat quietly pumping diesel through the demonstration. Perhaps he had heard it all before, and was just waiting for the old man to retire so he and his son could take over.

Carlos, owner of Top Banana Tours took "Bolero" and "Ciris," and us on a tour of the island. He spoke excellent English, as he had lived in the

States for years, and served us drinks all the way. Luckily, as our Dutch friends were big drinkers, after a while they didn't notice I couldn't keep up.

Carole: *A colorful church and a good seafood lunch under umbrellas on a beach, huge caged macaws at a tourist shop, and two inebriated cruisers—what a day!*

Ryan (13): *We saw a huge, black tarantula that lived in a house in the village and I got to touch its legs—like velvet. Mum didn't want to be in the same country.*

Juan checked us in and out at the same time, and we set sail for the Golfo de Cariaco, on mainland Venezuela. The big news was that, after a long drought, Ryan finally got back into catching fish—two within minutes of each other, and they were welcome eating.

The Golfo runs west to east for about 20 miles and has an interesting easterly wind of around 25 to 30 knots that came up around 11am every day and howled for the rest of the day. We headed for Laguna Grande, a huge bay with lots of anchorages around its perimeter. The surrounding mountains and cliffs were red and white rock, bare of trees, but with a beard of green mangroves at water level. In the early-morning and late-evening sunlight, the colors were astounding. Deserted, except for transient oyster-gatherers, we were very happy just to swing at anchor there.

A perfect place for Ryan to wakeboard, so we broke out the 25-HP outboard, which adamantly refused to start. I tried new plugs, new fuel, pats and kisses, kicks and swear words, but nothing changed its inoperative mind.

The next day we moved up-gulf to Puerto Nuevo, anchoring off a restaurant, and enjoying a fly-by of flamingos followed by the best sunset of the trip. What made it so great was the reflection in the still water—gold on black. A local dinghy circled us and the small waves made the reflections coalesce and circle like golden/aqua/grey/pink/crimson oil paint poured on the surface. Monet would not have been able to capture it with all his genius.

In the midst of a long dinghy exploration, attempting to find the elusive Venezuelan scarlet ibis, the 15-HP outboard ceased operating some three miles from DS. We hailed a passing local boat, loaded to the waterline with long poles, and were towed back. We paid them for their trouble, probably more than they would have earned in the day, but worth every penny. This time the cause of the stoppage was obvious, a broken connection in the fuel system. Who would imagine that, after five years of trouble-free operation, both motors broke down within two days of each other.

Carole: *Word must have spread because boats kept appearing and circling the crazy gringos who paid $US50 to be towed.*

Deciding that the Golfo didn't like us, we moved to Bahia Manare in the Mochima National Park. A pretty place, under the shadow of cliffs heavily undercut at water level, it had the added advantage, in our outboard-less state, that Ryan and I could swim from DS to the reefs for snorkeling.

Late in the day, we were a little distracted by a very fast powerboat, crewed by a young couple, which anchored nearby. Immediately the anchor was down, the couple, standing on the bow, became locked in a very close embrace. This lasted about 45 minutes. They then swam ashore and stood on the sand in another embrace for a further 30 minutes. Perhaps tiring, they then sat at the water's edge, and again entwined arms, legs, lips. We lost interest, and therefore can only record that some 40 minutes later they were embracing back on the boat, and up anchored and left some ten minutes after that. Ah, youth!

The next day we headed for Puerto La Cruz, past the biggest cement plant we have ever seen, perched right on the edge of the national park. A rain shower suddenly reduced visibility to 50 feet—we couldn't see the bow—as we were negotiating some tight passages between islands. Radar works, but doesn't show the little fishing boats and their nets. Carole held her breath for the whole time and saved us.

Maremares Marina was part of a five-star hotel complex, and marina residents received the same treatment and facilities as hotel guests, all for $US16 per day including power, water, cable TV, telephone, and 24-hour guards armed with shotguns. It was deep in a canal development that contained many hotels, a couple of huge shopping malls, thousands of houses, and three other marinas. When we called on VHF, they sent out a guide, which was just as well, as there was an unmarked rock in mid-canal at one spot, and the twists and turns of the canals were not immediately obvious to the newcomer.

A huge swimming pool with a wave generator and crossed by a large suspension bridge, gym, restaurants, room service plus four clean fresh towels every day—can a marina be better? The water around the boats was dirty, as might be expected in a man-made canal system, and grew stuff on props and lines faster than you can believe. The passing powerboats created a little wash, but not enough to be disturbing. The sunrise and sunset were slightly obstructed by buildings, but the electrical storms were the best we have seen since Australia. To make up for this lack of absolute perfection, the hotel management threw a cocktail party for marina guests with free drinks and food every Wednesday night,

Venezuela

Carole: There had been continuing political unrest in Venezuela, and the President was not friendly towards the U.S. I was very concerned that the narrow canals we had to negotiate to leave could have been easily blocked, leaving us trapped and helpless. The Army post at the channel entrance didn't help.

Deciding that Venezuela needed exploring, we hired Vicky to take us on a two day trip to see Las Cuevos de Guacharo, near Caripe, a five-hour drive away. These caves are huge, and the home for some eighteen thousand guacharo birds, which live in the dark, come out only at night, and echo-locate like bats.

Vicky, who did the laundry at the marina, was just starting her guiding business, and we discovered that she had been to Caripe only once before, by a different road. I had luckily brought along a road map, so was able to point us in the general direction. We stopped often to ask directions of the locals, always provided with a smile, and an invariable point of the finger back in the direction from which we had come.

Alongside the road ran several pipes. "Water," said I. "Oil," said Vicky. We then passed an oil field with flaring burn-offs everywhere. As the countryside was empty of people except for scattered villages, and it was so very third-world, we tended to forget that Venezuela was one of the bigger oil producers in the world. Many of the small towns consisted of concrete houses, built by the Government in past years. In the countryside, a common house had walls made of interwoven branches, covered with sun-dried mud. In our opinion, these looked nicer, and were in better repair, than the cement town houses.

All went well until we ran out of fuel, some ten miles out of Caripe. Apparently getting lost several times had caused Vicky to totally misjudge her fuel-tank capacity. In spite of all the oil, gas stations were notable by their absence. The friendliness of the Venezuelans became immediately apparent. Everyone passing (one vehicle every ten minutes or so) stopped to offer assistance, but none could help. Vicky finally persuaded a truck to take her to Caripe, get fuel, and bring her back. We sat by the side of the road (actually on the road, as there was no shoulder, only a drop into a ditch) and enjoyed the views.

We made it to Caripe for a late lunch—excellent Venezuelan dishes at a small roadside restaurant—and then further up into the mountains to check into our hotel, Niebla Azul. Built into the side of a cliff overlooking the valley and town, it offered panoramic views, comfortable rooms, but no restaurant, bar or other facilities.

The parking lot and office were at road level. A circular ramp, hung off the cliff, led down to the first level of rooms, and to the long walkway that went to the main apartments. Six in number, these cascaded down the cliff, connected by steep rock stairs. Luckily, we had the top one. It featured a unique, in our experience, sliding-glass door, which could be locked and unlocked only from outside. We had to unlatch a small sliding-glass panel in the door, step outside, lock the door with the key, then step back inside and close the panel.

The rooms were small, two-bedroom apartments with kitchen, and were somewhat expensive at $US70 per night for two people. Vicky now informed us that we had to pay for her accommodation, so she spent the night in our apartment on the couch, at no extra cost. Not a real inconvenience, just an irritation. She compensated in part by making me an excellent cup of coffee the next morning, and the truly gorgeous view from the verandah was priceless.

Perched as they were on the top of a cliff overlooking the valley, town and mountain ranges, the apartments had unrestricted views in every direction. Where the cliff began to slope into the valley were small farms, with workers tilling and tending the crops by hand, as it was far too steep and stony for any machinery. Birds flew everywhere. Venezuela had over 250 species of birds, more than all of Europe and the U.S. combined. We counted only about ten, but that was enough to keep us very absorbed, and almost ignoring the view.

With all the bird-watching and swooning over the view, we made it to the caves just in time for the last tour of the day. There was a paved path for the almost two miles that we walked into the caves, but no lights other than the propane lamp carried by the guide. Our group comprised three locals and the three of us, with a young lady guide who spoke no English. She had the disconcerting habit of speaking normally until she made a prepared speech, at which time her voice increased in volume about five times, and lost all inflection. We guessed she had been trained with large groups and couldn't adjust for small ones. Mostly we got the gist of what she said— big cave, birds, dark, look out for the hole, in various permutations. Unfortunately she hadn't been well light-trained and her lantern alternately blinded us, or left us stumbling in the dark.

The guacharos hang out about half a mile into the cave, high in the roof and unseen. As we entered the cave we gradually became aware of a distant hum, a vibration really. This built in intensity and volume as we penetrated further, and became a roar as we approached the section they were. Anyone not knowing that it was caused by birds would have every reason to get out quickly.

Occasional birds flew across the cave, heralded by a series of loud clicks, which was probably their sonar at work. The floor was covered with droppings, seed casings, seeds, and sprouted seeds. These latter seemed to grow to about a foot high, then die through lack of sunlight. We saw several adults and chicks on the floor, the adults probably sick and dying, the chicks fallen from nests. They were large birds with whiskery faces, a little owl-like. I thought them ugly, with dull coloring. Carole found them cute.

Ryan (13): *The guide put one of the birds on my arm and it crawled up to sit on my shoulder. I suppose it was sick, as wild birds wouldn't be so tame. Mum and Dad were very worried about lice, so they wouldn't let me hold it for long.*

Carole: *I saw a rat! We were a long way into the dark cave, so I couldn't run out like I wanted to.*

We do have to give every credit to Carole, who continued on even after she saw the rat. Probably the alternative of being alone in the dark with the rodents was a little less appealing. The caves themselves were rather uninteresting, huge, but with little in the way of stalactites or stalagmites. Because of this, the guide was reduced to giving shadow shows to keep up interest after we passed through the bird part. In a couple of spots we had to crawl through narrow passages (me with a great deal of difficulty), and in spite of the lack of drama, it was enjoyable

Several times the guide turned out the lantern, and our concern then became how do we find our way out, in the pitch black, if she couldn't light it again. For the record, our best plan was to take off our shoes so we could feel the path, with Ryan in front because he was more likely to survive a fall down the several sets of rock steps we had to negotiate. We never did determine how to work out which way was out. On the way back, Ryan persisted in walking ahead, just out of lamp range, to test his newly developing manhood. Carole and I were very happy to be in the light.

A small tour of Caripe—two one-way streets and a huge guaracho statue that looks a little like the eagle on the U.S. coat of arms—alerted us to the predominance of stands selling strawberries in various forms. We stopped at one for strawberries and cream, and very nice they were too. The proprietor gave us a glass of strawberry wine, and we bought a bottle as a good-will gesture, because he let us wash the strawberries we ate in bottled water. The wine was expensive, and a rather ghastly drink that still lurks in the fridge waiting for unsuspecting guests. This berry-dominance was a little strange, as no strawberries are grown in the area.

Back to the caves at dusk, to see the evening issuance of the birds in search of fruits and nuts. The build-up was dramatic, with the soft roar getting louder and more urgent, as the birds worked their way closer to the entrance. Finally, loud enough to make conversation difficult, the birds began to come out—an anti-climax. As the noise level dropped, we knew they were leaving, but instead of the mass exodus we expected, they flew in small groups, often below the tree line and therefore unseen. More entertaining were the fireflies, dancing and pulsing everywhere. Worth the visit for the noise crescendo alone.

Having come to Caripe by the inland route, we returned by way of our favorite Golfe de Cariaco, along the southern side where we could look across the water to our old anchorages. Vicky's vehicle began to exhibit alarming signs, such as the total inability to get up even small slopes in anything but first gear at maximum revs. Then the revs became less than maximum, and it began to appear as if we would be pushing the remaining 100 or so miles. Luckily we limped into Cumana and, leaving us at a restaurant, Vicky headed off to find a mechanic—did we mention that it was a holiday? Four hours later, she reappeared in a taxi, which took us, at her expense, back to Puerto La Cruz.

Ryan acted as our interpreter in Venezuela, his Spanish having become fluent. He dealt with conversations over the radio, went with me to the repair shops and helped every time the adults floundered with the language, which was often. The Venezuelan Spanish is very fast and some pronunciations differ, but Ryan picked it up well.

Carole: *Ryan began learning Spanish during our first year of cruising. I had my college books from when I last took Spanish eight years earlier. Although I am reasonably proficient in grammar, my pronunciation is poor, so we used a lot of CDs and tapes. A special favorite was "Nat King Cole Sings Espanol" that I had used in High School and now purchased on CD. Ryan learned all the songs and wrote them out in Spanish. We would sometimes have to check words with a local Spanish speaker. The only way we could get the second Harry Potter book was in Spanish, so Ryan had to learn fast so he could read it.*

I reflected that, back when I was teaching, my students would translate for their Spanish-speaking parents at Parent Conferences, and here we were having Ryan translate for us every day.

When we returned to the real world and Ryan started school in Grade 10, his Spanish was at such a level he was put into the AP class. At the end of that year, he received the top honor at the school, surpassing even the native Spanish speakers in his class. I am really proud of him and of the fact that I, really only an English speaker, taught him.

We got our outboards fixed at the local Yamaha repair shop in Puerto La Cruz. The 25-HP was soon running again, but the 15-HP was another story. Finally apparently fixed, we put it in the dinghy and headed off, only to have it immediately stop and refuse to start. Back to the shop, where they diagnosed a carburetor full of water—funny how the 25-HP remained unaffected using the same fuel tank. In the dinghy again, the motor worked perfectly, but the propeller didn't. Modern props don't have shear-pins, but a sort of rubber gasket that ruptures under stress. Therefore, instead of replacing a 50-cent pin and being underway again in a few minutes, we had to buy a new propeller—isn't progress wonderful?

Now I discovered that Yamaha, in their wisdom, have different specifications in different countries, for the same engine. The propeller for the Australian 15-HP (ours) was totally different from that of the Venezuelan version, which was different from the U.S. one. Makes real sense! An e-mail to my daughter in Australia, and we had a new propeller in six days. In the meantime, I got to be on first name terms with a lot of taxi drivers, who would stop in the street and ask me about progress with the outboard. Better still, if empty they would take me back to the hotel—free of charge. Looking pitiful has some advantages.

The good part of all of this was that we decided to fill in the time by making a day-trip to Angel Falls, the tallest in the world. Steve Patterson, an American living in Venezuela, flew us up and back in his four-seater, and arranged all the tours. It was one of the best things we have done, ranking right up there with Petra.

Vicky picked us up and drove us to the airport in the infamous vehicle, now fixed. We hadn't quite made it out of the hotel gate before the car caught fire, and filled with smoke. The flames were put out, we waved away the smoke and continued—what else?

Ryan got to sit in the co-pilot seat, and Steve gave him a continuous running commentary on everything he was doing. Ryan now believes he can fly a plane! Carole hates small planes, but put on a brave front, except when we flew into clouds. The bones in my hand mended quite well, thank you.

Carole: I had flown in a small plane only once before, with a friend who had just got his pilot's license. As a nice gesture, he obtained Air Traffic Control permission to fly over my house, and I was thrilled. This diversion apparently then meant he had to approach the landing in a different way, couldn't set the plane down, and had to quickly request permission to go up again. We just missed the fence at the end of the runway and scraped the trees just beyond it. The next try to land was successful and I asked my friend if he had been scared. "Petrified" was his not re-assuring reply.

I never made a sound during the whole ordeal, but did resolve to ask the pilots of any planes smaller than a 747 how many hours they had flown. Yes, I asked Steve.

We flew south, across the Orinoco River, into the heart of Venezuela. Camiama, the nearest town to the falls, was accessible only by air. Dirt airstrip, ramshackle, one-story shacks, rutted, dirt roads and loungers everywhere, it was a perfect movie set for the frontier town on the edge of the wilderness. The local character, a retired diamond miner (presumably unsuccessful), was there to meet us and add color to an already perfect scene.

The river bank was a white-sand beach shaded by swaying palms, more Caribbeanny than any island we had been to so far. It was almost a shock to look across the river to the line of roaring yellow falls. At the beach we boarded a large canoe, with a 48-HP Yamaha. This modernity could be overlooked, as the canoe was carved out of a single log. It took us along the foot of three falls, each about 100-feet high and several hundred feet long, all in full spate as it was the rainy season. The yellow color was courtesy of dissolved tannins from submerged trees and other growths. As we disembarked on the far bank, we were treated to the rare sight of several river otters rolling and diving in the foam from the falls.

An easy climb and a flat walk across a small mesa took us to the gorge of another fall. It was quite a scramble down to the bottom. I got Carole down by promising that she would not have to go back the same way—I lied. There we changed into swim suits (the guide obligingly turned his back), Carole by means of contortions under a sarong, and walked under the falls.

The water thundered down, occasionally scant inches away, creating a swirling wind that immediately soaked us. In one spot the wind was so strong, and the falling water so close, that it was difficult to breathe, and a real struggle to walk. Contact lenses wouldn't have stood a chance. Ropes had been installed at the worst sections just a few months previously. Before that people had to hold hands to negotiate the narrow, rocky track. Ryan was in his element, a sense of danger, and wet too! Carole did extremely well, getting through even the worst areas with scarcely a shriek (not that she could have been heard over the roar of the water). Out the other side, a few photos, then back again, retracing our path. It was cold, wet and wonderful.

The falls are called Frog Falls as they are the home of a brilliant black and orange frog. It secretes a poison behind its ears, used by the Indians to tip their blow-gun darts. We saw a couple and, despite Ryan's urgings, decided not to test the poison's efficiency. The only other animal we saw was a small dead snake. The males wanted an anaconda, and got a foot-long miniature!

We then scrambled up the gorge side to the top of the falls—photo-op—and into another canoe for a five-mile jaunt up-river. The almost total absence of bird and animal life was somewhat of a surprise, but perhaps understandable as the river levels were some 10 to 15 feet above normal. We disembarked at the foot of some rapids, impassable by boat, and walked up the hill to the sole dwelling—a souvenir shop. Its saving grace was that all the goods were made by the family living in the house, but were faithful copies of the usual tourist junk, if better made.

Back down the river we went, to the top of the first falls. Given our recent experiences with Yamaha outboards, we must admit to a little trepidation as we raced to within a couple of hundred feet of the drop before pulling into the bank. We did note that the canoes without outboards were the ones parked nearest to the edge. There was a small hydro-station supplying electricity to the town, but not to the surrounding villages.

Our guide lived in a village some miles away, with no power, which was why (his story) he had so many children. All of his kids, with the exception of the just-born baby, were living with his mother in Bolivar, a hundred miles to the north, so they could go to school. Only in the past few months have some of the park fees gone to the local Indians. They have used this income to provide village amenities, fly sick people to hospitals, and assist those without work. Our guide was on the Council and was very proud of the progress being made.

We strolled to Camiano for an excellent lunch at the only restaurant outside of the hotel.

Carole: *It may have been for Laurie and Ryan, but I got sick from it, the second time on the trip, the last being in Egypt at a McDonalds.*

The hotel was $US300 per person per night, and had a wonderful view of the falls from the outdoor restaurant/bar, which was reserved for guests, not riff-raff off boats. They did allow us to visit their souvenir shop, however.

Steve took us to a local handicraft shop—"buy these baskets, they will soon be museum pieces"—was the sales pitch. Perhaps they will be, as they were certainly well made. Carole almost bought something. That statement needs explanation. Carole never, but never, buys anything on first sight. She has to look, then find similar articles in other places, then come back to look again, then go home for a think, then look at still more, then go back and buy. This procedure does impose some restrictions on purchasing when we are on a tour, perhaps fortunately, as otherwise "Dolphin Spirit" would have been overloaded and sunk long ago.

Carole: *Thinking back on all the purchases I didn't make, like the Fijian special implements designed for eating human brains, the only one I really regret not making was a sandalwood carving we found in Indonesia, but at*

$2,400 I couldn't just impulse buy.

Ryan (13): *Several monkeys were running around. They were not friendly and bared their huge teeth every time I got close. Watching them was better than watching Mum window-shop.*

Then came the highlight of the day, the fly past Angel Falls. This is the land of huge tepuis, steep-sided mesas, which were the setting for Conan Doyle's *The Lost World*, the original dinosaur survival book. Looking at these dark, vertical-sided monsters, their tops often hidden in cloud and protected by slabs of stone reminiscent of the Easter Island statues, it was easy to visualize prehistoric animals still roaming there.

Every tepui was streaming water—waterfalls everywhere, an absolutely wonderful, breathtaking sight. They fell from the tops of the cliffs, and from part-way down, they were roaring torrents and misty veils, they bounced off rocks or fell straight, or were all of the above. Angel Falls was almost an anti-climax, as we were so filled with the sights that it just seemed to be a larger—much larger—fall. It really was magnificent, as we saw it in full flood, dropping from the tepui top to the mist and trees below. The clouds came down, and Steve decided that more flying up the canyons wasn't worth the possibility of a close encounter with one of the cliffs, so we flew the two hours back to Puerto La Cruz. Vicky drove us back to the marina without incident!

Carole: *I am nervous in a 747, and here we were in a tiny plane flying only inches away from cliffs. Then, on the way back, we skirted around a huge thunderstorm. Seeing lightning from the boat is scary, but at eye level it is positively petrifying. Not my idea of a good time. Looking back, the fly past was truly magnificent, I just wish I had known we would survive. Of course, I wish I had known that about our entire trip.*

Maremares hotel/marina was only a short walk from La Baguette bakery (great bread and to-die-for chocolate goodies), a gelato shop, five Italian restaurants in a row (we tried them all and liked them all), a very big enclosed mall, and was only a dinghy ride away from Plaza Major, a huge open air mall with supermarket, picture theater (in English mostly) and banks. Carole tried a butcher shop, unique in that we sat at a counter and sipped coffee while the butcher cut our meat specially, but didn't like the ambience, smell, or seeing chops and steaks cut from hunks of red flesh. We then found that the supermarket offered the same service, even to the coffee. The taste of Venezuelan beef was different, so when we provisioned we mostly bought chicken, New Zealand lamb, and smoked pork chops.

Venezuela

Staying at the hotel was a family from Texas, with a son Ryan's age, and another a little younger. Ryan and Jake became inseparable. Bob was in the oil business and the family was moving to Venezuela for a couple of years.

Carole: I went house hunting with Cathy and learned a lot about how the wealthy spend money. The houses and apartments we looked at rented for between $US4,000 and $US10,000 per month. One house featured thirteen (yes 13) bathrooms. All were in or around the El Morro development, where our marina was situated. This was the new "in" spot, particularly for expats and rich locals. Some of the houses were stunning, but I saw many a magnificent house next door to a lot covered with garbage, a peculiarity of a developing third-world country. If ever the political situation stabilizes here, Puerto La Cruz would be a great place for a vacation home, on a canal, boat at the door, great islands only an hour away. Actually, a three or four bedroom house on a canal could be bought for around $US300,000, much cheaper than renting.

We finally left Puerto La Cruz, very slowly as it turned out, because our propeller was a ball of barnacles after just three weeks of sitting still. To get out of our marina spot we had to reverse around a mooring buoy, and between two others, all three with lines attached to other boats. Given our usual propensity to reverse in any direction except that intended, we had two dinghies standing by to push and shove. "Dolphin Spirit" reversed out wonderfully, going exactly where required, as if on rails. The hidden benefit of a barnacle-ball prop.

The disadvantage was a slow passage to the anchorage at Chimana Grande Island, where Ryan and I dove and cleaned off the barnacles. Only four miles from Puerto La Cruz we were in another world—clean water, surrounded by pretty red and white cliffs, fish, birds, calm, no one around. While in Puerto La Cruz, we were subjected to rain and thunderstorms every day. At the island we were dry, watching the clouds hug the mainland.

Tropical storm/hurricane Chantel was lurking, so we stayed a couple of days until it passed, then sailed to Tortuga Island. This was an absolutely flat piece of land, some two feet above water level, with no trees at all. Herradura was a lovely anchorage, surrounded by a blinding, white beach. We arrived on a Sunday, when the rich and indolent from Caracas fly their private planes over for a day on the beach. The airstrip was defined only by the tire marks of previous landings, so each pilot did his/her own thing. Some even left after dark, presumably guided by starlight, as that was the only illumination. Most buzzed the anchored yachts at mast level.

The northerly swell rocked us a little too much, so we left for an overnight sail to Los Roques, a small island group renowned for its clear water and reefs. The passage was pleasant, except for a thunderstorm that chased us, came up beside us, and stayed there flashing and growling.

Carole: *Of course it was during my watch that the thunderstorm appeared on our stern and then caught us. I always run around unplugging everything as soon as any storm gets within ten seconds (time between lightning and when you hear the related thunder) and I make sure we maintain a constant radar watch—most storms are clearly defined on radar. We have known three boats hit by lightning, and the results were not pretty, so it pays to be cautious. At sea, our mast is the tallest thing around, so of course I am nervous.*

Grand Roque Island has big rocks—small mountains—the only ones in the island group. The rest of the islands are Tortuga high, but with trees. The wind was blowing 25 knots as we tried to anchor on the narrow shelf off the town (the only civilization in the island group). After three tries to get the anchor to set, we moved to the adjacent Francisquis Island, anchoring in a lovely lagoon with a lot of other sail and motorboats. The pretty beaches were filled every day with tourists brought over by large dinghies from Grand Roque. They were either staying in the several small hotels there, or had flown in from the mainland for a day of sun and sand.

When the wind dropped a little, Ryan and I dinghied over to Grand Roque to check-in with the authorities. As we had already checked out for Bonaire from Puerto La Cruz (with intermediate stops permitted), we expected this to be a formality. Not so. First the Coast Guard, where we were given a thorough grilling as to where we had come from, and why we were here. They inspected every piece of paper and made copious notes, finally keeping our Zarpe (exit document) and giving us a form to be filled out by three other offices, then returned to them so they could check we had done it.

Next it was the Guardia Nacionale, who also inspected every document and took copious notes. Then to the airport, where we paid $US2 per foot of boat length plus 10,000 Bolivars per person (approximately $US150 in total) as fees to stay in the area. This was all payable only in Bolivars, and there were no banks or formal money changers on the island. On to Imparque, the department that runs the National Park, where we were given documents allowing us to stay. Then back to the CG to prove we had done it all.

A couple of days before we arrived, the Coast Guard had detained 14 foreign-flagged vessels for illegally chartering, and escorted them back to Puerto La Cruz. This explained why we were asked, over and over, how many people we had on board. The transgressions of the few made it all a little difficult for the law-abiding majority, but then that's not new.

The anchorage was pleasant, the snorkeling between the two islands was excellent, but the wind never dropped below 20 knots and grew a little tiresome. We enjoyed watching the pelicans dive-bombing the fish, but eventually the constant passage of boats decided us to move to Sarqui Island, a great idea. Lovely clear water, nice coral, great fish, diving pelicans, pretty beach, all that was missing were the palm trees to make it truly perfect.

Lazing in a little protected pool, we met the people off "Volare" a Venezuelan boat. They spoke perfect English, were of German ancestry, lived in Venezuela all their lives, and had been coming to Los Roques for thirty-plus years. Apparently it was now once again cheaper to fly to Miami and shop, rather than do it in Caracas. This used to be the case in the 70s, when even houseservants would have enough money to shop in the U.S.

I became all excited one day when I spotted a flock of pink flamingos on a neighboring island, and wouldn't rest until we had gone over to get pictures. The island was marked as a "Do Not Anchor" zone in the charts, so we undertook a wet and bumpy dinghy ride. Carole insisted on our taking life jackets, food and water, and alerting another boat to stand by on the radio in case we needed help. She was about to load in the EPIRB, when I called halt—we were only going a couple of miles, even though it was into the open ocean.

"Do not Anchor" was an unnecessary warning, as the island was surrounded by a rocky reef that we got the dinghy over only with difficulty. The flamingos were at one end of the island, and we could find a landing only at the other. In the excitement over radios and EPIRB, we forgot shoes, but luckily most of the jagged lava and coral rocks that made up the ground were covered with a soft carpet of ice-plant. Delicately, we trudged up the island, through a swamp of ankle-deep sticky mud and took the requisite photos. A passing launch waved at us to get away, so we retraced the epic journey to find the launch contained Imparque park wardens; the island was forbidden to visit, and they gave us a citation. Nice men, they wanted us on Grand Roque in four hours to deal with the citation, but gave us three days when we pointed out that this was impossible given the wind direction and other sailboat-related problems.

To avoid a bash with "Dolphin Spirit" into the 25-knot winds, Ryan and I went to Grand Roque the next day by hired fishing boat. We smashed into waves for an hour and got soaking wet—Ryan insisted we would have been dryer swimming. First we went to the Coast Guard and checked out to Bonaire, receiving a brand new Zarpe. Then to the Imparque office to face the music, but it was closed for lunch. The only supermarket was also closed, so we found a restaurant and had a nice fish meal.

Imparques finally opened and the officers gave us the cold-shoulder treatment until the manager arrived. Ryan had been very helpful to him on our last visit, translating for an English couple, so he was really friendly. I received the obligatory lecture, and had to sign a letter saying that if I ever did it again I would be summarily shot, or some similar penalty (the letter was in Spanish), smiles and handshakes all round. The other staff continued to look sour. The supermarket never opened, and the trip back was a sleigh ride, with the wind behind, and the fishing boat surfing down waves.

Every day the water boiled in some part of the anchorage, as schools of large fish fed on schools of small fish. One morning it was our turn and the feeding frenzy was right around the boat. Dancing and bobbing above the melee was a flock of sea birds that seemed to be picnicking on the scraps the big fish left. We were fascinated spectators, totally ignored by the participants. Two pelicans then began diving on fish right at the boat. Did you know that the bottom of the pelican's beak inflates like a balloon when it hits the water?

An easy 40-mile down wind sail took us to Aves de Barlovento, a little spec of an island at the bottom end of a huge reef. Covered with mangroves, the island was home to thousands of sea birds. The water colors were magazine magnificent, with reefs apparently to the horizon. We took a dinghy ride to the main reef to check out an anchorage there, and to do a little spear fishing. Ryan and I were in the water, but soon scrambled back into the dinghy babbling about huge barracuda. Carole naturally then refused to enter the water, a pity as the coral and fish were exceptional.

Ryan (13): *We were in about five feet of water, swimming amongst the coral, when this shape appeared in my peripheral vision. It was the biggest barracuda I have seen, over five feet long, allowing for the magnification of water and mask, which made him seem even bigger. Dark silver in color, he simply swam past, keeping an eye on us, but not turning his head. We headed for the dinghy, straight into a second, smaller, three-foot long, bright silver one.*

Dad and I went spear fishing the next day on a nearby reef. I had wounded a fish that got away, and Dad had just finished saying it might attract barracuda, when over a coral head loomed the bigger brother of the five-footer we had seen previously. This time he circled us, then headed straight in, stopping only a foot or so from the spear Dad kept pointed at him. There was no doubt he was checking out the lunch. After a very long look, he smiled (Dad and I will both swear to this) and drifted away.

We have seen, and swum with, a lot of barracuda, but never face to face, never this big, and never this close. In my humble opinion, sharks are much more preferable company. Barracuda were present on every dive, but we soon learned their territories and stayed away from these.

Lobsters were under every rock, so why upset the big guys when you don't have to? Ryan and I developed the technique of one person watching out for the barracuda, and the other getting the lobster. Fish were ignored for the moment.

The bird life was fascinating, mostly boobies, with occasional pelican, frigate bird and smaller sea birds. They were nesting, most with single eggs, and allowed us to come within a few feet, simply staring at us. The day we arrived and were dinghying to shore, a booby flew only feet from us at eye level, turned its head and inspected us, quite deliberately, as if asking, "What are you?" It held the gaze for at least a minute before veering off. Since then we have had several recurrences, but never so close or so intimate. The pelicans perform vertical dives, but the boobies seem to be just learning how to do it. Their dives were more of a lurch, splash and stab. They also spent more time chasing others with a catch than fishing themselves.

Carole: *We saw it again—the Green Flash. Seen by us in Sri Lanka (twice), where some said its veracity was in doubt due to previous margarita intake, and then again in Cefalu. This one was unmistakable, but more like an emerald jewel sinking into the sea.*

All the bird life, beautiful water, reefs, and isolation, brought out the muse in me (Carole and Ryan want no blame for what follows) and I dashed off the:

Ode to the Aves

You must go to the Aves, we were told and retold.
To see the birds in thousands, unafraid and so bold
To check you out they fly and stare in your face,
Then poop into your dinghy, to prove it's their place.
The coral is simply terrific, the water is quite balmy,
With fish and lovely lobsters, enough to feed an army.
This promise of some lobsters, was all we needed to know,
To right then haul up anchor, and sail to Barlovento.

We're here, we're glad, it's just as promised and more.
We've been inspected by the birds, on our way to the shore.
The water is so very pretty, and the lobsters are so thick,
They cluster all around you, it's easy to take your pick.
The hunters, Ryan and Laurie, here learned a brand new feat,
How to walk on top of water, very quickly in bare feet.
Their incentive, a barracuda, length six feet at very least,
Who licked his lips and grinned at them, a really nasty beast.

It's now been more than three weeks, since we last saw a shop,
But Carole's food inventiveness goes on without stop.
Each day, three meals, plus snacks, or Ryan looks tragic.
From fridge, freezer and storage, food appears as if by magic.
Occasionally she takes a break, draws butter and just sits,
While Laurie serves fresh lobster, cut into tasty bits.
We'd all be just as thin as rakes without her as a cook,
Problem is, that's just the way she really wants to look.

We start each day in the cockpit, to watch the sun arise,
Then snorkel all the coral, every fish is such a prize.
It's time to watch the myriad birds, flying o'er the trees,
Swooping, diving, soaring, or just riding on the breeze.
We toss a line over the side, but don't check for a bite.
Read, then do some schoolwork, well Ryan just might.
Then get into the dinghy, and wander to and fro,
It's cocktails then at sunset, where did the whole day go?

The timetable caught up with us a little, so we moved on a few miles to Aves de Sotavento, not a good decision. The anchorage in the lee of Currican was protected enough, but we missed our boobies and the pelican patrols. The huge piles of conch shells ashore were the remainder of what must have been the equivalent of strip-mining the reef.

Curacao, Bonaire, Aruba, Columbia, Panama and the Panama Canal

Year Six
September 10 to December 14

Deciding we deserved some marina time, we checked into Harbor Village Marina, along the coast from Kralendijk, Bonaire's capital. This was a full facilities marina, water, electricity, cable TV, and telephone, so we splurged and got the lot.

The next morning started out well. The lady on the boat next to us was a scuba instructor, so we asked her to put us through the obligatory checkout needed before we could dive in Bonaire. Looking for our dive cards, I had to clean out the safe and found, right at the bottom, Carole's black pearl pendant that had been missing since Turkey. She was thrilled.

But then Carole's mother called and we spent the rest of the day watching the horrors of September 11 unfold. It was so unreal to be in our floating home, under blue skies, with an island devoted to pleasure outside the porthole, and see so much tragedy on live TV. So conditioned are we to onscreen violence, we had some difficulty in believing it was real, and not just another disaster movie.

Carole: *Home was brought close to us that day and the days after. Cruisers of all nationalities and the people of Bonaire gathered together for special services. We attended one that was broadcast around the world by a religious radio station headquartered less than a mile from us, followed by lighting of candles in memorial to those who had so senselessly died.*

After two weeks in the marina we moved to a mooring on the narrow shelf between the land and the drop-off that supports the reef. "Dolphin

Spirit" swung just over the reef, in crystal clear water, allowing us to snorkel and dive right off the boat. Ryan took lessons and became a qualified Advanced Open Water Diver and earned a specialty as an Underwater Naturalist.

Ryan (13): *I went on my first night dive. The fish were really unique, and behaved differently. The certification dives and the examinations were easy and the lady instructor was very nice to me.*

Although much of the coral had been destroyed by a hurricane, enough remained to make this a wonderful place to dive and snorkel. Ryan and I simply rolled off "Dolphin Spirit" and there was the reef, sloping down into the deep and running along the coast for miles. My problem was remembering which piece of coral marked "Dolphin Spirit's" position.

Carole: *We went on a wonderful snorkel one day, in and around a concrete pier that had been destroyed by the hurricane. It was inhabited by schools of fish that simply parted to let us through. We hovered over fish cleaning stations, and watched the large fish being serviced by the smaller ones, who even went in and out of the open mouths.*

One night out almost resulted in disaster. We were heading back in the dinghy, when the entire transom came loose from the hull. I was driving, and managed to grab the outboard, or we would have lost it all. Fortunately, we were not far from our boat, and managed to paddle home. Within the next few days, almost every piece of adhesive on our Zodiac gave way. To keep us semi-mobile I held everything together with lines, and tried every adhesive our stores and the island could offer. The combination sort of worked and we could get about, but not plane, or travel at any real speed. To this day, Zodiac denies any responsibility.

Ryan (13): *Bonaire was a great place for me because there were lots of kids. "Lady Starlight" had two boys, one 14, one 11, "Millennial Destiny" one boy, 14, and "Nyantja" three girls, 12, 11 and 6. This was the largest group I had been with for a long time. All of us had schoolwork, but we spent most of most days together in some combination. Being boat kids, all of the older ones, including me, could use dinghies, and were trusted to go ashore.*

"Millennial Destiny" was the subject of many long discussions amongst the other yachts. The family had bought it second-hand and had sailed almost immediately, hoping to make repairs as they went, and as their very limited budget allowed. That they got to Bonaire was something of a miracle, as the boat leaked badly and almost nothing worked. They were determined to sail around the world, and spent every day fully occupied trying to achieve that goal.

One of the great things about cruising was that we kept seeing old friends. We had met "Runaway" in Mooloolaba five years earlier and then again in the Canaries, where we spent a month with them. Now here they were on the mooring next to us. Showing up later was "Sunshine," an Australian boat we had sailed with to the Cape Verdes.

Friday, Saturday and Sunday were "rib days." A few yards off the beach, a BBQ place opened, serving ribs and chicken legs, all we could eat, for less then $5 per person. It was just a small back yard, with a couple of tables and chairs and a BBQ. We found we had to get there early, or they would be sold out. We ate there, took away, and generally became ribbed-out, all except Ryan, who inhaled them.

Carole and I went round the island on a rented scooter, admiring the piles of salt, photographing the flamingos, and back-tracking every time my hat blew off. Carole finally assumed the "arm around the waist, arm on top of head" position that enabled us to complete the drive before year's end. Later Ryan and I repeated the drive, sans hat. Naturally, Ryan had to drive for a while. I walked.

The timetable struck again and it was time to move on to Curacao, and the anchorage in Spanish Waters. This huge, calm bay was entered through a narrow, winding passage, but then offered a wide choice of anchorages. We motored around, finally choosing one in the middle, away from the large groups, but close enough to land so our crippled dinghy could cope.

Carole: *Many of our friends had gone before us and had planned a party on the night we arrived, at a funky BBQ place for ribs. It featured wooden tables and a strolling singer belting out American 50's rock and roll songs. Service was spectacularly bad.*

Even though Bonaire and Curacao are part of the same Dutch territory, we had to check out of one, and into the other. On Bonaire, this was quick and pleasant. The Customs officer handed out Bonaire pamphlets and the Immigration officer gave shopping tips. Curacao was different.

The offices were in Willemstad, a 30-minute bus ride from Spanish Waters in a delightful bus, somewhat reminiscent of a San Francisco cable car. The front was enclosed by windows and was not air-conditioned. The rear was completely open and had an air-conditioning unit! There was a little uncertainty as to where the Immigration office actually was. After all, only a 1,000 or so yachts visit every year, so there was no need for precision. We found an office in the Post Office, but it was closed. Enquiries to a local police officer elicited directions to another office, which had been closed for years. Further entreaties led to an office which was open, but which dealt only with immigrants, not transients like us.

Giving up, we meandered down town and found the Customs office, remarkably with a huge "Customs" sign. A very pleasant gentleman completed the formalities very efficiently and quickly, even directing us to the correct Immigration office, across the water, at the old cruise-ship dock.

This meant we had to walk across the Willemstad traffic bridge, which has outboard motors fitted and drives out of the way to allow ships to pass. Pedestrians and traffic are cleared off before the drive, but I think that they would do much better selling tickets for the unique experience of going for a boat ride on a bridge.

We crossed and tried to find Immigration by following the street, and it wasn't there. Then we obtained further advice, turned down a dead-end street, walked past the "Do Not Proceed" sign, through the "Authorized Personnel Only" gate, and along half a mile of deserted pier to a little building tucked between warehouses, and distinguished only by the effigy of a pelican.

We shouldn't have bothered. The lady officer took one look at our passports and declared us illegal. By her interpretation, we were allowed only two weeks in the Dutch Islands, and we had used up four weeks of that in Bonaire. Pointing out that the Bonaire officials obviously had a different view had no effect. Pointing out that the Post Office officials gave three months, even if you had been months in Bonaire, had no effect. Walking out wasn't an option, as she had our passports.

The compromise reached, after some wrangling, was that she wouldn't check us in, but would check us out if we left on Sunday (it was Friday). No way would she make it Monday, and Sunday obviously compromised her ethics irrevocably. We later heard that the correct thing to have done was to walk out immediately we saw the lady officer, and return later when her male colleague was there. He gave three months without a problem. Naturally in the above, "female" and "male" are used simply to distinguish between officers, and in no way reflect any gender bias, or aspersions about the egotistical, power-mad, unreasonable, ill-informed, and stubborn characteristics of the female sex.

The end result was that we left on Wednesday, not out of spite, but because the weather wouldn't let us go earlier. Actually, Curacao wasn't worth more than about a week.

Carole: *We found an excellent supermarket, and so were able to provision to my satisfaction with mostly U.S. brands. I wondered about my growing desire for the "familiar" when for years strange brands had been just fine. Fruit and vegetables were average. Everything was hugely expensive. As you may gather, Curacao isn't high on our list of places to return to.*

We decided to enjoy the "dark side" by not checking into Aruba, although we stayed there for three days, anchoring off a pretty beach just north of the hotel strip, and inside a wrecked freighter, assuaging our consciences by not going ashore.

Ryan (13): *I went ashore three times with people from the other boats. The "Lady Starlight" crew took me with them to dive on the freighter and on a sunken airplane. Although the water was a bit murky, we spotted an airplane engine with the propeller still on it almost as soon as we got to the bottom. Then we saw more engines and some air filters which had secretary blennies living in them—they looked like honeycombs.*

The main wreck was of a very large container ship. We could have gone inside, but Jim and I got separated from the others and I used up so much air getting back to them, I had to share with Chris.

Because the Colombian coast had such a bad reputation for drug smuggling, piracy and other assorted nefarious activities, the accepted way of sailing to Cartegena was a very rough passage, well off shore. In recent times some brave sailors had pioneered the coastal route and had survived, so together with "Lady Starlight" and "Nyantja," we set off to do the same, with hopefully the same results. These decisions are not like, "Do we take the 5 or the 405 freeway?" but are possibly life or death—well okay, it is like the 405!

The first leg was an easy overnight to Cabo de Vela, a huge bay decorated with fishing canoes and nets. We had to anchor a long way offshore because of the nets. It was a picturesque, desolate place, with only a few huts, and no apparent roads.

Ryan (13): *Local fishermen took "Lady Starlight" and me to a wreck for some diving. I was really surprised, and so was everyone else, when some huge, 80-pound or more, snappers appeared and came right up to us. We were worried that we would be knocked about by the fish, which obviously hadn't seen divers before. It was fun.*

Ryan caught a huge wahoo, about 50 pounds, whose white flesh made a nice change from the previous diet of red tuna meat. Apart from that, the Caribbean fish yield was disappointing. A few tuna, and a mackerel or two, separated by large amounts of water, are not what we were used to in tropical seas. The "Dolphin Spirit" standard is to decide when we want to eat, and put out a line a few minutes before that.

On the way to Guayrace Bay, a huge, solitary, scarred dolphin rode our bow-wave for several hours, our first solo dolphin, and certainly the longest time any have stayed with us. A major storm system came up in the middle of the night, so we tried to dodge it by heading out to sea. Naturally, it followed, so after a couple of hours we decided to head right through it, at the apparently narrowest point. An hour of lightning, thunder, rain, wind, and Carole not breathing, and we were through.

The morning brought snow, atop the Sierra Madre Mountains which suddenly appeared out of the mist and cloud. Even though we were expecting it, the sight was startling here in the tropics. Countless yellow and white butterflies chose the time of our entrance to Guayrace to fly from one side of the bay to the other. We drifted in as slowly as possible, to enjoy this treat. When we tore our eyes off the butterflies, the bay turned out to be a pretty anchorage surrounded by jungle covered hills, sloping down to white beaches and a small village.

Ryan(13): *We went windsurfing in the bay, which was cool, as we sailed through the butterflies which seemed to keep coming. I went with one of the villagers to an archeological dig. Actually it was just a lot of holes that the villagers had dug to get stuff to sell to us. Many of the burial pots and other pieces were still partially buried.*

Perhaps everything was genuine, as the place certainly wasn't a tourist Mecca, or even on the tourist maps. All sorts of pre-Colombian artifacts were exposed by the holes, including burial urns complete with bones and offerings, pots and other unidentifiable objects. To find the site, walk past the garbage dump, kill the snake crossing the path, turn left and there you are. The bay was once a major pre-Spanish settlement, apparently rich in gold, which the Spanish wiped out in typical fashion.

The afternoon wind, acting against the current, kicks up nasty waves at the entrance to the Magdalena River, so we left Guayrace around 3am to enable us to cross the river in the morning. The local fishing boats were lit, or got out of our way, so the exit was relatively simple in the dark. Even three miles offshore, the outflow of the Magdalena turned the water a muddy brown, and we had to cross about eight miles of it. Luckily there had been little rain, so the normal hazards of trees, logs, and occasional houses were almost absent, and all we had to contend with was the three to four-knot current. For once, we timed it right and had only a little chop.

Herradura sandbar, almost three miles long, in existence for long enough to sprout trees, roads, major houses and hotels, was totally unmarked on even the most modern charts. Guess it wasn't there in the 1800s when the surveys were done—a real lesson in trusting charts. The bay behind it was calm and obviously the haunt of the Colombian rich and leisurely, as it was surrounded by hotels and filled with jet-skis and parasails.

Cartagena, was only fifty miles away, an easy day sail that turned into a marathon. The wind, which had been conveniently with us all the way, spun through 180 degrees to be right on our nose. The current, benign to now, became two knots, against us. This combination meant that, for most of the day, we thought we would be unable to make Cartagena before dark.

The Boca Grande entrance to Cartagena was wide and easy, so the Spaniards built a wall across it, just under water, to keep out pirates and other unwanted items such as future sailboats. In a fit of do-good-itis, a couple of years before we arrived, the authorities blasted a narrow, shallow hole in the wall, and marked it with two buoys, both of which were notoriously absent or hard to find.

Depth sounders were useless in these circumstances, and the water was too murky to see anything, but we found the buoys, hoped for the best, and gingerly felt our way in (***Carole:** Laurie just drove in at speed between the buoys in spite of my impassioned pleas to slow down.*) through the buoys and around the fishing boats that seemed to think they had some rights to set nets across the only entrance.

Cartagena Bay is huge. No wonder the Spanish used it as the center for the bullion fleets, and no wonder the pirates had a hard time attacking it. We headed in, rounded the lighthouse and entered the inner harbor, to be met by the statue of the Virgin Mary, all alone in the middle. Past her was the welcome sight of the masts of the boats at anchor off Club Nautico. We thought we had a reservation at the next-door Club de Pesca, but didn't, so had to sweet-talk our way into a very nice spot at the end of a dock.

"Lady Starlight" arrived at the entrance after dark and spent a rolly night at anchor outside the wall. They had made the last few miles on the smell of an oily rag, so we got fuel to them the next morning. "Nyantja" had refueled off the "Dolphin Spirit" floating fuel barge at Herradura. They both found places at the Club Nautico docks. "Millennial Destiny" arrived a couple of days later in thick fog and had to anchor in the bay, rocked by the near misses of Navy and other assorted boats that could obviously see clearly.

Cartagena quickly became our favorite place in the Caribbean. The people were friendly, the old town was gorgeous, the restaurants good and cheap, and it was safe. We wandered the streets at night without a problem, or hint of one. Club de Pesca was in a small Spanish fort. We had guarded gates and an armed guard who sat at the bow of our boat all night.

The only downside, and Club Nautico docks were worse in this regard, was the wash caused by the water-taxis. These were 15-feet long, powered by 150 to 200-HP outboards, which, at speed, left only the rear quarter of the vessel touching the water even when fully loaded. They screamed by, feet away, oblivious to the carnage in their wake. I asked why they came so close to the docks, then made a long curve to their destination, when the straight-line distance was so much shorter. It was really simple. The straight line took them close to the Naval yard. The law stated that all passengers must wear life jackets, but most refused to put them on because they were wet and smelly. Therefore the operators dodged the enforcers by going the long way round.

Pelicano restaurant became our favorite. The evening fixed menu, six-course meal, all the wine we could drink, plus coffee, was $US9 per person. We also ate Chinese, Italian, Thai, even Columbian. There was a local pizza place near the marina, so Ryan got his regular fix.

On a tour of a monastery, set high on a hill overlooking the city, we were leaning against a wall enjoying the scenery, when a half plastic bottle suddenly appeared over the top of the wall. It was attached to a long stick, wielded by a young girl asking for money. The novelty broke my long-standing prohibition, and she got some. Apart from the view, the main interest was the museum, where the featured display was money from around the world. All the history around, and they don't promote it, other than by selling "real" pre-Colombian artifacts.

Carole: *At the monastery entrance was a man with a sloth, with baby sloth, that he hung on Ryan and me for a fee. Not as cute as a koalas, but how many people have cuddled a sloth?*

One of the squares had a number of very nice restaurants and an "emerald factory" which we naturally had to inspect. A very good salesman, a terrific range of emeralds, mounted and loose, a feeling that, after looking at Colombian emeralds all over the world, we were at the source, and Carole became the proud owner of some green rocks.

Carole: *The necklace features a unique woven gold chain holding an emerald surrounded by a cluster of diamonds. Matching ear-rings and an unmounted emerald completed the purchase, which we got for a song*

...and an arm and a leg.

We had the bottom of the boat and the prop cleaned (two weeks growth at the waterline was about two feet of algae) and some varnish work done. The people we employed worked very cheaply and well and, at Carole's insistence, were rewarded by extra money and a lot of clothing we didn't need.

We checked out and set off with "Nyantja" for the San Blas Islands. An uneventful two-night passage became eventful when we arrived within a few miles of the entrance. The clouds and fog rolled up, and down came the rain and lightning. We pressed on, and then had to circle for an hour or so, waiting for the rain to ease so we could attempt the entry with some visibility.

Carole: When I can see lightning actually hitting the sea, I become positively obsessive about being somewhere else. Laurie tries to calm me, then keeps on course. Can't he see that I want him to transport the boat at least 100 miles away instantly, or at least turn around?

With "Nyantja" close behind, we followed the way-points and made an easy entry, but then had to negotiate a winding pass through several reefs to an island anchorage. Clouds and poor visibility are not ideal in these circumstances, so I hailed a passing Kuna dug-out and asked them to guide us in. They did, for a small donation and some fuel.

These were picturesque islands and our anchorage was behind a reef, between two of them. In spite of the weather, we happily settled in for a few days to snorkel the very pretty coral and find the scarce fish.

The eleventh day of the eleventh month signaled the end of World War I in 1918, and this year signaled a major event in the cruise of "Dolphin Spirit." Lightning struck home—our home. It was a wild night, winds gusting to over 40 knots, continuous, blinding rain, lightning all around, but the worst seemed to be over, when, around 1am, we were hit!

Carole: Earlier in the evening the danger had seemed much greater. The "Nyantja" family had come over for cocktails and, sitting in the cockpit, we paid little notice to the small black cloud racing towards us. Suddenly it was all around, with wind, rain and lightning. "Nyantja" couldn't leave.

The thunder was deafening, and lightning struck several times between us and the island. I was scared, but calmly went below to organize a sing-along as reassurance for the kids (and me). Ryan played the keyboard, often inaudible over the rolling thunder.

To make things even more uncomfortable the cockpit became soaked early in the night, as the cockpit cover had been re-sown in Cartagena and all the new stitches leaked. When the storm hit, Ryan and I had to go out in the darkness, wind and rain, to wrestle down our awning, as it was threatening either to disintegrate, or to turn DS into a replica of Captain Hook's flying ship.

Carole: For three hours it raged, then died down. We had survived. "Nyantja" went home and, very relieved, we went to bed.

I heard the wind pick up, went up top to check, and was sitting in the cockpit when everything went white, followed by an instant of "negative vision" when black was white and white black, with no colors, followed by what seemed to be a very long time of no vision at all. I had enough time to be concerned that my sight wasn't going to return, and was so relieved when shapes began to appear out of the black.

Carole: *I was standing in our cabin wondering why Laurie was up. There was no thunder, rain or lightning. Then came one bright flash, and a simultaneous crash of thunder. Laurie didn't say anything; there was no jolt; no sparks; we were fine. Then I heard that calm "We've been hit," and my heart fell.*

Apart from my temporary vision problem, Carole, Ryan and I weren't hurt, but almost every piece of electronics on "Dolphin Spirit" was destroyed. We lost two radars, G.P.S., SSB and VHF radios (the VHF antenna at the top of the mast was melted), wind and boat speed instruments (both systems), battery monitoring system, inverter, propane control, auto-pilot, and the insulated back-stay had the insulation blown apart. Very strangely, the mirror in Ryan's bathroom in the bow had a corner broken off. The tri-color navigation light at the top of the mast was vaporized—not a piece of it was found on deck. Fortunately, the special dispersion unit (witch's broom), set atop the mast to prevent lightning strikes, was completely untouched, and remained poised to protect us.

The strike hit us, skipped the boat next to us, hit the one beyond them, skipped the island, and (obviously by now in a weakened state) partially destroyed the electronics on two boats anchored there. In that anchorage several boats dragged anchor, two going aground. It was a hell of a night all round. There was nothing we could do except feel depressed and keep lookout to ensure we didn't drag. Even the Kuna Indians who came by the next day, commented on the fact that they couldn't sleep because of the wind, rain and lightning.

The really good fortune was to discover that the main battery bank seemed to be operative and the engine and generator sets both started and ran. The next day we ran the refrigeration and water maker successfully, so the first shock of "everything is gone" was a little alleviated. We had a back-up inverter, and a spare for the one that was destroyed, so I replaced that. Our main G.P.S. and one depth sounder somehow escaped the carnage, and we had a spare control unit for the auto-pilot, so by the end of the day we were in pretty good shape, considering.

On the negative side, with no radios, we couldn't talk to anyone except over the limited range of our hand-held VHF. With the damaged back-stay, use of sails was problematical, although I rigged up a system with running back-stays and spare halyards that would probably have allowed us to sail in an emergency. Without battery monitoring systems, we didn't know if the battery charger was working, although the volt-meters indicated that it was. We could travel reasonably well.

During the week we were in the San Blas Islands we saw the sun for only a few hours on one day. The rest of the time it poured rain, or threatened to. In spite of that, we found them to be quite beautiful islands. The Kuna family we met at the first anchorage was very pleasant, not pushy, and always smiling. By way of contrast, we hadn't dropped anchor in Chichime, when we had three dugouts tied to us, with three others circling. "No" wasn't a word they understood.

Finally managing to drop the anchor without swamping a canoe, we actually bought molas (the Kuna specialty of artfully worked fabric), spreading the buying around every canoe. The Kuna approach was interesting. Prices were fixed, no bargaining. Then they asked for presents (sugar, milk, cloth, sweets, etc.), which they took without thanks.

Carole: *I handed out lots of toys (Ryan's stuff that was too young for him), made sure every child was given paper and crayons, gave every visiting woman a package of sugar (bought specially for this purpose in Cartagena) and bought lots of molas. I gave an old lady a package of sugar, and she handed me a small shell, which I took to be a return gift (as regularly happened in the South Pacific and Indonesia) until she started to haggle about the price. No more, I told Laurie, and didn't look at another thing.*

At the end of the transactions, they kept asking us to buy, and then left without a smile. One pair of old ladies, who arrived after we had bought more than enough molas, were most upset with us for not buying, even after they received the usual presents. We realized we were in their country, but we did pay for the privilege of anchoring, plus a fee for going ashore, plus a dollar a person a photo (expensive for a group shot), then bought molas, then gave presents, so we weren't exactly free-loaders. A smile and a nice word in return wouldn't hurt.

The weather sort of cleared, so we cautiously headed off for Portobelo, on the Panama mainland. This was a major Spanish port, raided several times by Drake, Hawkins, Morgan and sundry other pirates. A marvelous place, it is the wettest spot in Panama, so it rained solidly for the two days we were there.

Another cruiser offered to sail with us to Colon, to assist with radio communications if needed, and to provide the very necessary radar watch, as this was a high-traffic area with rain and fog impairing visibility.

Coming through the breakwater behind a huge tanker, and realizing we were in the Panama Canal was quite a thrill. We headed for the Panama

Canal Yacht Club (don't believe the name) in Colon and, thanks to the good work of our agent Peter Stevens, were able to get a place tied up outside another boat. PCYC doesn't take reservations, and it is always full. Some boats have been there for many, many years, and look it. It rained again, and again.

The Panama Canal Yacht Club docks were decrepit (being polite), as no money had been spent on them for years. PCYC leased their place on a month-by-month basis from the Panama Canal Authority, not a situation conducive to capital expenditure or maintenance. While we were there, a large man off a powerboat jumped onto a dock from the boat, went right through the decking, and broke off a considerable section of the dock. Several sailboats were tied to it, and they drifted away. Marvelous confusion for hours, right at our cocktail time, fortunately. The rain in Colon continued to fall, and fall, and fall. We couldn't stand still for any length of time, or mold would form. The inside of our cockpit cover turned black.

Carole: *Though we now had mold in the cockpit, we never had any below. Sailing books I had read before departure had depicted the horror of mold very graphically and many of our friends had to scrape it from their storage bins, not to mention the horror of moldy shoes. The badly affected hold-down straps in the cockpit were soaked in Nappisan and came out white again.*

We had checked into Panama in the San Blas. A boat containing Customs, Immigration and Port officials, all in Kuna civilian dress and bare feet, but with plastic-covered, shrink-wrapped IDs, came to us. We were stamped, accredited, cruising permitted, and charged, all in one easy series of transactions in the cockpit. The officials at Colon weren't all that pleased, and wanted to do the whole thing again. I mentioned the word "agent" and all problems vanished. Other cruisers, doing it themselves, weren't so lucky, and had a hassle.

I was soon occupied with getting equipment ordered and technicians arranged for the installations. Our wonderful, lovely, marvelous, insurance company, Pantaenius, agreed to pay for replacement of all damaged equipment with new equipment, and for the installation, without requiring an inspection. And still it rained, and rained.

We all hoped that the experience of a boat which was hit by lightning in the San Blas, again while anchored in the Flats waiting to get space at the Panama Canal Yacht Club, and again at that Club's docks, would not be repeated.

For those in the fast lane, and those who think Reader's Digest con-

densed books are a good thing, here is a summary of the rest of the book:
- Rain, rain, and more rain
- Lightning struck again
- Equipment mostly fixed
- Panama Canal transit mostly incident free
- Panama
- Costa Rica and crocodiles
- The dreaded gulfs of Papagayo and Tehuantapec
- Mexico and margaritas

Okay, now you can go back to your hectic life.

Carole: *To get a little respite from all the boat-repair traumas, we enjoyed a great day at Gamboa Nature Resort. The main building has a gigantic picture window overlooking the jungle and river. Huge mobiles of the local birds hang from the ceilings. One day we will go back there to stay a while.*

The reserve was almost at Panama City, so we taxied there and back across the Isthmus, as the train wasn't running, and the local bus service didn't go there. The resort was just off the Canal, and we took a two-hour Chagres River/Canal tour, ducking in and around the islands to see herons, toucans, hawks, crocodiles, howler and white-faced monkeys, and lots of big iguanas, Our guide took us under a tree and started to throw pieces of bread to a family of white-faces. The male refused to let the female (who was carrying a baby) have any. The guide tried to get around him, but to no avail. Probably getting upset at this potential threat to his dominance, the male startled everyone by leaping into the boat, grabbing the bread, and bounding off.

Ryan (13): *He landed just next to me and I thought he was going to take the bread and my hand as well.*

The Treetops Tram Ride, tame by comparison, was an open cable-car which took us slowly, at tree-top level, to the top of a small mountain. The views were great, but there were no birds, animals, or even insects to be seen. It is a very "green" operation, designed to minimally affect the trees and other growth. Perhaps no one told the wild life. At the bottom, on the return trip, our guide said he saw a sloth at the top of a nearby tree, but we didn't.

Colon, once a grand old city, had gone completely to seed. The architecture of some buildings was magnificent, but all were unpainted, unrepaired, occupied by squatters, and full of garbage and junk. We were warned about walking outside of the Yacht Club gates, even in daylight. Tourists were mugged every day when they ignored basic safety rules, and sometimes even when they observed them. The PCYC taxi drivers spoke excellent English, so we used them at all times, having them wait for us if we went shopping or used the Internet cafes. Others picked up a taxi off the streets, only to have themselves driven to the muggers—sort of like a delivery service.

We loved the local buses, from the outside. They were all ex-U.S. school buses, painted in psychedelic colors and designs—60s' flower-children would have felt right at home. Obviously they were put into use as soon as they arrived, as we saw some with the school name still there, others still yellow, but with the name blacked out, others with the bonnet painted, and other variations up to full glory. Seeing a hundred or so of these in a line at peak hour caused a little eye strain, made worse by the clouds of exhaust fumes.

Beggars were everywhere, but the guys we liked are the ones who staked out a piece of street and controlled the parking there, for a fee. Of course they had no official standing, but just try to park without using them! Curbside car washes at $1 per car lined a lot of streets. Kids selling Chicklets were persistent, as were the ones offering bracelets.

"Take out the money you are going to spend now, and put the rest somewhere safe," advised Rudi, our taxi driver, as we prepared to enter the market area. Great fruit and vegetables, excellent prices, weirdly colored chicken, good to unidentifiable meat—a typical local market. Colon was a little different as the market was the focal point for the pickpockets and similar thieves. Fanny packs were not safe, shoulder bags were open invitations, as were watches and necklaces.

Apparently the high crime rate—even locals get mugged—was the direct result of high unemployment, which in turn was a result of the U.S. transfer of the Canal to Panama. We were told that over 20,000 people lost their jobs almost immediately. Panama has subcontracted Canal maintenance and some operations to the Chinese, and they have introduced "economies." According to one taxi driver, who used to be a maintenance technician (so sour-grapes can't be ruled out here), they were using second-rate replacement parts and skipping essential maintenance. Several local gringos predicted a complete breakdown of some locks within the next few years, at the latest. Hopefully all are proven wrong.

At the other end of the spectrum was the Super 2000 shopping plaza, with a huge, American-style supermarket, up-market shops, and machine-gun armed guards. No beggars allowed here, only gringos and locals in expensive cars. The Panama Canal Free Trade Zone was a huge area full of fashion and electronic equipment shops, accessed only by non-Panamanians and Panamanians with influence.

Back to the lightning repairs: Buying all the necessary equipment in the States and shipping it to Panama was cheaper and quicker than sourcing it in Panama. We placed our order with Maritime Communications in Marina del Rey (thank you Ken and Joe) and started to look for installation technicians. To cut a long, painful story short, we found a New Zealander to do the rigging, and Panamanians to do the electronic, electrical and mechanical work. Fortunately Panama uses American currency, as everyone wanted payment in cash.

Ken air-freighted 10 boxes of equipment from Los Angeles on a Monday, it arrived in Panama City at 10pm Tuesday, and we had it on the boat at 12:30pm Wednesday, thanks to our agent, Pete Stevens, doing the customs clearing. He was worth every penny of his fee. We know of others who tried to do it themselves, and spent weeks and probably the same amount of money in taxis and bribes.

It continued to rain, which didn't promote the work too well. Backstay insulators, the radios and one radar were replaced, and some electrical work done, when I called a halt, just a little frustrated. The work was done well, just maddeningly slowly, and not all that cheaply. Enough was in place to make the boat safe and seaworthy, so I decided to go to Costa Rica to get the rest done.

In case you were wondering, total repairs, parts and labor eventually cost over $US35,000. Wonderful, wonderful Pantaenius, our insurer, paid for it all except for our deductible, and offering cash up-front.

Carole: *The day installation of radios, inverter, battery monitoring system, and radar was completed, a major thunderstorm hit. Laurie raced around disconnecting everything that had just been connected. With a flash and instantaneous boom lightning struck—the freighter tied up 100 yards away. People on shore had their computers wiped out, but we had no damage this time.*

That was the final straw—we were leaving ASAP. Pete Stevens arranged for our admeasuring. A Canal Authority measurer came to the boat with tape measure to get dimensions, check engine and canal lines (we had to have four, each 120-feet long), and make sure we signed the waiver relieving the Panama Canal Authority of all responsibility whatever happened. Another form stipulated that our boat was fitted with sub-standard equipment. It goes without saying that nothing on "Dolphin Spirit" was substandard in any way, but this must be signed whatever the equipment standard. The PCA makes sure that no one can sue them, regardless of circumstances.

Pete organized line handlers (four were required), lines and transit date—4:30am, December 12. I bought car tires covered in duct tape for additional fenders. The transit fee for "Dolphin Spirit" was $US750. We used an agent, so didn't have to pay the refundable deposit of a further $US650 (to cover damage our little boat might do to the canal). Here's a twist. Yachts smaller than us paid a $US750 deposit.

At around 1am, December 12, the transit time was changed to 4:30am, December 13. Another day of Chinese food at the Yacht Club dining room—actually good food and good value—and Carole had time to buy more molas.

Carole: *The delay caused me a little concern as I had to provide breakfast and lunch for us, the four line handlers, and the Advisor, and possibly dinner and breakfast the next morning, if we were delayed. Breakfast was the real problem, as we already had bought two dozen muffins. Luckily these were packaged, and no one noticed the extra day—always buy "quality goods," it pays in the long run.*

December 13 gave us clear, starry skies, and light winds, perfect for a transit. The line handlers (Ng, Rudi, Alfonso and Elvis) arrived on time—4am—removing the first of Carole's concerns. We pushed off into the deep darkness to stooge around the Flats anchorage and wait for the boat bringing our Advisor. Yachts less than 65 feet in length get an Advisor, those longer get a fully qualified Pilot. Tony arrived, leaping on board from the Canal boat. This was a critical time. A couple of days before, the Advisor on another yacht had sprained his ankle in the leap, and their transit was canceled for that day. Safely on board, Tony directed me to make full speed towards the first lock, about three miles away. We arrived a little after 5am, and were told to just float around, as the lock didn't open until sunrise (6am), and the container ship we were to follow hadn't appeared.

Staying relatively still in the current, not allowed to move out of the traffic lane, and trying to keep off the rocky shore the current was pushing us towards, kept me occupied, but I still had time to point out the rather large crocodile that swam across our bow. Howler monkeys yelled at us from the trees. All this while we were no more that 100 yards from the concrete and bright lights of the Canal locks. Ryan's excuse is the early hour, but he startled everyone by looking for the sunrise in the West. To this day we can still get him to blush when we remind him of it—not that we do so more than once or twice a day!

Ryan (13): *I wasn't really confused. Dad had turned the boat around when I wasn't looking, so I pointed at the correct side of the boat, but it wasn't in the right place. They didn't quit teasing me until the container ship with which we were to be up-locked arrived, and we had things to do.*

Canal primer: The Panama Canal is about the same longitude as Miami, runs north-south, not east-west, and is all fresh water—three wonderful pieces of trivia in the first sentence. Starting on the Caribbean side, the three connected Gatun Locks lift vessels 85 feet to Gatun Lake. After crossing 31 miles of the lake, the Pedro Miguel Lock drops boats 31 feet to Miraflores Lake. The double lock at Miraflores drops vessels a further 54 feet to the level of the Pacific Ocean. Gatun Lake, created by damming the Chagres River, holds all the water necessary for the operation of the canal, some 52 million gallons to take a ship from one ocean to the other. All this fresh water flows into the ocean.

We entered the first of the Gatun Locks with some trepidation. Yachts go through the up-locks behind a freighter or tanker, and through the down locks in front of one. We had a choice of being in the center of the lock (either alone or rafted with other yachts), side-tied to a tug, if one was available, or alongside the lock wall. The water, boiling up through 100 holes in the bottom of the lock, creates considerable turbulence and currents in the lock, so being alongside the very rough concrete wall in an up-lock is guaranteed to cause damage. We asked for a tug-tie, and luckily got one, as it is by far the easiest and safest method.

Blocked from our mind was the incident, a couple of months earlier, when a tug, with two yachts tied to it, lost its stern line and swung, driving both yachts under the stern of the freighter in front. One yacht was a total loss. Maybe the incident wasn't well blocked, as the first thing we did after tying up was to pass the tug crew freshly baked cookies and drinks, and station one of our line handlers to monitor the tug stern line.

The lock doors closed behind us—the same doors that operated when the first ship transited almost 90 years earlier. We were at the bottom of a dark, dank pit, with the huge stern of a container ship only feet in front of us. It was one of the big ones, and filled the lock almost completely from side to side. The pilots certainly earn their pay getting those monsters in place with such minimal clearance. Huge boils erupted in the water, and swirls went in all directions, as the inlets were opened. The mules (electric engines on rails that control the big boats) tightened their lines to the ship, and we all steadily rose towards the light.

At the top of the first lock the front gates opened, and things got interesting. Although the mules pull the big boats through, the ships always help by turning their props to start themselves moving. This drove a torrent of water backwards, right to us. Still tied to the tug, we kicked and bucked until the ship moved forward. The current became manageable, so we untied, and swung towards the wall. Carole screamed (she thought we would stay tied to the tug for the three locks and so was unprepared for movement away), but I had "Dolphin Spirit" under control. When the tug had motored into the next lock and tied up, we moved back into position alongside, and retied. Tony remarked to Carole, "A little nervous are we?" A sea eagle swooped down and grabbed a large fish from right next to "Dolphin Spirit." The gates closed and up we went for the second time.

A cruise ship, one lock behind us, was lined with people who all seemed to be photographing us. We returned the compliment. (***Carole:*** *Would someone on that ship please send us copies.*) Two locks went smoothly by. We started to relax a little. Then the third lock tie-up and the elevator ride was over. We were at the top of the last Gatun lock, and the ship had moved out. Our stern line to the tug was cast off, when we saw with horror that the tug bow crewman was not at his post. Our stern swung out, I tried to counter, but the current was too strong. Frantic yells brought the man running. He cast us off, just in time to bring our stern swinging into the tug and entangling our stern arch. Some screeches, bangs and sickening sounds later, we were free, with amazingly only a few scratches as damage. Perhaps we gave the tug crew only enough cookies for two locks!

A word about line-handlers: We had four very experienced ones—Tony said they were the best of them all—and it certainly paid off. Their quick actions, knowing what to do and when, made the transit very easy and saved us from potential disaster a couple of times. At a cost of $US60 per person, they were a bargain.

The Advisor: We chose the line handlers, the Advisor was delivered. Tony spent all of his time either on his cellular phone doing private business, or asleep. In the locks he told us when to enter, but then left everything else to the line-handlers, a very smart move on his part.

The third Gatun Lock spat us out into Gatun Lake, and once again Tony told me to make all speed. A requirement for being allowed to do a one-day passage was the ability to maintain a speed of seven-knots. We diverted through a small-boat shortcut called the Banana Cut, which was a well marked channel through the drowned forest and several small islands. A big boa swam across behind us and howler monkeys continued to yell. Tony fell asleep, and woke after we were back in the main Canal. He wanted to know if there had been any traffic when we rejoined the Canal, seemed quite impressed that we had managed the transition without his help, and got back on his phone.

Eleven am, and we were at the entrance to Pedro Miguel Lock, and requested once again to wait. This time we tied up at a dock and Tony went ashore, not to reappear until 12:30, missing the terrific buffet luncheon Carole served.

A powerboat that had spent the previous night in the Canal, was to go through the last three locks with us. He had refused to raft up with us because we were "too expensive a boat." On the advice of our line-handlers we had already agreed to go on the wall, so this did not delay us. The lock gates opened and the powerboat went in first, tying up center chamber, with four lines to the walls, to keep the boat in place. As the water level drops, the line-handlers let out line in a controlled fashion. It isn't easy, and requires real concentration.

Entering the lock was quite disconcerting. We were at the top, looking over the lip of the gates at the void below, and sighed in relief when the two lines securing us along the wall were in place. After "Dolphin Spirit" and the powerboat were in position, our container ship friend from the up-locks came in behind us—and kept coming and coming. The bulb at the bow finished up 20 feet behind our stern, and we looked straight up at a wall of steel. Even at its slow speed, the huge mass pushed a surge of water ahead of it that had our lines groaning and fenders straining (being pushed over the edge not so far in front of us was more than a passing thought). The powerboat line-handlers were enthralled by all this, and were so busy filming and photographing (a major Canal no-no for line-handlers) they didn't notice the water was being let out, until screams from the wall alerted them to the fact that they were becoming airborne. In a mad scramble they released lines and splashed into place.

Meanwhile, our professionals were letting us down and fending us off the rough, slimy wall. Going down isn't turbulent, and so a wall-tie isn't the danger it is in the up locks. Once down, the gates opened and we motored across the couple of miles of lake to the first of the Miraflores Locks. On our left was the Pedro Miguel Yacht Club, probably the safest place in the world to leave a boat. There is no way to get a stolen boat out, as it is inside the Canal and between two sets of locks.

I misjudged the wind and current, and only the prompt intervention of our line-handlers saved us from damage, and from going over the top of the lock gates. Again we watched, mesmerized (now we know how it feels to be a mouse waiting for a cobra to strike), as the container ship kept on coming and coming. Once again the powerboat stern-line handlers forgot their job, and the powerboat took an alarming bow-down tilt. Although being on the wall was easier down than up, it still took the full concentration of two handlers on the lines, two running back and forth fending off, and me applying engine power when necessary, to avoid hitting the wall.

Then it was the last lock. Our line-handlers informed us there were cameras there feeding an Internet site, so friends and family can watch transit of this lock. We didn't know about it before hand, or we would have told everyone, but we waved anyhow. By now we were experts and relaxed, so once again it was the line-handlers who saved our bacon when the Canal people were late securing our lines, and the freighter's surge propelled us towards the edge. Then it was easy until we were down and the gates opened. We had been warned about the turbulence caused when the salt water mixed with the fresh, but were surprised by its strength. I had to gun the engine to hold us in position. Lines dropped and we were out into the Pacific, about five years after we left it by passing through Torres Strait in northern Australia.

Carole: *I was sorry we were nearing home, but glad to be back in MY Ocean.*

Actually we were still some miles from the open ocean, but it was Pacific water we were in. A Canal boat swung by and picked up Tony and we motored under the Bridge of the Americas (the only link between North and South America), past the burned out Balboa Yacht Club, to Flamenco Island Marina. It will be a marina some day, then it was just an enclosed piece of water, with a fuel dock and some moorings.

All the moorings were taken, so we tied up alongside a huge, dirty dredge. The dredge was American, and the American operators lived on board. They had been operating it for over 25 years, most of the time in Costa Rica and Panama. They filled our water tanks before we left.

Across the bay, the Miami-like skyline of Panama City loomed, beckoning. What a difference from Colon. Huge hotels lined the shore, but otherwise it turned out to be just another big, South American, rainy, crowded, city. The ruins of old Panama, destroyed by Henry Morgan the pirate, were impressive, even though he did a pretty good job, and the weather almost finished the place off. Why anyone would decide on that site as a place for a major port was not evident. When the tide goes out, the beach/mud flat is over a mile wide.

For lunch we had been recommended to a restaurant in a large shopping center. All we could find, for our last Panama meal, were Dominos, Kentucky Chicken, and McDonalds. We chose the Colonel over the Scotsman and the Italian. Carole has never forgiven me for that, but we all did benefit from the grease injection.

Panama to Mexico to San Diego
Years Six and Seven
December 15 to April 10

Carole: *The knowledge that we were on the last leg of our journey provided a strange sense of urgency to finish. Strange, because none of us wanted to stop cruising, so why this feeling we had to press on? I was partly to blame, because I love calm weather and wanted to take every such opportunity to keep going.*

A pod of dolphins provided very special aerial acrobatics while escorting us, as we waved a soggy goodbye to the Bridge of the Americas. Wind and waves gave us a relatively mild midnight passage around the aptly named Punta Mala. Boats that were a day ahead of us reported a strong countercurrent, and burying their bows into the head seas. The good conditions lured us on, and we bypassed several marginal but pretty anchorages.

A large dorado (40 pounds or so) made Ryan happy again. He was suffering fishing withdrawal symptoms. We anchored in the huge, calm, Bahia Honda. Several miles in diameter, it offered innumerable anchoring spots around the shore, and at the several small islands dotted in its expanse. Anchored near us were "Far Out" and "Lady MJ," two powerboats we had last seen in Trinidad. They were delighted to receive some of our dorado.

A local Indian canoed by, and we bought bananas and paw paws. His father later paddled out to see if we needed anything else, and reeled off a list of possibles. Carole asked for cilantro and ginger. Not a problem. Off he paddled to his farm, to re-appear a few hours later with tiny fresh ginger roots and some huge leaves that looked like marijuana, but smelled and tasted like cilantro.

Ryan (13): *Schools of fish made the water boil as they fed around the boat, and as far out as we could see. I almost went nuts chasing around in the dinghy trying unsuccessfully to catch some. Nothing worked. I even tried the Cook Island jagging method, but the fish dodged. It was very frustrating.*

We dinghied around the bay, looking at the occasional house and watching monkeys play in the trees. It was one of our nicest times, calm and restful after the stress of the previous weeks and the canal transit. Yes, stress, a real-life problem, and we didn't need it.

Returning to our boat after a dinghy ride, we were called to shore by a local. He wanted us to take him out to his canoe, which was floating free about 100 feet off the shore. Apparently, he had forgotten to tie it up as the tide came in. We wondered if swimming had become a lost art, or if there was some religious thing about getting wet at 4pm on Mondays.

Reluctantly we left and sailed to Isla Parida, with Ryan back in his element once again, catching a 35-pound dorado. Another lovely anchorage, this time in a tiny bay, in a quite small, uninhabited island. Some fishermen came by and we bought four good-sized lobsters for $US10—one cannot live on mahi-mahi alone. A couple of kids paddled out (wasn't this an uninhabited island?) and traded some 50 lemons for pencils and paper.

This was our last Panama stop. In my usual fashion, I planned the next 85-mile passage to Golfito, Costa Rica, as an overnight, leaving at 4pm so as to arrive in the early morning the next day. It's lucky I did, as we found a contrary current that held us to a speed of less than three knots over the ground. At one stage we were seriously contemplating a second night at sea, but then Neptune/Poseidon (cover all bases) relented and we zoomed along, to arrive close to our planned time.

Golfito grew up on the banana trade, which died in the early 50s, and it hasn't found a niche since. Work was proceeding to transform the old banana boat wharf into something new, but no one was quite sure what. The town was charming, in a run-down, dilapidated, 1850s Texas cow-town sort of way.

Very up to date was the Port Captain, who seemed to change the rules every few days. When we arrived, he required yachts to anchor in front of the commercial wharf, and wait for an official. We did, and waited a few hours. Then he decided that we (everyone on board) had to come to his office. By then we had contacted Bruce Blevins at Banana Bay Marina, who agreed to act as our agent. He convinced the Port Captain to allow us to move to a mooring off the marina, and do the check in by car.

Bruce's fee of $US35, which covered check-in and out, and transportation around all the offices, was well worth it. Immigration came to the marina, and then we went by car to Quarantine, Immigration again because he forgot to stamp a form, Port Captain and Customs, all offices separated by several miles. Our driver got into a blazing row with the Port Captain, who wanted to charge a fee of $US100. Apparently this was not official, and if you protest properly (yell and stamp your feet), you don't have to pay. If alone I would have paid, as I never argue with the officials, so the $35 agent fee became even more of a bargain.

Banana Bay Marina had new docks that held some 20 boats, and were always full with "permanent" powerboats. The bar was extensive, and the restaurant served the best food in town—not that there were too many restaurants to choose from. We enjoyed strolling through the streets and greeting the locals, who were very friendly.

As we wanted to be in a marina for Christmas, and have a secure place to leave the boat for some land cruising, we moved on to Los Suenos Marina, in Bahia Herradura, at the entrance to the large gulf that contains Puntarenas. This was a very new marina, with U.S. style floating slips, power and water, but no other facilities, as everything else was still under construction. Security was excellent, with round-the-clock guards. However, the payable in advance charge of $US10 per foot per week ($US530 per week for us) was unwarranted, given the marina's bare-bones state. Boats that stayed a month were charged the same weekly rate, plus they had to provide an additional $US2,500 deposit. The place was full of deep-sea fishing powerboats, all owned by Americans, most of whom owned a condo in the associated Marriott Hotel/condo complex. We could have used the pool at the hotel, for a charge of $US40 per person per day—they provided towels! Are there clues here to indicate transient cruisers were not wanted at marina and hotel?

Ryan (13): *My parents are occasionally so weird. For Easter in Turkey, I received a blanket as a present; for Christmas in Spain, a black-foot ham; and now, in Costa Rica, a waffle iron. At least Santa understood my real needs and brought me a great cast net.*

The only way of getting around was by car, so we hired one at $US330 per week. So far the week had cost us $US860, and we hadn't moved. On Christmas Day we set off for an afternoon drive, and the rear tire went flat. An ancient pickup filled with people and kids immediately stopped to offer assistance, but 61-year old macho-man and 13-year old mini-Arnold had everything under control. A piece about two inches in diameter had blown off the tire. We changed to the three-quarter size spare, and drove to town to see if a garage was open. The road led past the Economy Car Rental office and they were open, at 5:30pm on Christmas Day! Our rental agreement stipulated that punctures were at our expense, but I pointed out that the damage to the tire couldn't be so classed, and they agreed to put on a new tire.

By this time, the owner/manager had appeared, stripped down to change the tire, and found that the new tire was on a smaller rim, and one of the wheel nuts had been damaged. Off went a flunkey to have the tire changed to an appropriate rim, while the manager set to work to reinstate the wheel-nut thread. Back came the tire on the correct rim, but with a huge bulge that would, within 100 yards, have resulted in the original problem. By now it was 6:30pm and getting dark.

I pointed to a rather spiffy-looking 4-WD SUV and said, "We would be happy to take that as an exchange vehicle, at no extra charge." Timing was everything, the 4-WD was given a quick wash, and we drove out in a $600 per week car that had less than 200 miles on the speedo.

About an hour's drive from the marina was a bridge lined with people staring over the edge, so we stopped to stare with them. The bridge spanned a river bordered with sandbanks covered with crocodiles, big 10-foot crocodiles. Some were motionless, sunning themselves, or walking about, or with just tail, eyes and nostrils above water. It was fascinating to see them silently sink and just vanish. There must be a good source of food, but apart from the herd of tourists, and a herd of cows in the distance, we didn't see any likely candidates.

Dragging ourselves away, we drove on north through pretty country, along the Pan American Highway (with only one short break in Panama, it allows you to drive from Alaska to the bottom of South America). Looking for a lunch place, we found a restaurant on the banks of a river, near some rapids and a waterfall. By chance we had discovered the starting point of a white-water raft trip down the river, a trip where the raft was guaranteed to stay upright and the riders almost dry—a Carole special.

The raft was a standard inflatable, which we shared with another family of three. Our guide stood in the stern and used oars to keep us pointed in roughly the right direction. The many rapids were exciting, the raft stayed upright, and we got wet. Huge iguanas, ranging in color from bright orange to black and green, seemed to be in almost every tree. Small crocodiles kept hands and feet inside the raft. Various birds flew about.

Carole: *Wait a minute! You mean that if we flipped over in one of the rapids............ Glad I didn't think of that then.*

Ryan and the other lady (not Carole) had to go to the toilet, so we pulled alongside the bank. They scrambled up and headed in opposite directions to find the His and Her trees. Both returned rather wide-eyed. Apparently a troop of howler monkeys chased them, and then watched, screaming abuse. All this was on top of the swarms of mosquitoes which surrounded them immediately they hit shore, and bit every exposed body part.

Carole: *In the 80s, I taught with a Costa Rican lady who had now returned home, so I got in contact, and we spent a couple of delightful days with Itzhel and her husband Victor. Thanks to them, we got to understand Costa Rica much better. They had cousins staying at the Marriott at the marina, so we walked over to visit. A guard stopped us, checked with reception that there were the appropriate guests in residence, then came back in a few minutes to confirm that we were with them. Keep out those marina riff-raff!*

One of the women around the pool was wearing a swimsuit that looked as if it was made from real silver. The top was covered in emeralds, diamonds and other precious stones. Definitely a suit for lounging, and being seen in, not for swimming.

The Manual Antonio Nature Reserve was quite boring. Our guide carried a powerful telescope, which brought us up close to the two and three-toed sloths and to the monkeys. Perhaps because we were there around midday, we saw no birds. To satisfy Carole, our guide found a small boa coiled up in a tree.

Ryan (13): *All the sloths were too far away to see properly, and the snake was asleep. Much better were the monkeys we found at one of the beaches. These tried to steal stuff from people's purses and back-packs, and ran about everywhere.*

The reserve contained three pretty beaches and was entered through a small town that seemed to be all trinket stalls. In contrast to the paved entrance, the exit was down a muddy slide and across a tidal stream by way of haphazardly placed rocks.

Hungry, we searched the back streets and found a sports bar that seemed to have reasonable food. The five TVs showed five different U.S. football games. The bar stools were branded with the names of the apparently permanent occupants. After all that, the food did turn out to be good.

Carole was driven to distraction by the high costs of the no-facilities marina (we had planned to stay for a month), so we moved on. New Year's Eve was spent in Punta Leona.

Ryan (13): *I saw in the New Year alone, as the old fogies barely made it to 9pm.*

Bahia Ballena was lined with restaurants and palapas, and very rolly. Our dinghy was fitted with wheels so we could easily pull it up the beach, away from breaking waves. Unfortunately the sand at this beach was soft, so all we did was bog, right in the surf.

We were happy to move on to Bahia Potrero, where we anchored just outside Flamingo Marina, in very calm water. The various reports we had heard suggested a nice marina, so we called in advance and were told it was full. When we got there, we were very happy to be outside. The marina entrance was tiny, the docks falling apart, the depth minimal, and the space to maneuver non-existent. "Hoptoad" (who names these boats?), with two boys around Ryan's age, anchored nearby.

The voyage from Panama to Mexico requires the crossing of two gulfs, Papagayo and Tehuantapec. Both are famous for their ferocious winds, caused by air from the Caribbean funneling through the mountains, picking up speed as it goes. Although there are now some predictions, the winds arrive on otherwise beautiful clear days, and last for hours, or days.

Tehuantapec is the most feared, as the winds scream down from the mountains, often at 50+ knots for days, and many boats have been severely damaged during the crossing. January is the worst month for winds, and it was January. The two "safe" methods for crossing the 200-mile wide gulf are to go 500 miles out to sea or to hug the shore ("one foot on the beach"), staying less than half-a-mile off.

Carole: *We met a boat which had sustained severe damage crossing the Golfe de Tehuantapec. Laurie had neglected to tell me about this place, one of the most potentially dangerous crossings of our trip. He had also somehow forgotten that January was statistically the worst month to cross. He certainly suffered for those memory lapses. In retrospect he did the right thing, as I would have been worrying about it for years, instead of for just a few days.*

To check out of Costa Rica, we had to go around the corner into the Gulf of Papagayo and anchor at El Coco, at the top of the gulf. Carole and Ryan celebrated their birthday by being blown back to the Ballena anchorage by the dreaded Papagayo winds. The next day we left earlier and made it. Coco was a fairly open anchorage, so we were a little rolly. There wasn't much ashore except lots of restaurants, so we did paperwork ($US50 for the Port Captain, $US6 for immigration) and prepared to leave.

Our intention was to get out of the Gulf of Papagayo early in the day before the winds came up, and have an easy four-hour trip to the next anchorage. We actually made it half-way down in a flat calm. Then I pointed out an approaching wind-line and we had instant 30 knots. As we were reasonably close to shore there were no waves, but the wind was such that we couldn't comfortably turn the corner to our proposed anchorage.

Panama to Mexico to San Diego

Being the adaptable cruisers that we are, we noted we were going sort of north-west, so decided to keep on to Puerto Madero, Mexico, some three days away. This kept the winds on our beam, and they stayed at over 20 knots all day. Dolphins escorted us on and off for hours. A mating pair of turtles was rolled over by our bow wave. They stayed upside-down for as long as we could see them—an admirable example of concentration.

Ryan (14): *I was pulling the lines in for the evening, when a black marlin hit the one that wasn't rigged for marlin. He danced in the air a couple of times, then took off, straight down. The choice was to lose half the line, or all of it.*

Off the coast of Nicaragua the next morning, a panga crossed our stern too closely and caught both our lines on his outboard. The reels were almost stripped before we both could stop. We did recover all our lines and lures, hand delivered by the panga crew. Ryan got back into the mode, and caught a 40-pound dorado soon after.

Carole: *As usual, Laurie tells half the story. I had my sarong up to block out the sun, so we didn't see the panga until it was right on us. We were miles out to sea, so were very surprised to see this type of boat. Our immediate thoughts were that they were going to board, and this was reinforced when they came to a stop. As it turned out, they stopped because our two fishing lines had wrapped around their prop. Then came the decision, do we go back to help, or keep going. What if they were pirates anyway, just having a bad-luck day? It was not an easy decision, but we just couldn't leave them, miles from shore, in a disabled boat. We turned to help, they got going at the same time, handed us our lines, and everyone was happy.*

The current relented and we surged ahead at our accustomed eight knots again. The winds fell into a pattern, right on the nose all morning, on the beam all afternoon, negligible all night. Listening to the radio, we discovered that there was a weather window which would stay open for a couple of days, just enough to get us across the Golfe de Tehuantapec.

Carole: *Our little four-hour jaunt to the next anchorage turned into five nights at sea. Luckily I was (those days anyhow) always prepared with plenty of food, including frozen canned fruit for the fruit-bats in the crew. Years before we had discovered that the bottom of the freezer was a bad place to store perishables as they sometimes didn't stay solidly frozen, so we lined it with cans of fruit. All our frozen goods stayed frozen, and we had treats on hot days.*

Because of the apparent weather window, we kept on past Puerto

Madero, and headed into the gulf, choosing the "keep one foot on the beach" option. The winds never got over 10 knots, and the seas were flat calm for the whole of the two-day crossing. We soon abandoned being close to shore and headed straight across, taking hours off our passage. The water was littered with hundreds of turtles, sunning themselves on the surface, some with sea-birds resting on top of their shells. Dolphins escorted us, and there always seemed to be rays leaping and twisting in the air. It was one of our nicer passages.

Without even the slightest hint of a problem, during the worst month to cross, the dreaded Papagayo and Tehuantapec were safely behind us. We were in Mexico, a little shaken by the realization that it was the 56th country of our trip, and the last. Our sadness at leaving one country had always been tempered by the anticipation of the next. This time was different. We were looking forward to being with family and friends, but not happy at all with the thought of being land-bound again.

Huatulco was our first Mexican port, so we had to do an international check-in. Mexico did somewhat strain our policy of tolerance to all officialdom. Check-in required visits to Immigration ($US21 per person), Agriculture, Port Captain ($US25), Customs, Navy, and API (the Mexican port authority) ($US21). Payment to the Port Captain had to be made at a specific bank. The Port Captain therefore had to type out a form, which we then took to the bank (close-by here, but in later ports several miles away in another town). Then it was back to the Port Captain with proof of payment. All of this took us two days, including waiting around for Customs and the Navy. Our last country before the U.S., and the longest check in on record!

All this would have been fine if it just had to be done once, but Mexico had introduced new rules requiring boats to check in and out of every port where there was a Port Captain. As we later found, this procedure took some four hours to check-in (Immigration to Port Captain to bank to Port Captain) and four to check-out (same procedure), which made a day-stop at a port impractical, and expensive at $US25 each way. Banderas Bay, for example, has three Port Captains (Puerto Vallarta, Nuevo Vallarta, and La Cruz), spaced about six-miles apart. A day-sail covering the three would therefore theoretically cost us $US150 and take 24 hours to go through the processes. Luckily, some Port Captains had realized the silliness of the system, and were selectively applying the rules, but we couldn't count on it. We therefore revised our cruising plan and decided to skip a lot of the places where we had planned to stop, and stay longer at others.

Although we enjoyed Mexico, we didn't have the great time we expected. The anchorages were crowded and rolly, the marinas crowded and expensive, the restaurants adequate and expensive, the scenery quite nice, the other cruisers interested only in their own little groups, and the "tourist rip-off" syndrome fully developed. Our "end of trip" malaise didn't help.

Huatulco was once a small fishing village until the Mexican Government decided to make it into another Acapulco. They had certainly poured money into the place. Shops, restaurants, hotels were all new, good looking, well tended, and empty. It was our first introduction to how expensive Mexico had become. It was also our introduction to the rolly anchorages that seemed to be the feature of the coast.

Acapulco. We broke all our rules and entered the harbor at night, picking up a mooring. A spectacular view after dark, the hills around the huge harbor looked tatty during the day. The Marina found a place for us, so we tied up at rather rickety docks, still not repaired after hurricane damage a few years ago. The advantage was that the marina checked us in and out, and we didn't have to pay the Harbor Master fees, which meant that we stayed at the marina almost for nothing, and they had a great pool.

Carole: *Acapulco was a name from my youth, when we all aspired to go to this glamorous place, playground of the stars and of the rich and famous. We went to the famous restaurant where the 50s film stars autographed the wall, and also saw the renowned cliff-divers.*

Zihuatenjo. This was the famous cruiser Z-Town that everyone raved about. The anchorages were crowded and even more rolly than usual. For once, the beach landing was sheltered and calm, not the usual white-knuckle zoom through the waves. Port Captain and Bank were a long walk apart, and Immigration was a taxi ride away, so the four-hour check-in became five, with a repeat on check-out. The restaurants were a grade above "average." We saw no reason to stay more than a few days, and none whatever to stay the several months that seems to be the norm for a lot of cruisers.

Carole: *If we had planned to cruise only Mexico, our reactions would probably have been very different, and Z-town may have been a highlight. We were going in the wrong direction (north), had a different itinerary, and so many different points of comparison. Laurie found it difficult to relate to cruisers who had never moved more than a few miles.*

Manzanillo. We entered the harbor and drove round to the anchorage in front of the Las Hadas resort, where "10" was filmed. Bo Derek didn't make an appearance, there wasn't enough room, it was rolly, so we left after taking the obligatory photos.

Bahia Navidad. After anchoring overnight tucked in behind some small islands, but still rolling, we went into the lagoon for fuel and a couple of nights in the marina. It was almost full of powerboats, mostly big fishing boats. I also need the time to try to get the water-maker going again.

Ryan really wanted to go fishing in one of these boats and he set out to make his wish come true. In his inimitable fashion, he made friends with a couple of guys who owned an Egg Harbor 60, and was invited out for a day's marlin fishing. He was a little frustrated at our having hooked a few marlin and sailfish without being able to bring them alongside. As it turned out, they had a great day, but no marlin.

Ryan (14): I was swimming in the pool and began talking with some men who told me they had a powerboat in the marina. They invited me to go deep-sea fishing with them the next day. It was a new experience for me, even though we didn't catch anything. I learned a lot, and that helped me later to catch my marlin. One of the men owned a tackle shop in Newport Beach.

Tenacatita. This huge bay has a great reputation amongst Mexico cruisers. Some boats love it, and stay at anchor for months. We found it to be pretty, with the usual roll. The dinghy ride up a mangrove-lined creek to a beach lined with restaurants, was notable only for the almost total absence of wild-life and birds, other than pelicans.

While we were there, the cruisers organized a boat race. Participants had to sail to several beaches, and at each take the dinghy, or swim ashore, to drink a beer. The winner either had a fast boat or had participated in many College drinking competitions as training.

Cabo Corrientes. This cape is feared for its often bad winds and current. The night before we went around, a sailboat had been driven ashore there, and one life lost. We passed the next night in light winds and flat seas, into Bahia Banderas, and on to Paradise Village Marina in Nuevo Vallarta, where we spent five weeks tied up at the low-rent section of the marina.

Carole and I gave a seminar there to the approximately 50 yachts about to set off across the Pacific. We were very well received, and it came as somewhat of a shock to realize that many of the things we have come to take for granted, as routine, were new to those about to set off. We thought back to the absolute novices we were just over six years before, and marveled at our survival that first year.

Carole: The ladies in the group said they appreciated my presentation. Perhaps they could empathize with my sea-sickness, with my "I've crossed my oceans," and with my decisions to go just as far as the next port, and decide there if I could go further. I committed to them, and to Laurie, that I was ready now to go as far as Cabo, but up the dreaded Baja, well, we will just have to wait and see...

Also a shock was the lack of some of the basics that we had come to think of as essential to both survival and comfort. A quick walk down the dock showed that at least 30 of the 50 boats set to cross the Pacific had undersized anchors. As an example, a lovely new 52-foot racer/cruiser had a 44-pound Bruce, and line rode, as its only anchor. I advised a minimum 105 pound CQR or Bruce, and all chain rode, and was told that this was not possible as it would detract from the boat's performance. As the owner was taking his wife and three teenage children with him, I couldn't, in good conscience, walk away, and managed to convince him (shamelessly playing on all of his wife's fears) to change to all chain rode. There was no way he would put on a bigger anchor. Perhaps he did the right thing, as they made it to New Zealand. All I know is that 105 pounds of anchor and 200 feet of chain on the bottom is the best insurance you can buy, and absolutely priceless when it comes to peace of mind.

The other big shock was the almost total lack of paper charts, and the complete reliance on electronics. I am the first to say that we wouldn't have made it around if we had to rely on my skill with a sextant, and that I absolutely rely on radio, radar, and G.P.S., but charts are something different. What if you were hit by lightning, as we were? What if you had an electrical fire, as happened on several boats we know? What if the damn thing just stopped working in the middle of nowhere—trust me, no electronic device ceases to work near a repair facility?

The Banderas Bay regatta was on and Ryan was invited to sail as crew on one of the racers. They didn't win the three races they were in, but Ryan played his part and earned the respect of the others. He has come such a long way, both mentally and physically.

Ryan (14): *I worked really hard and really enjoyed it. Racing is so different from cruising. I think we tacked more times in one race than we did on "Dolphin Spirit" in six years.*

One of our time-shares was in Puerto Vallarta, so we spent a week there, off the boat, hoping to ease the transition to land. Ryan played beach volleyball every day, while Carole and I cheered him on from poolside. We sat on our balcony and watched the cruise ships coming and going, or just stared at the ocean across the tops of the palms.

Back on the boat, we took dinghy rides up the canals looking for crocodiles in between the mansions. The only ones we found were those that swam past "Dolphin Spirit's" stern most evenings.

Carole and I responded to an invitation to look at a time-share in the apartments attached to the marina, not because we wanted an apartment, but because all sorts of wonderful free gifts were promised. They turned us away because we didn't have an airline ticket, and because we couldn't prove we were married (Carole's passport shows her maiden name).

I got our dinghy glued together here, and it held. We had been so long without a safe dinghy that we almost missed the lines that held us all in place. It was nice to be able to get up on a plane again. The repair shop owner said that the Zodiac tendency to fall apart was sending his children through University.

Carole: *A lady in a store near the dinghy-fixer owned a canal boat in England, so we spent a lot of time with her, as the English canals are possibly our next adventure. We found a market that made tortillas while we watched, and sold carnitas, so Laurie could have his favorite dish.*

Tired of sitting in the cockpit watching the sunset over the hotel and the crocodiles swim past, we decided to move. With the assistance of high tide and a strategic push by a helpful dinghy, we managed to turn the right way in the narrow channel and get out of the marina.

Motoring into the wind made the short hop to Punta Mita easy, but things started to break. The main G.P.S. stopped talking to the autopilot, and the backup G.P.S. was equally uncommunicative. The water-maker stopped making water again, and I broke a fitting off the pump box trying to find out why. A water hose on the generator set burst. Our boarding ladder wouldn't deploy. The furling line of the jib broke. Short version—fixed everything else, but the water-maker remained obstinately out of action.

We poked our nose into Chacola, but there were two boats already settled in, filling the tiny anchorage, so we pressed on to San Blas (the Mexican one) and anchored in Bahia de Matenchin at around 7pm, in time to watch the sunset. The next morning, just before sunrise, we headed out. Whoever John was, he was up early, and berated us soundly over the VHF for not checking in and out of San Blas. In our defense, there was absolutely no indication that Matenchin was part of San Blas and, if we had known, the dinghy ride in to check in and then check out would have taken most of the day. All we wanted was a night's sleep.

Whales were breaching beside us on the way to Isla Isabella, and we had to circle around the two possible anchorages before finding a spot. I wasn't really happy with the place or our anchorage, so we up-anchored, with two anxious moments as the chain caught on rocks, and motored through the night in a flat calm to Mazatlan.

Check-in and out was a speed record of three hours, including the obligatory taxi to the bank. We stayed a couple of days, just lazing on the boat and doing chores, as there seemed to be no attractions ashore to entice us.

Ryan (14): *On the first day of the passage to Cabo, a marlin came right alongside the boat and sort of swiped at the bait a couple of times with his sword. Then, just before sunset one hit my lure and jumped and fought, but with my new rod and reel I could handle him, and eventually got him right to the side of the boat. Dad tried to unhook him, but couldn't, so we cut the line and let him go. I had caught my first marlin, and he was probably over 300 pounds.*

For the record, I stopped the boat and let Ryan do all the work. There is no way that a sailboat can be maneuvered like a powerboat to reduce the strain on the fisherman, so Ryan did a great job. He was exhausted.

After a night of actual sailing, I was trying to raise the Cabo marina on VHF, when a very familiar voice called us. Kurt and PL on "Osprey" had sailed with us from Tahiti to Greece, when they kept going and we stopped in the Med for a year. Now here we were, three years later, about a mile from each other, both heading for Cabo. You just can't keep good friends apart.

"Osprey" had completed their circumnavigation in Mexico the year before. They had kept the boat in the Sea of Cortez while returning home to Oregon. Now Kurt was back alone to take "Osprey" north, assisted by various friends at each stage. He was heading to Cabo to meet one when we ran into each other. That evening was filled with "remember whens."

The Baja Bash up the coast of the Baja Peninsular from Cabo to San Diego has a reputation for breaking boats and people. Kurt and I were both dedicated and careful planners, so we had done our research a long time ago. In keeping with our philosophy of leaving nothing to chance, we sat down together to compare way-points, anchorage information, "what-ifs" and other basics. The weather can't be controlled, but we could reduce the risk by eliminating most of the other variables.

We waited six days for the "right" weather window, then left at 5am to avoid the winds around Cabo Falso. They were up earlier that day, and beat us up for about four hours before shifting and dying, just as we were about ready to say "Enough" and go back. Fingers crossed we kept going, and the winds obliged by staying below 20 knots.

Passed Punta Tosca the next morning in relatively calm seas and less than 10 knots of wind, and passed Cabo San Lazaro in the mid afternoon, conditions still the same. We couldn't believe our luck so far, and pressed on for another night. The next morning gave us a flat calm—was this the dreaded Baja Bash? We didn't dare say anything, as the Wind Gods have very acute hearing.

Ryan (14): *I caught three small tuna, all with lots of teeth. We let them go as they were less than five pounds. To make it more interesting, I started to use my light rod and line, but forgot to set the clicker on the reel, so, as Dad wasn't paying attention, all the line was stripped off the reel.*

The great conditions persisted to Turtle Bay, so we decided not to stop and pressed on to Cedros Island. Still perfect there, so we kept on for San Quinton. Someone must have whispered something, because the wind kicked up to 20 knots on the nose, with some quite nasty little seas. We are cruisers and versatile, so there was an immediate direction change, and we headed for San Carlos. The middle passage was rough and we slammed into waves for a few hours, but then they relented and we had a smooth last 30 miles to the anchorage. In five non-stop, easy days, we had covered the worst of the Baja Bash.

A panga came by with the unusual request for a fender, and we gave him one of our seldom used spares. He came back later with a bucket of crab claws, which made a delightful lunch. We motored an easy day to San Quinton and met "Hoptoad" again. "Osprey" arrived about six hours later after dark, with us guiding them in by radio.

Although that last sentence sounds rather simple, the practice is not, and requires experience on the part of the guider, and complete trust by the guidee. Radar is essential for both, as is a masthead strobe on the guider's boat.

Another problem surfaced. The engine would not rev past 1,500 rpm, a possible indication that there was a line wrapped around the prop. Ryan went over the side, into bitterly cold water, and he couldn't see anything. As our speed wasn't affected, we pressed on for an overnight to Ensenada, tying up at the empty, new Marina Cruiseport. We had conquered the dreaded Baja Bash in seven, easy days.

Wednesday, April 10, after an overnight from Ensenada, we arrived at the San Diego Custom's dock to complete our circumnavigation.

Carole: *On our last night out, we recorded a tape we hoped would sum up our experiences. It really was too sad an occasion to be deeply philosophical, so I just expressed the desire to throw up for the last time, Ryan asked to keep sailing, and Laurie wondered where we would find a slip to keep "Dolphin Spirit."*

Re-entering the Real World

Our first dose of reality arrived with the U.S. Customs officer who checked us in. Noting our Australian registration, he told us we would need special clearance from the Customs office downtown. He was totally unswayed by the reams of paper we had used to check out of the U.S., proving that "Dolphin Spirit" had been purchased here. The downtown officers were equally unmoved, and gave us 12 months to get "Dolphin Spirit" out of the country, and issued a total ban on selling her. It took me almost six months of emails, letters, lawyers, and finally researching and finding similar cases, before Customs would relent and reverse their decision.

The next shock was the total and complete absence of slips for "Dolphin Spirit." When we had left, the marinas were competing for business and offering deals. Now the only deal was whether the waiting list was one or two-years long. Thanks to an old friend, we found a temporary place in Dana Point, then moved to a broker's slip in Newport Beach.

"Dolphin Spirit" was put up for sale, we moved back into Carole's Burbank house, Ryan began Grade 10 at Village Christian School, Carole was offered and accepted a job as a Math Coach with her old employer, Los Angeles Unified School District, and I started up my consulting practice again.

After the first flurry of greetings and reunions, and the novelty of living in a house was past, things got really tough. Actually the problems started early, when we were emptying the boat of more than six years of living, six years of wonderful experiences, great people, and fantastic places. The dream life was over and nothing as good was replacing it.

Helping the malaise for us all was the total lack of any common frame of reference with non-cruiser friends, and even family. Far too many times, conversations went something like:

"Meet Laurie, he has just returned from sailing around the world."
"How wonderful. Did you have any bad weather?"

"No, not really."
"What about pirates?"
"We didn't see any of those."
"Well I'm sure you had a good time anyhow. What do you think of those Dodgers?"

Occasionally the pirate question precedes the weather one, and if Carole is being questioned, the latest Macy's sale might replace the reference to the Dodgers. It was really hard to come to grips with the fact that no one cared about what we had done. We were no longer part of a special group, but were swallowed up and absorbed without trace into the general mass of humanity.

Ryan had it especially hard. He had little experience with organized schooling, and had not played team sports since he was six. He had no friends, and only sporadic experience in mixing with people his own age. Very quickly he learned not to speak about his experiences unless specifically asked, and then to be brief. He was well ahead of his age group scholastically (thanks to Carole's home schooling) and light years ahead in most other aspects, except baseball, basketball and football. To his credit, after the initial traumas diminished, he found his feet quickly and surely, and is now almost "normal," not necessarily a good thing, but essential for survival in this world.

Carole had to cope with returning to the house she had lived in for more than 15 years, to working for the same employer, driving the same roads, shopping at the same shops. It was as if the six years had been just a fleeting dream. Her hair had grown down to her waist over the years of travel, and she resisted cutting it now, as to her that meant the trip was really over.

I had to cope with being over 60, unemployed and unemployable, so decided to return to my old love of consulting—those that can, do, those that can't, consult—and soon had several clients. Perhaps the years of chasing sunsets and watching them over the rim of a wine glass had made me more intelligent, perceptive and creative.

However well settled we now seem to be, we all want out of this land-based life and back to cruising. Yes it is pure escapism, a retreat from reality, an abrogation of responsibilities, and isn't that just great.

Thank you "Dolphin Spirit."

THE END

May a peaceful wave
of love and respect
circle the world
to honor the diverse ways
people travel life's journey.

ABOUT THE AUTHORS

Lawrence (Laurie) Pane

Born and raised on a sugar-cane farm in North Queensland, Australia, Laurie's earliest water experiences involved swimming to school during floods, and taking a small dinghy miles out to sea to fish on the coral reefs. With age came some sense, and he moved to racing catamarans in the Brisbane River and Moreton Bay. Two children, a job, and a house eventually won out, and for many years he was land-bound. A move from Australia to Los Angeles, and a second wife, stirred the salt in his veins. They began serious bareboat chartering, principally in Tonga and Whitsunday, Islands. A couple of Newport to Ensenada races completed the conversion. After a year of searching, "Dolphin Spirit" was purchased in 1993.

Believing his wife's fight against breast cancer was won, they began serious planning and preparation for a circumnavigation. Sadly, it was not to be together. Acting on her wishes, and on Laurie's determination to make life special for their then six-year-old son, Ryan, the planning continued. With a third wonderful lady in his life, Laurie finally decided preparations would never be completed, so they set off from Los Angeles.

Sailing-related articles and photographs published *in Sailing, Sail, Cruising World, Latitudes and Attitudes* and *Latitude 38* magazines.
Cancer-related articles published in *Coping* magazine.
Travel-related articles published in several local newspapers.
Unpaid editor/reporter for the *Johns Hopkins Alumni Newsletter*,
    1990-1993.

Past President: Australian-American Chamber of Commerce
    of So. California
Past President: National Australian-New Zealand-American Chamber
    of Commerce
Director of the Australian-American-New Zealand
    Association (AANZA)

Bachelor of Engineering and Bachelor of Science from
    Queensland University.

Carole Wells Pane

Born in Glendale, California, and spending most of her time in beautiful, downtown Burbank. Carole's only link with the sea was her regular holiday at Laguna Beach. An elementary school teacher in the Los Angeles Unified School District for more than 25 years, she spent only two years out of California, in Connecticut.

When her marriage suddenly ended, she spent a couple of years regaining her confidence and self-esteem, and succeeded to such an extent that, when Laurie appeared, she could accept, with equanimity, his proposal for a radical change in life style. Though prone to seasickness, had never sailed, had never been outside of the U.S., and was very attached to her home and family, she became an enthusiastic partner in the planning, and the eventual voyage. Her enthusiasm has only grown over the years. She has become a real mother to Ryan, the role she enjoys most of all.

Bachelor of Arts, cum laude, Clear Life Teaching Credential.
Sailing relating article published in *Latitudes & Attitudes*.

Ryan Alexander Pane

Born in Los Angeles, holding both Australian and U.S. passports, Ryan made his first international trip when he was just three months old. Other voyages followed, including one in Tonga and a three-week charter in Australia's Whitsunday Islands when he was less than a year old. By his fourth birthday he was a very experienced traveler. A dedicated fisherman, he has become renowned for his ability to catch fish in places where others have failed. Always the first to make friends with locals of all ages, he has provided his parents with a fresh and often different view of places visited. Since their return, he has tried to settle back into the real world, and became an AP honor student at Village Christian School, Sun Valley.

APPENDICES
APPENDIX 1
Frequently Asked Questions

How Did You Handle Money?

We had good friends and relatives receive, sort and forward mail for us. They became our U.S. address (you need to have one for tax purposes, if for nothing else). Wherever possible, we paid by credit card, with the monthly bills then being paid by our friends, from our bank account. We gave them limited power of attorney.

We always carried between $2,000 and $8,000 in cash on board to be used where credit cards didn't work, for changing to local currency for incidental expenses, and for emergencies. The fishing boat that tows you off a sandbank will not take a credit card or travelers check, neither will the repair man for the refrigeration. This cash should be in clean, un-marked bills, in $5, $10 and $20 denominations. Banks and money-changers will not take marked, torn, or sometimes even creased, bills.

We stored the cash in a well-hidden safe on board. It was so well hidden that we didn't know it was there for the first two years we owned "Dolphin Spirit." I called the previous owner to find out the combination, and he said, "What safe?"

Occasionally we had funds wire transferred to us. Always check with the receiving bank that they will give you U.S. currency, as many times this will not be possible. As a general rule, wire transfers attract large fees.

How Much Did It All Cost?

The simple answer is that cruising costs what you allow it to cost. We averaged around $40,000 per year for the six years, for everything. This included at least one trip back to the U.S. each year for the three of us, lots of land cruising with the associated expenses of hire cars, hotels and restaurants, boat maintenance, repairs, fuel, food and normal living expenses. "Dolphin Spirit" was fully paid for before we left, and we carried full insurance on her. We kept up Health Insurance for us all.

There are certainly cruisers who have lived on $500 per month, and good luck to them. We didn't live that way on land, so saw no reason to do so on a boat. Cruising is mostly cheaper than land living, and we did have one month where the expenditure was almost zero.

What About Pirates?

The only problems we had were with the ones on land. Most sea-pirates are more interested in freighters and tankers than in little yachts. Where pirate areas couldn't be avoided, such as the Malacca Straits, we traveled in convoy with at least one other yacht. In other instances, such as Socrota Island at the bottom of the Red Sea, we detoured so as to stay at least 100 miles away.

In common with all things cruiser-related, care, caution, communication, planning and patience will reduce the risk.

What Spare Parts Should We Carry?

We developed a simple rule. Put on board all the clothes, provisions and spare parts you think you need, then throw out half the clothes and half the food, and fill the spaces created with more spare parts. Food and clothes can always be purchased, but once you leave the U.S., Mexico and the Caribbean, you can forget manufacturers' warranties, there are no nearby West Marines, and service people are very scarce.

We also found that many absolutely essential maintenance tasks can be carried out only by a contortionist with the ability to ignore pain. Special tools may reduce the discomfort, so check them out before you leave.

Some parts and tools that we found to be important included:
- Starter motors for the main engine and gen set
- Fuel pump for the main engine
- Complete gasket sets for the main engine and gen set
- Complete hose sets for the main engine and gen set
- Raw-water pumps for main engine and gen set. It is often simpler to

change the pump in total than to change the impeller.
- Fan belts
- At least six of every hose clamp used on the boat—do a detailed check and find each one
- Engine oil for at least three oil changes
- Outboard motor oil if yours is a 2-stroke
- Two circuit breakers of every size used on the boat—check them out
- Fuses—most electronic equipment has a fuse somewhere. Find it, note its rating, and buy two spares. Put these in clearly marked baggies. Store the baggies where you can find them. Tell someone where they are, because you will forget.
- Rolls of electrical wire, connectors (squeeze type, not soldered type) and appropriate wire cutters and connector compression tool
- Soldering iron with a very fine tip
- Full sets of metric and U.S. open and closed end wrenches (spanners) and socket sets
- Adjustable wrenches (butcher's tools) in varying sizes, for use when you are just too frustrated to find the correct wrench, or after the last of the correct wrenches went over the side
- Long-nosed pliers
- At least three of every size and type of screw-driver, as two of them will be lost overboard or into the bilge
- Bolt-cutters, not for the usually expressed reason of being able to cut the rigging if the mast goes overboard (you won't be able to unless you possess gorilla strength), but to cut locks off when you lose the last key, or when the lock is too frozen to be opened. This WILL happen.
- Check every bolt and screw on board to see if a special tool is needed. Do this before you leave.
- Check every bolt and screw on board and be sure that you carry several spares. Many will be special (size and type), and the time to discover this is before you actually need the item in mid-ocean.
- Flexible coupling between gearbox and drive shaft. We didn't have a spare and nearly lost the boat because of it.
- Refrigeration gas
- Refrigeration gauges for checking and adding gas
- Funnels of varying sizes
- Flexible clear plastic hose of every diameter up to one inch
- Light bulbs for all interior and deck lights, including navigation lights
- Spare parts kits for each size and type of winch
- Winch handle to replace the one that will go overboard
- Winch grease
- Shallow pan for washing winch parts in petrol to remove old grease. Using a baking pan from the galley is a never-to-be-repeated mistake after the first mate finds out.
- Black electrical tape (like money, there can never be enough)
- Batteries for flashlights and portable electronics—double the quantity you think you will need
- WD40 or equivalent degreaser
- Hacksaw and replacement blades
- Collapsible canvas bucket for carrying tools around and up the mast
- C-clamps of various sizes
- Dinghy valves and pump
- Instant glue
- Wood glue
- Underwater epoxy
- Normal epoxy
- D-rings of various sizes

What Did You Do About Charts?

We carried paper charts. These formed a pile at least four feet high by the end of the circumnavigation. It frightens me to see so many cruisers setting off and relying entirely on electronic charts. These are great and wonderful, for as long as the equipment works. Back-up paper is essential. Besides which, I like to pretend

APPENDICES

I am a navigator, and draw lines and mark arcs. Plotting my position on a paper chart seems a lot more satisfying somehow.

We kept all our charts, but a brisk trade in charts goes on at many major ports.

What Did You do to Prepare to Leave Port?

By the end of the first few months of cruising, we had developed a pre-departure ritual which was posted in the nav station. Carole, Ryan and I each had assigned tasks (One of Carole's was to ask Ryan and I if we had done all of ours. We never had to ask her.) that covered everything necessary for an easy up-anchor and a comfortable passage.

Ryan's included putting away all books and games in his cabin, making sure the piano was properly stored and that his computer was locked in place.

Mine actually began the previous day with the establishment of way-points, setting these in the G.P.S. and auto-pilot, getting weather data from weather fax, SSB and other sources (this was an every-day task, not just before sailing), checking engine oil and water, checking all standing and running rigging and lines, checking that the dinghy and other on-deck items were properly lashed in place, getting out the abandon-ship bag, putting passports and ships papers in the floating bag, checking the weather again and making the final decision to leave.

Carole's principal tasks were to get below decks ready, closing portholes, latching drawers, tying up anything loose, packing paper towels and toilet rolls in the storage areas to prevent rattles and breakage and ensuring everything was properly stowed. Her last question always was, "Are you *really* sure we should be leaving today?"

What Did You Take Into Account When Planning Passages?

My first task was always to go to the charts and determine the way-points needed to get safely to the next anchorage. No way-point was ever closer than two miles from any possible danger, reef or land—three miles if the way-point was to be reached at night. I then entered these into the G.P.S. and had it calculate the sailing distance.

Assuming a six-knot average speed, I then calculated the time this would take. The conditions at the next anchorage, and this time, then determined when we would leave. We almost never enter new anchorages after dark; coral requires that the sun be behind us so that it can be seen; an area known for unlit fishing boats may have to be avoided after dark.

Then I looked at known currents, wind directions and other matters that would influence boat speed, to see whether these would change the first rough calculations. If the six knot assumption would have us arrive just at sunset, and there was the possibility of an adverse current, then the departure time would be adjusted to provide an additional safety margin.

The phases of the moon were also taken into account. It was nicer on night passages with a full moon lighting the way, but in some areas a full moon meant worse weather. The absence of a moon showed the stars in all their glory. Maybe this was why the moon was a late entry in the decision-making stakes.

No sailor, including me, will own up to being superstitious, and at the same time very few will start a long passage on a Friday. A number of times I deliberately avoided a Friday start, so therefore anything bad that happened on those passages was caused by other malevolent factors. Friday day-hops don't count.

What About Pets?

We had friends with two dogs on board. For the six years we knew them, they never tied up to a dock, as most countries will not allow pets ashore for fear of disease. We felt very sorry for the animals, and their total lack of exercise. Besides which, have you ever smelled wet fur in a closed boat?

Did You Trade With the Locals?

We did trade in many countries, and found that the most acceptable trade good was currency, local or U.S. Where trading with goods was possible, the goods (Tee-shirts, caps, cosmetics) had to be new. Fish hooks were often requested. Ball point pens were always needed, and we usually gave these as gifts to the children.

Crayons, paper, pens and children's books are welcomed by every school, but do not try to use these as trade items. As a gift, they often bring a greater reward than you might expect.

A word of warning. In some countries you will be asked for ammunition. If you carry this, do not, under any circumstances, say so. For one thing, you should have declared it, and had it taken off the boat when you entered the country. Discovery of non-declared guns or ammunition will most probably result in your boat being seized and you jailed. For another, ammunition dealing is almost certainly strictly illegal.

What Were the Best Places You Visited?

We have debated this long and hard and have no real consensus.

Best cruising areas:
- South coast of Turkey
- Tonga & Fiji
- Great Barrier Reef
  (in spite of our experiences)
- Indonesia

Most memorable anchorages:
- Lehok Uwada Desami, at the southern end of Rindja Island, Indonesia
- Asim Limani, Turkey
- Anchorage 6, Vava'u Group, Tonga
- Suakin, Sudan
- Southern end of Waya Island, Fiji

Places that have stuck in our memories:
- Petra, Jordan
- Lanzarotte Island, Canary Islands
- Temple of Karnak, Luxor, Egypt
- Barcelona, Spain
- Cappadocia, Turkey
- Cartagena, Columbia
- Ende, Indonesia
- Manihi Atoll, Tuamoto Group
- Cefalu, Sicily

What About Children?

Do not leave home without them. If you don't have any of your own, rent one. Having children on board is a definite plus for both children and parents. They will open more doors and provide access to more experiences than you can believe.

Children do reduce spontaneity and flexibility, and there were occasions when that was an irritant, but the overall benefits far outweighed this minor complaint. Children also require dedication by the parents; dedication to a regular schooling schedule; dedication to finding other children as playmates; dedication to disrupting your schedule whenever necessary to meet the needs of the child; and simply dedication to being a parent.

On a cruising boat parents must be teachers and playmates as well as parents, and the roles are sometimes difficult to separate. There is usually no baby-sitter at the end of a phone, although other cruisers fought for the right to have Ryan on their boat.

After six years of cruising over 40,000 miles and then two years on land, we feel competent to comment about the effect on Ryan. Academically, he is well ahead of his peers. Socially, he is at ease in adult company. He makes friends of all ages quickly, and has an unerring sense of character. Physically, he missed out on team sports, but plays tennis, water skis, snorkels, is an open-water qualified scuba diver, and is a wonderful swimmer. He is a voracious reader, a devoted video-game addict, and plays chess and piano. Undefined, as yet, are the results of in-depth exposure to 56 different cultures and life-styles.

How Did You All Survive the Togetherness for so Long?

We found one method to be for each of us to have our own space, where we could retire to from time to time, and be alone. Close proximity, 24 hours a day, seven days a week, palls in even the most loving and caring family. Ryan's space was his cabin, Carole's was the main stateroom, and mine the cockpit.

Another was hobbies. We all read voraciously. Carole entered recipes into her computer. Ryan played video games and fished. I did future planning. The most important was tolerance, recognizing when someone needed to be alone.

What Did You Have on Board That Was Absolutely Essential?

Ignoring the obvious such as food, sails, anchor, navigation lights, radios, dinghy and engine:

Laurie:
    G.P.S.—the "we would not have left port without this" piece of equipment.
    Radar
    Auto-pilot—we used the wheel only for entering and leaving port.
    Link 2000 battery monitor
    Blender for making margaritas
    Awning, completely covering the deck from the mast to stern.
    Special fish filleting knife.
    Gel batteries—we installed these in 1995 and looked at them again,
        for the first time, in 2004.
    Four Winds wind generator that simply worked quietly away
        24 hours a day.

Carole:
    Freezer, microwave, 110V appliances in the galley, computer, mosquito netting at each porthole and completely covering the cockpit, fans in every cabin, See's chocolate suckers, Books-on-Tape.

Ryan:
    Computer, video games, fishing rods, lures, hooks and line.

All:
    Books, snorkeling gear, videos, CDs. The complete cockpit enclosure.

What Unusual Things Did You Need?

Egg cartons, as eggs in most countries are sold loose
Sealable plastic bags, sandwich to one gallon sizes
Green plastic bags that keep vegetables fresh
A magnet to pick up things from the bottom of the bilge
Ties to keep glasses and sunglasses from vanishing into the deep
A battery powered reading light that clips onto a book, for reading
    while on watch
A propane tank connector adaptor to match U.S. connectors to European ones.
Dish and wine glass storage system to free-up cupboard space

What Medical Supplies Did You Carry?

Antibiotics including Cipro and other more specific ones with clear instructions from our doctor about when and how to use them.
Chlorox chlorine bleach. Immediately wash all coral cuts and scrapes in this (undiluted) as the ONLY way to avoid infection. Regularly add to the fresh water tanks to stop growths.
Antiseptic creams for cuts and scrapes
Band-Aids by the hundreds
Eye Drops for eye infections
Ear Drops for ear infections
NyQuil or equivalent
Robitussin or equivalent
Cough Drops
Asprin, Advil or your choice of headache pill

Aleve (or your choice of pain relief pill)
Benadryl
Sudafed
Cold sore cream
Lomotil for diarrhea
Laxatives
Sterile gauze pads
Gauze bandages
Elastic bandages
Sterile needles for injections
Sutures
Suture needles
Lip screen
Thermometers
Instant cold packs
Instant heat packs
Insect repellant
Calomine lotion or equivalent for itch relief
Tums or equivalent
Malox or equivalent
Vitamins for daily use
SPF 15 sunscreen
Emergency dental repair kit
Aloe gels and creams—lots and lots for sunburn relief and other soothing requirements

Apart from the colds and sore throats that we contracted when we were on land for a time, we were disgustingly healthy for the whole voyage. We didn't need to use one of the 18 Fleet Enemas for some reason we had stored on board.

What Did You Keep in the Abandon-Ship Bag?

Cans of Spam
Cans of tuna
Cans of nuts
Bottles of water
A PUR hand-operated water-maker
Can opener
Assorted knives, greased and wrapped in plastic
Fishing line, sinkers, hooks and lures, greased and wrapped in plastic.
A folding gaff
Sunscreen
Aloe cream
Band-aids
Antiseptic cream
Flares and flare gun
A small mirror, for signaling
100 feet of Spectra line

In a separate, floatable, ready-to-go bag:
Passports
Credit cards
Cash
Ship's documents
Essential prescription medicines
Extra pair of prescription glasses
Sunglasses

When on passages, we kept these bags near the companion-way. Permanently mounted on either side of the companion-way were the EPIRB and the portable VHF, both essential in an abandon-ship situation. Whilst we had an off-shore six-person canister life-raft ready for deployment on deck, we always regarded the inflated dinghy as our best "survival" asset.

Always remember the old rule—abandon the boat only when you have to step up to get into the life-raft.

What Do You Wish You Had Known Before You Set Off?

That we would survive!

APPENDIX II
Schooling and Having a Child on Board

"Dolphin Spirit" had been set up internally very much with Ryan in mind. He had two cabins, one for sleeping, the other for his work desk, computer, TV/VCR, electronic games, books, board games, and videos. One bunk had been removed from this cabin for extra convenience and comfort.

For the first year of cruising (Grade 3) we used the Calvert School system and found it to be excellent. Carole had been an elementary school teacher for more than 24 years, so in subsequent years she set her own curriculum, as she wanted to include lessons on the history, geography, culture and language of each country we visited, when we were there.

As his 9th Grade needed to be from an accredited school, we used the Texas Tech program, and Ryan received straight As. The problem we had was finding a place that complied with the stringent requirements necessary to hold his final examinations. In the end, he sat for all of the exams in one week in Los Angeles, after we got back.

Carole: Having an extensive background in education helped, and I did have many excellent resources I had used through the years. A more recent acquisition was the series What Your xxth Grader Needs to Know *which provided additional material.*

Weekends don't really exist for cruisers, so Ryan attended school every day. This allowed for days, sometimes weeks, free of school, without fear of his falling behind. Such flexibility was necessary to provide for rough passages, land cruising, playing with children, and those days when the snorkeling was just too inviting to be put off.

Sitting out the cyclone season in Mooloolaba, we put Ryan into a regular school for three months. Wintering in Barcelona, when the boat wasn't moving for months and he had children to be with every day, we reverted to a more traditional calendar—Monday to Friday, 8:30 am to 3:00 pm, with each subject allocated a specific time.

Other cruisers stayed with the formal systems, and were very happy. Some, non-teachers amongst them, have done as we have, using the formal system as a basis and developing a curriculum to suit. Whatever was used, the keys to success were the same—involvement by the parents, structure, and consistency. Teaching is time-consuming, but the rewards, for parents and children, more than compensate.

Every day, Carole prepared a formal lesson plan for Ryan, who worked until it was completed. After years in overcrowded classrooms, she was ecstatic about the advantages of a one-to-one teacher/student ratio. Ryan's work was corrected immediately, he was guided through difficult areas, with instant address to his problems, and he was kept focused and motivated. Knowing exactly how Ryan was performing, Carole could structure the lessons to fit his precise needs.

As part of the school day, Ryan was required to study the history, geography, culture and language of every country we visited. He wrote formal reports on most countries, and on specific items such as the Uffizi Gallery in Florence and the camel market in Suakin, Sudan, combining what he had read, with what he had seen and done. As an on-going project he prepared a time-line for each of the civilizations in Egypt, Turkey, Greece, Italy and Spain so they could be compared and contrasted.

It is impossible to over-stress the importance of tapes, videos and computer programs. Ryan learned typing, piano and languages from them. He now types at over 80 words per minute, and to our ears at least, has become a fine musician. In Venezuela and Mexico he found his cassette-learned Spanish pronunciation to be nearly perfect.

Away from school, he became familiar with all types of music, from Country and Western to Classical, because we played them, and he had little choice but to listen. To his surprise, he came to like some of it. We in turn, listened to his music.

This is not to say that boat/home schooling did not have its problems. Separating the parent and teacher roles was difficult. We went part way to solving this with an elaborate charade. Every morning Ryan formally said farewell to his parents and then greeted his teacher (Mum) and his Principal (Dad). After school, he "went home" and reported to his parents on the day's activities. He came home for lunch, or ate in the "school cafeteria." Sometimes "Teach" and "Prince" took Ryan on a field trip (snorkeling or an excursion to Rome). Often "Teach" telephoned the parents to discuss specific incidents or problems. Farcical at times, we found this separation to work well in the confined spaces of a yacht, and to help to relieve the tensions that inevitably arose.

Other problems were the lack of class discussions and facilities for bouncing ideas off, and interacting with, fellow students. Carole corrected Ryan's work immediately, so naturally his first focus was on what his errors were, regardless of the overall standard of the piece. Scoring his work, and thereby putting it into perspective, overcame this to some extent.

Cruising with kids is only partly about their education. The family is together, 24 hours a day, sometimes for months at a time, and this requires compromises from everyone, adults and children. In the absence of other children, the adults have to become playmates, a sometimes difficult transition. Repair and maintenance projects must be scheduled so as to minimally interfere with schooling. One child is an extra 50% added to everything—food to buy and prepare, dishes to wash, and clothes to launder, to mention just the obvious. The adults' time is not their own. Shore excursions, social get-togethers and similar activities with other cruisers are less spontaneous, and more difficult to organize. Occasionally it is hard not to envy the solo couple without responsibilities.

On the positive side, children provide by far the best way of getting to know cruisers and locals. Within seconds of the anchor going down or the dock lines being secured, Ryan was off, introducing himself to all. Carole and I became very accustomed to being known as "Ryan's Mum," and "Ryan's Dad." Many wonderful experiences would have been missed if Ryan wasn't there to break the ice. Having him learn about every country has provided us with more insights than we might have otherwise obtained.

Who knows what the long-term effect will be on a young person who has seen the enigmatic idols in the Marquesas Islands, the Temple of Karnak in Luxor, the ancient city of Petra in Jordan, the 25 layers of civilization in the excavations at Megiddo, the great cathedrals in Rome, Malta and Florence, the mosques in Indonesia, Malaysia and Turkey, the golden palaces of Bangkok, the synagogues in Israel? What will be the results of participating in village life in Fiji and Indonesia? How will he remember, and assimilate, all the women in a village lining up just to touch him, swimming every day with clouds of fish, dolphins and sharks, uncovering an undiscovered mosaic in Turkey, being arrested in Sudan, watching a mother whale teach her calf to breach in Tonga, stepping carefully around landmines in Egypt, and having an elephant carry him around wrapped in her trunk in Sri Lanka? From the profound to the mundane, Ryan has seen and been exposed to more of the world than most of his contemporaries, and probably most adults. Can this be anything but beneficial?

Overall, for us, the whole experience with Ryan has been wonderful, bringing us firmly together as a family, more than we ever anticipated or hoped. Long term cruising is not for everyone, but children should be an incentive, not a deterrent.

Planning Ryan's Lessons

Ryan's Lesson plan was divided into three parts, plus homework:

A. Core subjects: Math, Reading, Language Arts, Spanish, Science, Social Studies and Geography (about 45 minutes for each subject depending on how diligently he worked). He selected the four he wanted to work on each day, with the two not chosen having to be chosen the next day.

B. Supporting subjects: Handwriting (including Calligraphy), Bible, Memorization of poems and Bible verses, Typing, Spelling (he picked two subjects a day, about 10 to 20 minutes per subject. We marked the ones he chose and they could not be chosen again until all in this category had been completed.

C. Electives: Art, Music and Home Economics: Drawing, Famous artists, Guitar, Classical Music, Famous Composers and Their Compositions, Country Western and Ballroom Dancing, Cooking, Sewing (buttons), and knitting (at his request). He had the freedom to choose which ever one he wanted to do that day.

D. Homework : Piano (Four days a week for 45 minutes from prepared lesson). We kept lists of books he read, poems he memorized, and a notebook of pictures he drew. The boat was often decorated with his latest drawings or art projects. We kept track of the number of hours he did at school each day. Thirty hours of school, gave him two free days, equivalent to a week end. These he would save up to use when he wished. When we traveled off the boat— we tried to limit the number of books we had to carry—he mainly had to write reports on the countries we were visiting, read newspapers, a selected book, and study Spanish.

Carole: *With a little knowledge—not proficiency, any parent can become the teacher of a child who does become proficient. Two examples:*

My Spanish was limited to three years of high school and much later I took another year in college (first year Spanish) when the children I was teaching became increasingly Spanish speaking. I do not speak Spanish—my accent is very poor—but I do have a working knowledge of the grammar.

Using Spanish tapes, music, and my College Spanish book, Ryan became so proficient that he always translated and spoke for us in the Caribbean and Mexico. Upon returning to a land-based school for his sophomore year, he took AP Spanish and received top honors in his class (some of his classmates were Spanish speaking natives).

When we could not find HARRY POTTER in English, we bought a Spanish copy. It took us more than a year to read it—first year only being able to get through a few paragraphs a day, but in the last few months he was able to easily read and translate each chapter.

My piano ability is very limited—I began when I was thirty and have taken the first year of piano on and off over the years. I can read music a little, but I could not sit down and play a piece. After twenty years, I have made myself memorize Fur Elise and can play it for pleasure. With my limited knowledge and his consistent practice, Ryan learned to read music, and can play the piano well.

APPENDIX III
Description, Specifications and Equipment List
"DOLPHIN SPIRIT"

Description

Type:	1987 Mason 53 Center Cockpit Cutter
Length Over All:	53'6"
Length at Water Line:	39'9"
Beam:	14'10"
Draft:	6'8" (empty), 7'2" (fully loaded)
Displacement:	39,600 pounds (20 tons)
Fresh Water:	330 gallons in four tanks
Diesel:	204 gallons in two tanks
Holding:	60 gallons in two tanks
Main Engine:	Perkins 4-236, 85-HP
Generator Set:	Westerbeke 8-KW
Staterooms:	3
Heads:	2

Overview

"Dolphin Spirit" is a semi-custom Mason 53, center-cockpit cutter, launched in 1987. She was built and equipped for extended offshore cruising and has been rigged to be safely single-handed and easily cruised by a couple. Seven feet headroom below deck and over seven feet between deck and boom add to her comfort and safety.

Walk Through (below deck)

Right at the bow is the huge chain locker, accessed by two louvered doors from the forepeak. The forepeak was originally the crew's quarters and is now storage space, with folding sink with hot and cold pressurized water, plumbing for a washing machine, and many shelves and lockers. The second head is next, with shower, sink with hot and cold pressurized water, a fresh-water foot pump, mirror, Groco manual toilet, large linen locker, under sink locker, exhaust fan, and electric sump pump.

Then come the two forward staterooms. The port stateroom has one bunk, hanging locker, two sets of drawers, lockers below and alongside the bunk, book shelves, reading lamps, mirror and fans. The starboard stateroom has two bunks, a hanging locker with shelf storage behind the hanging section, a set of drawers, reading lamps, fans, mirror, and lockers below and alongside the bunks. Both staterooms are separately heated from the central heating system, and each has a smoked acrylic hatch.

The salon has a U-shaped settee and dining table to port, and a long settee to starboard. Above the starboard settee are the built-in entertainment system, TV, VCR, CD player, tape player, and AM/FM radio. Behind, below and above all settees are very well designed storage units and lockers. All exposed lockers have louvered wooden doors. There are special storage units for videos, CDs and books. The table may be raised and lowered. A large mirror, forward of the table, makes the already extensive area seem even more expansive. The room is heated by the central heating system (two radiators and fans), has many reading lamps and fans, and a large hatch.

The companionway leading to the cockpit is flanked by the 406 EPIRB and a hand-held VHF radio. On the starboard side is the nav. station. A padded bench seat, large chart table (whose top hinges to reveal a storage area), easily removed instrument panels, and special navigation lighting makes this a navigator's delight. Large storage lockers surround the area. The extensive switchboard is here, featuring hinged front panels, individual circuit breakers and meters for every function.

On the port side of the companionway is the in-line galley with double bowl stainless steel sink, hot and cold pressurized fresh water, drinking water treatment system, salt and fresh water from foot pumps, six cubic foot refrigerator (top and front opening), six cubic foot freezer (top opening), stainless steel gimbaled propane stove with three burners, separate grill and separate oven, over stove exhaust fan, built-in microwave, spice rack and large storage lockers.

The master stateroom has a queen-sized bed on the starboard side, a desk on the port side, hanging locker, 13 drawers, bulk storage under the desk and bed, a large teak framed mirror, several storage lockers and bookshelves. Separately controlled heating, reading lamps, fans and a large hatch add to the comfort. The attached bathroom has a sink with hot and cold pressurized fresh water, fresh water foot pump, mirrors, Groco manual toilet, exhaust fan, and storage lockers. The shower cubicle has a seat, teak grill floor, electric sump pump, hanging locker, linen locker, and locker under the seat.

Walk Through (on deck)

Stainless steel mounts at the bow hold the 105-pound CQR and 75-pound CQR anchors ready for deployment. Both are raised by the Maxwell electric anchor winch set behind them. Harken roller furling units for the jib and staysail have control lines led to the cockpit. The raised forepeak hatch and the flush port and starboard stateroom hatches are forward of the mast. Stainless steel rails are on either side of the mast to protect the area, provide storage for the outboard motors, halyards and lines. A swivel davit, with its own winch, is mounted on the port side, in position to launch or retrieve the dinghy.

Between the mast and cockpit, the canister life-raft is set in a quick release stainless steel cradle. The system allows it to be security locked in place when in port. A stainless steel folding ladder with teak steps is permanently mounted on the starboard rail. Port side fittings allow it to be easily moved to that side when necessary. The ladder is designed to cope with large people fully loaded with Scuba equipment.

The center cockpit is completely covered by a canvas dodger and bimini, zipped together so that they can be used as a single unit or separately. Isinglass curtains, individually zipped, provide a weather proof enclosure when needed. Teak seating, covered by cushions, covers the entire 1-foot by 6-foot cockpit. A box at the forward end contains the radar, VHF radio, hailer and second instrument set. Waterproof speakers allow full stereo enjoyment of the entertainment system below. The Edson steering pedestal holds the main depth, speed and wind instruments, a folding teak table and drinking glass holder. Around the cockpit are three electric winches and four manual winches, allowing almost every sail adjustment to be made by a single person, from the cockpit, with ease and safety.

Accessed by an acrylic-topped teak hatch is the huge lazarette which contains the stern anchor locker, the Webasto heater, 110-volt refrigeration system, water-maker, hydraulic manual steering and autopilot systems. Right at the stern is the separate propane tank locker, with screw-down teak hatch and space for two 20-pound tanks.

At the stern is a stainless steel arch which holds all the antennae, wind generator, main radar dome, light actuated-anchor light, propane Bar-B-Que, table, and teak seats. A 44-pound Bruce anchor is permanently mounted with an electric anchor winch.

Specifications

Hull
Laminated fiberglass, laid to Lloyds + 100 A1 specifications, with eight full length foam and GRP longitudinal stringers and 23 GRP transverse members.

Ballast
11,360 pounds cast iron and 3,000 pounds of lead.

Deck
Hand-laid fiberglass with vertical end-grain balsa core. Deck-to-hull flange sealed with polysulfide and two alternating layers of one ounce matt and woven roving. Additional mechanical fastening is provided by full length stainless steel flat stock running full length, and across the transom, sandwiching the bonded flanges and secured by 7/16" stainless steel bolts on 4" centers, covered by a teak toe rail.
9/16" x 1" teak deck.

Deck Hardware
All exterior stainless steel is 316 grade electro polished.
Chain plates are stainless steel, heavily through bolted to structural GRP hull chocks.
Lifelines are supported by stainless-steel stanchions, through bolted. Port and starboard gates are provided.
Closed stainless-steel chocks are fitted into the toe rail on both sides, forward, after and amidships. Open stainless-steel chocks are fitted on each side at bow and stern. There are a total of 10 chocks.
Six cleats (12" and 10" Merriman stainless steel) are fitted fore, aft and amidships.
Stainless-steel gallows frame with teak boom chocks.
Stainless-steel stern arch with built-in teak seats.
Stainless-steel arches on either side of the mast.

Standing Rigging
All standing rigging is stainless steel 1 x 19 wire with swaged terminals.

Equipment List—Electronics
Radar
Furuno Model 1832, 36 mile, cockpit display
Furuno Model 1712, 24 mile, nav-station display
G.P.S.
Robertson Shipmate RS5800, connected to Furuno 1832 radar and Robertson autopilot.
Garmin 128, connected to Furuno 1712 radar.
Magellan hand held.
Radio
SSB—Icom 7100 with AT-130 tuner
VHF—Icom M402 —2 units, one in cockpit, one in nav-station, with antenna switch.
VHF—Icom M11 hand-held with leather case.
Hailer
Standard LH5 hailer in cockpit with mast-mounted Newmar PA40/30 speaker horn
Autopilot
Robertson AP300DLX
Autohelm 6000 linear drive with plug-in remote unit.
Instruments
Simrad IS15 Combi depth/boat speed display with bronze removable transducers, wheel-pedestal display
Simrad IS15-WD. wind speed/direction system, wheel pedestal display.
Datamarine Link 5000 depth, boat speed, wind speed/direction instruments in the nav station with repeater in the cockpit.
Weather Fax
Furuno weather fax with integral printer and separate antenna.
Navtex
Furuno NX-300 Navtex

Electrical
Batteries (12 volt)
House bank—Six 8D gel batteries
Engine starting—One 8D gel battery
Gen set starting—one 6D gel battery
Engine and gen set batteries may be paralleled to the house bank by separate switches
Inverter
Heart Interface 2,500 watt, 110 volt

Heart interface 1,800 watt, 110 volt
Both inverters separately switched and connected to all 110-volt outlets
Battery Charging and Monitoring
Link Interface 2000R which monitors the house and engine battery banks
Heart Interface battery charging (smart unit) contained within the Heart inverters
Lewco 80-amp silicon-diode marine battery charger (stand-by unit)
Generator Set
Westerbeke 8-KW, 110-volt, fresh water cooled
Remote starting and stopping switches mounted on the switchboard
Self-bleeding after fuel filter changes
Groco raw-water strainer
Alternator
150-amp, engine-driven
Wind Generator
Four Winds, two blade, high output
Switchboard - nav-station
All circuits are circuit breaker switched and protected.
110-volt AC circuit breakers are separate from the 12-volt circuit breakers and distinctly colored.
Each 12-volt DC and 110-volt AC function is separately switched.
Meters for the 12-volt and 110-volt systems
Shore Power
Separate 50 Amp inlets for 110-Volt and 220/240-volt.
3,000-watt 220/110-volt transformer permanently connected to the 220-volt shore power inlet.
110-Volt Outlets
Standard household outlets in every cabin, salon and galley.
Waterproof marine outlet in cockpit.
Fans
Nine 12-volt fans mounted in all cabins, salon and galley.
Lights
Dome ceiling lights in all cabins, salon and galley, engine room, forepeak, lazarette, anchor locker.
Individual reading lights over every bunk and strategically placed in the salon.
Night-vision (red) lighting system at sole level.
Exhaust Fans
In each head and above the stove in the galley.
In the engine room.

Safety Equipment
Alden Satfind 406 EPIRB
Fire Extinguishers
2 in the galley
1 in the nav station
1 in the starboard stateroom
3 in the forepeak
Halon automatic systems in the engine room and lazarette
MOB pole and horseshoe
Lifesling system at stern
6-man Avon offshore life raft in hard canister mounted on deck
All Coast Guard required equipment

Deck and Running Lights
Bow and stern navigation lights, switched from the cockpit
Masthead tricolor with anchor light and strobe, switched from the cockpit
Bow light at first spreader, switched from the cockpit

Spreader lights, switched from the cockpit
Anchor light at stern arch, light activated
Deck lights at gallows frame, one pointing forward, one aft
Deck light on stern arch

Bilge Pumps
Electrical
Low level 10-gallon-per-minute pump with automatic switching
High level 10-gallon-per-minute pump with automatic switching
Manual
Henderson pump in the cockpit
Henderson pump below the sole in the galley area
Emergency
Valve to allow the main engine to draw water from the bilge rather than from outside

Steering
Edson console in the cockpit with Wagner hydraulic system
Emergency back-up tiller accessed through a plate in the deck above
    the lazarette

Compass
Ritchie, 6-inch Globemaster, cockpit mounted

Engine
Perkins 4-236 diesel rated at 85-HP, fresh-water cooled
Cockpit panel for engine starting and stopping, tachometer,
    engine temperature, engine oil pressure, voltmeter and hour-meter
Start button at the engine for easier bleeding
Separate electrical fuel pump to facilitate bleeding
Groco raw-water strainer

Transmission
Borg Warner hydraulic, 1.91 : 1
Flexible coupling between transmission and drive shaft.

Propeller
Max-Prop VIP, 3-blade, 20-inch, feathering, with external pitch adjustment.
Original fixed 3-blade 20 x 13 (spare).
Hydraulic shaft brake.

Fuel
204 gallons in two black iron tanks.
Each tank has a pneumatic fuel gauge.
Each tank has an inspection and clean-out plate
Both tanks feed into a selection manifold with separate valving for all uses
    and sources

APPENDICES

Fuel Filters
Perkins main engine
Two Racor 500 series in parallel with valving allowing for switching
    from one to the other with the engine running
Westerbeke
Racor 200 series
Webasto Heater
Racor filter

Refrigeration
Six-cubic-foot refrigerator, top and front entry - one storage plate
Six-cubic-foot freezer, top entry—3 storage plates
All four storage plates connected in series
All four storage plates are cooled by separate 110-volt driven
    and engine-driven systems
110 volt "Stone Cold" refrigeration system, salt-water cooled, with timer
Engine driven refrigeration system, salt-water cooled, with timer
Refrigerator has stainless-steel shelves and door-activated light

Water maker
110V AC HRO System 9—500 gallon per day

Cabin Heater
Webasto Model DWB 2010, 40,000-BTU, diesel-burning, forced hot water
    with fan convectors—2 in salon, 1 each in master, port and starboard
    staterooms. Fans switched from nav station

Entertainment System
Magnavox 15-inch color TV
Sony AM/FM stereo receiver and control unit
Sony CD player
JVC stereo VCR
JVC cassette player
Rabbit system for operating remote TV
(All the above are permanently mounted in the salon.)
Two speakers in the salon
Two speakers in the main stateroom
Two Cybernet waterproof flush-mounted speakers in the cockpit
(The above six speakers are selected, individually or in groups, through a rotary switch mounted in the nav station)

Galley
Stove—Propane, 3-burner, separate grill and oven, stainless steel, gimbaled
Microwave—Panasonic 1,100-Watt, built-in
Sink—double, deep basin, stainless steel, pressure hot and cold water, foot-operated fresh and salt-water pumps
Separate treatment system for drinking water
Propane sensing and switching system
Exhaust fan

Propane
Two 20-pound tanks
Separate sealed and vented locker at the stern
Sensing and switching system

Plumbing
Fresh-Water Tanks
330 gallons in four stainless-steel tanks

Each tank has inspection and clean-out plate
All tanks feed a single manifold with selection valves
Pressurized Water
12-volt fresh-water pressure pump—40 psi.
One-gallon accumulator tank for even flow to all outlets
Hot and cold pressurized water in both heads, forepeak sink and galley
Deck outlet with hose fitting
Hot Water
11-gallon heater,110-volt and engine cooling water heated through separate systems
Showers (2)
Each shower has a sump with electrical discharge pump
Heads (2)
 Groco manual toilets with Y-valve to separate holding tanks
Two holding tanks, one for each head. Each holding tank has manual and electric (macerating) evacuation pumps
Deck pump-out fitting for the holding tanks
Exhaust fans in each head
Deck Washdown
Salt-water pump with deck outlet and hose fitting at the bow

Ventilation
Hatches
Three teak deck hatches with smoked acrylic tops (salon, main stateroom,
    lazarette)
Two Bomar No. 130 semi-flush aluminum alloy hatches over port and starboard
    staterooms
Teak sliding hatch with smoked acrylic top over forepeak
Teak sliding hatch over main companionway
Dorade Boxes
Four teak boxes with smoked acrylic tops and stainless-steel cowls
Each box has two stainless-steel plates
Portholes
Salon, galley and master stateroom—ten 7" x 14" rectangular chromed bronze
    opening portholes with toughened glass
Salon—two circular forward facing chromed bronze opening portholes with
    toughened glass
All portholes are above deck level.

Insect Screens
All portholes are fitted with aluminum-framed removable screens
All hatches are fitted with hinged, teak-framed screens
The cockpit can be protected by a removable screen that covers it completely allowing full use and access at all times

Deck Prisms
Four oblong prisms—over galley, nav-station, port stateroom, and forward head

Winches
All winches except the Maxwell are two-speed, self- tailing, chrome-plated bronze.
All are oversized for their application.
Cockpit
Two Lewmar 55 electric two-speed winches
One Maxwell single-speed electric winch (not sell- tailing)
Two Lewmar 43
One Lewmar 30
Mast
Three Lewmar 43

One Lewmar 30
One Lewmar 16

Mast
Forespar Stowaway, two spreader, height 64 feet
Forespar main sail in-mast roller furling system
Spinnaker pole is track-mounted on the front of the mast
Storm trysail track is welded to the starboard rear
Forespar spring-actuated boom vang

Roller Furling
Jib is roller furled by Harkins #3 unit
Stay sail is roller furled by Harkins #2 unit
Mainsail is roller furled by Forespar in-mast system

Sails
Main
715 square feet—roller-furling, UK Sails, new March, 1996.
715 square feet —roller-furling, Sobstad, refurbished March, 1996, unused since.
130-Percent Genoa
882 square feet —roller-furling, UK Sails, new March, 1996.
882 square feet —roller-furling, Sobstad, refurbished March, 1996, unused since.
90-Percent High Aspect Staysail
282 square feet—roller-furling, UK Sails, new March, 1996.
282 square feet—roller-furling, Sobstad, refurbished March, 1996, unused since.
Cruising Gennaker
1800 square feet, with snuffer, red, white and blue, UK Sails, new March, 1996
Storm Trysail by Hood, unused
Storm Jib by Hood, unused

Ground Tackle
Bow Anchors
105-pound CQR with 400 feet _ inch ABCO high tensile chain
75-pound CQR with 30 feet 5/16 inch ABCO high tensile chain and 200 feet one inch Samson double braid nylon rode.
Nilsson V 3,000 electric anchor winch.
Stern Anchor
44-pound Bruce with 250 feet 10-gauge high-tensile chain and 300 feet _ inch Samson double-braid nylon rode.
Lofrans Leopard electric anchor winch.

Canvas
Cockpit covered with canvas dodger and bimini, zipped together and supported by stainless steel frames. Isinglass curtains, individually zipped provide complete weather protection
Covers for the three hatches over salon, master stateroom and lazarette
Covers for bow and stern anchor winches
Complete toe rail cover
Covers for all isinglass curtains
Cover for the outboard motor
Awning that covers the deck from mast to stern. Full length side curtain that can be moved from side to side
Awning that covers the deck from mast to bow. Rain catcher fitting

Miscellaneous
Boarding Ladder—custom, stainless steel, teak steps, folding, permanently in place but can be moved to either port or starboard side

CHASING SUNSETS
APPENDIX IV
BIBLIOGRAPHY

World Cruising Routes	Jimmy Cornell (useful for planning)
American Practical Navigator Vols. I/II	Bowditch (seldom used)
Chapman's Piloting	Elbert S. Mahoney (useful)
Ocean Passages for the World	British Admiralty (seldom used)
Charlie's Charts of Polynesia	Margo Wood (essential)
Charlie's Charts of Costa Rica	Margo Wood (essential)
Charlie's Charts of Mexico	Margo Wood (essential)
A Cruising Guide to the Kingdom of Tonga in the Vava'u Island Group	The Moorings (essential)
A Yachtsman's Fiji	Calder (essential)
Cruising in New Caledonia	Marc, Rambeau, Blackman (essential)
Vanuatu	Tiews & Hearne (essential)
Cruising the Coral Coast	Alan Lucas (essential)
Cruising the New South Wales Coast	Alan Lucas (useful)
100 Magic Miles	David Colfelt (essential)
Northern Territory Coast	John M. Knight (excellent)
Sail Thailand	Thai Marine Leisure (essential)
Red Sea Pilot	Davies, Morgan (really, really essential)
A Yachtsman's Guide to the Red Sea	Robin Bell (unreliable)
Turkish Waters & Cyprus Pilot	Rod Heikell (absolutely essential)
Greek Waters Pilot	Rod Heikell (essential)
Italian Waters Pilot	Rod Heikell (essential)
Mediterranean Spain	RCC Pilotage Foundation (essential)
Islas Baleares	RCC Pilotage Foundation (essential)
North Africa	RCC Pilotage Foundation (essential)
Atlantic Islands	RCC Pilotage Foundation (essential)
Canary Island Cruising Guide	World Cruising Publications (useful)
A Cruising guide to the Caribbean	Stone and Hayes (useful but dated)
Sailor's Guide to the Windward Islands	Chris Doyle (essential)
Cruising Guide to Trinidad and Tobago	Chris Doyle (essential)
Cruising Guide to Venezuela and Bonaire	Chris Doyle (essential)
Yachting Guide to the ABC-Islands	Gerard Van Erp (useful)
The Panama Guide	Zydler (essential)
Cruising Ports: Florida-California via Panama	Rains (essential)
Cruising Guide-Acapulco to Panama Canal	Goodman (useful)
The Forgotten Middle – Pacific Coasts of Guatemala, El Salvador, Honduras, Nicaragua	Roberts (useful)
Lonely Planet Guide Books	(essential)
Switzerland	Michelin Green Guide (useful)
Germany, Austria, Switzerland	Rick Steves (follow religiously)

USEFUL REFERENCES

The Dive Sites of the Great Barrier Reef	Neville Coleman
The Dive Sites of Thailand	Paul Lees
The Dive Sites of Indonesia	Guy Buckles
Red Sea Diving Guide	Ghisotti and Carletti
Mariner's Weather	Crawford
Offshore Cruising Encyclopedia	Dashew
Celestial Navigation	Toghill
Repairs at Sea	Calder
Boatowner's Mechanical and Electrical Manual	Calder

BACKGROUND READING

The Capable Cruiser	Pardey
Care and Feeding of Sailing Crew	Pardey
Dolphins at Sunset	Thurston
Gentlemen Never Sail to Weather	Moore
Pacific Wanderer	Hinze
Landfalls of Paradise	Hinze
World Cruising Handbook	Cornell

A World of Photographs

Sunset in Moorea.

No better school room. Mid-Pacific

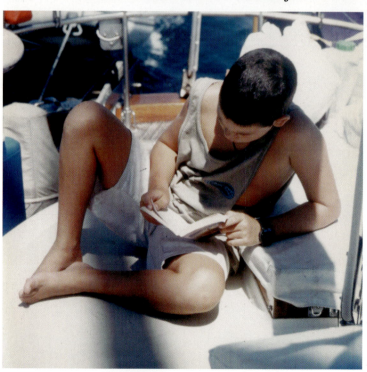
Bora Bora lagoon, and he has to study.

Our first dorado.

Training for the marlin to come. Manihi Atoll.

No "No-Nos" please. Huahine Island.

Enjoying Tonga. The ready-to-use stuff on the deck is our reason not to day-sail.

Drop-dead-gorgeous Tonga.

Ryan and friend. Tonga. Note the Singer sewing machine anchor.

Just one of the guys. A gathering of Captains. "Marita Shan," Ryan, "Osprey," "Sky Bird."

*Our own disappearing island. Musket Cove, Fiji.
I wanted to get married on it.*

*Cruisers wedding on "Marita Shan." "Pilgrim" officiating.
Great Keppel Island.*

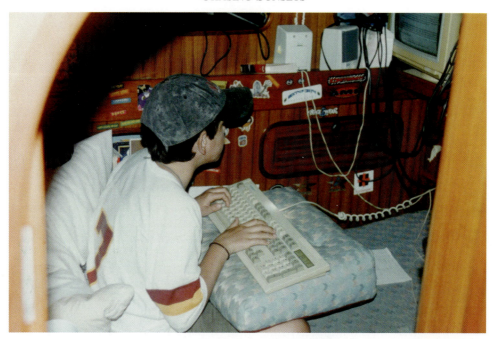

Ryan working in his cabin.

The "Touching Ryan" ceremony. Indonesia.

A World of Photographs

Christmas in Thailand. Good reindeer protection.

Carole walks one of the Maldives.

Lawrence of Australia and wife in Cairo.

Camel Market, Suakin, Sudan. Considering the offer.

A World of Photographs

A serious art student, any ruin. Turkey.

Turkey. "Did you get the picture yet, Dad. It's cold!"

Before the tourist buses came. Myra.

The best show in town. Roman theatre. Asim Limani, Turkey.

A World of Photographs

Driving home. Elba Island. ▲   ▼ *School's out. Mallorca.*

"Please let it start, and please let Carole forgive me for working in a white T-shirt again."

The end of our first dive together.

A World of Photographs

Objects in your mirror are closer than they appear.

Window shopping. Portugal.

The return. Dana Point, California.

Chasing Sunsets in the Mid-Pacific.